Living in the Shadow of the Large Dams

African Social Studies Series

VOLUME 11

Living in the Shadow of the Large Dams

Long Term Responses of Downstream and Lakeside Communities of Ghana's Volta River Project

by

Dzodzi Tsikata

BRILL
LEIDEN • BOSTON
2006

This book is printed on acid-free paper.

Library of Congress Cataloging-in-Publication Data

This book has been made possible by a grant from the *Stichting Wetenschappelijk Onderzoek in de Tropen* (WOTRO) of the Netherlands (Grant number WB 52 776).

Tsikata, Dzodzi.
   Living the shadow of the large dams : long term responses of downstream and lakeside communities of Ghana's Volta River Project / Dzodzi Tsikata.
      p. cm. — (African social studies series ; v. 11)
   Includes bibliographical references and index.
   ISBN 90-04-14144-8 (pbk. : alk. paper)
      1. Volta River Valley (Ghana)—Economic conditions. 2. Volta River Valley (Ghana)—Social conditions. 3. Ghana—Economic policy. 4. Volta River Project (Ghana) I. Title. II. Series.

HC1060.Z7V658 2006
330.9667—dc22   2006042507

ISSN 1568-1203
ISBN 13: 978 90 04 14144 5
ISBN 10: 90 04 14144 8

CONTENTS

ABBREVIATIONS AND ACRONYMS

ARS	Apostles Revelation Society
CSIR	Council for Scientific and Industrial Research
DANIDA	Danish Development Organisation
DCE	District Chief Executive
DFID	Department for International Development (UK)
DWM	31st December Women's Movement
EIA	Environmental Impact Assessment
FAO	Food and Agriculture Organisation (United Nations)
GLAACO	Ghana Libya Arab Agricultural Company
GoG	Government of Ghana
GNA	Ghana News Agency
GNPC	Ghana National Petroleum Company
GRIDCO	National Grid Company Limited
GWCL	Ghana Water Company Limited
GWSC	Ghana Water and Sewerage Corporation
HEP	Hydro-Electric Power
HIPC	Highly Indebted Poor Country
ICOLD	International Commission on Large Dams
IDAF	Integrated Development of Artisanal Fisheries
IMF	International Monetary Fund
IPP	Independent Power Producers
IUCN	International Union for the Conservation of Nature
KVIP	Kumasi Ventilated Improved Pit
L.I.	Legislative Instrument
LVEIS	Lower Volta Environmental Impact Studies
MEST	The Ministry of Environment Science and Technology
MLA	Modified Livelihood Approaches
MW	Megawatts
NEDCO	Northern Electricity Distribution Company Limited
NGO	Non-Governmental Organisation
NLC	National Liberation Council
OED	Operations and Evaluation Development of the World Bank

PIP	Policies, Institutions and Processes (used in the sustainable rural livelihoods approach)
PRSP	Poverty Reduction Strategy Papers
PURC	Public Utilities Regulatory Commission
SAP	Structural Adjustment Programme
SL	Sustainable Livelihoods
SRL	Sustainable Rural Livelihoods
TAPCO	Takoradi Power Company
TCDM	Tree Cover Depletion Minimization Project
UC	Unit Committee
UCC	Unit Committee Convenor
UNCED	United Nations Conference on Environment and Development
UNDP	United Nations Development Programme
UNICEF	United Nations Children's Fund
USAID	United States Agency for International Development
VALCO	Volta Aluminium Company Limited
VLRDP	Volta Lake Research and Development Project
VLTC	Volta Lake Transport Company
VOLTACOM	Volta Telecommunications Company Limited
VRA	Volta River Authority
VRP	Volta River Project
WCD	World Commission on Dams
WRI	Water Research Institute

GLOSSARY

The glossary contains two kinds of words and expressions which are used more than once in the book. The first are related to large dams and dam impacts. The second are Ewe expressions and words which are written in the standard Ewe orthography. Throughout the book, however, the names of settlements are written as they appear in official documents.

Adversely affected people/ Dam-affected communities	These are collectives who suffer negative effects of the project. In the case of the dams, this includes peoples whose economic, social and cultural lives are negatively affected by construction works, impoundment, alteration of river flows, and any ecological consequences. The term includes displaced people, host communities, downstream and upstream populations. It may also include people affected by the transmission lines or the development of irrigation schemes, water transfer canals, and sanctuaries.
Abɔ wuieve ka asideke	An indigenous way of measuring the size of land. It literally means a rope measuring 12 outstretched arms multiplied by 9. It is said to be equivalent to one acre. 2.5 acres is one hectare.
Abusa	A customary tenancy in which the landlord is paid a third of the outputs as rent.
Abusa labourer	A hired hand who is paid a third of the outputs as his wages for a variety of farm maintenance activities.
Abunu	A customary tenancy in which the land lord is paid half of the outputs as rent.
Adegbɔvi	Literally a servant of hunter or fisherman.

Akpa	tilapia
Amedzrofia	Stranger chief. This expression is used for community leaders of migrants.
Asabu	A cast net
Asisiwo	Regular customers
Atsatsa	A reed mat
Benefit sharing	Transfer of a share of the benefits generated by a project, such as a dam to local communities or authorities. Mechanisms for benefit sharing include preferential rates e.g. for electricity, revenue sharing or royalties, and equity sharing (through which local populations or authorities own all or part of the project).
Blume	The areas which are home to the Akan who are known as *eblutɔwo* by Ewe speaking people.
Chorkor Smoker	A fuel saving fish smoking oven made up of wooden and mesh trays stacked in an oven. It allows the smoking of much more fish at a time.
Compensation measures	Alternative resources (land, property or money) provided to displaced people and others adversely affected by a project as mitigation for losses suffered.
Dzigbe	Upwards. A generic expression for any location in the upper reaches of the Volta River. Popularly refers to areas around the Volta Lake.
Deme	Literally means farm and share. It is the Ewe expression for share-cropping. Similar to the Abusa and Abunu.
Dzenkpe/Akpatogui	The Ewe words for salted and sun dried tilapia.
Displaced people	Communities required, often involuntarily, to abandon their settlements (homes, agricultural land, commons and forests) or suffering loss of livelihood due to construction of a dam, submergence

	of the reservoir area, downstream impacts, building of dam related infrastructure such as roads and so on.
Dununɔla	The leader of a settlement. A broader expression which is used when this head is not a chief.
Edzo	Literally means fire in Ewe. In this con text, it means a minor arrangement for spiritual protection, distinct from *etrɔ*, which is a god that is worshipped at a shrine. It can also be used to harm people and whoever is involved in invoking such harm habitually is known as *dzo du ametɔ*. To invoke the harm is "*du dzo amé*").
Efe/efu	hook, as in hook and line
Eka	rope
Exa	basket trap
Etrɔ	A traditional god which usually has a shrine with officers who perform ritual functions and also adjudicate cases in the name of the god.
Ewedome	Literally means middle Ewe, and refers broadly to the Ewe groups who reside in the northern half of the Volta Region as well as the various dialects of Ewe spoken in this area. This description distinguishes them from the Anlo and Tongu Ewe who are found in the Southern parts of the Region.
Fiatefenɔ(la)	a regent
Impoundment	Body of water formed by collecting water, as by dam.
Kpodzigble	hill top farm
Large dam	A dam with a height of 15 m or more from the foundation. If dams are between 5–15m high and have a reservoir volume of more than 3 million cm3, they are classified large by the ICOLD.

Major dam	A dam with height of over 150 meters, or with dam volume of over 15 million cubic meters, reservoir volume of over 25 billion cubic meters or installed capacity of over 1,000 megawatts.
Mitigation measures	The reduction of potentially significant adverse impacts.
Mill	The cost of power is denominated in mills and one mill is US $0.001.
Precautionary approach	According to the Rio Declaration on Environment and Development (1992), where there are threats of serious or irreversible damage, lack of full scientific certainty shall not be used as a reason for postponing cost-effective measures to prevent environmental degradation.
Recession agriculture	A system of agriculture that depends on the moisture of the soil as the floods recedes. Recession agriculture takes place in the floodplain, which is the area subject to seasonal flooding by the river.
Reservoir	Any natural or artificial holding area used to store, regulate or control water.
Reservoir draw-down	The extent to which the water level in the reservoir changes on a daily or seasonal basis due to release of water from the reservoir for operations (such as irrigation or daily peaking for power generation). Emergency drawdown may be for safety reasons, or in anticipation of a major flood event.
Resettlement	Physical relocation of people whose homes, land or common property resources are affected by a development such as a dam.
Riparian	Lying on or adjacent to a river or lake. Used to denote people, plants or wildlife living along the water's edge.

River basin	The area from which a river system naturally receives its drainage water. It may include a series of tributary rivers and their sub-basins.
Riverine	Features or habitats relating to, formed by, or lying within a river; living along the banks of a river.
Tɔgodo	Literally means behind a water body. Refers to any place across a water body, which implies that to get there, you have to cross the water body in question. It also suggests distance.
Tɔkɔ	Water front, the banks a river.
Tɔnugble	A farm by the edge of a water body
The VALCO Agreement	A set of contracts, documents and regulations involving, in addition to the consortium, foreign governmental and international financial agencies for the construction and management of an aluminium smelter.
Zikpuitɔ	Literally, the "owner of a stool." This is a person from a segment of the royal lineage so designated. This person has a special ritual and jural relationship with the stool.

CHANGES IN THE GHANAIAN CURRENCY (1958–2002)

14 July 1958   Ghana decided to establish its own National Currency, the Ghana Pound (£G), to replace the West African Pound. (The £G was issued at par with the West African Pound; therefore at par with UK Sterling).

August 1960   Parliament passed the Exchange Control Act: hence forth all transfers of funds out of Ghana required permission from the Bank of Ghana.

19 July 1965   A new currency known as the Cedi (¢) was introduced. It replaced the Ghana Pound at the following rates:
(i) ¢2.40 = £1Stg.
(ii) ¢1.00 = US$1.67 (1US$ = ¢0.60)

24 February 1966   Nkrumah was overthrown.

17 February 1966   The Cedi was replaced by a new currency, the New Cedi (N¢) at the following rates: Old Cedi ¢1.20 = N¢1.00; ¢1.00 = US$1.40 (i.e. 1US$ = N¢0.71). The old Cedi ceased to be legal tender on 23 May 1967.

8 July 1967   The New Cedi was *devalued*; the following rates of exchange became applicable: N¢1.00 = US$0.98 (i.e. 1US$ = N¢1.02).

4 November 1971   The Bank of Ghana announced that the New Cedi will not be pegged to the Pound Sterling but to the US Dollar (at N¢1.00 = US$0.98).

27 December 1971   The New Cedi was *devalued*; the following rates of change became applicable: N¢1.00 = US$0.55 (i.e. 1US$ = N¢1.82).

13 January 1972   Col. Acheampong seized power.

7 February 1972   The 27 December devaluation is cancelled: the Cedi is, in effect, *revalued*; the following rates of exchange became applicable: N¢1.00 = US$0.78 (i.e. 1US$ = N¢1.28).

8 May 1972   The US Dollar was itself *devalued* by nearly 8% in terms of the unit price of gold. (As the New

Cedi was pegged to the US Dollar, it was automatically devalued in terms of gold by the same percentage).

15 February 1973   The US Dollar was *devalued* but the Acheampong administration decided to maintain the value of the N¢ in terms of gold. This decision resulted in an appreciation of the N¢ with the following rates being applicable: N¢1.00 = US$0.87 (i.e. 1US$ = N¢1.15).

March 1973   It was announced that, henceforth, the New Cedi would revert to its original name and would be known simply as the Cedi (¢).

20 June 1978   The Bank of Ghana announced the introduction of a Managed Flexible Exchange Rate Regime.

July 1978   Col. Acheampong was overthrown in a 'Palace Coup'.

28 August 1978   The Cedi was *devalued*; the following rates became applicable: ¢1.00 = US$0.36 (i.e. 1US$ = ¢2.75).

1 December 1981   Flt. Lt. Rawlings staged his second coup.

11 October 1983   The Cedi was *devalued*; the following rates became applicable: ¢1.00 = US$0.033 (i.e. 1US$ = ¢30.00).

September 1986   Foreign exchange auction with two tiers introduced.

February 1987   Two-tier system unified with exchange rate at 150 cedis to the dollar.

February 1988   Private Forex bureaux introduced. Average exchange rate was 229 cedis to a dollar.

1992   Inter bank market created. Created a free market in foreign exchange. Average exchange rate 520 cedis to the US$1.

1995   Average exchange rate was 1,449.28 cedis to the US$1.

1999   Average Exchange rate was 2,674.03 cedis to the US$1.

2000   Average exchange rate was 5,321.68 cedis to the US$1.

2002   Average exchange rate was 8,500 cedis to the US$1.

Sources: Anin, T.E. (2000) Banking in Ghana, Harrigan and Oduro, (2000), ISSER, The State of the Ghanaian Economy, 1999, 2000, 2001.

ACKNOWLEDGEMENTS

This research is the fulfilment of a longstanding interest in what happened to the Lower Volta after the Akosombo Dam. The opportunity finally came after years of unsuccessfully trying to find the resources to research this topic. I am grateful to the Netherlands Foundation for the Advancement of Tropical Research (WOTRO) for the grant (No. WB 52 776) which enabled me to research and write this book.

I am truly grateful to the people of Mepe, Sokpoe, Surveyor Line, Kudikope and Kpando Torkor for their warm welcome and kindness. I want to acknowledge the following persons who facilitated the logistical aspects of my research and in some cases, were also informants. Dankudi Akaho-Tay and Prosper Adamali of Accra let me live in their homes at Mepe and Sokpoe respectively. At Mepe, Mr. E.O. Adukonu, Gladys Adukonu, Kwasi Ego Akumani, Mama Awusi Sreku, queen-mother of Mepe, Andy Gbedzeke, the late Mankralo Togbe Asidi and the late Togbe Atise did whatever was necessary to ensure that my interviews went smoothly. Togbe Anipati IV, my first informant and colleague at the University of Ghana, encouraged me to go to Mepe and Surveyor Line and his name opened doors. At Sokpoe, Esther Goh, Solomon Eworyi, Jerry Kaleku, Margaret Fiadzigbe and Togbe Zogah I assisted me. I wish to thank John Akpese, Alice Zotor, K. Korkor, and Togbe Ekuvor Mensah at Surveyor Line, Togbe Awuku Adzor and Gershon Akorli at Kudikope and Togbe Adze, Togbe Nutakor, Amavi Ahumata and Larweh Atsu at Kpando Torkor. Mr. Kobla Kalitsi, former chief executive and Board Chairman of the Volta River Authority deserves special mention for his generousity with his time and for putting his vast knowledge of the Volta River Project at my disposal.

I owe a debt of gratitude to Prof. Carla Risseeuw, without whom this book might never have been written. She steered me through funding and visa applications and draft chapters with much skill, care and kindness and tempered my legal bent with large doses of anthropological insights. Dr. Piet Konings facilitated my visits to Leiden in many important ways and made sure I always received my money on time. His critical comments on my drafts inspired me to work harder at making myself understood. To Prof. Leo de Haan, my special thanks for agreeing to support my funding application even before we met and for staying the course and showing great diligence in reading my chapters and always giving me thoughtful and insightful comments. Ann Whitehead of the University of Sussex was very generous with her time, her vast experience of my subject matter and her hospitality. She read my drafts, discussed them extensively and made substantial contributions. I am truly grateful to Prof. Jacob Songsore for good advice on writing strategies and his constant encouragement and moral support. Prof. Kojo Amanor read some of my earliest drafts and gave me sound advice about length which, if I had taken, would have saved me much heartache down the road.

The CNWS Research School at the University of Leiden hosted me for four years and the Africa Studies Centre (ASC) provided me with the resources and space to finish writing up the research. I am especially grateful to the administrative staff of the CNWS and the ASC for their practical, logistical and technical support—from help with visa applications through preparing seminar presentations to office clips. My thanks to Drs. Dick Foeken and Marcel Rutten of the ASC, and Drs. Robert Ross and Sabine Luning of the CNWS, who at different stages helped me to work through some of my ideas.

Prof. K. Asenso-Okyere, Vice-Chancellor of the University of Ghana, who was the Director of ISSER during the period of this research gave unstinting encouragement. Charity Dzormeku helped me with the accounts and also took an interest in my constantly slipping time-table.

I wish to acknowledge the assistance of Yaw Oppong-Ampofo, Augustina Adukonu, Atsu Apetorgbor, Agbodzi Gborgbor, F. Asare-Thompson, Joseph Ecklu and Isaac Owusu-Mensah with fieldwork data collection, transcription of tapes, secondary data collection and data analysis. Nana Eshun went beyond friendship and proof read my text. Kafui Denkabe produced the bibliography. Hellen Agbesi-Sunu typed my interview transcripts and type set the book, and in her usual unflappable style, made it all look very easy. Sam B. Duodu produced all the beautiful maps I used in the text by hand. I thank Dr. K.M. Cranu of the Ghana Universities Press for technical advice in the preparation of the manuscript for publication. I am also grateful to Mr. Normanyo for copy-editing the text and to Mr. S.K. Attah for producing the book's index. Dr. Nana Akua Anyidoho generously read through the first proofs of the book at very short notice. I thank the team at Brill—Dr. Joed Elich, Ms. Sasha Goldstein and Ms Renee Otto for overseeing the publication of the book.

My thanks and appreciation to Bunie M. Matlanyane Sexwale, Felix Ameka, James and Joscelyn Essegbey, Marijke Steegstra, Ellen-Rose Kambel, Fergus MacKay, Nana Baiden, Salome Asem, Nana Oppong Banson and Merra Tegegn Melesse in the Netherlands, Nana Eshun, Angela and Sam Bruce, Tony and Evelyn Aheto in the United Kingdom for being my family away from home and making my long absences from Ghana bearable and pleasant. Henrietta Heimgaertner and Imani Tafari-Ama, fellow participants at the ISS over a decade ago and Amrita Chhachhi my favourite teacher from those years provided me with much needed continuity, reminiscences and uplifting conversations at different times during the period.

My mother Janet Fiadzigbe, facilitated my fieldwork by travelling with me to my research communities. I thank my siblings-Senanu, Novisi and Setorme and their families for managing to remain my primary support base in spite of their being away from Ghana. My dear friends Rose Mensah-Kutin, Takyiwaa Manuh, Gertrude Torkornu and Naa-aku Acquaye-Baddoo have in different ways supported me. I am especially grateful to Afi Kokuvi, Ama Adzinku, Selina Obess and Rejoice Adavwu for childcare beyond the call of duty.

Finally, I dedicate this book to Yao Graham and to our son Susu. To Yao, I owe a debt of gratitude for his unconditional commitment to the life we have together and the countless ways in which he demonstrates this. To Susu, who can now read this, my deep appreciation of his brave acceptance of my long absences and for his faith that it would all end one day.

Accra, June 2005

CHAPTER ONE

INTRODUCTION

The Akosombo Hydroelectric Power Dam, constructed over the Volta River between 1961 and 1965 and commissioned in 1966, is not visible from much of the Lower Volta and the Volta Lake settlements. However, few in these places are unaware of its long shadow. The profoundly negative impacts of the Akosombo and also the Kpong Dam on lives and livelihoods are visible all around the Lower Volta—in the polluted state of the Volta River, in the high poverty levels and the ongoing struggle to make a living, in the migration patterns and household demographics and in the bilharzia infections. It can also be inferred from the experiences of those who settled around the Lake—in the near absence of health, education and communication facilities, in the poor state of housing and living conditions and in the terrible living conditions of hordes of child fishermen. That these realities are not shared by most people in Ghana is partly a function of the research and policy invisibility of the Lower Volta and the Volta Lake settlements. As well, many Ghanaians are only now recovering from a long love affair with the Akosombo Dam, which until recently, was seen as a technological triumph and a symbol of modern nationhood. The Kpong Dam, constructed over a decade and half later in 1982 and situated 25 kilometres downstream from Akosombo, never excited the same level of interest partly because of its smaller size[1] and less dramatic architecture and also because

---

[1] Both Akosombo and Kpong are part of Ghana's Volta River Project (VRP). Other parts of the VRP are power stations, the electricity distribution network, townships, roads, a port and an aluminium smelter. The International Commission on Large Dams (ICOLD) defines a large dam as one with a height of 15 metres or more from foundation (Goodland, 1994; Report of the World Commission on Dams, 2000). Also, dams between 5 and 15 metres with a reservoir volume of more than 3 million m³ are also classified as large. By this classification, Akosombo and Kpong are among the 45,000 existing large dams in 2000 (World Commission on Dams, 2000). The Akosombo Dam is 244 feet (74.39 metres calculated at 3.28 feet to 1 metre) above the level of the river (Volta Lake Research and Development Project, Phase II, 1973).

it was constructed long after Akosombo and did not produce a reservoir the size and significance of the Volta Lake.[2]

Apart from their showcase status, the Dams supplied the bulk of domestic and industrial electricity and also revenue from the sale of electricity to the largest single consumer, the Volta Aluminium Company (VALCO), neighbouring countries—Togo, Benin and La Côte d'Ivoire, and local commercial and domestic consumers.[3] Once it became clear that the dream of industrialisation engendered by the Project would not materialise, the Volta River Project's star dimmed somewhat. Recent problems with the reliability and price of electricity and the indebtedness of the Volta River Authority have also damaged its credibility as one of the important achievements since Ghana's independence in 1957.[4]

From the start, there were two concerns about the Volta River Project. One of these was the growing unhappiness among certain sections of the population about the agreements governing the Project on account of the serious imbalances in the enjoyment of project benefits (Sawyerr, undated, a; Graham, 1986). In 1972, university students in a demonstration outside the US Embassy in Accra had demanded a review of the VALCO Agreement[5] and some gold mining concessions (Sawyerr, undated, a). During the regular demonstrations of workers and students in the early period of the Rawlings Regime (1982), the VALCO Agreement was a focus of protests and demands for renegotiation and nationalisation. These protests cul-

---

[2] The Volta Lake which formed after the Akosombo Dam was considered the largest man-made lake in the world for years—3275 sq. miles (3742.8 sq. kilometres), 250 miles long (285.7 kilometres) and a storage capacity of 120 million acre feet of water (Jopp, 1965). It inundated 4% of Ghana's land area (Jopp, 1965). Other studies have put the percentage of land inundated at 8% and 10% (Johnson, 1971; Williams, 1991; Blackwelder, 1983) based on different calculations.

[3] There is nothing particularly Ghanaian about the iconic status of large dams in the national imagination. McCully (1996) documents American pride in the Hoover Dam and President Nehru's eloquence about the Nangal Canal and the Bhakra Dam in the Punjab in the 1950s. However, it may be that in Ghana, the many failures of the post-colonial project have put this particular achievement in sharp relief.

[4] The Volta River Authority announced in December 2002 that it had secured a loan of US $30 million to repay its debts to its creditors such as La Côte d'Ivoire for the supply of power.

[5] The VALCO Agreement is a set of contracts, documents and regulations involving the Aluminium Companies, foreign governmental and international financial agencies and the government of Ghana which govern the sale of VRP power to the aluminium smelter among other things (Sawyerr, 1990, 83–86).

minated in the Rawlings Regime's decision to demand a renegotiation of the VALCO Agreement. The agreements, which were renegotiated between 1982 and 1985, will be discussed in more detail in another chapter of the book.

The second concern, long articulated but mostly ignored in policy circles, was about communities adversely affected by the Volta River Project. They were the over ninety thousand persons who were evacuated and resettled to make way for the Volta Lake and the Kpong Headpond, the unknown numbers of communities established along the Volta Lake from 1965,[6] and their hosts whose lands were submerged or commandeered to resettle others. There were also the downstream communities, which experienced profound environmental and socio-economic impacts and major disruptions in their pre-dam livelihood sources and patterns (Moxon, 1984, p. 162).

In August 2001, what appeared to be a routine meeting of researchers, policy makers and community representatives to discuss the findings of research took place at the Accra Conference Centre. The meeting, however, was totally unprecedented in that it was the first in the over three decades since the construction of the Akosombo Dam on the Lower Volta. Three government ministers were present, each expressing commitment to solving the development problems of the area. The Volta River Authority, the statutory corporation in charge of the VRP, also took this opportunity to claim a long-standing concern for downstream communities, thus attempting to rewrite its history of neglect of the Lower Volta. In what was a departure from the format of the meeting, the then Member of parliament for North Tongu read a statement in the name of concerned citizens of the Tongu area. The statement expressed dissatisfaction with the research findings and scepticism that the recommendations being made were strong enough to tackle the deep-seated livelihood and health problems of dam-affected communities. Once the statement was read, the meeting returned to its format of presentations by the researchers and comments by the participants. No direct

---

[6] In 1962–63, the Volta River Authority enumerated 20,000 Tongu fishermen in a census to determine the population to be displaced by the Lake (Lawson, 1986 (a), p. 45). Kumi, writing a decade later, noted that the majority of the 12,500 fishermen with 12,000 canoes operating and living with their families in about a thousand villages along the lake with a total population of up to 60,000 were Tongu fishermen (Kumi, 1973, p. 918).

response was ever made to the concerned citizens' statement. The statement, together with the lack of a response, captured the running sore of state neglect of the Lower Volta in all its symbolism. Once again, the people of the lower Volta had spoken and received no response or acknowledgement. Four years after the event, not much has changed in the Lower Volta and there is no visible attempt to implement even the weak recommendations of the conference.

How dam-affected communities in the Lower Volta have survived dam impacts and state neglect is the subject of this book. The book examines the long-term impacts of the VRP, state policy responses to these impacts and the everyday responses and livelihood trajectories of Downstream and Lakeside Communities—two related categories of dam-affected communities. The downstream of the Akosombo and Kpong dams is an area stretching 5 miles in width on both sides of the Volta River between Amedeka/Akuse and the estuary at Ada. This area, which was also the floodplain of the Volta, is the last 54-mile (61.7 kilometres)[7] stretch of the river as it enters the sea in the Gulf of Guinea on the Atlantic Coast of West Africa.[8] While this area is home to a number of groups—the Krobo, Osudoku, Ada (of the Ga-Adangbe socio-linguistic group), and the Anlo Ewe, the Tongu Ewe[9] is by far the largest single sub-group.[10] The Lakeside, the extensive shoreline of one of the largest man-made lakes in the world, was settled by thousands of fishing and farming people from the 1960s when it formed. These communities are predominantly from the coastal and inland fishing communities of Southern Ghana, with the largest single sub-group being the Tongu Ewe.

The book addresses a number of gaps in the scientific literature and policy focus on the impacts of large dams in general and the Akosombo and Kpong dams in particular. These include the physical

---

[7] Converted from 54 miles at 7/8 miles to a kilometre.

[8] There is controversy about the 5 miles width with inhabitants arguing that the area, which should be covered because of its riverine character, stretches further than that. This point came up at a national conference on the Lower Volta in 2001, as did a complaint by the people of the Amedeka that while administratively they were now within the Manya Krobo administrative district, they were an integral part of the Lower Volta.

[9] Tongu, which literally means "along the river", denotes the people, their language and their location.

[10] The four districts covered by the Lower Volta—North Tongu, South Tongu, Dangme East and Dangme are estimated to have a population of 139,000 living in 403 communities (Volta Basin Research Project, 1999).

scientific and engineering bias in dam literature and policy which has relegated affected populations to secondary status, and a preoccupation of the literature with those physically dislocated and subsequently resettled and with short term impacts (Chambers (ed), 1970; Johnson, 1971; Kalitsi, 1973; Kumi, 1973). This is in spite of the fact that the few studies on downstream and lakeside communities who form the majority of dam-affected communities point to serious long term adverse impacts (Yeboah, 1999; Volta Basin Research Project, 1999; Geker, 1999) in keeping with the findings of similar studies around Africa.[11]

The book is situated within a national context, particular elements of which are significant. These include the expansion in local demand for power, anxieties about the physical condition of the Akosombo Dam and public resistance to escalating domestic electricity prices in the face of continuing enjoyment of low tariffs by the Volta Aluminium Company (VALCO). These have resulted in a number of policy shifts in the power sector. One of these is the promotion of private sector involvement in power generation and management. More recently, there have been discussions about the construction and management of a new large hydroelectric power dam at Bui on the Black Volta, a tributary of the Volta. The proposed Bui Dam, the cost of which has been estimated at US$1 billion, could generate 300 megawatts of electricity, about a third of Akosombo's 833 megawatts.[12] More recently, the wrangles over the cost of power between Ghana and VALCO resulted in the sale of the Aluminium smelter to the Ghana government. The government recently entered into agreement with ALCOA, another US company, for the sale of the smelter. Interestingly, these debates about the cost of power are

---

[11] Thomas and Adams, for example, note that "reviews of impacts of large dams on the inhabitants of floodplains in Africa nearly all stress their adverse impacts" (1999, p. 920). Studies of different floodplains have documented the decline in agriculture, fisheries, forests and other sources of livelihood (Goldsmith and Hilyard, 1984; Drijver and Marchand, 1985; Drijver and Rodenburg, 1988; Adams, 1992; Horowitz and Salem-Murdock, 1991, McCully, 1996; Collier, Web and Schmidt, 1996; Atakpu, 2000).

[12] M.A.O. Addo, Director for Organisational Services, VRA in a Ghana News Agency (GNA) interview, *Daily Graphic*, July 20th 1994. The Ghana Government announced in 1994 that dams would now be constructed by the private sector (President Rawlings's Sessional Address to Parliament, 1994). The Bui Project was shelved in the first year of the New Patriotic Party (NPP) government in 2001, but was reinstated in 2002 and bids invited from prospective dam building consortia.

being conducted without any consideration of the costs represented
by the problems of dam-affected communities. The rest of this chapter introduces the book and sets out the national context and conceptual framework for studying lives and livelihoods of downstream
communities.

2. *The National Context*

The setting for the Volta River Project is Ghana, a small country
of just over 18 million people,[13] situated on the Atlantic Coast of
Africa in West Africa. Ghana is bordered to the North by the
Republic of Burkina Faso, to the West by La Côte d'Ivoire and to
the East by the Republic of Togo—three of the countries with whom
it shares the Volta River. At least 40% of the Volta Basin, though,
is within Ghana. The Volta with its tributaries is one of the defining
characteristics of the Ghanaian landscape and an important source
of fish, drinking water, water for farming and transport. Rainfall is
from medium to poor in most parts of Ghana and while southern
Ghana has two rainy seasons, the North has only one.

At the time of the VRP, Ghana was a low income developing
country with much of its population based in rural areas and engaged
in food crop and export crop farming, fishing, small scale trading
and indigenous artisanship and this has remained so over three
decades later. After years of political instability, intermittent coups
d'état and military rule from the mid-1960s to the 1990s, Ghana
entered a period of parliamentary constitutional rule in 1992 (for
more detailed accounts of different aspects of these periods, see
Graham, 1989; Hansen and Ninsin, eds, 1989; Gyimah-Boadi, ed,
1993; Nugent, 1995). This had been preceded by the adoption of
Structural Adjustment Programme (SAP) in the 1980s in an attempt
to halt the economic decline, which had accompanied political instability. In the late 80s and early 90s, the SAP strategy was declared
a success because it restored economic growth and the regeneration
of infrastructure. However, as analysts pointed out, this success was
bolstered by aid and rapidly accumulating debt and did not change

---

[13] Ghana Statistical Service, 2002. At the time of the VRP, Ghana's population
was estimated at around 6 million, a third of this figure.

the essential character and structure of the economy (Aryeetey and Harrigan, 2000; Killick, 2000; Hutchful, 2002). By the end of the 1990s, Ghana had applied to join the Highly Indebted Poor Countries (HIPC) initiative which was designed to aid indebted countries reduce their indebtedness. Throughout the periods of political instability and economic crisis, the Volta River Project was viewed as an island of success. Indeed, the Kpong Dam was commissioned on schedule in very uncertain political and economic times by the last in a long line of coup d'etat regimes. However, by the late 1990s, the Volta River Authority had begun to experience and reflect the crises in the larger political economy.

These problems of the Ghanaian economy have their roots in history. Formally colonised by the British in 1901 through a process which began in 1471 with the arrival of Portuguese traders on the coast and involved trade, treaties and wars of conquest, the Gold Coast, as it was known in the colonial period, gained independence in 1957 as Ghana. As a colonial entity, it had consisted of four parts cobbled together in different periods and by different means. They were the Colony on the coast, Asante in the middle belt, the Northern Territories and the ex-German trust territory of Togoland, which was administered as part of the Gold Coast after World War I. This last territory, which became part of Ghana through a plebiscite just before independence, placed a significant portion of the middle and lower sections of the Volta River within Ghana instead of on its international borders.

Other elements of colonial policy were to be important for the Volta River Project (VRP) which was conceived in this period. Although executed as a post-colonial project, colonial imperatives had shaped the VRP. Policies such as the establishment of native administrations under chiefs to administer parts of the territory under the overall supervision of the Colonial State resulted in the creation of chiefs where there were none, and weakening and strengthening of different aspects of their powers where they existed. Their legitimisation as representatives of their people and the repositories of customary law and practice by the Colonial State came to influence the conduct of the struggles of dam-affected populations for redress. Colonial economic policy focus on the export of primary commodities created an export oriented agricultural economy with very poor internal linkages and virtually no industries. The establishment of a colonial bureaucracy created a class divorced from its rural roots

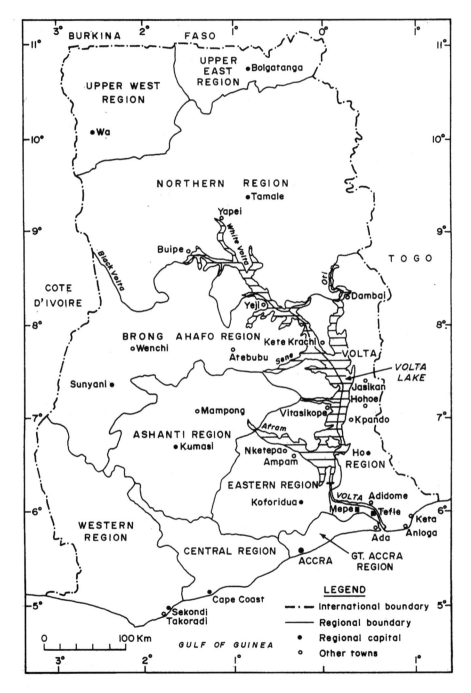

Figure 1: Map of Ghana showing the Volta Lake and the Lower Volta

and interested in the modernisation project of the colonial and post colonial States for its own ends (Hinden, 1950; Phillips, 1989; Mikell, 1989).

At independence, Ghana's leaders embraced the Volta River Project as a way to acquire cheap electricity to catalyse rapid industrialisation, which they and the development economics establishment of the day considered critical for the modernisation and development of the country. The result was an ambitious and technologically impressive project that involved the marshalling of a staggering range of international players in a world riven by cold war conflicts and experiencing the beginnings of what is now understood as the vast power and influence of trans-national corporations on governments. The VRP's long gestation also meant that its proponents had to respond to constantly changing conditions and challenges, with the result that the government of Ghana lost sight of its original goals, one of which was the mitigation of dam impacts on local communities. Successive governments have also been unable to address this issue.

3. *The Conceptual Framework and Research Methods*

The starting point of the conceptual framework for studying downstream and lakeside communities is whether their specificities set them apart. In other words, how different are they from other rural populations struggling to survive under difficult environmental and social conditions? Two other questions arise here—whether dam impacts are the most important factor shaping livelihood trajectories in the Volta Basin and what livelihoods would look like without the Volta River Project. This last question probably cannot be fully answered, but all three questions need to be kept in view in devising a conceptual framework.

The first assumption of the framework is that the people of the Volta Lakeside and the Lower Volta are no different from millions of rural people in Ghana and elsewhere living under adverse environmental and socio-economic conditions. Indeed, some of their responses have resulted in livelihoods similar to those in other rural areas. This in itself gives the study wider applicability. However, the damming of the Volta River represented a highly significant moment in the life of post-colonial Ghana and indeed sub-Saharan Africa in which the particular constellation of the forces and players active in shaping the present and future of the country and the continent were presented in sharp relief. There were the bilateral and multilateral agencies and banks, trans-national corporations, foreign governments, one of them the erstwhile colonial power, the Post-colonial State and the people of Ghana. Each of these players had their own interests and as the history of the Volta River Project shows, it was a moment of converging but also irreconcilable interests that were somehow held together by the single-mindedness of one individual—Kwame Nkrumah. It was also the Ghanaian Post-colonial State's first serious exercise of the principle of eminent domain to commandeer local resources for a national project. Its conduct in this instance set the tone for future practice.

Another point of difference between the Lakeside and Lower Volta on the one hand, and other rural areas on the other hand, is the drastic redesign of the environment of dam-affected communities almost overnight, something that for most other rural communities is usually a process of attrition. This, together with the dramatic changes arising from the creation of the Volta Lake, was important for the directions people's livelihoods took. Whether people were resettled, migrated to the Lake or remained in the Lower Volta, they were responding to the changes downstream and upstream. So while these communities might have responded as other rural dwellers do when faced with environmental stress, the particular choices they made took the conditions created by the dams into account.

The foregoing is not to suggest that the Volta River Project was the only factor at play here, but that it was critical and definitive. Therefore, a second set of concerns is to identify the multiplicity of factors that have shaped and are shaping livelihoods in the Lower Volta and around the Volta Lake. This would capture the experiences of communities in a way that shows their specificities as dam-affected communities as well as the differences between and within them taking into account the larger national and international political economy.

Murray recommends that livelihoods must be discussed "within an analytical framework most simply described as the political economy of change" (2002, p. 491). To elaborate this framework, a modified livelihoods approach has been constructed from the sustainable rural livelihoods framework, pioneered by Ellis (1999) and others and modified by the theoretical work of researchers such as Kaag et al., 2003; Arce and Hebinck, 2002; Chimhowu, 2002;

Murray, 2002; O'laughlin, 2002; Whitehead and Kabeer, 2001; de Haan, 2000; Francis, 2000; Beall and Kanji, 1999. In the absence of analytical frameworks designed specifically for the study of dam-affected communities, this approach offers a useful way of analysing the long-term survival strategies of such communities and their members. This is because the livelihoods approaches recognise the multiplicity of influences, actors, strategies and outcomes in the making of a living, allow the consideration of both macro and micro processes, and transcend dichotomies such as urban/rural, industrial/agricultural and formal/informal. They are also credited with taking account of both intra-household and extra-household social relations (Grown and Sebstad, 1989; Murray, 2000) and giving recognition to the fact that livelihoods may not occur within a fixed time and place of work, involve an employer-employee relationship, admitting seasonality and multiple, sequential and overlapping tasks (Grown and Sebstad, 1989, pp. 941–942) and recognising the equal importance of production and reproductive activities in the making of a living. The definitions of livelihoods and livelihood strategies show clearly these advantages of the livelihoods approaches. There are several of these (Sebstad and Grown, 1989; Ellis, 1998). In this study, Painter's definition of livelihood strategies as "how individuals, households or corporate groups gain access to, use and exercise control over any number of resources that they identify as important for their well-being. Resources may include, for example, income, commodities (ranging from food to tools and utensils, clothing and medications), arable land, wooded areas and water resources needed for agro-pastoral production" (Painter, 1996, pp. 80–81) combined with Beall and Kanji's definition of livelihoods as not just earning an income, but involving a wider range of activities including "gaining and retaining access to resources and opportunities, dealing with risk, negotiating social relations and managing social networks and institutions within households, communities and localities" (Beall and Kanji 1999, p. 1) are adopted.

The Department for International Development (DFID) of the UK is one of the pioneers of the sustainable rural livelihoods approaches (SRL), one of the earliest livelihoods approaches (Carney, 1998). Ellis (1998; 2000a), Bebbington (1999), Painter (1996), Lyon (2000), through a micro-level focus on livelihoods, have added analytical depth to the DFID approach. The DFID scheme is rendered by Ellis as follows:

Assets	→	Access	→	Activities
		(Mediating processes)		
Social		PIP/ Vulnerability Context		Farm, non-farm
Human		policies	trends	transfers
Financial		institutions	shocks	
Physical		processes	seasons	
Natural				

Source: Ellis, 2000.

The SRL framework postulates that the ability of individuals and families to construct livelihoods depends on their assets, which allow a range of possible strategies, each strategy being a bundle of activities. The SRL approach sees livelihoods as consisting of three interconnected parts: a) assets, b) access (mediating processes) and c) activities. Livelihood activities are realised through the interaction of assets with access (the mediating processes). There are five kinds of assets—social, human, financial, natural and physical—and they are critical as are the factors that determine people's access to both assets and activities. Two categories of mediating processes are recognised in the SRL framework. One is the policies, institutions and processes (PIP) and the other the vulnerability context, composed of the risks, trends, shocks and seasonal factors. Livelihood activities include farm, non-farm activities, transfers, etc. (Ellis, 2000). The SRL approaches have been heavily critiqued for not making good some of the promising aspects of the livelihoods approaches, particularly their failure to take serious account of the macro level and institutional issues within the livelihood contexts and their limited treatment of the relational and process dimensions of livelihoods. What follows is a discussion of the various elements of the critique which form the building blocks of this study's conceptual framework, which can be described as a modified livelihoods approach (MLA).

The Macro Context of Livelihoods

In response to their critique of the SRL, Murray and others have taken up the consideration of international and national macro-economic and political processes policies and institutions and environmental factors as a point of departure. Some of their analysis has drawn attention to the importance of accounting for the interaction between the macro and micro contexts and processes shaping liveli-hoods (Beall and Kanji, 1999; Whitehead and Kabeer, 2001; Francis, 2000; Chimhowu, 2002; Kinsey, 2002; Murray, 1998, 2000; 2002). Apart from the scientific relevance of this view, it has policy impli-cations as it challenges the focus on micro-level interventions to the exclusion of macro-policy and institutions as well as the structural constraints, which frame many livelihoods (Beall and Kanji, 1999; Narotzky, 1997).

Considerations of the macro context as both context setting and as constitutive allow analysis of the interaction between the broad socio-economic and political trends at different levels and trends of livelihood changes (Beall and Kanji, ibid.). As well, it enables analy-sis to go beyond livelihoods and discover the underlying structural processes which lead to poor livelihood outcomes (Chimhowu, 2002; O'Laughlin, 2002). However, as Beall and Kanji (1999, p. 1) point out, one side of the interaction, i.e. the impact of policy on house-holds and communities has received more attention than the ways in which "livelihoods systems and their attendant social relations are constitutive of wider socio-economic processes". The interaction between macro and micro processes sometimes results in unintended consequences, according to O'Laughlin (2002). In the analysis of livelihoods in the Lower Volta and around the Volta Lake, the main macro contexts are the Volta River Project and policies towards affected communities. As well, it includes environmental changes, national, regional and local institutions which govern livelihoods, international and national influences of the Ghanaian state's devel-opment policies and macro economic policies. In the study, the most important elements of the macro context have been large-scale out-migration and in-migration, drastic environmental change, and state neglect of dam impacts in particular, and development in general.

The Environmental Context

The second element of the modification of the SRL approach by Murray and others is the more serious consideration given to envi-ronmental change as a context and a product of livelihoods. In a study of post-dam livelihoods, environmental change is a particularly pertinent issue. That environmental factors affect livelihood traj-ectories is widely accepted (Kinsey, 2002; Ellis, 2001). This is not surprising given the natural resources base of most rural livelihoods.

There are many definitions of the environment, some limited to the
physical and natural surroundings in which humans live and others,
including, to different degrees, the socio-economic and political contexts of human existence (see Dietz, 1996; de Haan, 2000 for a discussion of various definitions). Leach et al., for example, define
environments as "landscapes under constant change, emerging as the
outcome of dynamic and variable ecological processes and distur-
bance events, in interaction with human use" (1997, p. 4). This view
of the environment, which sees it as a setting for social action as
well as a product of such action, is the definition used in this study
(Leach, Mearns and Scoones, 1997). It is a departure from the more
inclusive definitions of the environment that embrace, to different
degrees, institutional and socio-economic elements.

Our definition enables us to focus attention on these factors separately while acknowledging their inter-connections. It also recognises that the environment is constantly undergoing small and large
changes as humans interact with it. These changes have to be substantial and generally irreversible to be seen as environmental change.
Thus it has been suggested that drought, however long and severe,
may not amount to environmental change (Odegi-Awuondo, 1990).[14]
The term environmental degradation has been used extensively in
dam impacts and other literature on rural livelihoods. However, there
is dispute about its definition and what indicators would signify its
presence (Bhalla, 1992; Ghai, 1994). It has been suggested that irreversible changes in the physical environment amount to degradation
when they adversely affect or impair the ability of the environment
to support the livelihoods of the populations residing in it at the levels existing before degradation. As this has long been established in
the case of downstream communities, we use the term environmental degradation in this framework (Adams, 1992; McCully, 1996).

The Social Relations of Livelihoods

A third key element of the modification is the recognition of the
centrality of social relations of class, gender, kinship and generation

---

[14] The term stress has been used instead for both long and short-term drought
(Odegi-Awuondo, 1990; Sefa-Dei, 1992).

to livelihoods. Murray (2002) argues that livelihood trajectories of individuals and households in one social class are often related to those in another social class and this demands an understanding of livelihoods in structural and relational terms. Therefore, proper emphasis has to be given to the role of social relations and inequalities of power in livelihood trajectories in a specific historical context (see also O'Laughlin, 2002). In much of the literature on livelihoods, class is often replaced by terms such as "income", "social status" (O'Laughlin, 2002. See also de Haan & Zoomers, forthcoming). This tends to obscure the structural and relational dimensions of class. On the other hand, Scott has critiqued the privileging and treatment of class in purely structural terms in the Marxist and neo-Marxist traditions, noting that such an approach does not allow enough space for human actors, the specificity of class relations, and the presence of other social relationships which might or might not affect how class relationships are manifested (Scott, 1985). He argues:

> Class after all does not exhaust the total explanatory space for social actions. Nowhere is it truer than within the peasant village where class may compete with kinship, neighbourhood, faction and ritual links as foci of human identity and solidarity. Beyond the village level, it may compete with ethnicity, language group, religion and region as a focus of loyalty. Class may be applicable to some situations, but not to others; it may be reinforced or crosscut by other ties; it may be far more important for the experience of some than of others . . . the messy reality of multiple identities will continue to be the experience out of which social relations are conducted (1985, p. 43).

While this point is correct, the disappearance of class analysis, whether of a structural or more agency oriented kind, from much of the discussion of livelihoods is problematic in that it hampers the analysis of differentiation in livelihood trajectories by creating the erroneous impression that the only social relations at the level of the household are gender, kinship and generation. Given the intersection of social relations, this silence on class affects the quality of analysis of other social relations.

Gender, unlike class, is often discussed in the livelihoods approaches. However, its full implications are rarely analysed. Some of the writing on the gender and livelihoods focuses on differences in access to resources and the implications of women's concentration in low return and ease of entry activities (Koopman, 1991; Whitehead and Kabeer, 2001).

Kinship relations are central to organisation of livelihoods. As Slater (2002) argues, "the capacities of households to respond to change and spread themselves across space were a function of household circumstances and intra- and inter-household relations of gender, kin and generation" (2002, p. 216). These relations, which are a source of credit, payment in kind, employment and physical security, enable people to respond to risk and contingencies. Thus the differences in the livelihood trajectories of two persons of the same gender and their current levels of vulnerability may be a function of their ability to call on these social and kin relations (Slater, 2002, pp. 612–613). These findings notwithstanding, kinship and interaction relations are often hierarchical and not always fully reciprocal. Familial systems privilege age, kinship status and maleness (Whitehead and Kabeer, 2001). Also, while they might appear to be stable and fixed, they are most diverse and changeable (Risseeuw and Palriwala, 1996). Besides, the meaning and implication of these social relations can be complicated by their intersections. Thus while age might bring some privileges which enhance livelihoods, old people, especially women have to care for young grandchildren without adequate resources in the Lower Volta. More specifically, Whitehead argues that as a source of labour exchange, the value of kinship and social networks is tempered by the increasing social differentiation they engender (Whitehead, 2002).

Some of the literature on gender, kinship and generation also discusses the role of reproductive activities and intra-household relations in the organisation of livelihoods. The focus on reproductive activities can be extended to the examination of class and other forms of social and economic differentiation. It can also enable the consideration of how various social relations intersect in the organisation of livelihoods both within and between households. This issue of intersection has been an important insight of gender analysis and is also implied by Scott's critique of class cited above (Scott, 1985; see also Koopman, 1991; Folbre, 1996). In this connection, studies of child-care and other domestic work of older women and children in households have also provided insights useful for the study of livelihoods (Elson, 1992; Beall and Kanji, 1999; Risseeuw and Palriwala, 1996). Related to this, changes in inter-generational relations, especially those between adults and children, are increasingly recognised in the literature (Risseeuw & Palriwala, 1996; van der Geest, 1997). An aspect of this is in the studies of child labour. White (1996) has written extensively about the problems of children working under unregulated and informal labour arrangements. While there is agreement that child labour is most driven by economic factors, the specificities and trends are also important. Van der Geest has observed that over the years in several African settings, children have shifted from being seen as assets to being economic passengers who would only bring returns as very well-educated adults (1997). This has implications for childcare practices and the role of children within households and families. This additional dimension of intergenerational relations is relevant to the conditions of children in the Lower Volta.

In this framework, the analysis of social relations is structured by examining the various social relations implicated in livelihoods through labour relations and the institutional arrangements which govern these relations. Thus labour relations between men, between women and men, and between women as master/mistress and worker or apprentice, husband and wife, parents or grandparents and children are considered within and outside the household and in the virtual and physical work places.

In our view, the intersections of the social relations allow certain persons access to and control over the labour of others, an issue arising from some of the case studies in the book. We also consider institutional arrangements such as the conjugal contract, labour contracts and master-apprentice relations in keeping with the idea of the embeddedness of these relations in the general organisation of societies and their reinforcement by ideological and cultural constructs. The ways in which the culture and practice of particular institutions affect livelihoods is considered. The institutions include markets, state and regional policy-making institutions, community level governance, as well as social and economic institutions.

Chimhowu has argued that there are conflicts generated by differences in livelihood strategies of different types of communities, as well as conflicts between different uses of particular resources (2002; see also Leach et al., 1997). In both the Lower Volta and around the Volta Lake, these conflicts between fishermen and farmers as well as between the use of the dam for hydroelectric power and its use for fishing and farming were being played out in the livelihoods of communities and their members.

Making a Living: livelihood trends, responses and outcomes

Several authors take issue with the concept of livelihood strategies (Devereaux, 2001; Murray, 2002; de Bruijn and van Dijk, 1999; Kaag et al, 2003). Devereux (2001), for example, criticises its use ex post facto to describe observed behaviour, distinguishing this from its usage to describe ex ante actions. Murray adopts the notion of livelihood trajectories as used in a study of long term change and livelihoods by Blaikie and others (2002). Livelihood trajectories are defined "as a path through time, and refers to the consequences of the changing ways in which individuals construct a livelihood over time" (Murray, 2002, p. 496). De Bruijn and van Dijk (1999, see also Kaag et al., 2003), for their part, suggest the notion of pathways as being in keeping with the more open-ended approach to livelihoods (2002). In our view, the notions of livelihood trajectories and pathways need not preclude strategies. This is because while trajectories imply the plotting of livelihoods over time, strategies refer to particular livelihood decisions at any point in time. It has been said that the planning and deliberation implied by the term strategy may not be present in particular situations (Devereux, 2001; Kaag et al., 2003). While we agree that not all behaviour qualifies as strategic, some of the criticism takes a somewhat grand view of the term strategy. The knowledge of limits, constraints and what is possible, even when constraints are overwhelming and people appear to have no other options, afford all persons the ability to strategize. It does not imply success or any particular outcomes. Therefore we have retained strategy for the description of particular combinations of activities while using trajectories to describe livelihoods over time.

The framework also uses the broader concept of responses which includes both traditional livelihood responses such as intensification, extensification, changes in the practice of multiple livelihood activities, coping and adaptation. It also admits responses from other traditions which are useful for considering both community and household level responses such as social security mechanisms and resistance.

In keeping with the livelihoods literature as well as the evidence from earlier studies, multiple livelihood activities at the level of individual household members and at the level of the household are distinguished. As well, changes in livelihood activities such as the practice of multiple livelihood activities or diversification are distinguished from what Chimhowu describes as "a radical restructuring of livelihood portfolios" (Chimhowu, 2002, p. 562). Restructuring in this context refers to significant changes in livelihood portfolios and in the organisation of livelihoods which are a response to shocks and irreversible environmental changes as occurred in the Lower Volta and in the decision to migrate to the Volta Lake.

Livelihood activities have been classified in various ways. For example, as a counterpoint to farming, certain rural activities have been variously called "non-agricultural rural employment", "non-farm" or "off-farm" activities.[15] Some of them, firewood and fodder sales, charcoal burning or even the episodic sale of grain and cassava are rooted in the land and labour relations of farming. Others, such as trading, carpentry, masonry, metal and leather work, and to a certain extent mining and pottery, are either removed from the land or imply different land and labour relations.[16] For our purposes, taking into account the range of livelihoods in the Lower Volta and the critique about the assumption that all rural dwellers are farmers, a more simple classification would suffice. This would be: a) farming, b) fishing, c) extractive, e.g. mining, quarrying, charcoal making; d) traditional and contemporary artisanal activities, e.g. carpentry, masonry, pottery, mat making, e) services, e.g. beer brewing, cassava processing, fish preservation, petty trading, corn and flour milling, etc. As well, our framework adopts the classification of anchor and supplementary activities because it allows the examination of their status within a livelihoods portfolio and a determination of their importance in terms of earnings, status and identity and time use. This way, it helps to explain the purposes and changing positions of different activities and their interrelationships.

Other key concepts of the analytical framework are risk, coping and adaptation. Livelihood decisions are a response to various risks in the environment that individuals, households and other groups face as they organise themselves to access resources for survival and prosperity. Risk is defined as "the subjective probability attached by

---

[15] Some studies have however argued that diversification can be within agriculture or outside agriculture. Diversification strategies within agriculture include changing crop mixes, introducing livestock or changing the balance between livestock and farming.

[16] Fishing is particular in the sense that in some cases it is highly contractual and involves hired labour, while in other cases family labour is involved.

individuals or by the household towards the outcomes of the various income-generating activities in which they are engaged" (Anderson et al., 1971, cited in Ellis, 1998, p. 12). Risks differ from context to context, but also have several common features for rural populations. For example, Cernea's risk model in relation to people who are physically displaced by dams identifies eight main risks, which together could lead to impoverishment. They include landlessness, joblessness, homelessness, marginalisation, increased morbidity, food insecurity, loss of access to common property and social disarticulation (Cernea, 1996, 252). The model resonates with certain conditions in the Lower Volta.

The social security literature has an expanded notion of risk in the making of livelihoods. Benda Beckmann (1998) argues that the achievement of social security involves countering and overcoming conditions of insecurity which can be brought on by various factors such as political instability, wars, climatic factors or specific conditions such as unemployment, old age, pregnancy and illness. This conception of social security, which is based on a combination of past experiences, current resources and the promise of future resources, ties in with the concept of livelihoods trajectories, which suggest that livelihoods have a past, present and future. It also includes both community wide and more household specific situations in its definition of risk.

Adaptation and coping are considered in the literature as both livelihood responses outcomes. Coping, considered to be on a lower scale than adaptation, is defined as "the distress and crisis reasons for the emergence of new livelihood patterns" (Ellis, 1998, p. 14). Coping strategies include cutting down on consumption, eating gathered and hunted food, liquidating savings and stripping assets, crop diversification, livelihoods diversification to include self-employment and wage labour in both farm and non-farm sectors (Whitehead and Kabeer, 2001; Beall and Kanji, 1999). Ellis defines adaptation as "the continuous process of changes to livelihoods which either enhance existing security and wealth or try to reduce vulnerability and poverty. Adaptation may be positive or negative: positive if it is by choice, reversible, and increases security; negative if it is of necessity, irreversible, and fails to reduce vulnerability. Negative adaptation occurs when the poor can no longer cope with adverse shocks" (Ellis, 1998, p. 14). In a preliminary study of economic recession in South Eastern Ghana, Chisholm (1982) suggests that local Tongu communities have adapted to ecological changes in the area as a result of the two dams on the River Volta. However, his observation that households had peculiar features raises questions about the validity of his conclusion. Thomas and Adams (1999) also argue that while in the short term, downstream communities of the Tiga Dam (which was constructed in 1974) might suffer shocks, in the long term, they could adapt to dam impacts. While it is not said, there is an implication that the adaptation is positive. The evidence they found in the Hadejia Jama'are floodplain included significant agricultural production increases, population growth at a higher rate than Nigerian averages and the adoption of new technologies. While this conclusion is open to question,[17] their findings—the recovery of agriculture, population increases and the increased use of technologies and the growth of wage employment, contain criteria which are useful for concretising and testing the concept of adaptation.

The working definition of adaptation adopted within this framework is made up of Ellis's definition of adaptation and the criteria identified by Thomas and Adams (1999) in their study of the Hadejia Jama'are floodplain. Therefore the presence and absence of such factors in the research settlements in the Lower Volta are examined. As well, factors which might point to the absence of adaptation have also been identified and applied to the study. Thus the continued environmental decline, the decline in the main livelihood resources, increased conflict and competition over resources, the intensification of the use of hitherto marginal resources, changes in nutrition and consumption, and social problems related to poor livelihood outcomes and the lack of adequate livelihood activities are all factors which could signify the absence of adaptation.

In relation to the practice of multiple livelihoods or diversification, in cognisance of the debate about what its presence and absence signified, we adopted a very simple definition—the presence of more than one livelihood activity within a person or a household's livelihood portfolio at any point in time. This was operationalised in the survey by asking people to list all their work activities and what other members of their family did. We also asked who were involved

---

[17] For example, the focus on just farming does not provide the basis for a conclusion that adaptation has taken place. Also, as they themselves point out, the observed agricultural boom might not be sustained. Chimhowu (2002) has argued that rural livelihoods are characterised by cycles of accumulation and liquidation of assets, which are related to the performance of livelihood activities.

in what reproductive activities such as sweeping, childcare, cooking, procuring fuel and water. We also tried to get a sense of how productive activities were prioritised by asking which was first, second and third in terms of income, time use and status. Through the case studies, we examined in more detail the different implications of the presence of multiple livelihood activities at the level of individuals, household members and the household as a whole, what factors made it possible, the outcomes and the reasons for poor or better outcomes.

Diversification is considered as a sign of both adaptation (Ellis, 1998) and coping (Whitehead and Kabeer, 2001). Some have criticised the use of the concept as arising from a misconception that rural people are first and foremost farmers who then switch to or add on other activities to improve their situation (Arce and Hebinck, 2002). And yet, multiple livelihood activities have been more the norm than the exception in several parts of Africa for a long time (Ellis, 1998, 2000; Kinsey, 2002; Foeken, 1997; Bagachwa, 1997; Gaidzanwa, 1997). This has policy implications. Francis, for example, has observed that if policy makers start from the assumption that rural people's livelihoods are diverse, then the fictive farmer or farm household would disappear from policy calculations (Francis, 2000; see also Arce and Hebinck, 2002; Zoomers, 1999; de Haan and Zoomers, forthcoming). This critique of diversification expands the possibilities for analysing the role of different activities in livelihood portfolios. However, if livelihoods are understood to have both their material and ideological elements, then the status of every livelihood activity has to be analysed in those terms. Thus farming has to be discussed beyond its position as one of several activities in the livelihoods portfolio. This might yet lead us to the conclusion that in some cases, people engaged in multiple activities still identified themselves first and foremost in relation to one of these. The experience of being told by respondents that they are farmers, only to find out that they are engaged in petty trading and other activities, is telling. The idea that Sub-Saharan Africa's economies are predominantly agricultural does have a basis even if it is overstated. In this book, the phrase "the practice of multiple livelihood activities" is used except when referring to literature which uses the term diversification.

While the practice of multiple livelihood activities is old and widespread, there have been changes in its practice. In keeping with this realisation, the focus of the book will be the changes in the character and organisation of livelihood activities since the Volta River Project. In his analysis of diversification, Ellis reflects the debates about what diversification means in particular situations. Diversification is generally considered a desirable livelihoods outcome and those whose attempts to diversify do not work well, or those who do not diversify at all, are among the poorest households. This is because diversification offers the possibilities of flexibility, synergies and protection from misfortune, shocks and failures (Foeken, 1997; see also Gaidzanwa, 1997; Francis, 2000, Chimhowu, 2002; Whitehead and Kabeer, 2001; Whitehead, 2002). There are however many qualifications to this view of diversification (Kinsey, 2002; Slater, 2002).

Meagher and Mustapha (1997, also Whitehead and Kabeer, 2001) have suggested that the difference between poorer and richer households is not whether or not they diversify, but the kinds of activities they diversify into. They argue that poorer households are forced to diversify into marginal non-farm activities resulting in fragility rather than flexibility (1997, pp. 79–80). Most off-farm activities are low-return but with few entry constraints, e.g. charcoal making, while a small number are high-return but with serious entry constraints, e.g. livestock. For the few who access the high end of the off-farm market, diversification is not just a risk management device, but also a way of finding investment capital (Whitehead and Kabeer, 2001). A conclusion, articulated by Bryceson, has been that reliability of earnings was as important as diversification (Bryceson, 1997). Another conclusion has been that diversification has different outcomes because households may have different goals—risk minimisation, maximisation of flexibility and income stabilisation (Bryceson, 1997; Meagher and Mustapha, 1997; Ellis, 1998, 2000).

An important element of multiple livelihood activities is that they sometimes involve multiple spaces. Most of the examples in the literature concern livelihoods which straddle rural and urban areas (Francis, 2000; Foeken, 1997) and they are discussed in terms of the synergies between the different resources and possibilities of the two locations. The study brings an added dimension to this issue in the sense that some of the cases of multi-spatial livelihoods involve two rural areas—the Lower Volta and the Volta Lakeside. As well, it explores the implications of migration for livelihoods.

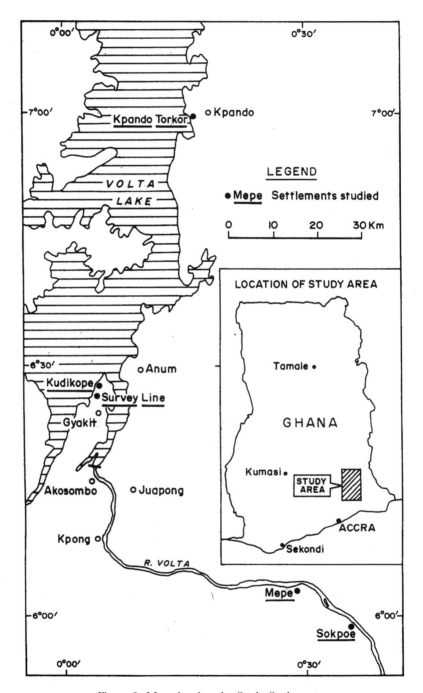

Figure 2: Map showing the Study Settlements

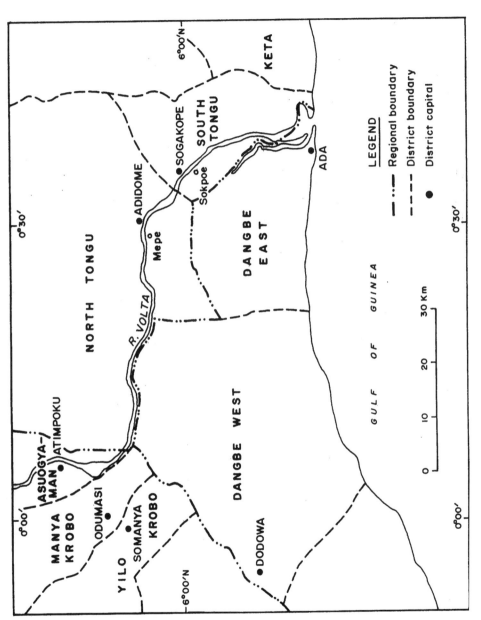

Figure 3: Map Showing the Districts Within the Lower Volta Basin

Notwithstanding the fact that the migrant-hometown relations discussed in this book are rural-rural relations, there are certain common elements of hometown-migrants relations, whether they are rural-rural or rural-urban. Attention has been drawn to both the concrete and normative elements of the links between migrants and their hometowns, the significance of hometown burials and the implications of gender, age and economic success for hometown-migrant exchanges. The stresses in multi-spatial relations particularly when they involve marital relations have also been discussed (Geschiere and Gugler, 1998; Trager, 1998). As well, the distinctions drawn between a) the individual and collective elements of the linkages and b) the links with family/kin and community are useful as is the observation that insecurities in migrant settings have implications for the interest in links with hometown (Trager, 1998).

The more public and long range responses discussed in the livelihoods and social security approach can be distinguished from Scott's list of the weapons of relatively powerless groups such as "foot dragging, dissimulation, false compliance, pilfering, feigned ignorance, slander, arson, sabotage" (1985, p. 35). These are characteristics of inter-household relations but can also be extended to intra-household relations. In distinguishing between public/on-stage from private/off-stage scripts of both the powerful and their subordinates, he alerts one to the fact of responses that may not be public. In spite of some of the questions raised about Scott's concepts,[18] they have been deployed in analyses of gender relations because of their salience for covert and indirect forms of resistance (Agarwal, 1994).

As Kandiyoti argues, this is because, "the fact that resistance did not necessarily have to take overt and organised forms but could be expressed through covert and indirect forms of bargaining was particularly well-suited to women's contestations of domestic power structures involving as they do face-to-face relations with intimates such as husbands, mothers-in-law, sons and daughters rather than encounters with the more impersonal workings of bureaucracies and state apparatuses" (1998, p. 141). Kandiyoti, however, cautions against the

---

[18] Among them is the critique that in characterising the decision of poor peasants to conform rather than resist openly as a rational response to the danger of sanctions or failure, Scott ignores the evidence of hegemony. Also, gender relations as well as intra-household relations are missing from his analysis (Kandiyoti, 1998).

extension of frameworks developed to explain the relations between different social categories to account for gender relations.[19]

The conceptual framework outlined above has influenced the approach taken in this study. The concept of livelihood trajectories suggests a historical approach to the investigation of livelihoods. Secondly, the focus on macro-micro linkages, relations, processes and institutions requires the use of qualitative methods (see Whitehead, 2000, p. 7). In keeping with the work of Murray and others, the study uses both circumspective and retrospective approaches and a combination of qualitative and quantitative techniques.[20] To examine the workings of social relations of class, gender, kinship and generation, the study focuses on labour relations in the organisation of livelihoods both within and outside households. In selecting a purposively sampled group for the histories, it has been possible to identify how these social relations have played out in the livelihood trajectories of men and women of different ages, keeping in mind the multiple identities people embodied. In addition to its role in labour relations, kinship was examined through relations between households and the compounds in which they were situated and compound-level cooperation and collective processes.

4. *The Books's Sources*

The book is based on research conducted between 1998 and 2003. It involved two broad categories of research to enable an examination of the interface between the political economy of the Volta River Project (VRP) and household level impacts and responses. The first, which sets out the historical record examines the context, conception and execution of the dams and dam impacts and policy

---

[19] For example, she argues that concepts such as resistance and doxa in spite of their explanatory power, are better-suited to power relations which are quite stable and permanent, for example, landless peasants in relation to their landlords. Gender relations on the other hand are fluid, fluctuating and present changing possibilities for power and autonomy even for the disadvantaged (Kandiyoti, 1998).

[20] Murray identifies three methodological approaches to the study of livelihoods—circumspective, retrospective and prospective. Circumspective studies are those which study livelihoods in one moment of time; the retrospective tries to look at changes over time while the prospective distils past experience into future policy, focusing on project monitoring and evaluation (Murray, 2002).

responses, is a close reading of the secondary and grey literature of
the Volta River Project. This research relied in no small measure
on the 1956 Report of the Preparatory Commission of the Volta
River Project and a study of the Lower Volta which the Commission
contracted the economist Rowena Lawson to carry out.[21] The
Preparatory Commission noted that there was very little information
about the area, which had also seen "very little Government activity" partly because of the parlous state of its communications
(p. 142).[22] These and more recent studies of the political economy
of the Volta River Project (Hart, 1980; Graham, 1986) were supplemented by in-depth interviews with informants within the Volta
River Authority. These important sources confirmed, provided tex-
ture, alternative or particular viewpoints, expanded, contradicted and
in summary, provided a window from which the written material
has been viewed. That material was important for the first four chapters of the book.

The second component which tackled long-term dam impacts and
responses was largely executed by a survey, life story and informant
interviews in five affected settlements, two downstream (Mepe and
Sokpoe) and three around the Volta Lake (Surveyor Line, Kudikope
and Kpando Torkor). The downstream settlements were selected
from two of the six districts in the Lower Volta Basin identified as
dam-affected (Volta Basin Research Project, 1999), North and South
Tongu respectively,[23] and two of the districts around the Volta Lake
(Asuogyaman and Kpando). They were selected to provide similarities (size and composition) and contrasts (spatial features and resources).

---

[21] As the Preparatory Commission said of the report, it "should be of value in
dealing with the Tongu communities who feature so prominently both above and
below the dam site . . .". Ten years later, this study was updated and published as
"The Changing Economy of the Lower Volta", the most comprehensive study to
date of the area (Lawson, 1972). The Preparatory Commission Report also conducted a wider survey of the area, which is featured in Appendix VII of the Report.
The report covered the physical characteristics of the river, agriculture in the area,
fish production and the two major lagoons in the Area—the Songaw and the Keta
Lagoons.
[22] The situation does not seem to have changed much since this assessment. Over
four decades after the Preparatory Commission presented its report in 1956, the
Lower Volta Environmental Impact Studies found that communications in the area
were very poor, describing it as an enclave (Volta Basin Research Project, 1999).
[23] The affected communities are Dangme East, Dangme West, North Tongu,
South Tongu, Manya Krobo and Asuogyaman Districts and the Anyanui and Attiteti
areas.

Although dam affected communities in the Lower Volta and the Volta Lake are found in a number of districts and among different socio-linguistic groups, the research has concentrated on Tongu settlements. Thus while both for the survey and in-depth interviews respondents have been selected irrespective of language, the choice of settlements has meant that Tongu Ewe respondents are in the majority.

The focus on the Tongu Ewe is in the interest of coherence and to allow the comparison of strategies of communities with significant pre-dam commonalities such as environment and culture. The Tongu are the largest single group affected by the Volta River Project. At least 10% of those resettled after Akosombo were Tongu and 4,349 of the 6,656 of the resettled population after the Kpong Dam, represented in four of the six communities, were Tongu Ewe. The migrants who settled along the Volta Lake and the Kpong headpond were also mainly Tongu Ewe. As Moxon (1984) noted "in a very real sense, the Tongu are the people of the lake". The socio-economic study of the Lower Volta Environmental Impact Studies (LVEIS) found that the North and South Tongu Districts made up 2/3 of both the dam-affected population and settlements (Volta Basin Research Project, 1997). Apart from numbers the Tongu are represented in three of the four categories of affected communities of the Volta River Project—resettlers, migrants and downstream dwellers.

For the survey, which took place between January and May 1999, two hundred and twenty (220) households were interviewed in each of the two downstream communities bringing the total for this category to 440 respondents. As table 1.1. shows, the sample was composed of almost 40% male and 60% female, reflecting roughly the composition of the population of the communities. In the migrant communities, a total of 220 persons, about 52% male and 48% female, reflecting the composition of the population in these settlements were interviewed.[24] Thus a total of 660 household interviews were conducted with about 40% male and 60% female respondents.

Persons interviewed were usually the heads of households, but in their absence, a spouse or sibling was considered suitable. The plan

---

[24] Two communities, Surveyor Line and Kudikope, were chosen instead of one because of their small size. For the purposes of sampling, they were considered to be one community.

Table 1.1: Respondents in The Lower Volta

Sex of respondents	Absolutes			Percentages		
	Mepe	Sokpoe	Total	Mepe	Sokpoe	Total
Male	85	84	169	38.6	38.2	38.4
Female	135	136	271	61.4	61.8	61.5
Total	220	220	440	100	100	100

Table 1.2: Respondents in Migrant Settlements

Sex of respondents	Absolutes	Percentages
Male	116	52.7
Female	104	47.3
Total	220	100

to interview two persons in each household, i.e. the head and his or her spouse had to be abandoned because in the Lower Volta, households composed of husband, wife and children was not the norm. Instead, more households were covered. The households were randomly selected, but every quarter within each community was sampled. In the migrant settlements where men headed the vast majority of households, the sample had 162 male and 58 female household heads (73.6% and 26.4%). A decision was taken to interview more females within households to maintain some balance between population composition and respondent proportions and also between the Lower Volta and the Lakeside (Table 1.2). However, some of the survey results were based on household heads.

Life-story interviews with a total of sixty (60) persons selected from the survey sample on the basis of their gender, age (up to 30s; 40s–50s; 60s and over) and their livelihood trajectories were conducted from January 1999 to April 2000. There were 15 such interviews in each community.

In addition to the household-based survey and life stories, there were informant interviews, discussions with special groups to provide information on the prevalence of particular strategies and factors determining such prevalence and to provide triangulation. Respondents included community leaders and members, leaders of economic institutions, school children, apprentices, young unemployed persons, roadside sellers and young men working on a commercial farm. Community litigation records were also consulted. District Administration Officials at Sogakope (South Tongu) and Kpando were interviewed and their archives and complaints files consulted.[25]

In addition, I sat through judicial processes at Mepe, Surveyor-Line and Kpando Torkor, crossed both the Volta and its tributary, the Aklakpa River, to conduct interviews at Dadome, a Mepe community. I also visited markets in both the Lower Volta and around the Volta Lake and attended church services and festivals at Mepe and Sokpoe. While this was not the total immersion practised by some anthropologists, there were many opportunities to observe everyday life.

One problem was the absence of uniform information on the pre-dam conditions in the Lower Volta. Important sources of pre-dam information had a focus and used methods quite different from the approach of this approach. Therefore, while they were important in the reconstruction, there were gaps, which could only be partially recovered through in-depth interviews. The limitations of these studies notwithstanding, they were vital to the historical record. Without the Preparatory Commission Report, the task of reconstructing life in the Lower Volta before the Volta River Project would have been much more difficult and more open to challenges. The inclusion of downstream communities in the Preparatory Commission's Report is even more remarkable because it was not part of its original brief.[26] Interestingly, the Preparatory Commission assigned both precautionary and positive reasons for its interest in the Lower Volta. The Commission noted that:

---

[25] The two other districts, North Tongu and Asuogyaman, were not visited because they were carved out of older districts only in the 90s, and therefore, it was felt that the additional expense and time was not justified.

[26] In its introduction, the Commission writes that while the United Kingdom (UK) Government White Paper of 1952 had noted that the VRP would entail expenditure arising from the creation of the Lake, the Commission "had been unable to find evidence, however, that similar consideration was given at that time to the parallel problem of the effects which the new dam might have on communities between its site and the mouth of the Volta River" (Appendix VII, Chapter 1, p. 139; see also chapter 13, paragraph 268 of main report, p. 45). In choosing to focus some attention on this issue, the Commission was far ahead of its time. It is therefore not surprising that its recommendations were easily dispensed with.

The collection of this information would be an essential step in preparing to meet the claims for compensation which would undoubtedly
arise, where cases of direct financial loss resulting from the changes in
the flow of the river could be established. Failure to do so could pre-
cipitate a situation in which the Gold Coast Government and the Volta
River Authority were later faced with a large number of claims for
compensation for alleged loss, not all of which might be justified, but
which might be very difficult to refute. On a more positive approach,
the information gained from the surveys could provide a sound foundation for plans for the future development of the area (p. 140).

The above statement was prescient. The Commission's findings and
judgements were deployed by the Volta River Authority (VRA) in
its defence and also were influential in policy towards affected communities.[27] On the other hand, few of the statements and petitions
from or about the Lower Volta have referred to the Preparatory
Commission's recommendations in their favour (see 1967 letter sent
by Konu, MP for Tongu, to the VRA for a rare reference to the
Commission).

Another aspect of the difficulties of recollecting the pre-dam situation relates to the paucity of material on the social and political
organisation of the Tongu people. Even more serious is the challenge of periodisation and the tracking of social change in the discussion of Tongu institutions such as chieftaincy, kinship and religion.
The neat device of distinguishing pre-dam from post-dam situations
is more suited to mapping environmental change than to discussions
of social institutions. Informants discussed these institutions in terms
of past and present when questioned in that vein. However, they
tended to speak in terms of an ideal past corrupted by change or
non-changing custom which was being breached by bad office holders,

---

[27] For example, the Preparatory Commission's findings on the pre-dam salinity
levels of the Volta River were deployed by the VRA in its defence years later. Also,
the Commission's expectation that fishing in the Lake would more than compensate for losses in the Lower Volta became a cornerstone of policies towards affected
communities (p. 140). Lawson's valuation of houses in the Lower Volta in the early
50s at less than £ 20 on the average came to influence notions of what was a fair
compensation for houses which were lost through the Project (Lawson, 1968). Even
more influential was the idea that, with the exception of a few houses built for
renting in larger villages, most of the houses in this area were a depreciating asset
with no market value. And yet, some laterite block houses were important investments—blocks were made, laid and held together by a mixture which included a
little cement. In some cases, the walls and floors were plastered with cement and
painted black. The roof could be thatch or iron sheets.

young people and migrants. Also, some disagreements among informants about practices reflected their own positions, particularly in
situations of contestation. This was complicated by the unevenness
of change in institutional practices as well as the ossification of certain principles through their reinforcement in legal processes and
their designation by state institutions as customary law. The problem is not particular to Tongu social relations.[28] To address, albeit
partially, the difficulties of accounting for changes in the function-
ing and practices of these important institutions, they are described
based on informant interviews and secondary literature. In addition,
the few indications of change, the disagreements among informants
and the gaps between stated and observed practice are highlighted.

5. *The Structure of the Book*

The book has nine chapters. This introductory chapter is followed
by an account of the history of the Volta River Project focusing on
the role and contributions of the different players involved in the
Project and the interactions between them. These include the Ghanaian
post-colonial state, the bureaucracy it created to administer the dams,
the Volta River Authority, the World Bank, the various commercial
banks and the aluminium companies. The chapter also discusses the
preparatory processes of the VRP as agreed and implemented. The
predictions and recommendations on dam impacts on local populations is also tackled in this chapter. The central argument in this
chapter is that the VRP's conception as a colonial project implemented by a post colonial government negotiating from a weak position ensured that the benefits and costs of the Project were unfairly
distributed and the Project failed to protect the interests of dam-
affected populations.

Chapter three focuses on life in the Lower Volta on the eve of
the Volta River project with particular emphasis on Tongu societies
and economies as they were organised around the annual flooding

---

[28] Much attention has been drawn to the invention and reinvention of customary law, presided over by the colonial judiciary and its implications. It is generally
agreed that customary laws even when they are enunciated as certainties are constantly changing in response to internal and external social and economic pressures
(Chanock, 1982; Ranger, 1989; Woodman, 1985; Manuh, 1994).

cycle of the Volta River. The chapter also discusses how pre-dam seasonal migration upstream fitted into this cycle and also created the conditions for the mass migration of Tongu fishermen after the Akosombo Dam. Dam impacts on the Lower Volta receive attention. Issues such as the creation of the Volta Lake, the environmental changes in the Lower Volta and their impacts on livelihoods are explored. The main argument of the chapter is that the Akosombo Dam resulted in a drastic restructuring of the environment and resources of the Lower Volta. As an immediate response, there was mass out-migration to the new Volta Lake. This altered the prospects and conditions of those who continued to live in the Lower Volta, creating serious problems which could not be properly addressed without state intervention. Chapter four discusses state policies towards dam-affected populations. The chapter explores the VRA as a public sector organisation and assesses its responses to dam impacts and affected populations. The chapter chronicles the Ghanaian state's inability to make proper institutional arrangements to tackle the problems of dam-affected communities, thus leaving the VRA with this task, which it has performed selectively and with reluctance. The changing responses of communities to dam impacts and state neglect are also tackled in this chapter which explores why community responses have been largely ineffective.

Chapter five tackles livelihood patterns and trajectories at Mepe and Sokpoe in the Lower Volta focusing on the changing resource base of livelihoods which has resulted in the over-exploitation of various resources as well as changes in the structure and organisation of livelihoods. Strategies such as the intensified use of certain resources and the unstructured deployment of multiple livelihood activities are examined as are some of the indications of poor livelihood outcomes. Chapter six explores the social relations implicated in the organisation of livelihoods—kinship, gender, class and generation—and examines their implications for livelihood outcomes. This is to account for differences in trajectories and outcomes within a generalised situation of livelihood crisis. The discussion focuses on the labour relations within and outside households as well as the use of informal and formal associations in the construction of livelihoods.

Chapters seven and eight focus on livelihoods in Surveyor-Line, Kudikope and Kpando Torkor, three migrant settlements along the Volta Lake. Chapter seven traces the history of their establishment and development of institutions as a background to discussing liveli-

hoods as they have changed over the years in chapter eight. In particular, the movement of Tongu communities from fishing to farming along the Lake is explored. In the last chapter, the Volta River
Project in the broader perspectives of the large Dam literature, the
international politics of large dams and their implications for future
policy on dam-affected communities are tackled. The chapter concludes that while processes such as the World Commission on Dams
have opened a new chapter in the discussion of the impacts of large
dams, national processes such as the deregulation of the energy sector have mixed implications for dam-affected communities. The chapter concludes with a summary, conclusions and the policy implications
of the study.

CHAPTER TWO

THE VOLTA RIVER PROJECT:
HISTORICAL PERSPECTIVES

1. *Introduction*

In this chapter, the history of the Volta River Project as it was conceived, negotiated and executed is set out. Certain aspects of this history are well documented (Hance, 1958; Rado, 1960; Nkrumah, 1961; Futa, 1961; Hilling, 1965; Barnes, 1966; Birmingham et al., 1966; Moxon, 1984; Hart, 1980; Dickinson, 1982; Adu-Aryee, 1985; Faber, 1990) and these sources have been used extensively in this chapter. As well, the chapter has benefited from extensive discussions with Mr. E.K. Kalitsi, then chairman of the Board of the Volta River Authority.[1] This chapter sets the context for evaluating state policies for addressing the profound socio-economic and environmental impacts of the Volta River Project in subsequent chapters. The chapter begins with an analysis of the post-colonial state in Ghana and its imperatives. The positions and motivations of the different players in the project—the government of Ghana, the World Bank, the commercial and investment banks, the aluminium companies and their governments—are examined. The Volta River Project as agreed and executed and the subsequent debates about its merits are examined.

The chapter also discusses the various predictions made about how the Lower Volta would experience the VRP. It will become clear that while the Preparatory Commission was aware of the high expectations of inhabitants and did not want to raise them further,[2] it was

---

[1] Mr. Kalitsi worked at the Development Commission, the Volta Secretariat and the VRA where he held the positions of Resettlement Officer, the Director of Finance, Deputy Chief Executive and Chief Executive at different times. He was also once the chief executive of the Electricity Corporation of Ghana. This unique position in relation to the Volta River Project afforded him particular and interesting views which were helpful for recreating the history.

[2] As the Preparatory Commission notes about perceptions in the Lower Volta, "it is a well-known proposition in these parts, and one on which considerable hope

not fully cognisant of how its own research activities contributed to keeping those expectations high. The chapter demonstrates that the history of the Volta River Project has been important in its relationship with communities affected by the dam, and this in turn has been important in how communities and their members have responded to dam impacts on their livelihoods.

2. *The Players and the Volta River Project*

The main actors in the planning and implementation of the Volta River Project were President Kwame Nkrumah, President John Kennedy, Edgar F. Kaiser, the World Bank under its president Eugene Black and Prime Minister Harold Macmillan of Britain (Faber, 1990). In this discussion, the players will be considered as part of their institutions and or countries—the Ghana government, the Volta River Authority, the government of the United Kingdom, Kaiser Aluminium, the United States of America government and the World Bank.

The United Kingdom government

The United Kingdom government was a marginal player in the Volta River Project as it came to be implemented. However, this belied the nature of British involvement in the conception and planning of the Project. In 1952, the British government presented a White Paper to its Parliament about the Volta River Project in which British interest in the Project was stated in terms of securing more supplies of aluminium at good prices within the sterling area. At that time, 4/5 of the United Kingdom's aluminium came from dollar sources and thus a shift to colonial or "soft currency" sources would be beneficial to the UK. It would also boost development within the Commonwealth, a grouping of the UK, its colonies and ex-colonies. Concerns about the safety of such a large investment resulted in the establishment of the Preparatory Commission in 1952 by the UK

---

appears to be placed, both as providing individual employment, and as likely to introduce more active economic conditions to the locality such as may curtail the existing drift of the population" (1956, p. 143).

and Ghana to continue the work of preparing the VRP for implementation. By the time the Report was published in 1956, the British
government and the aluminium companies had lost interest in the
project, partly because of the massive increases in the world supply
of aluminium which had apparently caught up with demand (Rado,
1960). This loss of interest in effect shelved the project until it was
resurrected with the help of the USA government and business.
However, even though officially outside the Project, the UK continued to be a player. For example, the government of the USA
sought British advice when it had concerns about the anti-American
stance of the Nkrumah Regime and had to decide whether to go
forward with its support for the Project (State Department, 1964).

The Government of the United States

Hart argues that the USA government's involvement in the Volta
River Project was for both political and economic reasons. The USA
was seeking to increase its influence in Africa as part of its cold war
considerations but also to expand the market for US goods, services
and companies (Hart, 1980). The declassified correspondence of the
State Department in this period supports this view. In the middle
of the Project, the USA government considered pulling out of the
Project on account of the Nkrumah government's unreliability as an
American ally. The decision was taken to continue with the Project
partly because Kaiser's interest remained strong. The USA government's involvement was mainly through loans supplied by the US
Export-Import Bank which covered much of the construction costs
of both the power station and smelter (Faber, 1990, p. 66; State
Department, 1964). The difference, which was made up by Kaiser
and Reynolds, two American aluminium companies, was fully guaranteed by the USA government. Years later, the Overseas Private
Investment Corporation (OPIC), a USA government agency which
insures and helps to finance American private investments in developing countries, was to honour the Volta Aluminium Company
(VALCO) with its first annual development award (Hart, p. 45).

The World Bank

Once the British and aluminium companies lost interest in the VRP,
it was felt that the World Bank's intervention might be decisive.

(Hance, 1958; p. 83). The World Bank's role as lender and referee
was very significant in the Project. In 1960, after the Kaiser Reassessment Report, the World Bank was requested by the Ghana
government to make a preliminary appraisal as part of the process
of finding additional financial support for the Project (Parks, 1960;
Barnes, 1966).[3] The World Bank was prepared to make the "largest
loan in its history to any single project in Africa"[4] and was involved
in negotiations around the pricing of electricity. Hart argues that
while the World Bank acted as buffer between Ghana and the aluminium companies and gave useful advice to Ghana, which sometimes ran counter to VALCO's proposals, it had its own interests in
the Project and liaised closely with the Americans. For example, the
World Bank's preoccupation with the feasibility and profitability of
the project was in the interests of successful debt servicing. It urged
the Ghana government to seek the highest possible tariffs in order
to shorten the time it would be operating at a loss and the time
needed for earning enough to service the debts. The Bank's assessment was that at US 2.5 mills per kilowatt/hour (kw/h), the power
revenue from the Aluminium Smelter would not be enough to service the debt (International Bank for Reconstruction and Development,
1960, p. 16).

As we shall come to see, VALCO was able to secure power rates
only slightly higher than the figure the World Bank had found unacceptable before. And yet, the Bank went ahead and granted the loan,
choosing to safeguard its repayment by ring-fencing VRA's foreign
exchange earnings instead and making debt servicing the first charge
on the VRA's earnings (Barnes, 1996). Other lenders followed suit
with the result that the repayment of loans became the Project's top
priority. Indeed, notwithstanding the economic crises of the 80s,
Ghana continued to service its debts under the VRP (Faber 1990).

Beyond financial conditionalities, the Bank's critical role in securing various guarantees designed to protect the foreign investment in

---

[3] Parks notes that even before the World Bank Report survey had been completed, there was news that Kaiser Industries, Reynolds Aluminium, ALCOA and
other Canadian and British Aluminium companies had formed a consortium to
build a smelter (1960, p. 28).

[4] In earlier financing plans, the WB had been scheduled to provide a £30 million loan. At 6% interest, it was considered in that period to be fully commercial.
However, the loan was cut to £14.25 million to reduce the servicing charge as part
of the measures taken to reduce the cost of the project (Faber, 1990, p. 67).

the project is revealing. Among other things, the Bank's approval was needed for the appointment of the Authority's Chief Executive and the fixing of the power rates. As well, the Bank was influential in the establishment of procedures for the financial records, operations, organisational structure, staffing policies and accounting system of the Authority (Killick, 1978 pp. 250–251).

While it was the practice in some cases for the same organisation to be responsible for both generation and distribution of power, the Bank recommended that the VRA focus on generation and transmission of electricity and supplying the smelter, and leave distribution to the Electricity Corporation.[5] The Bank also advised that the transmission of power be done using standard voltage instead of the special voltage proposed by the aluminium companies. It also recommended a "use or pay" system for the power contract with the aluminium companies, i.e. that they commit to purchase a fixed amount and pay the full cost whether or not they use it. This was one provision that Ghana was able to secure from VALCO.

Some have attributed the relative success of the VRA to World Bank control. Kalitsi on the other hand suggests that it was due to the imperatives of providing power to a customer as technically demanding as an aluminium smelter (Interview with KK, Accra). Hart for his part has remarked that the Bank's domination by the USA's foreign policy concerns muted how much it interrogated the VRP Agreements (Hart, 1980). This impression was fed by the close links between leading Bank officials and the Kaiser Empire.

The Kaiser Corporation

The Kaiser Corporation, which by the time the Volta River Project came to be implemented owned 90% of the smelter, was at the time of the project a large conglomerate—total assets at $3,600 million and the forty-fifth largest manufacturing industry in the USA in 1977. Different parts of the Kaiser Empire were involved in a wide range of businesses including aluminium, engineering, manufacture and mass media, specifically broadcasting. While it had undergone many

---

[5] This was perhaps to insulate the VRA from the added uncertainties of having to deal with a myriad of small-scale consumers and the particular challenges of retailing electricity.

changes, it remained a significant organisation with its total revenue in 1973 almost as large as Ghana's GNP in that same year. A number of factors shaped Kaiser's relationship with the Volta River Project. These include the interests it already had in the aluminium industry worldwide and the different roles it played in the Volta River Project. One of its components, the Kaiser Aluminium and Chemical Corporation, the fourth largest producer of aluminium in the world, owned aluminium facilities including bauxite mines, alumina plants, aluminium smelters, rolling mills and fabrication plants in Europe, the Caribbean, South Asia and the Pacific (Hart, p. 47). Thus Kaiser was much more interested in its own holdings than in Ghana's goal of establishing an integrated aluminium industry. All Kaiser needed then was cheap power to smelt alumina to be brought in from different parts of its far-flung business empire. According to Faber (1990), Kaiser was motivated to take the Volta River Project plunge with all its risks because of the promise of cheap power over a long period and the prospect of owning and operating a smelter without having to pay more than a small fraction of its costs up front with state protection from expropriation.[6]

By the commencement of the construction of the dam, different sections of the Kaiser Empire had been involved in different capacities in the Project. As Faber notes,

> Kaiser's role had changed greatly and quickly. Originally brought in by the USA and Ghana governments to reassess the Volta Scheme, the company produced a series of consultancy reports, the fees from which amounted to some £9 million pounds. At that early stage, Kaiser's were also interested in the major contracts that might be expected for the dam and powerhouse construction. Again at the request of the Ghanaians, however, Kaiser had been asked to act as the promoter of a consortium of aluminium companies who would be willing to undertake the financing of a smelter, to own and operate it and to provide a market for its product. By 1960 Kaiser's president found himself not only the main designer of the project but the only potential owner and operator (apart from Reynolds' 10% interest) with sufficient enthusiasm and confidence to commit his company to a major involvement in it (1990, p. 71; see also, Hart, p. 49).

---

[6] As the US State Department explained in one of its documents, the US government had guaranteed the $100 million Kaiser investment against expropriation and had loaned the company money to assist in the financing of the smelter (Department of State, Vol. XXIV, 1964–1968).

As will be discussed later in the assessments of the VRP agreements, Kaiser's changing roles were considered by some analysts as a source of conflict of interests in the VRP negotiations (Hart, 1980).

The Ghana Government

> Newer nations, such as ours, which are determined by every possible means to catch up in industrial strength, must have electricity in abundance before they can expect any large-scale industrial advance. Electricity is the basis for industrialisation. That, basically, is the justification for the Volta River Project (Nkrumah, K: 1961).

Industrialisation has long been seen as the cornerstone of economic development in the largely agricultural ex-colonies in Africa and the rest of the developing world.[7] In Ghana, various post-independence development programmes have sought to diversify the economy's reliance on cocoa and other agricultural commodities through industrialisation. The first of these, the Nkrumah regime's economic programme, has been characterized as economic modernisation. It consisted of structural transformation to be achieved by state-led import substitution industrialisation, agricultural mechanisation of a small peasant-based agricultural economy and the expansion of formal education to secure the supply of skilled labour (Killick, 1966; Songsore and Denkabe, 1995). Having identified the availability of a cheap source of hydroelectric power (HEP) as key to industrialisation, the Nkrumah government set about seeking financial support for the construction of a HEP dam over the Volta River at Akosombo. However, this proposal to dam the Volta had been inherited from the colonial period when it had been shaped by other imperatives. As will be seen from a discussion of the balance sheet of the Project, some analysts felt that this origin was decisive in settling its essential features (Hart, 1980).

The project to achieve development through modernisation and industrialisation coincided with both the dominant ideas of development economics of the sixties and Nkrumah's politics, a combination of nationalism and socialism (Killick, 1978). Throughout the

---

[7] Killick argues that there are strong empirical and apriori connections between industrialisation and development and this has led in some cases to the equation of industrialisation with development (Killick, 1978, p. 20).

life of the Nkrumah regime, modernisation and industrialisation remained national goals. These goals were anchored in a political philosophy, which while explicit about the interests of ordinary people, approached development projects as though all citizens in Ghana would benefit equally. This ignored the burgeoning class, rural-urban and North-South dichotomies in Ghanaian society and the situation that those who would benefit from the VRP would not be the same as those who would be adversely affected (Brown, 1986; Konings, 1986; Songsore and Denkabe, 1995). There is general agreement in the literature that there was much continuity in development policy after the overthrow of the Nkrumah regime and this included the policy towards the Volta River Project, which remained a centre-piece of development policy for decades. As a result, the Volta River Project (VRP)'s impact was likely to be greater on Ghana than on any of the other parties. Ghana would either be a major beneficiary of the project or the biggest loser and this made it the weakest player in the whole equation, a situation not helped by the fact that it also had the most ambitious aims and objectives.

3. The Volta River Project: Conception, Planning and Implementation (1915–1966)

Between 1915, when it was first mooted, and 1966 when the Akosombo Dam was commissioned, the VRP proposal went through various modifications. These include:

- the Kitson proposals,
- the Duncan Rose/St John Bird modifications (1939–49),
- the Halcrow and Partners proposal and the Preparatory Commission Report commissioned by the British and Gold Coast governments,
- the Kaiser Reassessment proposals (1959–1966)

Below is a table setting out the various proposals in terms of their features and costs. The most significant of these proposals was contained in the 1953 Preparatory Commission Report. The Commission, headed by Sir Robert Jackson, was established to continue feasibility work in order to carry forward the planning of the Project to a stage where a decision could be taken on its implementation. In 1956, the Commission presented its Report along with an Engineering

Report prepared by the consulting engineers to the project, Sir William Halcrow and Partners.[8]

Hart notes that the Report, which arose out of the closest collaboration among the Ghana government, the British Government and the two aluminium companies who were interested at this stage in the Project, was widely regarded as one of the "most exhaustive preliminary investigations for such as project" (Hart, p. 21). It considered the technical engineering issues as well as the economic and social matters arising from the proposed project. These included future demand for aluminium, water loss from the reservoir through evaporation, labour for dam construction, questions of resettlement as well as the situation of downstream communities.

While the Commission's thoroughness was lauded, the Report was criticised for starting from the point of view of the aluminium companies and minimising the potential benefits of the Project for the Gold Coast (as Ghana was then known) through its proposals and omissions.[9] As well, the proposals were considered too expensive, especially since the British government and the aluminium companies were not willing to put up such sums (Nkrumah, 1961; Hart, 1980; Killick, 1979).

In 1957, the year of Ghana's independence, through the offices of President Eisenhower, the International Co-operation Administration took up the task of making the Volta River Project possible. It had advised a reappraisal of the Project and Henry J. Kaiser Company, an American firm of Engineers, was selected for this exercise. In 1959, The Reassessment Report on the Volta River Project was presented to the Government of Ghana. The Reassessment Report, which was funded by the Ghana and US governments, made some changes to the plans and recommendations of the Preparatory Commission. These included a proposal to increase the amount of

---

[8] Report of Preparatory Commission, Introduction, 1956, p. 1. The Report had 16 appendices on various issues of concern to the Project. The seventh (Appendix VII) was on the Lower Volta Basin. Most of the subsequent references to the Report are to Appendix VII.

[9] Some of these are the proposal to minimise the labour force for dam construction, the failure to interrogate the proportion of the electricity being reserved for the companies and the proposal by the aluminium companies to use Jamaican bauxite (Hart, p. 24).

power to be produced and the shortening of the time frame for dam construction from seven to four years to save costs. It also recommended a change in the location of the dam from Ajena to Akosombo. Altogether, it was estimated that the proposed increase in capacity by 25% coupled with the 17.5% reduction of the capital cost of the project to £55.7 million had the effect of reducing the cost per kilowatt from £110 to £72.5, a saving of 34% (Rado, 1960, p. 14; Barnes, 1966). The site of the smelter was also shifted from Kpong to the port of Tema and the future provision of another power station at Kpong recommended. The Report also recommended that a national electricity grid system be established for a major part of Southern Ghana instead of the original scheme of providing only a small proportion of electricity for local consumption (Nkrumah, 1961, p. 4; Government of Ghana, 1963; p. 1; Barnes, 1966).

On the use of Ghana's bauxite within the Volta River Project, the report noted that there were large reserves of good grade bauxite to "support a substantial aluminium industry in Ghana". It therefore recommended that the aluminium producers examine the feasibility of building additional alumina capacity for sale and export (Kaiser Report, 1959, quoted in Hart, 1980, p. 25). In subsequent discussions with Kaiser and ALCAN, it was decided that the proposed smelter should initially use imported alumina as a measure for cutting capital costs. This postponement of the use of Ghana's bauxite also saved the project an estimated amount of 60 million pounds on the cost of the mine, the rail system and the alumina plant. All the savings allowed the possibility of selling electricity at 2.5 kWh (Faber, 1990). Last but not the least, project components which were not directly concerned with power production such as the resettlement of displaced persons had to be tackled by the Ghana government outside the main project. Hart notes that the details of this modified project were never published (Hart, 1980 p. 26).

In spite of the Nkrumah government's unhappiness about the changes being proposed in the Kaiser Report, they were accepted as the best deal under the circumstances. As Kalitsi was recently to argue, there were no other proposals on the table at the time, and before this the Project had been shelved (interview with KK, 2000). The terms of the Kaiser Report as well as the recovery of the world aluminium market created very favourable conditions from the point of the view of North American and British Aluminium companies (Rado, 1960; Barnes, 1966).

Nkrumah defended the project in terms of the common interests of the parties involved, arguing that the Reassessment Report had made the Volta River Project more attractive financially.[10] He also stated that as early as 1953, the government had already decided on the construction of some project components such as the Tema Port and township, regardless of whether or not there would be a dam. Therefore, even before the Project had taken off, Ghana's resources were used to provide infrastructure, a move also explained in terms of saving time on the initial preparation of the work-site, including the provision of roads, housing, water and power (Nkrumah, 1961). The Nkrumah government accepted the recommendation of the Reassessment Report that it would finance power development, including the dam, from public resources, while the smelter would involve private sector investment. The Kaiser Corporation was urged by Nkrumah to establish a consortium to build and operate the smelter. A meeting was convened in 1959 to form VALCO to which five major aluminium companies were invited.

In the end, only Reynolds Metal Company, which took 10% of the new company and Kaiser Aluminium and Chemical Corporation (a subsidiary of Kaiser Industries Corporation) which was left with 90% interest in the company, became shareholders (Nkrumah, 1961, p. 3; Moxon, 1984; Hart, 1980).

As early as 1952, Ghana's Legislative Assembly had passed a motion allowing the negotiations for financing and constructing the VRP to begin. Hart, however, points out that negotiations had begun six months earlier. In November 1960, the Ghana government published a statement about the Volta River Project, followed a day after by a statement in the Legislative Assembly. This statement elicited fulsome praise and unsubstantiated claims about what could be achieved through the construction and operation of the dam. Critical questions were brushed aside. In 1961, when the Volta River Development Bill, which established the VRA, came to the Assembly, the opposition again expressed its unhappiness that the Government had brought it under a certificate of urgency. The Bill was passed

---

[10] The Kaiser estimates were said to be 42.2% lower than the Preparatory Commission estimates. In 1966, the VRA was of the view that the year saved on dam construction would further lower the Kaiser estimates by 14.6% (Barnes, 1966, p. 9).

through a first and second reading, a consideration stage and third reading in less than one hour, according to Hart (1980).

Clearly, this was no time for debate. Soon after this, in August 1961, work on constructing the dam began. At that point, the US loans for the project had not been confirmed. The loans were later approved in December that year. By February 1962, the legal and financial terms of the Volta River project had been settled (Hart, 1980). Bypassing Ghana's parliament thus became normal practice in matters about the VRP, and this, as well as the substantive provisions of the agreements, was the subject of acrimonious debates in the house. The defensive stance adopted in Parliament by the government deprived the country of the opportunity to discuss the issues raised about the Project.

4. *The Volta River Project as Agreed and Executed*

It cost the Ghana government £70.5 million (pounds sterling) to finance the Dam, a power house, transmission lines, sub-stations, the establishment of the Volta River Authority, the resettlement of people whose homes would be flooded by the Lake and health measures to deal with anticipated diseases in the lake area (Nkrumah, 1961; Government of Ghana; 1963). The money came from the Government's Development Fund and through loans from the World Bank and three foreign governmental lending agencies.[11]

The Volta Aluminium Company Ltd (VALCO), formed by Kaiser Aluminium and Reynolds Metal Company in 1959 to construct the Smelter, entered into agreement (The Master Agreement) with the Ghana Government which set out the obligations of the two parties under the Project.[12] The Master Agreement exempted VALCO from

---

[11] These were the Agency for International Development of the US, the Export-Import Bank of Washington and the Export Credits Guarantee Department of the Board of Trade of the British Government (Nkrumah, 1961; Moxon, 1984).

[12] The Master Agreement consisted of a power contact and other provisions such as those for financing the smelter, the dam and hydro facilities, the obligations of the Volta River Authority and the arrangements VALCO could enter into for the tolling of alumina into aluminium. Attached to the Master Agreement were schedules covering the Smelter Site Lease, the Water Agreement, the Port Agreement, the Immigration Quota, the Currency Agreement and the Income Tax Laws of Ghana as at 1961, which covered various areas of relevance to VALCO's operations.

Table 2.1: The Volta River Project proposals at various stages

Year	Proposers	Details of project	Estimated Cost	Additional comments and Circumstances
1915	Scheme 1 Sir Albert Kitson,	A Dam 15 metres high at Akosombo with a large enough lake to transport bauxite deposits on Kwahu plateau to a power station and smelter located near the dam.	Not estimated. No detailed economic and engineering studies to back up proposals.	Discovery by Kitson of bauxite deposits in 1914. Idea of dam first publicly mooted at the 1st World Power Conference, London, 1924.
1939–49	Scheme 2a Duncan Rose	Dam slightly higher upstream at Ajena Island, 40 metres (120 ft) high and a railway and a rope-way bringing bauxite from Yenahin and Kwahu to a port on the Afram River. Alumina refining plant and smelter adjacent to the power station on the west bank of the river at Ajena. Improving riverbed of 72 miles from Ajena to Ada at the estuary to carry inputs and aluminium ingots to the new port at Ada	£2.5–3.5 million	
	Scheme 2b C. St. John Bird	Dam 75 metres (250 ft) high	£6.5 million	Hired by Duncan Rose to carry out a survey. Scheme won the approval of a joint mission of ALCAN and BAC. Progress of this proposal interrupted by WW2. After war, Rose returned to Ghana and formed syndicate to propose Volta River Dam

Table 2.1 (*cont.*)

Year	Proposers	Details of project	Estimated Cost	Additional comments and Circumstances
1951	Scheme 3a Sir William Halcrow and partners	Dam of 80 metres and power station at Ajena and Alumina plant and smelter at Kpong. Bauxite now to be brought by rail to Kpong. Irrigated rice and cotton production envisaged downstream. New Port at Tema.	£144 million £40 million of that for dam and power house	Project now seen as a multi-purpose project with irrigation and a new port. The estimated costs included public works and some social costs. Proposed lake was 2000 sq. miles, 25 times as large as Rose's guess of 80 sq. miles.
1956	Scheme 3b Sir Robert Jackson's Preparatory Commission	Proposals remained largely the same	£231 million for dam, power station, smelter, harbour and other infrastructure plus 45% contingency margin making the total estimate £309 million	Considered too expensive at 40% of GDP of Gold Coast at the time. Estimated cost of electricity at 5 mills, twice as high as ALCAN wanted to pay.
1959–66	Kaiser Reappraisal Report	Dam site shifted back to Akosombo à la Kitson and smelter site moved to Tema.	£130 million	Smelter for an initial period would use imported alumina (saving £60 million on mine development, railway system and the alumina plant). Almost total exclusion of public works and social costs. This last proposal was implemented.

Sources: Barnes, 1966; Hart (1980), Faber (1990), Ghana Government (1962).

export duties on processed aluminium and import duties on alumina and other materials needed for the operation of the smelter not available in Ghana. It stipulated that the tolling[13] charge would increase from 56% to 60% of the basic world price of aluminium after 10 years of operation unless Ghanaian bauxite was used exclusively. Also, VALCO would be exempted from duties on imported construction materials and minerals if it decided to mine or process Ghanaian bauxite (Government of Ghana, 1963, p. 7).

For the first thirty years of its operations, VALCO had a tax holiday on its operations, (except for its income tax at the rate of 40% of chargeable income and for certain minor taxes). VALCO was also granted pioneer company relief in respect of the funds contributed by shareholders to the construction of the smelter. This exempted it from all taxation of its income for at least five years and for a maximum of ten years depending on its profits. In addition, VALCO's imports of alumina and materials for building and operating the smelter were duty-free for thirty years (Articles 15 and 20). Its aluminium exports were also made free of taxation and any other restrictions (Article 19). The Export-Import Bank and the owners of VALCO were guaranteed their share of VALCO's earning in foreign exchange (Government of Ghana; 1963; p. 8). What VALCO was charged for power (2.625 U.S. mills for each kilowatt-hour of energy) was 5% of the average world price in 1983 (Blackwelder, 1983) and one of the lowest in the world.[14] In addition, the Agreement did not contain a firm provision that VALCO construct an alumina plant in Ghana (Birmingham, et al., 1966). Also, it was the Ghana government rather than the aluminium companies that had to provide

---

[13] The tolling charge or fee was what VALCO's shareholders paid the company for smelting services, i.e. converting alumina to aluminium. The tolling charge was an important issue because it determined VALCO's profit margins and what it could pay for electricity. In the ensuing disputes about VALCO's electricity tariffs, some have charged that the low electricity prices the company was paying were because it was subsidising its customers who were also its owners by keeping the tolling charges low.

[14] By 1983, it was 5.0 mills/kWh. Between 1982 and 1985, Ghana successfully renegotiated the price of energy to VALCO to 17 mills/kWh, a figure that could be reduced if VRA could not supply power to run four pot-lines, but with a floor price of 10 mills/kWh. In those negotiations, Ghana won the right to review power prices every five years (Sims and Casely-Hayford, 1986). By 1991, the price was 20.8 mills/kWh.

housing and general services for smelter employees, contrary to the recommendations of the Preparatory Commission (Rado, 1960).[15]

In 1961, the government of Ghana passed the Volta River Development Act, 1961, Act 46 to establish the Volta River Authority (VRA) as a statutory corporation to oversee the construction of the dam and the generation of electricity (Jopp, K: 1965; Futa, 1963). That same year, a contract was awarded to the Italian Consortium IMPREGILO for the construction of the dam. Kaiser Engineers was awarded the overall engineering contract for the project, the design and construction of the work-site and procurement of materials. Work on the dam started in 1961. Two dams, the main dam and a saddle dam which sealed a gap in the surrounding hills, were constructed. This phase of the VRP was completed in 1965 and commissioned in 1966.

At the commissioning of the Akosombo Dam, Nkrumah's emotional speech spoke of his pride in the dam and his optimism about its revolutionary potential and symbolism for Ghana and the rest of Africa (Nkrumah, 1966). Barely a month after this, in February 1966, he was overthrown in Ghana's first coup d'état, an event of epic proportions for Ghana. In spite of the opposition's concerns about the terms of the Volta River Project agreements, the National Liberation Council (NLC) government and subsequent regimes explicitly committed themselves to honouring the terms of the Volta River Project. In a review of its first hundred days in office, the National Liberation Council appropriated the VRP, describing it in even more optimistic terms than the Nkrumah regime had done. In a sixty-nine page document which condemned most of Nkrumah's policies and projects as part of the justification for the coup d'état, that five pages were devoted to the VRP was significant.

Nowhere in the document and the speech before it did affected communities feature. Thus the expectations generated by the promises of the overthrown government, for which there were no concrete plans or financial arrangements, disappeared from the frame. From the totality of statements and concerns expressed, it was clear that

---

[15] The Preparatory Commission had estimated this expenditure at £14.7 million. These special terms were justified in terms of the size of investment represented by the smelter, estimated to be about US$100 million. As Nkrumah noted, "for so large an investment special arrangements are necessary" (Nkrumah, 1961, p. 33).

the obligations to foreign capital were the preoccupation of the new government. The Volta River Authority itself was not sure of its position in this new dispensation. From a special and privileged relationship with the Nkrumah regime, it found itself having to adjust to a changing political climate. The VRA's relations with various regimes in Ghana and policies towards affected communities will be discussed in chapter four.

Since the 1960s the VRA has successfully implemented its mandate of producing reliable electricity for the aluminium smelter and for local commercial and domestic consumers. Between the late 1970s and early 1980s, it successfully oversaw the construction of the Kpong Dam. This smaller dam, 20 metres high to Akosombo's 80 metres with only a fraction of the latter's capacity (160 MW maximum), augmented Akosombo's guaranteed capacity of 750 MW, representing power from five of the six generating units (Hart, 1980). As with Akosombo, the Kpong Dam also necessitated the resettlement of communities, but on a smaller scale. Between 1982 and 1985, VALCO's agreements with the Volta River Authority (VRA) were renegotiated and new agreements reached after difficult negotiations which sometimes broke down (Tsikata, 1986; Sawyerr, undated). The issues under negotiation were power costs and amounts, the tolling fees, taxes, legal matters and other aspects of VALCO's operations.

Among other things, the new agreement increased the power rate from 5.6 mills to 17 mills per kWh. It also provided a five-yearly review of power rates and increased the tolling fee. Taxes as well as the annual payment to the VALCO fund were increased. The law of the contract was changed from the law of Ghana as it stood in 1962 to the current law together with applicable international law. Ghana was now entitled to representation on the VALCO Board. The economic value of these changes was estimated at US$43.2 million in a "normal" year, "i.e. in a year during which the smelter operates four potlines and the price of the metal averages US$0.75 a pound" (Faber, 1990, p. 82). As at 1996, the two hydropower dams together supplied over 95% of Ghana's electricity needs, including those of VALCO's 200,000 ton aluminium smelter. Since then, the demand for power has risen above the supply, throwing the power sector into turmoil (Kalitsi, 1999). That story, however, belongs to chapter seven of the book. At this stage, we return to the discussion of the terms of the Volta River Project as agreed by the Nkrumah regime.

5. *Assessing the Terms of the Volta River Project*

Two broad types of assessment have been made of the Volta River Project. The earliest assessments tended to focus on the fairness or otherwise of the Project's agreements. These only discussed affected populations tangentially, if at all (Nkrumah, 1961; Killick, 1978; Hart, 1980; Dickinson 1982; Tsikata, 1986; Faber, 1990). More recent assessments have tended to focus on project impacts on affected communities, most usually resettlements (Diaw and Schmidt-Kallert, 1990; van Landewijk, 1988; Yeboah, 1999). A more fruitful approach should combine assessments of project agreements with impacts on affected communities. However, this section focuses on the terms of the VRP Agreement. This is because of its importance for the historical record of the Volta River Project. Also, it demonstrates the narrow focus of dam builders and their supporters and critics and also lays a good basis for the rest of the book, which focuses on affected communities.

There is general agreement among commentators that the Volta River Project did not result in the same level of benefits for all the parties concerned and Ghana benefited less than the aluminium companies (Killick, 1978; Faber, 1990). Faber, who gave technical support to the Ghana team during the renegotiations of the 1980s, however argues that the unhappiness in Ghanaian circles had more to do with unrealistic ambitions such as a fully integrated and nationally owned aluminium industry and industrialisation of the economy than with proper economic assessments (Faber, 1990, p. 66). Thus Faber argues that while Nkrumah's dreams could not be realised and the VRP resulted in the suffering of the resettled communities and ecological damage, it did not mean that Ghana would have been better off without the Dams. This view is strongly supported by Kalitsi (2000). This category of arguments which use the counterfactual in defence are problematic. The claim that there is no evidence that Ghana would have been better off without the Volta River Project does not advance the debate as there is also no evidence that Ghana is better off with the Akosombo Dam. Secondly, and more importantly, the argument should be and indeed has been about the terms and character of the particular project that was agreed and not whether or not Ghana should have pursued a power project at all. Some of the issues raised in this regard are discussed in subsequent sections of the chapter.

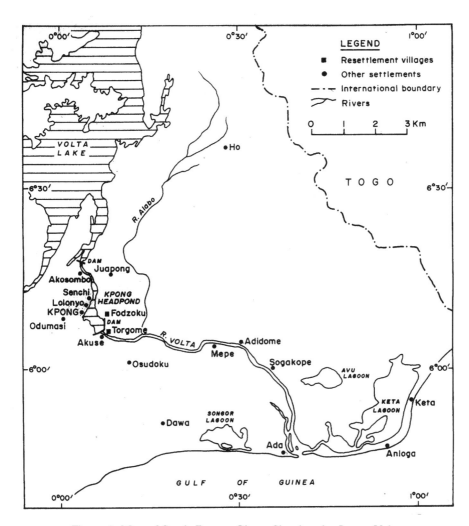

Figure 4: Map of South Eastern Ghana Showing the Lower Volta

Anticipated benefits and problems of the VRP

A number of advantages of the VRP were anticipated. Chief among them was industrialisation. The smelter was seen as a signal to potential private investors about investment possibilities in Ghana. Dam construction would provide employment for Ghanaians, as would the smelter (estimated at 1,500 jobs when in operation). The smelter would have the added advantage of becoming a source of tax revenue in addition to its purchase of 60% of electricity at the estimated cost of £2½ million. The Lake for its part would enhance river transport, improve access to Northern Ghana, provide significant amounts of fish and fertile farmlands on its shores, and serve as a tourist attraction. Its shores would be fertile farming lands (Nkrumah, 1961; Dobson, 1963). Furthermore, it would result in the expansion of port traffic, an overall increase in economic activities and revenue in the form of taxes and user fees (Dobson, 1963). Other potential benefits were that the VRP would reduce the dependence of Ghana on cocoa revenue.[16]

While the direct employment possibilities were not particularly significant, they offered the possibility of training and promotion for Ghanaians. As well, the envisaged improvements in agriculture and fishing and the creation of townships were expected to increase the numbers of beneficiaries and also the regional development possibilities (Parks, 1960; World Bank, 1960; Dobson, 1963). The real benefits turned out to be more modest.

Not all commentators had a positive assessment of the VRP. The World Bank in its preliminary assessment report written even before dam construction began, had been decidedly less upbeat. This was because in spite of all the identified benefits, it estimated, based on the various assessments, that the VRP's contribution to Ghana's national income in 1960 would be 1%, and probably less than that in 1970. Also, in terms of overall costs and benefits, the VRP would have a modestly positive balance sheet at best. According to the Bank, the returns on the VRP for Ghana over the estimated 50-year lifespan and annual smelter capacity of 120,000 tons would be

---

[16] Cocoa was providing 2/3 of export revenue and a third of government revenue. Even the development plans were to be funded largely from cocoa exports. Fluctuations in cocoa prices and the ravages of swollen shoot disease as well as a growing population had underlined the need for diversification.

7–8%, depending on tariff levels. The Bank considered these returns poor and off-putting for potential lenders. For these reasons, the Bank's approval of the Project was qualified in the sense that it is left to the Ghana government to decide whether the benefits out-weighed such a large investment in a single project, given the uncertainties and what had to be foregone. As the Bank concluded:

> It is clear that there would be no net gain, and probably a net loss, during the first decade of operation, when financial returns would be very low and net tax benefits, if any, would be small. However, the benefits in later years would be greater, when the power capacity is more fully utilized, when the tax deferral period has expired and when (and if) the aluminium enterprise has become a balanced and inte-grated operation . . . (International Bank for Reconstruction and Development, 1960, p. 21).

There were a number of other questions raised about the VRP even before its implementation. These include, to paraphrase Hance (1958), the problems of obtaining capital, the inflationary potential of the project, the possible disruption of other development programmes and the threats to economic control posed by the levels of foreign borrowing required (p. 79). However, these problems were considered to be amenable to solutions. The Government was confident that it could find the money and this confidence was not misplaced as Ghana paid for its contribution to the VRP from its own resources as well as from loans. Of these, only a USAID loan of G£9.6 million at 3½% was considered below commercial rates. The loans were long-term (for between 2½ and 3 decades) with substantial interest payments estimated at £3 million a year payable in foreign exchange. For this reason and the fact that expected revenues from the project were going to be quite small, estimated at 1½% of GDP, Ghana's capital in the VRP was provided in the form of equity (Birmingham et al., 1966).

The dangers of inflation were discounted partly because much of the heavy spending on the VRP would be external. Local fears about foreign economic control were also dismissed with the explanation that since the project was situated in Ghana under the supervision of a Ghanaian organisation and was expected to pay its way, the fear of foreign domination was unjustified, particularly with the involvement of the World Bank (Hance, 1958).

The expenditure planned under the VRP was expected to have implications for the government's ability to execute various projects under the Ghana's Second Seven Year Development Plan (1963–70) because the government had pledged to give priority to the VRP. The cost of the dam and power station, estimated at £55 million was about 4/5 of the cost of implementing the Plan, thus much of the latter had to be postponed (Rado, 1960; Barnes, 1966).[17]

Agreed and disputed problems arising from the Volta River Project

To advance his thesis that political interference has been central to the failure of state enterprises in Ghana, Killick discusses the Volta River Project as an exception to the rule. As he argues of the Volta River Authority, "in terms of its main duties, it was a success story" (Killick, 1978, p. 249). Though the resettled communities are mentioned, they do not seem to detract much from the success story. "It is true that attempts to resettle the former residents of inundated areas ran into serious difficulties, especially (and characteristically for Ghana) the creation of improved agriculture" (Killick, 1978 p. 249). Some of the successes include a) the finishing of the dam ahead of schedule and below original estimates, b) the power sold and its profitability exceeding projections in the first five years, and c) the established credibility of the VRA to secure additional World Bank and bilateral loans. Killick attributes the VRA's success to three factors—the thoroughness with which the Volta River Project was planned and evaluated before its commencement, the fact that the Act which established the Authority was unambiguous about its functions and its freedom from political interference (Killick, 1978 p. 251). The last point about political interference, though, is debatable. Kalitsi's account of the VRA's privileged position in the 1st Republic and Nkrumah's personal interest in its affairs suggests that there was plenty of political intervention. The difference here was that it was seen as supportive and beneficial and therefore not interference!

With the benefit of fielding criticisms of the VRP for decades, Kalitsi's assessment was more moderated. He has argued that the objective of providing a reliable source of electricity in Ghana was

---

[17] Paradoxically, the postponed elements of the Development Plan, such as the ambitious and probably unrealisable aim of establishing 600 factories to produce over 100 products (Parks, 1960, p. 21) was to have been made possible by hydro-electric power (HEP) from the VRP.

largely met for thirty years. This he contrasts with many unfinished projects around Ghana, arguing that as an investment, VRA brought more returns than many other enterprises and projects in Ghana and elsewhere (KK, Accra). Faber for his part has argued that:

> Even before the renegotiation the scheme had been a net provider of foreign exchange, a provider of employment, a source of additional domestic product and the supplier of electric power to domestic users at a price cheaper than would otherwise have been attainable. The renegotiation enhanced most of these advantages (1990, p. 88).

Some of the benefits cited by the more positive assessments are the subject of contestation in the literature. For example, the VRP as a source of cheap power has been hotly debated over the years. The World Bank had recommended 4.5 mills per kWh for the Aluminium Companies and a flat rate of 15 mills for all other consumers. Kaiser found this unacceptable and the initial base rate that was finally agreed was 2.625 mills. Faber has argued that this was comparable to the prices being charged by the Bonneville Power Corporation in the USA.[18] Others have disputed this. Barnes, for example, described the power rates as very cheap, comparing favourably with the lowest power costs at other Kaiser smelters.[19] Hart notes that at the time VALCO was paying 2.625 mills per kWh, the average cost of industrial power in the USA was 7 mills.[20] In the 1970s Kaiser was paying 12 mills for coal-based electricity for its smelter in the USA.[21]

---

[18] However, in the same article, Faber also reported that Jackson, author of the Preparatory Commission Report of 1956, later commented in a personal letter to him (2 August 1984) that "Gbedemah, who led the delegation, was clearly under instructions from the President to come to an agreement with Kaiser's negotiators— and the latter had little difficulty in extracting many concessions, including an unreasonably low power rate" (p. 90).

[19] He has, however, suggested that it could not be otherwise because that was key to Kaiser's decision to invest in the VRP. Compared with local consumers whose demand for power from the electricity department was estimated at between 26% and 30% of peak demand on the average, VALCO would be able to consume power on a 24 hours basis (Barnes, 1966, p. 15).

[20] Although the power rates were for 30 years, they were negotiated upwards to 3.25 mills/kWh in 1977, backdated to 1973.

[21] That VALCO continued to operate at full capacity during the slump in the world aluminium market when parts of various smelting operations around the world were shut down is seen as an indication of the VRP's profitability for the aluminium companies. Indeed, Hart has argued that revenue from the sale of electricity to VALCO was lower than what it cost to produce it. This was even considering that it was a consumer of great importance, one whose needs were predictable and well understood (Hart, 1980, p. 64; Dickinson, 1982).

In a league table of average revenue per kWh sold, Ghana had the lowest figure of 6.2 and the next lowest was El Salvador, with 14.2 and the highest being Ethiopia whose installed capacity was much smaller than the Volta River Project's (Hart, 1980, p. 67; see also Birmingham et al., 1966). From the foregoing, it can be said that the electricity prices VALCO was paying did not take into consideration the full cost of production.

Therefore, while low power tariff might have been advantageous for the aluminium companies, it was detrimental to Ghana in terms of its earnings from power and the fact that its own industries could not benefit from such favourable terms. Hart came to argue years later that among other things, the VRP contributed to the balance of payments problems of Ghana and the growing debt burden. A lower than expected profitability of VRA's operations slowed down debt repayments. Also, the value of aluminium exports did not make much of a difference to the essential character of the Ghanaian economy, which was based on primary commodity exports.[22] While the Volta River Authority, the Electricity Corporation and VALCO employed about 10,000 persons, some of them casually, it made no serious difference to unemployment rates and expected multiplier effects in industry and employment did not materialise. Even the decision to site the smelter at Tema has been criticised as convenient for VALCO but inconvenient for Ghana because it meant electricity and water had to travel longer distances. Tema thus became a dual-purpose settlement, both port and aluminium town, putting a strain on housing and leading to the formation of a squatter town, Ashaiman.[23]

The failure to achieve integration between the VRP and the Ghanaian economy has been cited as a key factor in the relatively poor benefits of the VRP for Ghana (Hart, 1980, p. 59). For VALCO, on the other hand, the terms, particularly the power tariff and tax exemptions, were so generous that it recouped its investments quite quickly (Hart, 1980).

---

[22] The exports, consisting largely of cocoa, timber, gold, diamonds and manganese, throughout the sixties and seventies never fell below 83% of total value of all exports. In any case, aluminium exports had to be offset against the value of the imported inputs used in production (Hart, 1980, p. 57).

[23] Interestingly, Ashaiman is a popular destination for migrants from the Lower Volta and Lakeside communities.

Accounting for the Volta River Project: The how and why

If the terms of the VRP were so problematic, how did that happen and why did Nkrumah accept and defend them? Faber, for example, would argue that while Ghana did not benefit as much as the other parties, there was enough in there to make it worthwhile. Kalitsi would say that it was the best deal on offer and Ghana needed to build the dam. According to Hart, on the other hand, Nkrumah's sometimes hard-to-comprehend stances in the protracted and complicated negotiations leading up to the final agreement had to do with his belief that the conflicting interests could be reconciled and his exaggerated expectations of what was possible (Hart, 1980, pp. 40–42).

The issues raised by the differences in the explanations of the how and why need some consideration. They include the power imbalances among the parties to the VRP, questions of conflicts of interests and the status of the aluminium smelter in the conception of the VRP. Other issues were the externalisation of costs represented by the treatment of non-power projects within the VRP and the climate, timing and the conduct of negotiations.

Power imbalances and conflicts of interest

Hart has argued that the outcomes of the Volta River Project were the result of the differences in aims and expectations of the parties to the Project. While the aluminium companies and their backers wanted to primarily secure a cheap source of aluminium for their markets and the continued integration of their own aluminium industries, the Ghana government had more elaborate but less specific developmental goals. These included the securing of a source of cheap power for industrialisation, the possibility of an integrated project utilising Ghana's bauxite and power to produce aluminium for the world market, irrigation of the Volta Basin and an additional source of transport between Northern and Southern Ghana. These aims and objectives were to prove incompatible. Being the weakest party in this array of forces which included the aluminium companies, foreign governments, the foreign banks and the World Bank as referee, the Ghana government was not able to fulfil many of its expectations. The aluminium companies had many options for their supply of power, bauxite and alumina. Within such a scenario, the deal represented by the VRP had to be extremely attractive for the aluminium companies. As far back as 1958, even before Kaiser had entered the scene, Hance noted, "it should be apparent that Ghana needs capital more than capital needs Ghana" (1958, p. 67).

What was considered attractive enough to make a deal also depended on location. It has been argued that if the bauxite deposits and the river had been in New Jersey, then the Preparatory Commission's more cautious estimates of costs, and therefore, profitability would not have been such a turn-off, since the risk element would have been considered much lower (Hance, p. 68). As it was, risk was a consideration, which was not dropped even in the face of all the reassurances of the Nkrumah Regime. The problems with the negotiated outcomes of the VRP, it has been argued, were exacerbated by a lack of attention to potential conflicts of interest. An example of such a conflict involved the use of interested parties to conduct feasibility studies. As Killick argued:

> ... using interested parties to undertake feasibility studies sometimes killed potentially sound projects as well as promoting unsound ones. A case in point was the use of companies who were supplying Ghana's cement industry with imported clinker to study the possibility of replacing the clinker with domestic limestone. This was done twice and it can come as little surprise that both companies arrived at negative conclusions. The same mistake was made regarding the creation of the alumina plant, where the company studying the project had a clearly established interest in producing a negative result and duly did so (Killick, 1978, p. 230).

Faber, for his part, identifies the calculations of the cost of the project and the power rate as another source of conflict. As he argues, "the larger and more expensive the dam, the power station and the accompanying infrastructure, the greater would be the loans required; and the greater the loans, the higher the power rates to the smelter would have to be to service them. But too high a power rate meant that no one would be prepared to build and operate the smelter, for that part of the scheme was to be left to private enterprise" (1990 p. 72). Related to this, Birmingham et al. have argued that the low tariffs weakened Ghana's negotiating position with regard to the use of local bauxite by the smelter. This is because the low cost of power made it still economical to use imported alumina. Had the power been more expensive, using locally produced alumina would have made more economic sense. Besides, fixing of the price of power for thirty years also removed Ghana's ability to use power prices to leverage VALCO to establish an alumina plant (Birmingham et al., 1966, p. 403). For the owners of VALCO, investing in an alumina plant involved some predictions about the demand for alumina and aluminium, which were never completely certain.

A third source of conflict identified in the literature, which was more general, was the changing role of Kaiser within the Project, as was noted earlier in the chapter (Hart, 1980). Kalitsi denied that there was a conflict of interest or that it was an issue in the outcomes of the Project, arguing that while the Nkrumah government was very clear about its interests, it was constrained by the lack of a better offer on the table. Given the number of times the project had had to be shelved, it was important for the government to make the deal when it did at a time when the aluminium industry was going through hard times. Furthermore, the Project's benefit as a reliable source of power until recently was too easily forgotten in the assessments (KK, Accra; but see Hart, 1980, who argues that the range of technical options was deliberately narrowed to serve certain interests).

The aluminium trap

The Volta River Project was always linked to aluminium. It was the discovery of extensive bauxite deposits in the Western and Ashanti Regions, linked with the idea that the Volta River gorges would be a great location for a hydroelectric power dam which concretised the most salient features of the VRP.[24] From quite early on, feasibility reports argued that the VRP was economically feasible only if it was guaranteed a large industrial consumer of power such as an aluminium smelter (Halcrow, 1951; World Bank, 1960). The smelter requirement was so regularly restated that it became something of an orthodoxy (Balogh, 1956; Hilling, 1965; Barnes, 1966; Dobson, 1963).

The belief in the link between project viability and the aluminium smelter continued to prevail even in the face of contradictory information. For example, non-smelter consumers such as the mines, local

---

[24] Ghana's good grade bauxite reserves were estimated at 225–229 million tons and it was envisaged that they would be mined by surface mining (Hance, 1958, p. 53).

industries and domestic consumers and possibly neighbouring countries, were expected to bring in much more revenue in the first
twenty years than the smelter as a result of their having to pay about
five times the smelter tariff rate. The smelter was expected to account
for less than a third of the total revenue generated between 1966
and 1976, while consuming nearly two thirds of the power. Therefore,
the profitability as well as the securing of resources for future expansion of power supply lay more with the non-smelter demand and
level of tariffs (World Bank, 1960; see also Birmingham, 1966,
p. 398). The World Bank had recommended that non-smelter tariffs
be kept high in order not to jeopardise the already low returns and
even losses expected from the Project especially in its first decade
when it would be paying interests on loans and dealing with depre-
ciation and other losses (World Bank, 1960). The tension between
keeping tariffs high enough to generate the money to repay debts,
but also low enough to make them worth the while of the aluminium
companies and all other industrial and domestic consumers was always
present in the VRP.

While the Ghana government wanted cheap power for its industries, the aluminium companies wanted it for their smelter. The idea
of using cheap power to promote industrialisation, irrigation and
commercial agriculture implied not charging full market rates. It also
meant producing enough power in order that after supplying the
smelter, there would be enough left to pursue the promotion of industries and increased domestic consumption through increasing the
numbers of consumers and also their use of electrical appliances.
The World Bank did not share the "cheap power as a spur to industrialisation theory", believing that development could not be forced
with that approach (Barnes, 1966, p. 17). It also understood that
there was a limit to how much the aluminium companies would pay
for power. Therefore, it suggested that cheap power not be made
available to non-smelter consumers whose only option was relatively
more expensive thermal power (Barnes, 1966, p. 19).

There were good reasons for seeing aluminium production as the
central linking project. It has been argued that the combination of
huge bauxite deposits in close proximity to terrain on which power
could be produced and a port for import and export was unique.
Constructing an aluminium smelter close to these natural facilities
would complete what has been described as one of the most "ideally
integrated operations" of the industry with the potential for enor-

mous savings in transport costs, among other things (Hance, p. 52). What Hance had not considered was that what was the most integrated operation in the world could be integrated for only one of the parties involved in it. Integration for Ghana was not the same set of conditions as integration for the aluminium companies and did not have the same economic implications. On the other hand, given what is known about the environmental and socio-economic impacts of mining today, perhaps it was a blessing in disguise that Ghana's bauxite deposits were not exploited under the VRP.[25]

What is a central problem about the VRP was that alternatives to an aluminium smelter-tied project were never seriously considered. For example, the possibility of a smaller scale project was dismissed on grounds of higher unit costs for electricity as well as difficulties with attracting the kind of consumer represented by an aluminium smelter (Hance, 1958). Interestingly, a cost-benefit analysis of the VRP has suggested that the Project would be more advantageous to Ghana without the smelter if local consumption were to grow by Kaiser's estimates of growth (Parks, 1960). It therefore recommended a more gradualist approach to increasing dam capacity in co-ordination with growing levels of demand. This way, power costs would be lower and benefits higher if all the power could be sold to local consumers instead of a smelter (Parks, 1960, p. 85).[26] While the Parks study was not conclusive, his findings suggested that there might have been other options for maximising the benefits of the VRP for Ghana with or without a smelter.

Barnes, writing at the time the VRP was being considered, also raised another possibility to anchor the VRP—the West African market. Beyond the sale of power, many of the industries being mentioned in relation to the VRP would be more viable if they were established jointly with neighbouring countries, in recognition of the small size of the Ghanaian market (Barnes, 1966). However, though

---

[25] That state of mining technology of the sixties and the relative lack of attention to environmental impacts would have held real dangers for local communities. Even more importantly, the terms on which bauxite mining would have taken place were likely to have been as unfavourable as for other contracts within the VRP framework.

[26] The World Bank on the other hand declared the Kaiser estimates over-optimistic, arguing that the growth of local consumption was not going to be profitable enough to warrant investment in transmission lines beyond Accra, Tema, Takoradi and Kumasi, a triangular route from West to North to East (World Bank, 1960).

the development of a West African market was considered economically very interesting, it was not being vigorously pursued because
of political differences between Ghana and her neighbours,[27] leaving
VALCO, the mines, and other local commercial, industrial and
domestic consumers as the only realistic market (1966, p. 14).

The status of non-power projects and the externalisation of costs
The status of the non-power projects within the VRP is another factor which affected the outcomes of the Project. For those who really
mattered, the VRP was a Hydro-Electric Power (HEP) Project and
not a multi-purpose one, as the more optimistic have tried to claim
sometimes. Hilling, for example, described the Volta River Project
as the "largest integrated development scheme in Africa" (1965,
p. 841) citing Nkrumah's view that it was the beginning of industrialisation in Ghana. Futa (1963), a VRA employee at the time,
argued the opposite on grounds that the demands of running a multi-
purpose project would have been too onerous given the capabilities
of the VRA and Ghana's development priorities. Birmingham et al.
(1966) have argued that in so far as the economic viability of the
Volta River Project was based on the dam and the aluminium smelter,
then it was misleading to think of it as a multi-purpose project. Other
possibilities were to be seen more as "by-products than integral parts
of the whole concept" (Birmingham et al., 1966, p. 407). Dobson
agreed with this characterisation, but held out the hope that other
benefits were possible. Abhyankar (1964), writing in the same period,
while accepting that the primary character of the VRP was a hydroelectric project, was also of the view that its multi-purpose aspects
be pursued and nurtured to increase the overall benefits of the
Project.[28] As well, it would promote the development of the Volta

---

[27] Barnes notes that both Togo and Ivory Coast (now La Côte d'Ivoire) which
have to depend on coal and oil imports for producing power were interested in
the neighbourhood of 170 million kWh of Akosombo power.

[28] These included the inland water transport, the fisheries, the use of Ghanaian
bauxite, irrigation, charcoal and fuel from the 146 sq. miles of riverine forest which
was under threat from flooding by the lake, lake transport and manufacturing industry. Abhyankar also mentions the 146 square miles of riverine forest to be inundated by the Lake as a source of large quantities of charcoal and fuel if felled
beforehand, and the forest reserves adjoining the future Lake as the basis of saw
milling and logging concerns (Abhyankar, 1964).

Basin as an integral part of national economic development (Abhyankar, 1964; see also Hilling, 1965).

On occasion, VRA officials have alluded to a multi-purpose agenda while not fully committing to it.[29] This confusion about the Project's status affected the analysis of its benefits and costs as these non-power "components" were thrown into the equation without a proper assessment of their feasibility and compatibility. The issue of affected communities often arose tangentially in these discussions because the benefits they were expected to derive from this project would mitigate their disadvantages. For example, Abhyankar recommended the creation of fishing villages along the Lake as well as the provision of financial and organisational assistance and storage and marketing facilities to resettle migrant fishermen. Around the Lake, he recommended afforestation to support both conservation and charcoal-making and for the downstream, the rescue and development of the clam industry, the Volta River creeks and the Songaw (now spelt Songor) Lagoon salt industry (Abhyankar, 1964, p. 31). The stress on the hydropower approach to the project meant that while these other projects were never seriously considered, they came to be regularly cited as potential benefits of the Project. This helped to create some of the many unfulfilled expectations of the VRP, such as industrialization, irrigation, food processing, afforestation and lake transport. In the case of irrigation, which was one of the more seriously considered projects, there was talk of irrigating 200,000 to 300,000 acres of land. It was subsequently reported that a pilot irrigation scheme on 1,000 acres had been established at Kpong with a second phase involving 18,000 acres envisaged (Hance, 1958, p. 60).[30] By the same

---

[29] For example, E.L. Quartey, Dobson's Ghanaian successor to the post of chief executive, declared at the opening of an international symposium on man-made lakes in Accra in 1966 that "the Volta River Authority has always conceived the Volta Lake not only from the viewpoint of the production of electric power but also in relation to the many other benefits that can accrue from a multi-purpose dam" (Quartey, 1969).

[30] As early as in 1960, the World Bank had argued that the waters of the Volta would be adequate for a six-unit power plant, provided there was no substantial diversion or consumption of the water (International Bank for Reconstruction and Development, 1960). Dobson also suggested that there might be little or no scope for using the waters of the Lake for irrigation. Even in relation to the possibility of using downstream water, he anticipated some problems such as water logging and soil alkalinity in the long term (Dobson, 1963, p. 13). In spite of these questions, irrigation continued to be touted for a long time as one of the potential benefits of the VRP.

token, there was no interrogation of whether there would be power available for all the other development plans. This was a serious issue given the anticipated 60% VALCO consumption.

In relation to new industries, an additional issue was the size and availability of the Ghanaian and West African markets. In the case of lake transport, Barnes' assessment was that the tonnage of cargo at the time raised questions about the Project's viability (Barnes, 1966).[31] An important question posed about all the projects was that they would cost money to implement. Thus, although it was stated in the Nkrumah Government's Seven Year Development Plan that some of these projects would begin, there were no financial provisions made for them (Birmingham et al., 1966).

The tendency to externalise costs, now widely accepted as a problem with hydroelectric dam projects the world over, was recently reiterated in the report of the World Commission on Dams (2000). In the case of the Volta River Project, externalisation of costs is almost as old as the Project itself. This is notwithstanding Kalitsi's view that the VRP's benefits tend to be forgotten, a position he shares with Obeng, a pioneer Ghanaian aquatic biologist who has consistently argued that the adverse impacts of dams are often overemphasised (Obeng, 1975). Hart reports that as far back as 1949, St John Bird, the author of the first VRP proposal, argued that the land to be flooded by the dam was of low value and therefore £1 million (one million pounds) would be more than enough to cover legal costs and compensation. Secondly, the proposals contained calculations of savings to be made on segregated housing for project staff and outrageous wage differentials between European and African workers. Again, clearing the area to be flooded by the Lake of its forests was rejected solely on grounds of cost and a confidence that the dam could be protected from floating debris. No consideration was given to the fact that fishermen and other users of the Lake would be able to navigate its waters and exploit its resources more easily without the standing and submerged forests.[32] What is significant here is that all these proposals found some expression in the Volta River Project's arrangements. For example, housing for employees

---

[31] This, he suggested, could be solved by the transportation related to mining the iron ore deposits at Shiene (Barnes, 1966).

[32] As Hart points out, this disregard for local communities was only partly due to St John Bird's South African origins. Most colonial and post-colonial institutional housing projects and wage policies in Ghana have this character.

at Akosombo and other townships and stations of the Volta River Authority are in sharp contrast to resettlement housing. As we shall see in the next chapter, this has been a source of tension between the Volta River Authority and settlers. The land, which came to be submerged by the Lake, was not cleared of vegetation and this has become a factor in Lake Transport safety and fishing methods.

Interestingly, the World Bank had argued that "substantial ancillary projects such as resettlement, compensation, housing, water facilities at Tema and the new dredging and port works, which were directly attributable to the project but not chargeable to it and hence not included in its costs, had to be factored into assessments of the overall returns on the Project" (International Bank for Reconstruction and Development, 1960 p. 18). The Bank, in 1960, had been confident that the revenues from these so called ancillary investments could be the largest single benefit of the VRP and, therefore, the Ghana government was being urged to maximise it, as well as the tax revenue from the smelter. Unfortunately, the so-called ancillary investments came to be ruthlessly cut out of the Kaiser Reassessment Report. On a number of occasions, Nkrumah spoke positively of the substantial reduction in the cost of the entire project made possible in this Report (Nkrumah, 1961; Nkrumah, 1966). While this may have been the case, these reductions were to prove very costly. It has been noted that the result of the Reassessment Report was that the social and public works expenditure, which was not directly related to power production, was abandoned (Diaw & Schmidt-Kallert, 1990, pp. 10, 28).[33] The recommendations for irrigation and the dredging of creeks made by the Preparatory Commission in 1956 were also not retained by the Reassessment Report. They were,

---

[33] These ancillary investments had been estimated at £G 11.4 million. The breakdown was as follows:

Compensation and resettlement (excess over the £G 3.5 million to be charged to the project)	- £G 0.7 million
Downstream compensation	- £G 0.5 million
Housing for smelter labour	- £G 4.0 million
Water supply for smelter	- £G 0.7 million
Port works allocable to project	- £G 5.0 million
Extra dredging	- £G 0.5 million
Total	- £G11.4 million

Source: World Bank Preliminary Appraisal, 1960.

therefore, dropped from the financial arrangements for the dam. This tradition of excluding non-power costs has been continued in some of the literature. Faber, for example, mentions ecological damage and the problems of the resettlements, but discounts these costs in his substantive assessments.

Timing and the conduct of negotiations
Timing proved to be an enemy of the VRP from Ghana's point of view. We have already discussed how British interest in the VRP rose and waned with developments on the world aluminium markets. The resulting long period of gestation and the uncertainties around the VRP meant that by the time the American government and its aluminium companies entered the fray, Ghana was desperate for a deal. Secondly, because the project was intimately linked with aluminium, its attractiveness at any point in time continued to depend not only on the size, terms and security of the particular investment, but also on the state of the world aluminium market (Barnes, 1966). As Hance argued, the elaborate assessments and deliberations in the 1950s were partly to buy time for the British government and the aluminium companies to consider all their options carefully. While this was a reasonable course of action, also from the viewpoint of the Ghana government, the delays culminated in a weakening of Ghana's position in the negotiations (Hance, 1958).

Birmingham et al. (1966) confirmed this assessment. Eight years had passed between when the British Government White Paper was issued in 1952 and when it became clear that the Project would be implemented. Under these pressures, the conduct of the negotiations from the Ghana side was problematic. Not everyone shared Nkrumah's optimism. A case in point was the concerns expressed by some opposition members of the Assembly discussed earlier in the chapter. However, various tactics silenced dissenting voices. The Assembly was not expected to do more than rubber stamp the process and learn its details so that MPs could educate their constituents. The terms of the reassessment report had been accepted and the Master agreement drafted at the time of Nkrumah's speech to the Assembly in 1961. The speech was to seek the Assembly's approval for the arrangements that had been made and its advice with respect to the contracts to be executed. The President expressed the hope that MPs would learn the details to explain its benefits to their constituents in order to get national support for the project. It was striking just how much was already underway even as agreements were being negotiated:

> I have been confident throughout that we would succeed in bringing the Volta scheme to life and the Government has accordingly under-taken, by arrangement with the Kaiser group, for the bulk of this preparatory work to be completed in advance of the letting of the con-tract for the dam and power house, so that when the contractor arrives to start work, he will find a site ready for his occupation. Our faith in this scheme is now visible at Akosombo in the shape of houses, a power station, water supplies and a first class access road . . . (Nkrumah, 1961).

The negotiating strategy represented by this way of proceeding was at best too enthusiastic. In addition to the absence of debates in the Legislature about the Project, the government was awarding con-tracts for the construction of the highway from Tema to Akosombo, access roads to the dam site and housing for workers while negoti-ations were in progress. Furthermore, there was a pre-occupation with the comfort of the contractors and the beauty of the new town-ship, which was not matched with concern about the communities to be affected. Had more thought been given to affected communi-ties, their situation may have been different. Hart (1980) and others (e.g. KK, Accra) have argued that the anticipated boom in indus-trialisation did not happen partly because the electricity factor in industrialisation was exaggerated. Studies in countries with similar conditions as Ghana, e.g. Tanzania, Uganda and Kenya, have shown that because electricity costs are a relatively minuscule part of indus-trial costs, electricity is not sufficient to promote industrialisation. Thus while a project the size of Akosombo might have stimulated industry, the faith in electricity per se was too high.

6. The Volta River and Dam-Affected Communities: Predicted Impacts and Recommendations

A key element in the conception of the VRP was its impacts on dam-affected communities. The Preparatory Commission Report's segment on communities to be affected by the Akosombo Dam is the most comprehensive source of information about the thinking within the VRP about how to approach this issue. As the Reassessment Report did not address this issue, the Commission's predictions and assessments have remained unchallenged, even if not implemented. The Commission recommended further study on a wide range of issues including dam impacts on affected communities. This recommendation was to be implemented mainly by the Volta Basin Research Project (VBRP), which was established in 1963.[34] Because of the time it was established, the VBRP found itself struggling to catch up with the pace of dam construction and the resulting changes. Therefore, the research agenda set for it by the Preparatory Commission could not be implemented. In spite of this, both the Preparatory Commission and the VBRP had to make some predictions about the impacts of the Akosombo Dam and the Volta Lake on local communities.

The Commission's approach to project costs and benefits, especially in relation to affected communities, had a number of interconnected elements. These included:

- caution in the calculation of losses through downplaying both the existing value of the resources in question as well as the likely negative impacts of the dam;
- pointing out mitigating or beneficial effects and making recommendations to realise and strengthen benefits, e.g. fish losses downstream being matched against fish gains around the Lake, and measures proposed to realise fully the fisheries potential of the Lake;
- suggesting measures to repair or reduce any anticipated damage to resources, e.g. dredging of creeks;
- and if all else failed, compensation.

The Preparatory Commission struck a note of optimism about dam impacts in its very first chapter. It concluded that the local effects of the dam and Lake could be addressed satisfactorily (Chapter 1, paragraph 21, p. 3). The main effects it identified were the area of 3,500 sq. miles to be flooded, changes in the pattern of flow of the river from the dam to the sea, problems of health and sanitation on the new Lake, the effects on agriculture, forests and fisheries and

---

[34] The VBRP is described as a multidisciplinary project working in three main areas—"the archaeology of the area to be flooded, socio-economic changes and problems caused by resettlement and the hydro-biological features of the transformation of the river into a lake (Lawson et al., 1969, p. 966). By 1969, the hydrobiological work consisted of studies of the physical and chemical character of the Lake, microbiology and the productivity of the Lake.

the changed conditions in the Lower Volta. In addition to estimating the potential liabilities to communities arising from these effects, the Report made the explicit assumption that the government would set up administrative machinery to address these issues (Chap 13, paragraph 265, p. 45; Chapter 14, paragraph 274, p. 46). Post Preparatory Commission assessments also tended to be positive about dam impacts on communities. Dobson, the first head of the Volta River Authority (VRA), for example, notes:

> The Volta Project in its final operation stage will not only create new job opportunities for Ghanaians, but will lead to a fuller development of the industrial and agricultural potential of the area and thus help to increase the total level of production and incomes. The resettlement of nearly 80,000 persons who are likely to be displaced by the lake in new farms and new townships will also stimulate healthier living and scientific mixed agriculture in these communities (Dobson, 1963a, p. 41).

In relation to resettlement, Parks (1960) argued that it should not be a problem if the people could be persuaded to settle around the Lake to continue fishing which was their main occupation as well as engage in draw-down agriculture[35] (1960). Hilling, for his part, hoped that the benefits of resettlement would make up for the disruption it represented (1965). Birmingham et al. (1966) however provided a rare dose of realism when they argued that the forced removal of about 70,000 persons from their homes should be counted as a social cost. In spite of the fact that they shared some of the elements of the then dominant modernisation paradigm, their views were probably tempered by the fact that the resettlement programme was underway when they were writing.

While the Commission stressed the need for care in investigating what existed and what changes were anticipated, some of the activities of the VRP raised local expectations in the Lower Volta. An

---

[35] The draw-down area has been defined as "all the land bordering the Volta Lake, which is alternately flooded and then exposed as a result of the seasonal fluctuations in the level of water in the Lake" (Amatekpor, 1970; see also Ahn, 1970). The size of the draw-down is estimated at 211,000 acres (85,455 hectares) assuming a ten foot fall in the water level in the Lake between seasons (Amatekpor, 1970). Ahn found that while 20% of the area was too steep and narrow for agriculture, it was a significant addition to agricultural land (1970). Draw-down agriculture is farming which occurs on the draw-down.

article written in the Legon Observer, an influential publication of the University of Ghana community in the 1970s, recalled the promises made by those who toured the communities which were expected to suffer adverse effects (Aduamah, 1971). Secondly, in weighing the clams being picked by the women and recording fish landings over a whole season, the expectation that losses would be compensated was cemented (Interviews with Mama Sreku and others, Mepe). Many persons believed that they would be compensated individually for losses and new job opportunities would be created for their communities. As one informant explained:

> Before the dam was constructed, the government sent people around to examine all the streams around us from which we fished. People were also sent to weigh and record the fish harvests. The clams we landed daily were also weighed. They did that for the whole season. We were told there was going to be a change after the construction of the dam so they have to take account of all our operations and pay us some amount. They recorded our names in their books (Mama Sreku, Mepe).

In the following section, the Preparatory Commission Report's positions on subjects such as the Lake Fisheries, draw-down agriculture, the cessation of the seasonal floods in the Lower Volta, Lower Volta agriculture, the clam industry, creek fishing, conflicts over the use of the Volta and health and sanitation are examined.

Maximising dam benefits: The establishment of the lake fisheries

The Volta Lake Fisheries were long predicted as a valuable by-product of the Volta River Project. This was the one benefit of the Lake which was underestimated. It was generally estimated that 18,000 tons of fish would be produced annually, an amount equal to what was caught off the coast of Ghana. The Lake Fisheries came to be over three times this estimate (Parks, 1960; International Bank for Reconstruction and Development, 1960).

The Preparatory Commission recommended various steps to realise the potential of the industry. These included stocking the Lake, finding the fishermen, supporting them to adapt to the new environment, providing stronger fishing vessels and supporting the establishment of market infrastructure. It was envisaged that the Fisheries Department would establish stations for Lake fishing (Preparatory Commission, 1956; Hance, 1960, p. 61). Barnes (1966) went even further with recommendations to secure both Lake and downstream fishing. Noting the lack of the needed investment to secure the benefits of the fisheries, he suggested credit and technical assistance among other things.

Scientists from the nascent Volta Basin Research Project (VPRP) at the University of Ghana and the Institute of Aquatic Biology became involved in studying the Lake once it began to form. As early as in 1964, a VPRP study was suggesting that large-scale or co-operative fishing methods be emphasised and the fisheries regulated to ensure their sustainability. The study also predicted that mechanised fishing was not on the cards in the Volta Lake because most of the species of fresh water fish expected to survive the transition from river to lake were the so-called bottom living species. Also, that most of the fishermen who would settle around the lake in small isolated settlements would be Ewe fishermen in need of support because lake conditions would be a novelty to them. Therefore it was recommended that the Fisheries Department's Training Programme be introduced to the Lake (Roberts, 1964, 1967).

The cessation of the seasonal floods and its impacts on river flow

One of the issues the Preparatory Commission considered was the expected change in river flow. The Report had noted that changes in the pattern of flow of the Volta would have "an appreciable effect on the levels which lie on both sides of the river below the dam site" (Appendix VII, paragraph 2, p. 139; see also Obeng, 1975, who argued that the changes brought by Lake formation would have an unpredictable effect on the downstream of the river, with impacts on micro-organisms, plants and animals depending on the quantities of water flowing downstream and the timing and pattern of flow).

River flow, as already indicated, ranged between below 1,000 cusecs in the driest months to between 125,000 and 390,000 cusecs at the height of the floods in September and October. In the first phase of dam construction when the lake was filling, there was concern to keep enough water in the river to protect drinking water from excessive salinity. Subsequently, the expectation was that there would be more water in the river, reaching a constant flow of 38,000 cusecs throughout the year once power production was established. The Preparatory Commission wanted the implications of these changes investigated with a view to protecting the livelihood of riverine communities while at the same time ensuring that the water was not wasted. The expectation that damming would result in a more steady flow of the Volta throughout the year and improve the penetration of salt water beyond the estuary, were seen as improvements (Hance, 1960; but see Barnes, 1966, who argued that the all-year-round steady flow of the river after damming might have a negative effect on downstream fishing). There was also optimism that the salt and onion industries in the Keta Lagoon could be improved and any adverse effects on salt production in the Songaw Lagoon mitigated.

Agricultural production in the Lower Volta: Business as usual

The Preparatory Commission took the position that the cessation of the annual floods would not create immediate changes in agricultural production, although yields would decline in the long run, in the extreme event of there being no further seasonal flooding and no fertiliser use.

While the Commission estimated the gross value of crops grown in that period on creek land at £160,000, it also insisted that this would be considered a loss only if seasonal flooding ceased completely and only if the floods contributed substantially to the yields, two conditions as yet unproven in its view (Appendix VII, paragraphs 207–208, p. 174). The Commission also suggested that perhaps the floods were not needed every year to secure their beneficial effects on agriculture and in any case, the floods might be considered as only one of the factors in agriculture. Moreover, the floods were not an unambiguous blessing since their timing was sometimes detrimental to agriculture, either hampering production if they were late or harvest losses if they were early (Appendix VII, paragraph 208, p. 174).

Thus the Commission considered river control arising from the damming to be beneficial in creating the context for "planned agricultural development" (paragraph 373, p. 58; see also appendix VII, paragraph 209 for the Commission's statements about the advantages of "taming" the river). Thus the Preparatory Commission recommended the promotion of good farming rather than cash compensation, because of the scattered nature of plots "and communal nature of land rights" (Appendix VII, paragraph 210, p. 175). However, no amount was set aside for compensation for losses in agriculture, but with a proviso that proven losses would be paid from a general fund (paragraph 422, p. 65; Appendix VII, paragraph 200, p. 173). Agriculture was one area where Lawson's conclusions differed from those of the Preparatory Commission. Certain that creek farming was going to be adversely affected, Lawson recommended support to farmers in the Lower Volta in the form of irrigation, capital and technical know-how to assist them (Lawson, 1961). Abhyankar (1964), writing a decade after the Preparatory Commission Report, was even more detailed, recommending that public lands be identified around the Lake and in the Lower Volta to establish "state agricultural, vegetable, dairy and poultry farms" and develop the cultivation of commercial crops such as sugarcane, rice, cotton, tobacco and groundnuts "with a suitable crop rotation pattern".

Arresting the decline of the clam industry

There was general agreement that the clam industry would suffer (Preparatory Commission, 1956; Lawson, 1963; Abhyankar, 1964; Barnes, 1966). Lawson noted that the predicted level of flow when the dam was complete corresponded to conditions just before the annual floods when the volume and turbulence of the river were not favourable for clam picking. She therefore recommended the transplantation of clam beds to a point around Aveyime and Mepe where the river was wide and where large sandy stretches were exposed during the clam season. She envisaged a switch from clam diving to clam farming as part of the process of saving the industry given the success of the clam breeding practices of the clam divers. The provision of suitable transplantation sites had to be done before the clams became inaccessible with the changes in flow which were envisaged. This would also involve rescuing the river sand from the bed of the river to be used in future transplantation sites. As she argued, the clam pickers themselves could not save the industry without outside help in the form of capital and technology. (Lawson, 1961, 1963; see also Abhyankar, 1964 and Barnes 1966 who endorsed these ideas.) The Preparatory Commission took a different view. While agreeing that studies about the habits of clams were needed and that clam beds could be moved to new sites (paragraph 362, p. 57), the Commission argued that in the upper sections of the Lower Volta, clams were likely to continue to flourish, but in slightly different places. The topography of the river with islands and shallows suggested that clam diving would still be possible, although the rate of flow of the river might make it more difficult (Appendix VII, paragraph 141; paragraph 212).

Creek fishing: Minimising and compensating losses

Another industry for which fears were expressed was creek fishing. It was considered more economically important than fishing in the main river and clam picking (Preparatory Commission, Chapter 15, paragraph 354). Apart from being a source of revenue for families and individuals, the Tongu District Council in 1954 and the Sogakope Local Council in 1963 both took steps to earn some revenue from the creeks (Minutes Book of the Tongu District Council, 1968).

The Preparatory Commission predicted, based on a preliminary assessment, that at least 1/3 and possibly 2/3 of the 394 ponds and channels listed in the area could dry up or be submerged by a larger downstream flow. The Commission, therefore, recommended a general programme of restoring and improving existing channels including the dredging of a number of important creeks to either safeguard or enhance their production as a way of reducing compensation claims (Preparatory Commission, paragraph 364, p. 57; see also Barnes, 1966; Abhyankar, 1964 for similar recommendations). For the creeks that could not be saved, the Preparatory Commission recommended compensation (paragraph 368, p. 58). Both Lawson and the Preparatory Commission also downplayed the value of fishing in the main river. For example, Lawson declared it to be mainly for subsistence (Lawson, 1961) while the Preparatory Commission concluded that "any losses or re-orientation in the present fresh water fisheries below the dam should not be serious" (Appendix VII, paragraph 200, p. 173). Therefore, no recommendations were made for addressing any possible losses.

Predictions about conflicts over river use, salinity and flooding

By the 1950s, there was an awareness of potential conflicts in the possible uses of the river after damming. As Lawson argued, the Volta was valuable for agriculture, fisheries and industry and it was important that each aspect be realised without jeopardising the success of others. One possible conflict was the threat posed to the fisheries in the main river and creeks by the disposal of effluents from a proposed sugar refinery and a tannery. The effects of salinity levels on drinking water, fishing and farming as well as future irrigation plans was another conflict this time between electricity production and these other uses (Lawson, 1961). The Preparatory Commission underlined these concerns, arguing that the quality and quantity of water had to be maintained during and after the construction of the dam to secure the drinking water and also the way of life of communities (Preparatory Commission, Chapter 15, paragraph 356). Another recommendation was the provision of more wells at Agave and Ada and the ferrying of water from upstream. There was however great optimism about salinity because of advice from the consulting engineers that after the Dam, there would be no salt beyond the Estuary. Thus, water would become permanently good at Agave, a situation which would improve agriculture and irrigation in the area (Appendix VII, paragraph 175).

Other recommendations to address potential conflicts in river use were the establishment of a flood warning system and the control of the amounts of water going into the Lower Volta, which would have the added advantage of drastically reducing the risk of unexpected heavy flooding (Preparatory Commission, paragraphs 357–361).

Predictions about health, sanitation and aquatic weeds

Pre-dam studies suggested that that the new Lake would increase the incidence of certain diseases because of the increase of population as a result of labour recruitment for the VRP and Lakeside migration (Macdonald, 1954; Lawson, G, 1963). The Preparatory Commission considered the anticipated health problems to be amenable to solution (Chapter 16, paragraph 387, p. 60). Thus, it recommended research on the health situation of inhabitants of the area to be flooded as well as its surrounding neighbourhood. The Commission thought that only four of the existing diseases in the area— malaria,[36] trypanosomiasis (sleeping sickness), onchocerciasis (river blindness) and schistosomiasis (bilharzia)[37] would be affected, one way

---

[36] Malaria is caused by the bite of infected anopheles gambiae and anopheles funestus mosquitoes, which breed in stagnant water. Medical experts researching the issue had advised that because malaria levels were already high, the predicted increase was not likely to be in epidemic proportions also because there was some immunity within the population (Macdonald, 1954).

[37] Schistosomiasis or bilharzia is caused by a worm (schistosome) whose life cycle involves water snails, water and human beings. It attacks humans as schistosomiasis

or another, by the Akosombo Dam (Derban, 1999). Onchocerciasis was endemic just above the Lower Volta, especially around the then existing rapids at Senchi, where the presence of the vector, the *similium damnosum*, also known as the black fly, had been identified.[38] There were fears that the Project's workers would be in danger from the disease because the construction site of the proposed Akosombo Dam was close to this area. As well, a significant proportion of the dam building labour force was expected to come from Northern Ghana where the disease was endemic in parts (Macdonald, 1954). At the same time, it was suggested that onchocerciasis could be reduced or eliminated by the Lake because many of the breeding grounds of black fly would be submerged, leaving only a short stretch of the river below the dam to be treated with insecticides to kill its larvae.

The Commission also expected schistosomiasis and malaria to increase, but was not certain about trypanosomiasis (sleeping sickness). While schistosomiasis in Ghana pre-dated the VRP, there were fears that the Lake could become an important habitat of the snail vectors of the disease as a result of an anticipated explosion of aquatic weeds. An aquatic weed control programme integral to Lakeside health control administration was to be established (Abhyankar, 1964).

Institutional recommendations included the establishment of a Lakeside Health Section within the health and safety division of the Volta River Authority to oversee all the prevention and control programmes. The Preparatory Commission Report stated that all the parties to the project had agreed that disease control would be paid for by the Project (chapter 16, paragraph 415, p. 64). These costs included, in the case of trypanosomiasis control, bush clearing at £150,000 for capital costs and £30,000 recurrent costs, costs of sur-

---

mansoni (which affects the intestines) or haematobium (which causes urinary schistosomiasis, the more common form of the disease in Ghana). It has been described as "a cumulating and debilitating disease. The first symptoms include skin complaints, fever, coughing and at later stages blood in the urine" (Hart, 1980, p. 90; See also Grant, 1965). In its chronic form, it results in hypertension, calcification of the bladder and even heart failure and death (Oasis, Spring/Summer 1994).

[38] 68% of the population in one community, Atimpoku, was found to be infected, while in another, Agbotia, the figure was 82%. Males in these communities had higher rates of infection than females. At Atimpoku, percentage of the infected population was 92% for men and 57% for women, 51% for boys under 12 and 19% for girls under 12.

veillance and drug control and the costs of relocating villages. However, the costs of securing the health of new populations that might be attracted to the Lake for economic reasons were to be borne by the health budget of the government. The VRA was only to provide technical data, facilities and supervision as paid agents (Appendix VIII, paragraph 10).

Predicting costs, estimating compensation for losses: Treading with caution

Even at this stage, the consideration of affected communities was biased towards those to be resettled. The principles developed by the Commission for calculating compensation, for example, focused on the land to be submerged by the Lake. Potential losses were classified into public and private rights.[39] The Commission recommended a detailed study of land rights in the Lake area and the compensation of permanent losses such as the rights to the surface of land, perennial crops and buildings. Such compensation was to be calculated on the basis of the current market rate of such resources in a normal transaction between a willing buyer and seller. Housing was treated slightly differently on the basis that its current value could not take account of its real value to occupants and what it would take to build a similar house in a new location (Chapter 14, paragraphs 290–299).

There was a tendency to underestimate what the losses represented to those to be affected. For example, the 3,500 sq. miles of land to be inundated was described as "relatively poor and unexploited" with very little population, cultivation and no economic mineral deposits except for a small limestone deposit. As well, 50 sq. miles of riverine forests to be affected were judged not to contain many trees of serious value and 6,000 acres of cocoa were considered to be in poor condition on marginal soils.[40] In the same vein,

---

[39] The Commission recommended replacement in the case of losses of public rights, which included roads, ferries, schools, government and local council buildings other than schools and places of religious worship. Special rites were recommended for the loss of fetishes and burial grounds. Private rights were identified as those related to the surface of land and the things growing naturally on it, minerals, perennial crops, seasonal crops, the rights to prevent others from using the land, buildings, waterways, passage, rights held in common with others, e.g. the collection of snails, firewood, hunting and fishing.

[40] It was, however, mentioned that significant tracts of oil palm would be lost in the floods.

while it was acknowledged that 54,000 persons were dependent on
the Lower Volta to some degree for their livelihood, it was argued
that the area was isolated, with poor soils and a stagnant economy
(Preparatory Commission, 1956; Hance, 1960, p. 74). All losses were
to be mitigated by draw-down agriculture and lake fishing.

The Commission recommended that all the land needed for the
Lake and resettlements be acquired outright to give the Project the
freedom to exercise control over conservation and health issues. At
the same time, it was recommended that the present owners be
allowed to continue to use the margins of the Lake according to the
pre-dam systems of land tenure and inheritance (Chapter 9, paragraph 399, p. 133). These particular recommendations provided a
justification for lower levels of compensation.

Compensation for losses around the Lake was pegged at £428,580
for the public sector and £2,045,208 for the private sector. This
together with administrative costs estimated at £700,000 took the
cost of compensation to £3,173,788. This was distinguished from
resettlement, which was to cost £751,880.[41] According to the Preparatory Commission, the extra liability had to be borne by the Gold
Coast Government unless alternative arrangements were made. A
figure of £500,000[42] estimated for liabilities for changes in the Lower
Volta was also considered to be the business of the Gold Coast government since it had not been a subject of the UK Government's
White Paper (Chapter 9, paragraphs 414–418, pp. 143–135).

More than the question of responsibility was the amounts assigned
to different project costs. For example, the Preparatory Commission
had estimated that by 1964, an amount of £1,100,000, representing about 2% of the cost of the Akosombo Dam and power station
would be spent on securing health around the Dam and Lake. An

---

[41] The total figure, £3,925,668 was about £500,000 higher than the amount
stated in the British Government White Paper as the agreed figure for compensation and resettlement among the parties to the Project.

[42] £350,000 of this amount was earmarked for compensation for the loss of creeks
and channels and £20,000 for the cost of staff to conduct further research. Unspecified
amounts of the rest of the amount would be used for payment of compensation to
people whose land was proven to lose productivity as a result of the dam and the
cost of keeping water supplies in good condition, e.g. widening channels, installing
a pump and supplying fresh drinking water during the dam filling stage. These
were seen as alternatives to compensation (Preparatory Commission, Appendix VII,
paragraphs 236–238, pp. 180–181).

annual cost of £135,000 representing ¼% of the capital expense on the Dam and power scheme would be necessary for the maintenance of health (Appendix VIII, paragraph 86, p. 207). Thus estimates for bush clearing and the Lakeside health programme were more generous than the £500,000 allocated to all of the Lower Volta. This stark indication of the very different standards and levels of responsibility being assumed for the various aspects of the Project was to become the hallmark of state policy.

All in all, the conclusion was that the VRP would not dramatically change the way of life of people in the Lower Volta. While it was expected that there would be some changes in certain features, some for the better (e.g. health and communications), the Preparatory Commission stated that the only clear evidence of a negative change was the loss of the creeks. However, this reduction in the fishing potential of the Lower Volta would be more than offset by the anticipated increase in Lake Fisheries, the greatest beneficiaries of which would be Tongu communities of the Lower Volta (Appendix VII, paragraph 239, p. 181).

7. *Summary and Conclusions*

This chapter has set out a historical perspective on the Volta River Project in terms of its conception, processes and its agreements. The chapter has sought to demonstrate that a number of factors including the imperatives of a post-colonial modernisation project, specifically the drive to achieve development through industrialisation, were important in shaping the Volta River Project. The relative capital poverty of newly independent countries such as Ghana necessitates their dependence on others to finance large projects such as dams. The chapter demonstrates that in the case of the VRP, this did not favour the Ghana government and all those who had to depend on it to protect their interests, especially the dam affected communities. One result was that project issues such as the effects on local communities were relegated to the background. In the sixties, this was made even easier by lack of information on the part of all the parties concerned about the long-term environmental and socio-economic impacts of such large-scale undertakings.

The chapter discussed the benefits and costs of the Dam to the parties. It was noted that while there was disagreement about whether the agreement was generally beneficial or disadvantageous to Ghana, most commentators were of the view that the aluminium companies benefited more than Ghana did. That this judgement was without the benefit of a proper consideration of environmental costs as well as the impacts on affected communities is significant. The chapter also examined the factors that influenced what the parties could and could not derive from the Project. These included power imbalances among the parties, conflicts of interest, poor negotiating strategies and exaggerated expectations of the Project on the part of the Ghana government.

The last section of the chapter focused on how affected communities were considered in the conception and planning of the VRP. Early on in the conception of the VRP, there was a consciousness of three types of communities to be affected by the Dam. These were communities which would be submerged by the Lake and therefore had to be resettled, those whose lands were being acquired for resettlement and downstream communities. The Preparatory Commission in 1956 examined their situations, made predictions about dam impacts, computed losses and made recommendations for redress and compensation. The Commission's underlying assumption was that most dam impacts were amenable to correction, whether it was Lakeside health problems or hiccups with agriculture, fishing or clam picking in the Lower Volta.

The VRP went through a reassessment which resulted in the issues of affected communities being shifted from the main agenda and the Project being pared down to the Dam, power stations, transmission lines and the Aluminium smelter. In the next chapter, the accuracy of the Preparatory Commission's predictions will be addressed in a discussion of the Lower Volta before and after the Volta River Project.

CHAPTER THREE

THE LOWER VOLTA AND THE VOLTA RIVER PROJECT:
DAM IMPACTS AND ENVIRONMENTAL CHANGE

1. *Introduction*

This chapter is an account of the society and economy of the Tongu
Ewe area of the Lower Volta before and after the Volta River
Project. The Tongu Ewe, consisting of 13 sub-groups, described in
the literature as traditional states (*dukɔwo* in Ewe) and known in popular parlance as traditional areas, settled along this stretch of the
river from Agave in the south to Fodzoku in the north. In-between
these two outposts are Sokpoe, Tefle, Vume, Fieve, Bakpa, Mafi,
Mepe, Battor, Volo, Dorfor (also rendered as Duffor) and Torgorme,
in that order (Amenumey, 1997; Geker, 1999). The chapter discusses
how within the wider political economy of colonisation the inhabitants of the area organised their pre-dam livelihoods and how they
experienced the Volta River Project (VRP).

The purpose of the chapter is to lay the basis for analysing the
changes which occurred in the area as a result of the VRP and also
to establish a context and background for discussing the responses
of communities and their members.

The chapter is in two main parts. The first consists of an account
of the Lower Volta between the fifties and early sixties. The 1950s
were at the tail end of the colonial period, which had witnessed
momentous changes in the larger political economy of which the
Lower Volta was a part. While the Lower Volta had a more marginal role in the colonial project, its inhabitants had developed a
successful system of livelihoods organised around the seasonal flooding
of the Volta. This system included seasonal upstream migration,
mainstream and creek fishing, itinerant clam picking, floodplain farming and long distance and sedentary trading within the Lower Volta.

The Lower Volta before the VRP was already undergoing social
and economic changes (Lawson, 1968, 1972). However, the damming
of the Volta River was of such import that analysts have had no
difficulty in attributing the momentous environmental and socio-

economic changes in the Lower Volta to this particular occurrence. The second part of the chapter focuses on these changes, which include the establishment of the Volta Lake fisheries and draw-down agriculture, the great floods in the Lower Volta in 1963, the cessation of the seasonal floods and the decline of farming, fishing and the clam industry.

2. *The Lower Volta in the 50s and 60s*

Background

In physical terms, the Lower Volta was part of the coastal savannah with its riverine forests largely depleted by 1954. Its tree population was sparse, made up of silk-cotton trees, mangoes, baobabs, borassus palms, oil and coconut palm-trees.[1] Oil-palm production had been an important activity in the area, but this had largely declined by 1954 (Lawson, 1968; Preparatory Commission, 1956, p. 146). Rainfall was quite low. Mean annual rainfall in the 1950s was 34 inches (Preparatory Commission, Appendix VII, paragraph 89, p. 155). However, the Volta River dominated this landscape that it flooded annually from July/August to November, watering the land on both sides of the river and the numerous watercourses known as creeks that criss-crossed the area. In 1954, three hundred and ninety four (394) of these creeks were identified in a study commissioned by the Preparatory Commission of the Volta River Project. The variability of the Volta framed the organisation of the livelihoods in the area.[2] The main livelihood activities—agriculture, fishing and clam-picking as well as the seasonal economic migration patterns of both men and women—were established around the river's annual cycle of flooding and recession. The shallowness of the Volta, its particular combination of salinity and freshness as well as the

---

[1] These trees can still be found today although there is now a proliferation of neem trees.

[2] It has been remarked that the Volta is striking for its variability in this lower section. At the height of the floods, the volume of the water could be over 300,000 cusecs while it could be as low as 1,000 cusecs in the dry season. Again, not every annual flood was the same size. In some years, not all the creeks were flooded while in others most compounds could be flooded, entailing the loss of property.

sandy character of its bed created excellent conditions for the clams (Lawson, 1968; Preparatory Commission, Chapter 15, paragraph 349, p. 56).

Lawson described the Lower Volta in 1954 as "economically static, remote and in some areas, only on the fringe of a cash economy", with its four major markets (Akuse, Tefle, Adidome and Aveyime) trading in a limited range of goods (1968, p. 3). The social structure of the area in the same period was described as strongly egalitarian, dominated by chieftaincy and a clan-based system. The egalitarianism of a dominated chieftaincy and clan system is open to question. However, by the 1950s, economic and social differentiation was less striking in the Lower Volta than in the parts of the colony that had been more deeply penetrated by capitalism. Like in other peripheral areas, the combination of labour migration and local independent agricultural production—upstream and downstream—had delayed processes of proletarianisation and the development of capitalist agriculture. Lawson argues that most of the changes in the area between 1954 and 1964 were the result of the creation of non-agricultural employment and not an expansion in agriculture (1968).[3] The movement from seasonal to permanent migration in the Lower Volta has been attributed to this situation as well as the demands of economic activities such as cocoa cultivation (see Denkabe and Songsore 1995 for similar analysis of the impact of labour migration on Northern Ghana). Other developments in the Lower Volta between the 1950s and 60s include growth in employment, better established markets, improved infrastructure and improved nutrition.

Housing and housing technology were simple and appropriate for the hot climate, although there was a problem of durability. Compacted soil—usually laterite—made into blocks were used for the walls and thatch for the roof. The practice of using cement for the floors as well as galvanised iron sheets for roofing was becoming possible in 1954.[4] Both household and expert labour were deployed in the construction and maintenance of houses. The Preparatory Commission

---

[3] For example, the more rapid growth of Sogakope and Tefle was attributed to the improved ferry services across the Volta between these two settlements, while the growth of Adidome was due to its role as conduit for goods going into the interior.

[4] At Battor, for example, it was estimated that between a quarter and half of houses had iron-roofing sheets (Lawson, 1968).

suggested that the standard of housing might have been a little lower than the average for the south of the country. The meaning and basis of this assessment is not clear, but it was an example of the kind of commentary that influenced the low valuation of the houses in this area (Appendix VII, paragraphs 74–76).

In 1954, there were several primary schools in the large villages but only three middle schools in the whole Tongu District, all supported by the Christian churches. Even at this stage, there was concern about the education of the children of itinerant clam pickers.[5] By 1964, there were more schools, although the 1960 census showed that 56% of males and 80% of females were illiterate.

The Preparatory Commission thought that although the standard of health care and education in the Lower Volta was the same as in the rest of the Gold Coast, there probably was a higher incidence of malaria there. In 1954, there was no hospital, clinic or doctor in the Tongu District, except for a small hospital at Akuse. The incidence of malaria was 33%, bilharzia, 27% and onchocerciasis, 7.5% on the average in Central and Lower Tongu (Lawson, 1968). The water in the Volta was considered good although there was a problem of salinity around the Volta estuary (Preparatory Commission, Chapter 15, paragraph 352, p. 56; appendix VII, paragraph 73, p. 151).

An important factor in the state of the Lower Volta in the 50s and 60s was how the area experienced colonial and early post-colonial periods and processes. Colonial economic interests—the cocoa farms, gold mines and timber concessions—were found in the forest zone while the coastal areas provided administrative support and the ports to export commodities and import consumer goods. This area, which was carved out by rail and road, became central to colonial economic, political and administrative endeavours. It became a magnet for the in-migration of forced and voluntary labour from outlying areas and places as far afield as Northern Ghana and served as a source of money and new consumer goods. Colonial policy thus created a "golden triangle" bounded by Accra in the south-east, Takoradi in the south-west (both on the coast) and Kumasi within Asante in the heart of the middle forest belt.[6] Areas outside the tri-

---

[5] Minutes of the meeting of the Tongu District Council, 6/4/1957.
[6] The Akwapim and Akyim Abuakwa cocoa growing areas fell within this triangle.

angle such as the Lower Volta were connected to it through labour migration and long distance trading. In addition, Lower Volta communities participated in the wider economy through their seasonal migration upstream.

Most parts of the Volta Basin were not at the centre of colonial economic policy. However, its potential for opening up the interior of the country was not lost on the colonial government. Indeed, the British fought some of their colonising wars along the Volta as did local groups such the Akwamu and Asante before them.[7] Also, important colonial trading posts such as Ada and Akuse were established along the Volta River while the ferry-crossing at Tefle was a vital link between the western and eastern banks of the Volta and beyond. Tongu Ewe men and women were engaged in trading activities at Akuse, Tefle and other market towns, which were established in the colonial period.

In spite of the rapids at Kpong and Senchi and the seasonal variations in its volume, the Volta and its tributaries were potentially important for linking the coast in the South with the northernmost parts of the Gold Coast for trade and colonial administrative control. The Tongu area, while not central to the colonial economic effort, was not untouched by the economic and social processes within the colony. However, it and other peripheral areas, particularly Northern Ghana, suffered neglect in the development of infrastructure, social and economic services.

3. Political and Social Institutions

By the 1950s, the various Tongu Ewe groups in the Lower Volta were governed locally by a hierarchy of chiefs organised according to the clan structure. There was no single Tongu paramountcy. Each Tongu traditional state had its own chief who was assisted by a council made up of the heads of all the constitutive divisions/clans of the state. The chiefs were all males and by the 1950s, the more prominent of them had female counterparts known as "*nyɔnufia*", an

---

[7] The Tongu Ewe, because of their riverine location, had become involved in some of the local wars. Informants in Tongu have mentioned alliances with the Akwamu in wars with the Asante.

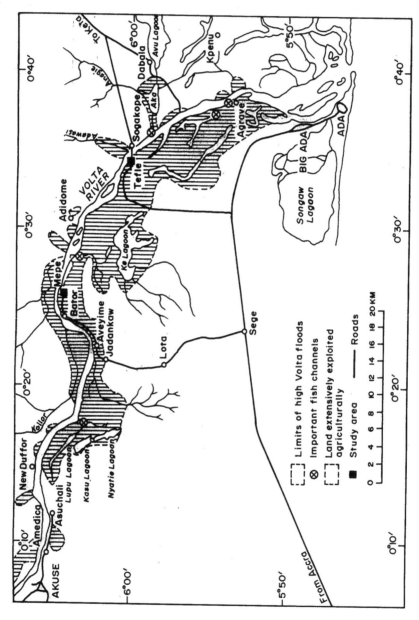

Figure 5: Lower Reaches of the Volta River from Akuse to Ada

ambiguous phrase that could either mean a female chief or a chief of the women. In terms of powers and influence, they appeared to be more chiefs of the women than female chiefs. That some of their positions were vacant at both Mepe and Sokpoe suggested that they had not quite taken hold. Among other Ewe groups, the *nyɔnufia* did not have the status and powers of their Akan counterparts. While they were members of the decision-making councils among the Tongu, their status was not always clear-cut.

In addition to the political and executive functions of the chiefs and their councils, there were also judicial aspects of the chieftaincy institution. Chiefs settled disputes among individuals and groups. These disputes were about a wide range of issues—land disputes, quarrels involving the trading of insults and accusations of witchcraft and wrongdoing, marital disputes, debt, fraud and other commercial cases and cases relating to the destruction of crops or farms by animals.

There were also various shrines of gods (*etrɔ̃wo*) which were an important component of the judicial set-up of many Tongu communities. Some of the gods were believed to have been brought from the original home of the Ewe (known in Ewe as *hogbe trɔ̃wo*, meaning "the place of origin gods" while others were found on the way or in the new settlements).[8] At Mepe for example, there were about five major shrines—Adido, Aklakpa, Dedzi, Dzoxɔ and Dali, and while each of them was based in a Division, they were each considered as belonging to Mepe as a whole.[9] The shrines were organised in a hierarchical order similar to chieftaincy principles with a number of officers—*ngɔgbe, zikpuitɔ,* and *trenɔ.* There were female officers whose main task was to keep the shrine in a state of repair. Shrines could be consulted for a variety of reasons. For example, when people lost valuables, they sought the assistance of the shrines to retrieve them. Or the shrine might be called upon to prove or

---

[8] A distinction has been made between established shrines (*etrɔ̃wo*) and private arrangements for supernatural protection (*edzowo*). The edzowo did not have elaborate shrines and were not engaged in judicial processes and were consulted for the protection of individuals, kin groups and particular occupational groups such as hunters (interview with TKA, Accra).

[9] For example, Dzoxɔ was at Dzoxɔnu, Dedzi and Dali at Dzagbaku, Adido at Gbanvie and Aklakpa at Sevie. This was in keeping with the history as told that one or two of these originated in one Division but was given to another one for safekeeping.

disprove accusations of wrongdoing. In addition to their judicial functions, shrines were engaged in religious functions related to well-
being, security and economic success.[10] Some of the state shrines also
specialised in the affairs of different economic occupations. The chief
priest of the Dedzi shrine was in charge of rituals around clam-picking. The clam-picking season could not start before certain rites were
performed and women had to contribute clams for these events.

Since colonisation, which was accompanied by active Christian
missionary proselytising, shrines have lost some of their religious and
judicial powers. On the other hand, at the state level, shrines continued to have undisputed critical ritual powers. Some of the state
shrines were represented at meetings of the chiefs and were consulted regularly by the community development association. They
kicked off the annual festival with their rituals and continued to be
key in stool rituals.

By the 1950s, however, the influence of the colonial national judicial and law and order system was being experienced in the Lower
Volta. This system came to serve as a kind of appeal court for local
cases and disputes. When chiefs could not settle cases, one of the
parties could seek the intervention of the police or the courts. If it
was a chieftaincy matter, the Regional and National Houses of Chiefs
could be consulted. As well, the decentralised structures such as the
District Administration and the District Chief Executive, known in
the past as the District Commissioner, also became important in the
governance of local communities. These national institutions have
been part of the Tongu landscape since the colonial period. In 1912,
recommendations from a commission set up by the Gold Coast government to investigate relations among the South Eastern Ewe as a
whole led to administrative arrangements which divided the Tongu
people among three units under the jurisdiction of the Ada, Akwamu
and Anlo Ewe. It was only in 1945 that a separate Tongu Confederacy
Native Authority was created. In 1951, with the reorganisation of
the local government system, the Ewe in south eastern Ghana had
two administrative units, Anlo and Tongu, and Mafi, the only Tongu
State under the Anlo unit, rejoined the Tongu District Council.

---

[10] See also Lawson who notes: "shrines had several purposes. Some are said to
bring rain, others are believed to give protection against illness and safety in time
of war. Some shrines are visited only during the clam diving season, others are for
the exclusive use of hunters" (1968, p. 8).

Currently, the Tongu are administratively divided into the South and North Tongu Districts and are part of the five administrative units constituting the south eastern Ewe area, the rest being Anlo, Ketu and Akatsi (Amenumey, 1997).

Land and water relations

No part of the Volta or its tributaries was owned by any group of people. At Mepe for example, while sections of the riverbank were named for the various divisions, it was theirs to keep clean, to fetch water from, to bathe and wash clothes from. The river itself was open to all persons using it and fishermen criss-crossed its length and breadth looking for the best fishing sites.[11] Clam-picking was also open to all who were interested although the most active clam pickers lived in the villages closest to the best clam sites, and were largely women. The main explanation offered for women's domination of the industry was that it would have been a breach of etiquette for men and women to work so closely together in a situation where they had to wear very few clothes. Unlike the main river, the creeks (*tɔvu* in Ewe) were a different story. They were owned as part of the land around them by particular lineages and clans. Lawson reports that fishing rights in the larger creeks was a serious source of income and could also be pledged against loans (1972).

Land relations in the Lower Volta were established on the basis of kinship. Some clans and lineages controlled much of the land. Non-land owning clans and their members had to negotiate their use of land with the owners. Clan land tended to be in dispersed parcels instead of being one large continuous piece. In the 1950s, permanent alienation of clan land hardly ever took place and land sales were rare. Thus even when land belonging to one clan was given to members of another clan, certain rituals and payments continued to give recognition to the original owners of such land. Such payments could be in the form of an alcoholic drink or levies to support litigation. These could be distinguished from when members of a lineage or clan gave out their assigned portions of lineage or clan land, usually land which had been handed down for generations

---

[11] The Preparatory Commission confirms this, but reports that dues were levied in some stretches by the local authorities (Appendix VII, paragraph 65, p. 149).

(what has been described as *nudufe*, meaning source of livelihood in Ewe) to others. These might also be members of their clan or lineage, but also outsiders. Here payments included a portion of the crop, sometimes a third or a fixed sum of money. Such land, once it continued to be cultivated, remained under the control of the "tenants" who could pass this interest on to their descendants. It however reverted to the land-owning group in question if it was not used for a number of years.

Lawson notes that while the clans originally owned much of the land, extended family rights had developed by 1954. Land was generally easily accessed except in places such as Mepe and Bakpa where much of the land was controlled by a few clans from whom others had to acquire it by various arrangements and tenancies. Even in this period, the terms on which farmlands were acquired could be distinguished from how land for residential purposes was acquired (Lawson, 1968; Preparatory Commission, Appendix VII). Farms were established on small pieces of dispersed land. It has been suggested that this was a strategy for promoting food security in the sense that a poor harvest on one piece might be offset by good yields on another. Land inheritance patterns have also contributed to this fragmentation of land. In the 1950s and 1960s, the most intensively used lands were those in the immediate vicinity of the river and the creeks and small pieces of land farmed seemed to secure the subsistence needs of households.

Kinship, descent and inheritance

The kinship and descent system of the Tongu Ewe in common with other Ewe groups was patrilineal and based on clans[12] and lineages. Tongu clans were dispersed throughout the villages and hamlets within each traditional state although some villages were founded or dominated by particular clans.

In terms of nomenclature and numbers, Tongu clans differed from one traditional state to the next. At Mepe, there were five clans

---

[12] Clans were composed of a group of people who believed they were descended through the patrilineal line from a single putative ancestor. Clan membership was, therefore, by birth and members shared a totem, ancestral shrines, names, taboos and avoidances and various rituals (Nukunya, 1997). Clans were composed of lineages which were made up of men and women who traced their ancestry to a known male individual.

known as divisions (Dzagbaku, Dzoxɔnu, Akɔvie, Sevie and Gbanvie), while at Sokpoe, there were two (Dzavie and Fodze). Tongu clans were not exogamous. Clans in Tongu owned land and other resources and were headed by chiefs with political and ritual powers. Within each state, different clans had particular political and ritual functions. In Mepe for example, the chief was from a particular clan, the Mankralo, and the queen mother from two others. In Sokpoe, the position of chief rotated between the two clans. Particular clans were also in charge of the state shrines. In spite of these particularities, the functions, character and importance of Tongu Ewe clans was largely similar to those of clans in other Ewe states. They were the grid around which "the social fabric is woven" (Nukunya, 1997, p. 1).

At the core of settlements such as Mepe and Sokpoe, members of various lineages lived in contiguous compounds in the quarter belonging to their clan. Newer sections of the village were not settled along clan and lineage lines and members of the various clans lived side by side. The lineage had a male head, usually the most senior member of its oldest surviving generation. Lineage membership was important in the organisation of livelihoods. Lineages had common property resources to which every member was theoretically guaranteed some form of access. Members were allocated portions of land over which they and their descendants had control.

The patrilineal principle was applied to inheritance, succession to office and various rites of passage—birth, marriage, adulthood and death. A man's property in cases where he was polygynous was shared equally according to the number of widows, regardless of the number of children each of them had. However, matrilineal kin were critical. Informants, however, insisted that the Tongu Ewe inherited from both parents. There was evidence that a number of people were farming and living on land belonging to their mothers' lineages. Both sons and daughters were said to have an equal stake in the property of their father and mother.[13]

During some religious and mortuary rites, bilateral principles were very much in evidence. In times of disputes and struggles over

---

[13] This is similar to what pertains with the Anlo Ewe. Nukunya notes that while Anlo kinship is patrilineal in legal, ideological and emotional terms, bilateral principles apply in relation to issues such as residence, ancestral worship, mortuary rites, reincarnation, kinship terminology and inheritance.

resources, the two principles of patrilinity and bilaterality were both cited in support of positions. There were, however, suggestions that inheritance through the maternal line had limitations. For example, some informants said that while you could inherit your mother's property, you could not pass on that property to your children on your death because it could be lost to your mother's lineage. This position was disputed by others who argued that it was due to greed, poverty and the growing scarcity of resources that the rules of inheritance were being rewritten to discriminate against persons inheriting through the maternal line.

Marriage and conjugal relations

Marriage and conjugal relations were an important aspect of gender relations, which were also relevant for making livelihoods in Tongu societies. Among the Tongu, marriage residence was virilocal. While the rights and duties of the parties to a marriage were broadly reciprocal, there were elements which were specific to either spouse and it was in some of these details that the co-operative as well as the unequal and potentially conflictual character of the marriage contract could be seen. Women owed a duty of respect extending to the kin of a male spouse, obedience, biological and social reproductive functions and fidelity in return for maintenance and consideration. Men owed a duty of maintenance including housing and care, biological and social reproductive functions in return for being obeyed and having access to the labour of their wives and children, and having political and social power as household heads and chief decision-makers.

Contracting a marriage used to be a long-drawn-out process involving various steps at which particular payments were made. Several informants remarked that marriage procedures were these days honoured more in the breach than in compliance. Familiar complaints were that young women would move in with men before the latter had made the marriage payments. In times of crises and rites of passage, the non-payment of marriage drinks could become an issue and a man could be asked to make these payments on the death of the woman, especially if they had children, in order to entitle him to treatment as a widower. In times of marital conflict, such a man was not entitled to being treated as a husband and the father of his children.

Divorce could be initiated by either party to a marriage at either the chief's court or more commonly at "home", i.e. before an assembly of representatives of relations of the parties. While the chief's court might have advantages for a woman because her chances of being awarded a financial settlement if the divorce was not her fault were better there, the family forum was preferred as the more normal forum for both contracting and dissolving marriages. The items used to contract the marriage could be demanded back by a husband depending on the duration of the marriage, whether there were children and who was considered responsible for the breakdown. In some cases, the husband was required to make a financial settlement in the nature of a send-off for his wife. Once the divorce was finalised, a woman was free to begin another relationship.[14]

The custody of children was normally given to the man. If, however, he was not interested, some or all of the children remained with their mother. Although leaving children with their mother was considered a sign of a man's lack of capacity, it happened very often in practice. Awarding custody to a father is seen as an extension of children's membership of their father's lineage and his duties of maintenance and training of his children. While these responsibilities extended to all children, the socialisation and training of young persons was gendered in some of its aspects.

While all informants said marriage was virilocal, it was observed at both Mepe and Sokpoe that many married women were staying in their own family compounds. Polygyny was said to be one of the reasons for this.[15] However, there was no uniformity in how polygynous households were composed. While some men lived together with all or some of their wives, some lived with only one wife at a time. Informants suggested that the ability and willingness of the man to provide a home for his wife and children was an important factor in marriage residence. Marriage residence could also be cyclical in that a woman sometimes lived with her natal family or with her husband and moved back and forth at different points in her

---

[14] Without a divorce being finalised, if it came to light that she was in a new relationship, her estranged husband could successfully sue the other man for compensation known as "*ayifare*" (derived from the Akan).

[15] Other informants mentioned the contribution of the great floods of 1963 to some women returning to their natal compounds on the loss of their marital homes.

lifetime.[16] These life-cycle movements at marriage, childbirth and widowhood complicated women's interests in land and other resources within both natal and conjugal compounds. Informants cited marriage residence and the fact that women's children were not members of their mother's lineage as the reasons for discriminatory inheritance rules and practices. In the Tongu area, seasonal male and female migration was an additional complication in marital residence patterns of the pre-dam period.

Lineage compounds and households

Households were established within lineage compounds at the geographical core of both Mepe and Sokpoe. However, with the expansion of the settlements, people began to build and settle outside their lineage compounds. There were very close links between the different households within a compound of a lineage. According to informants at Mepe, in the past, households were established within the quarter of a division or clan with lineage members living close to each other in contiguous compounds. The male members of a lineage ate their meals together although the food was cooked separately within each household. The women and very young children also ate together with boys graduating from being carriers of food and eating leftovers to a place at the table when they were considered socialised enough in the conventions of eating with other adults. Children of different households played together and were socialised by all adult members of a compound. Some compounds had shared water pots, with children and women having responsibility for filling the pots with water from the river.

In spite of the linkages described above, there were demarcations which set each household apart. Each household farmed separately and labour-sharing and other forms of co-operation notwithstanding, its members could have their own separate farms. Women farmed land either given to them by their husbands, or belonging to either of their parents if it was available, within reach, more abundant or fertile. It has long been remarked that in many parts of Africa and

---

[16] For example, she could spend a year after the birth of a child with her own relations or she could be required to live with an ailing parent and provide care.

Ghana, men and women within a conjugal union maintained separate economies. This was the situation with the Tongu Ewe (Lawson, 1972). Lawson has noted that there was not a concept of household income in the Lower Volta. Men and women within the same household had separate earnings, but worked together on the farms that provided food staples for subsistence and the money to purchase certain items. In spite of this, the labour of other household members, both adults and children, was critical to some economic activities especially farming. By 1964, Lawson observed a reduction in the contribution of children to economic activities. This was as a result of an expansion in access to education and coincided with the increasing labour deficit created by migrant wage labourers (1968).

In terms of the sexual division of labour within households, women were more heavily involved in reproductive work (household chores and childcare) than men. Even when they were household heads, women did more of this kind of work than their male counterparts. Male household heads also had more access to unpaid household labour than their spouses did. In return, food from farms owned by them were considered to be the household's primary source of nutrition and women theoretically had more freedom to decide what to do with their own earnings although, in practice, much of it went into the maintenance of households. In any case, men and women had different responsibilities within the household. There was some uniformity in how the responsibilities were designated, but in practice, it was quite complicated. For example, some women informants said that they were in charge of paying for the training of their female children while men took charge of their male children. But paying for artisanal training was only one of the many expenses parents incurred in relation to children. In Tongu in the 50s and early 60s, when seasonal migration was an established part of life for both men and women, the fact that women migrated for shorter spells and for much shorter distances meant that they maintained households on a day-to-day basis. In this scenario, male incomes could be accumulated for capital-intensive undertakings. This was also in keeping with local beliefs and practices about what men and women did with their earnings.

4. *The Economy and Livelihood Activities of the Lower Volta*

Introduction

Before the dam, the major livelihood activities in the riverine communities of the Lower Volta were farming, fishing and clam-picking (Lawson, 1972; Moxon, 1984). Other activities included petty trading, processing and selling of cassava and other surplus farm produce, craftwork, cotton spinning, native soap making, gin distillation, basketwork and manufacture of nets and fish traps. Women collected firewood and made pottery in a few pockets of the area. The vast majority of persons, both male and female, considered fishing (mainstream, creek and clams) and farming to be their main or secondary activities in the 1950s and 60s. In 1954, Lawson estimated that together, they represented 70% of the total real income of the riverine population (Lawson, 1968).[17]

Having multiple livelihood activities was an important part of the pre-dam Lower Volta economy and different activities were undertaken in particular periods of the year. As Lawson notes, "a woman who considered the largest portion of her cash income to come from clam diving, might when this season is over, turn to petty trading or to processing and selling her surplus farm produce or to small craft work and manufacture" (1968, p. 14; The Preparatory Commission Report, Chapter 15, paragraph 352, p. 56; also Appendix VII, paragraph 67, p. 150). The following is an account of the organisation of the main livelihood activities—women's clam-picking and men's seasonal migration upstream to fish, hunt, farm and build boats. Farming, fishing, trading and artisanal activities in the Lower Volta itself are also discussed. Clam-picking is discussed in much more detail than other activities. While this might create some imbalance in the account, it is being done to recover some of the history of the one activity that experienced the most drastic transformation. As well, it illustrates the differential impacts of development projects.

---

[17] In 1964, 25% of direct aggregate income derived from the river and the annual floods at Battor, for example. It was argued that this figure, which represented fishing and farming, would have been much higher if linkages and multiplier effects were taken into account (Lawson, 1968, p. 3).

Upstream migration and the Lower Volta in the 1950s

Migration upstream, a largely male occupation which involved few women, was organised to tie in with other livelihood activities in the Lower Volta. In December, many men travelled to various places upstream. There they engaged in one or more of the following— fishing, rabbit hunting, farming (either food crops or cocoa) and boat building. In June/July when the river began to flood, they returned to the Lower Volta. From March, creek fishing began. In July, August and September, people harvested all the crops before the floods reached the Lower Volta. Creek fishing also peaked in this period. In October, the floods began to recede. In November, the land around the river and elsewhere was prepared and planting of the year's crops would begin. In December, the first weeding of the farms would take place and upstream migrants would also begin to leave around the end of December and early January. Of the four types of fishing in the Volta Basin—estuarine, upper fresh water, tidal fresh water and creek—the latter three were the preserve of the Tongu Ewe (Lawson, p. 45). It was fishermen from the Lower Volta who did most of the upper fresh water fishing in the Volta River's tributaries such as the Oti, Afram and Black Volta and the main river itself above the Lower Volta (Lawson, p. 49). The inhabitants of the upper reaches did very little fishing themselves (Hance, 1958).

Lawson found that the upstream fishing was particularly important to fishermen from Mafi, Mepe, Bakpa, Tefle and Battor. It was estimated in 1954 that each year, some 1,000–1,500 fishermen and their families went upstream for the fishing season and returned in time to engage in creek fishing and farming. Upstream economic activities provided subsistence during a period when farming could not be undertaken.

River fishing upstream was done with seine, set and cast nets, lines and basket traps. However, set and cast nets were the equipment of choice because seine nets were expensive and very few fishermen had the capital resources. Lawson argues that only fishermen who owned seine nets earned good incomes from fishing (Lawson, 1968). While the majority of fishermen engaged in upstream migration earned less than £50 a year, each seine net yielded on the average about £840 a season and was operated by about 12 fishermen and their dependants (Lawson, 1968). Lawson described fishermen as living "an almost hand-to-mouth existence, borrowing money at the commencement of the season and repaying at the end if they were able" (1968, p. 44). The majority of them brought very little money downstream which they then spent mainly on celebrations, but also on farming and building (Lawson, 1968).

Seasonal migrants often combined economic activities upstream and downstream. As one informant reported of her husband, he constructed boats and hunted rabbits upstream and was engaged in farming for subsistence downstream. Whatever their limitations in monetary terms, upstream economic activities were an integral part of livelihoods in the Lower Volta. While clam picking and other Lower Volta-based economic activities provided subsistence and monetary support for households for the first half of the year, once the season ended, upstream earnings were important for the second part of the year. In addition to household subsistence, upstream earnings financed ritual obligations and other responsibilities around funerals and the annual festival.

It was already being noted in 1954 that some of this seasonal migration had led to permanent migration and Tongu communities were found in "widely scattered villages" and engaged in subsistence agriculture upstream (Lawson, 1968, p. 42).[18] Some fishermen did not return home at the end of the season as expected in order to undertake "off-fishing season" farming. Others stayed because they could not repay debts incurred downstream in the organisation of migration, could not pay transport costs or wanted to avoid expensive ritual and other social obligations.[19] The Preparatory Commission, however, noted that "they all maintain their links with the Tongu area in which many of them have left dependants" (Appendix VII, paragraph 66, p. 150). Thus in the pre-dam period, there was a continuing expectation that migrants would return seasonally. When and how such expectations would have changed is anybody's guess and one can only speculate how the connections seasonal migrants

---

[18] Lawson's statistics from Battor are instructive. Out of an adult male population of three hundred and fifty three (353), eighty one (81) men and twenty one (21) women had gone upstream in 1954 and less than half of them returned downstream that year (Lawson, 1968, p. 42).

[19] The discussion of debt and migration reveals the place of credit in the organisation of livelihoods in the Lower Volta. Different kinds of credit arrangements were in existence in the Lower Volta. For the most part, these were debts incurred to fund travelling and short-term maintenance costs until fishermen were able to begin to earn an income from their upstream activities (Lawson, 1962).

had with the Lower Volta would have developed had the Volta River Project not intervened. Indeed Tongu migrants were 10% of those resettled, an indication that they were seen as permanent migrants with a stake in their communities upstream. In 1962, the VRA had enumerated 20,000 Tongu fishermen in a census of those to be affected by the rising floods of the Volta Lake and as already indicated, the Tongu were 10% of those resettled (Lawson, 1968, p. 42).

Livelihood activities in the Lower Volta: The clam (Aforli) industry

The economy of clams

Lawson takes credit for the "discovery" of the clam (popularly but incorrectly known as oyster) picking industry.[20] Clam picking has been described as "easily the most valuable activity in the fishing industry" (Moxon, 1984, p. 190) and "the economic mainstay of downstream riverine communities" (Barnes, 1964, p. 2; see also Geker, 1999). This position is shared by Kwei (1965), who has argued that unlike most large rivers, the Volta had not supported any fisheries of economic importance except the clams. Lawson ranks the clams as the third most important industry after agriculture and fishing (1970, p. 51). The clams were as important to women in the Lower Volta as trading was in other parts of Ghana. They were collected along the thirty-five mile stretch between Kpong (near Akuse) and Tefle. However, the most important beds were in the upper parts of the Lower Volta, at Torgome, Asutuare, Aleboke, Volivo and Duffor (Lawson, 1963; Preparatory Commission, paragraph 98).

A mainly female occupation, clams were picked for six to seven months a year, when the river was not in flood.[21] Clams along with fish, provided a reliable and cheap source of protein, especially in times of hardship or fish scarcity throughout the Lower Volta.[22] The

---

[20] Her 1954 economic survey in the Lower Volta drew attention to the importance of the clams (1963). Certainly by the 1950s and early 60s, it was no longer possible to discuss the Lower Volta's economy without mentioning the clams.

[21] The Preparatory Commission put the clam season from January to June (Paragraph, 100) while Lawson and Moxon put it between December and June/July (Lawson, 1972, pp. 51–56; Moxon, 1984, p. 191).

[22] One report on clams notes that the protein content of clams at 54.3% was extremely high and experts were recommending it for use in protein-hungry areas (Kwei, 1965).

ability to preserve them meant that they could be consumed beyond the clam-picking season. At Battor, in 1954, Lawson reports that half the female adults were engaged in clam-picking and two-thirds of these considered it their main source of income (Lawson, 1968). Studies in 1954 estimated the capital input into the industry at G£10,000. The clams provided an annual income of more than G£100,000 a year to about 2,000–3,000 clam divers, about 2,000 doing it full-time (1963; 1968).[23] This was a considerable sum of money in an economy the size of the Lower Volta. The Preparatory Commission observed that unlike the local catches of river fish, about ⅔ of the clam harvest was exported every year (Appendix VII, paragraph 100, p. 157). In 1963, clam incomes were estimated at £G110,000, a figure expected to rise by another £G60,000–£G100,000 if retail figures were included in the estimates. Between 1954 and 1964, trade in clams had increased and cash incomes had tripled. These figures did not include the value of clamshells which were and still are a valuable source of high-grade lime (Kwei, 1965). Lawson argues that the clam picking industry had been overtaken by farming and casual wage employment in income levels by 1963 and a brief revitalisation in 1964 had tapered to an almost complete disappearance of clams from this stretch of the river by 1967 (Lawson, 1968). The following account of the clam picking industry comes from in-depth interviews with several older women who were involved in the industry until its demise.

Clam picking technologies and practices
A day in a clam picker's life began early in the morning. It was important not to leave it too late because the tide could change and make the water unfavourable for diving. They travelled by canoe

---

[23] The numbers of clam pickers were estimated from the calculations of the Fisheries Department and the 1960 population census. Variations were recorded for different years as well as for different days within each season, with numbers tapering off towards the end of the season when the floodwaters began to rise. Earnings were also estimated as there were intra and inter-seasonal variations in prices as well as differences in prices along different places along the river at any point in time. Also, earnings were different depending on the involvement of the clam pickers in marketing. However, Lawson's figure from earnings was calculated using the lowest estimates of 1,515 women and the average earnings of 40 women recorded by a Fisheries Department survey in 1956 calculated at G£70 each. This was the value of the catch at the riverside and did not include wholesale market price (Lawson, 1963, pp. 282–283).

and anchored at a chosen location on the river. The anchor also enabled the women to know how deep the river was at each place.[24] The divers then went into the water. Net pouches tied to the waist were used as the receptacle for the clams while underwater. From the boat, a clam picker would enter the water and swim towards the bottom with one hand holding her nose and swimming with the other. Eyes were either open or shut depending on personal preference. When her feet touched the bottom, she would continue holding her breath, kneel and collect the clams into the pouch with both hands until she could no longer hold her breath. Then she would rise to the surface for air and to deposit the clams in the canoe. A light rope tied to the foot of the canoe floated on top of the river and was used to pull the canoe towards a clam picker who surfaced far away from it. Two diving trips to the depths of the river usually filled a small bucket that became a standard measurement. Buckets were sold at 1,200 cedis by the time clam diving in the Lower Volta stopped. A clam picker could make a number of such trips until she was exhausted or cold.

The clam pickers developed the technology for storing and growing the clams they harvested early in the season. Clams were deposited in shallow water with clearly demarcated sections for each clam picker. The clams could increase their weight by 60% after four months of storage. Not only did they grow bigger, but also they reached their apex size faster than those that grew in the river (Lawson, 1963; 1968; Kwei, 1965). Once harvested, clams could be sold fresh or smoked to preserve them.

Successful clam picking meant an itinerant life.[25] In one season, women typically moved from area to area within the Lower Volta, literally chasing tales of large clam harvests. These movements were interspersed by periodic visits to their homes to check on their dependants, to stash money and possessions bought with clam earnings and to replenish food stocks. In a variation on this pattern, some returned home between the 3rd and 4th months to farm. At this

---

[24] It was estimated that the clam picking parts of the river were between 7–12 feet deep.

[25] Lawson for example found that ten Battor women who had migrated during the 1954 season to Alaboke, Damaleme and Torgome earned over two times as much as those who had stayed at Battor picking clams the whole season (Lawson, 1963).

time, clams were picked close to home. The clam industry migration, like seasonal upstream migration, was between the twelfth and
seventh months of the year, the return home coinciding with the
annual seasonal floods in July. The rest of the year was spent at
home resting, celebrating the festival, funerals and farming until the
floods had properly receded at the end of the year.

Migrant clam pickers established their own temporary dwellings
on the sandbanks at the places where they worked. These dwellings
were usually constructed by the women themselves who travelled in
groups of between ten and twenty or in some cases where none of
them had roofing skills (the construction of houses was men's work),
men were found and hired to do this. It would appear that the clam
pickers held themselves separate from the communities on whose
shores they settled. While independent dwellings were considered
preferable, it was not always possible. Another informant suggests
that in some cases, they had to live with the locals. Wherever they
settled, clam pickers had to adapt to the religious conventions around
the use of the river. The days when clam picking was not allowed
were used to find firewood for the roasting of clams. Pregnancy,
childbirth and child-care were woven into the fabric of the clam-
picking industry. Many clam pickers began before they had children
and continued throughout their childbearing years and way into late
adulthood.

Labour relations and forms of co-operation within the clam industry
The labour relations between the clam pickers and their child min-
ders (*evitsɔvi* (*sing*) *evitsɔviwo* (*pl*), literally a child who carries a child)
was critical. Women had to find accommodation between the productive and reproductive roles and without child-minders to look
after children during the day, clam-picking was not possible for some
of them. Family members such as sisters and older children were
deployed as child-minders. Most of the informants had used close kin
as child-minders at one point or other in their clam picking work. Clam
pickers who did not have a daughter old enough or a sister young
enough to be a child-minder would hire a young girl from their village or outlying villages for the season. The terms of the labour contract were agreed with the parents or guardians of the girl and she
accompanied the clam picker on her travels and took charge of the
children when the clam picker was away for the day. The work of
a child-minder consisted primarily of feeding, bathing and minding

the child and helping with some of the cooking. At the end of the season, the girl was returned to her parents and the hiring fee paid.

When small children were considered old enough, they were left behind. Different child-minding arrangements were made in home villages. Children were left in the care of older kin such as sibling, maternal grandmothers and other relations. Some of these older kin were themselves young, but considered mature enough to oversee the house. Leaving children behind meant returning home regularly to check on them and also to ensure that the food farms were cultivated. Beyond child-care arrangements, there were conjugal duties and the maintenance of the homes that the men could return to. One informant reports having to take a break from clam picking for some seasons to accompany her husband upstream. However, the majority of men took their sons and young male relations.

Besides the child-care arrangements around picking clams, there were some other labour relations in the industry. Typically, two or three clam pickers shared a canoe owned by one of them. She would let the others use it either for free because of their kinship or for a small fee of clams each day or a sum of money at the end of the season. According to Lawson, in 1954, over half of clam pickers owned canoes, which were sometimes given to them by their husbands as part of the marriage settlement. Others had made their own canoes from clam earnings. Women taught clam picking to their daughters and those of their sibling and other close kin. More experienced clam pickers also initiated the younger ones in many things including how to measure and sell clams to traders. In spite of such co-operation, clam pickers had control over their earnings, even when it involved mother and daughter.

Clam picking was physically strenuous and as a result of that and various hazards in the river and the technique of the clam picker, women did drown occasionally. One such hazard was the crocodiles. Encountering one at the bottom of the river did not necessarily result in injury or death. In addition to the crocodiles, there were large fallen trees in whose branches and roots divers could be entangled. There were also huge rocks on the riverbed on which a diver could land accidentally. Also, a part of a diver's body could be stuck in a small opening in a rock and this could be fatal.

Clam pickers sold their own clams to traders. They were mostly smoked before sale, but could be sold fresh. The fresh clams were loaded into sacks and taken to markets in Accra, Kpong, Akuse and

Koforidua and fried there. Sometimes a number of buyers would together hire a truck to take them. The fresh clams had to be processed in three days after being harvested because they would go bad otherwise. Clam pickers themselves also went to markets in places such as Accra to sell their clams and also purchase the consumer items they needed. Some clam pickers began to trade in clams themselves, sometimes combining this with trading in other goods if they were not involved in clam picking full-time.

The clam economy spawned its own service industries. They included boat making, producing clam picking equipment such as the net pouches and foodstuffs and cooked food selling. In addition, there were jewellers, traders of consumer goods such as cloth, other items of clothing, enamel pots, pans and basins, powder, pomade, perfume and shoes. Their presence at the beaches was convenient in bringing the market to the clam pickers. As well, they influenced the use of clam earnings. The collapse of the clam industry therefore closed an important channel of commercial activity in the Lower Volta.

The uses of clam earnings
The absence of banks in most communities and the position of women in Tongu society meant that earnings were largely stored in consumer goods. These were then displayed during the festival periods in a competitive spirit. As one informant said:

> Those days when we were picking clams, besides caring for our children, we competed in the buying of jewellery and cloth and everyone wanted to beat her friend to it. So we had a lot. During festivals, we displayed our gold jewellery in the town to the admiration of many.

Some clam pickers had houses, which were destroyed in the great floods of 1963. While some clam pickers were able to rebuild their houses and even invest in cement block houses, the bulk of the building boom which followed the 1963 floods was financed through Lakeside fishing and related economic activities. The most mentioned use of clam picking incomes was the care of children and dependants—on food, education and healthcare. Male seasonal migration meant that many responsibilities, even those traditionally considered as men's fell on women. This situation was not helped by the multiple responsibilities some men acquired as a result of polygyny. Men were regularly criticised during interviews for their lack of interest in the maintenance and reproduction of their households, particularly the welfare of children.

Fishing in the main river and in the creeks

Fishing in the main river was mostly for subsistence and not as lucrative as fishing in the numerous creeks around the Lower Volta. Here again, it was mostly the few seine net owners whose yields and incomes were significant. This evaluation was supported by the Preparatory Commission's finding that fishing was basically for subsistence, as evidenced by the small amounts of river fish available for sale at Aveyime, a Lower Volta market (Appendix VII, paragraph 96, p. 156). There was one technology employed by some fishermen to enhance their yields. This was known as the *atidza*. As one informant explained:

> In those days, groups of fishermen used a method of fishing known as "atidza". They would cut fresh branches of trees preferably the afafali tree, and arrange them in the river for some time. The fish would hide under the vegetation. The fishermen would come to fence the whole place with a mat (made of sticks and palm-fronds woven together with a rope called adzɔ) to keep the fish within the enclosure and to fatten them. After the branches were removed systematically, a fishing net was placed around the mat to catch all the fish. A lot of fish was caught with this method. The day any group was due to remove their branches, it was generally announced so many women traders would go and wait around with their pans to buy fish. From around Christmas, they put in the tree branches and at Easter, the various groups would start harvesting the fish. After the harvest, the tree branches were put back in place and the mat removed. After a while, the harvesting process was repeated, sometimes in that same month, so they could fish in this way about ten times before the 7th month (i.e. between December and July). Many fishermen especially at Mepe and Battor used this method.

Creek fishing was done throughout the year until the creeks dried out or the fish stocks had been removed. In 1954, the value of fish from the 5 major creeks in the area was estimated at £627,600 with the value of fish at 6 d (pence) per lb. The value of creek-fishing lay in the fact that it fetched higher prices than sea fish. This, according to the Preparatory Commission, was because they were tastier, less bony and their season coincided with a seasonal lull in sea-fishing (paragraph 217). The amount of litigation around the ownership and leasing of creeks to individuals was an indication of the value of the different creeks to various lineages. Most of the creeks had been pledged and, therefore, their owners did not have fishing rights. Instead, they received rent for the use of the creeks by others. Fishing methods in the creeks depended on the character of the creek.

Farming

Farming was more time-consuming and generated more income than fishing in the Tongu area in 1954.[26] The main crops grown in the Lower Volta were cassava, groundnuts, maize, sweet potatoes, sugarcane and vegetables. Sweet potatoes were the most valuable crop in terms of the monetary value of yield per acre (Appendix VII, paragraph 88, p. 154) although the main cash crop was groundnuts. The groundnuts, sweet potato and maize were harvested mainly in January/February and August and sold almost immediately with very little of it stored, according to Lawson (1968). The staple crop, cassava, was left on the farm and harvested as and when it was needed for food. The crops on creek-land though had to be harvested before the floods reached the Lower Volta. In times of hardship, some of the crop could be sold to purchase protein, vegetables and other needs. Part of the cassava crop could also be peeled, cut up and sun-dried[27] and exported in bulk during and after the seasonal floods.

There were two major types of land used for cultivation æ land surrounding the creeks and land that was on higher ground (upland). Creek-land was preferred because of its higher fertility, which has been attributed to its moisture levels as a result of seasonal flooding. Half of agricultural earnings came from crops grown on creek-land.[28] Another advantage of creek-land was that it could be used from year to year without rotation or fallow.[29]

Crops were grown on small dispersed plots that could be as small as 0.1 of an acre in size. At Battor in 1954, the average plot size

---

[26] At Battor, which was one of the larger villages and which therefore had a more diverse population, two-thirds of the adult population farmed and one third considered it a main occupation. 20% of households did no farming at all and the heads of these households were classified as strangers, usually wage employees (Lawson, 1968).

[27] This product, *kokonte*, a Tongu Ewe and Dangme staple, was ground into flour and cooked in a pot on a fire through the addition of hot water and stirring. The resulting product, a stick brown paste, was eaten with soup or pepper and fish.

[28] Sixty-five percent of crops were grown on creek-land in the riverine communities. The figure for Battor in 1954 was put at 55%. Experiments showed that creek-land was more productive. According to Lawson, groundnut yields on creek-land were over two times that of other land and cassava grown on creek-land did better after only six months than that grown for 14 months on upland soil (Lawson, 1972, p.32). If the floods subsided quickly, two groundnut crops could be grown on creek-land (Lawson, 1968).

[29] Land in upland areas on the other hand, had to be rotated. After 3–5 years of cultivation, the land was rested for 10–15 years (Lawson, 1972, p. 32).

was 0.4 of an acre, with households using an average of three scattered plots. The Preparatory Commission states that this was common to the Lower Volta (Appendix VII, paragraph 86, p. 153).[30] A study of markets in the Lower Volta indicated that a third of the cassava and sweet potatoes were exported outside the area (Lawson, 1968).

Farming was the one economic activity which saw co-operation between the different members of a household. Both men and women worked on farms, but there was a traditional division of labour with men doing the clearing and women weeding and harvesting (Lawson, 1968). Households typically had one set of farms that were considered to be the staple providers. These farms belonged to the household head and every member of the household who could was expected to provide labour. The surplus from this farm belonged to the household head. Farms belonging to other household members did not have the same status although their proceeds did in practice contribute to household welfare, whether through direct consumption of produce or the use of the money for household needs.

5. *The Lower Volta in the 1960s: Growth of Trading, Artisanal Activities and Waged Employment*

In 1954, most production in the Lower Volta was for subsistence.[31] Savings and the seasonality of livelihood activities kept households going during different times of the year. Roads were quite poor and river transport was the major means of travel. Trading and market activity were quite minor with only a few markets at places such as Akuse, Tefle, Adidome and Aveyime and small daily markets in several communities mainly sold local produce. By 1964, trading, artisanal activities and wage employment had become significant. This was accompanied by a process of centralisation[32] in parts of the area.

---

[30] As noted, the unit of measurement of farmland is a rope, rendered in the Ewe as *abɔwuieve eka*, (literally a 12 arm rope, estimated as 12 spans of a man's arms. This is said to be approximately 22 yards and therefore 1/9 of an acre. Interestingly, this is still the unit of measurement used in the Lower Volta.

[31] In many places, 70–75% of production was for domestic consumption, although in larger villages the figure could be as low as 30%.

[32] Centralisation has been defined as the increase in the population of a community through the depopulation of outlying communities. Four Tongu communi-

Centralisation was strengthened by the provision of infrastructure for the administration of communities and districts by the government. These developments which resulted in the building of roads, police stations, schools, clinics and health centres had resulted in the creation of wage labour and improved transportation. This in turn boosted agriculture in creating a market for food-crops locally and elsewhere and opportunities for artisanal occupations such as vehicle repair and driving. The Lower Volta markets had in the ten years between 1954 and 64 become larger and more established.

In the 1960s, farming was still described as the most important source of income in the Lower Volta. In this period, half the adult population considered farming as their main source of livelihood while a further third of the remaining saw it as a secondary activity (Preparatory Commission, Appendix VII, paragraph 85, p. 153). In addition, some state farm schemes had been introduced in the area, schemes which were no longer functional by 1967 as a result of collapse or being halted after the 1966 coup d'état. While some of these interventions did not affect the Tongu peasantry directly, they had an impact on the Tongu economy. For example, the injection of State capital and political presence into the area led to improvements in the standard of education, increases in wage employment and secondary economic activities such as trading, and artisanal work such as sewing, carpentry and masonry. Other new occupations observed in the area were the collection of shells for glass making, breaking stones in quarries and collecting sand for building projects. Lawson has noted that these new occupations were considered very attractive because they provided diversity of sources of income, greater personal mobility and could be combined with primary occupations (Lawson, 1968).

While this led to a proportional reduction of the agricultural population, the Lower Volta economy retained its essential character as one based on primary economic activities such as farming and fishing.[33] At Battor for example, Lawson reports a doubling of the land under

ties (out of 35 in the Volta Region)—Sogakope, Adidome, Tefle and Battor æ were identified as having experienced centralisation (See Lawson, 1970, pp. 16–23 for a discussion of processes of centralisation).

[33] Households at Battor, for example, had an average of 2.4 different occupations compared with 1.2 in 1954. Also, 20% of the adult-working population had a regular cash income throughout the year from sources other than farming, fishing and trading, as opposed to only 10% in 1954 (Lawson, 1967, 1968).

cultivation and the amount of land each household had as well as a higher labour input due to the fact that more persons were employed in farming. The intensity of cultivation increased from 10% in 1954 to 30% in 1964, a figure way above the national average of 10% (Lawson, 1968, p. 26).[34] The technology and farming techniques remained unchanged in spite of the introduction of a few tractors and the doubling of land acreage. The visible increase in agriculture was attributed by Lawson to the fact that farming was an "essential form of security in a situation of uncertain economic change" (1968, p. 17). After all, the demand for the services of rural artisans was not sufficient to make a break with fishing and farming attractive.

Fishing in the Lower Volta had suffered a decline between 1954 and 1964 because of competition from sea fishing, which was expanding and forcing down fish prices. However, fishing for subsistence remained important. Lawson reports that by 1964, a form of specialisation, which had been emerging in 1954, had become established as a result of the increase in volume of the clam trade. This was the separation between clam diving and the sale of clams. A number of clam divers had become largely clam traders, spending most of their time trading. In this same period, there was a three-fold increase in clam incomes because the Akosombo Dam had resulted in the cessation of the seasonal floods creating an extended clam season. As well, many more women were farming clams, i.e. transplanting and growing them, with the result that there were higher incomes for all parties.

Lawson observed that in 1964 the amount of time women spent in the river picking clams had affected the "economic organisation of the traditional family" (1968, p. 41). Women had not been able to fulfil their farming obligations and in some cases had to draft in extended family members to perform these roles. Lawson argues that this "posed another threat to the stability of traditional households with the culturally determined roles it allocates to various members of the household". This is an interesting observation. One male informant at Mepe wryly observed that but for the collapse of the clam industry, women of the Lower Volta would have no use for men. Some of these challenges to the traditional sexual division of labour

---

[34] As Lawson argued, "The riparian people were still mainly farmers and fishermen with a high degree of mobility between these occupations" (1970, p. 28).

might have become significant for women's views of themselves and
the society's view of them.

In spite of the intensification of farming and clam picking, there
was an expansion in markets and the goods they sold in the 1960s.
This was attributed to increased production and incomes as well as
improved road communications. Markets such as Aveyime quadru-
pled the amount of local foodstuffs they were handling and there
were new markets at Sogakope and Tefle. The markets also stocked
goods such as fish from the coast as well as a much wider range of
imported goods. In turn, local produce was purchased from these
markets and exported to far-flung places within the country. Many
of the food-crop traders in the markets were from the farming households that produced the crops.

There was also an increase in the numbers of small businesses
and trading stores, some more dramatic than others. At Adidome,
which had acquired urban characteristics in the ten-year period
between 1954 and 1964, these businesses had grown from 34 to 93
and included transportation, sewing, baking, corn-milling, construction, cooked food concerns, general trading, alcohol distillery and
gold-smithing (Lawson, 1968, p. 59).

The expansion in trading and the range of goods being traded
was accompanied by an expansion in the variety of foods consumed.
Lawson found in the 1960s that at Battor, the consumption of protein had increased significantly with more than 50% being obtained
from animal sources. Also, there was a marked increase in the availability and consumption of foodstuffs from other parts of the country,[35] processed foods such as *garri*[36] and rice, as well as bread, maize
and maize foods. Imported foods such as sugar and evaporated milk
were also more commonly consumed (Lawson, 1963, 1967).

Other noticeable socio-economic changes observed in the area
were the reduction of days spent away from economic activities and
the appearance of class structures based on wealth and ownership
of material goods. It was noted that while these structures had not
replaced the traditional clan and lineage-based ones, a decline in the
status of traditional leaders had occurred (Lawson, 1970, pp. 92–94).
These changes were attributed to the political institutions of the cen-

---

[35] Such as plantain and cocoyam which came from the forest areas through
Koforidua market.
[36] Grated and pan-roasted cassava, which, if well processed, can last for a year.

tral government, the presence of stranger wage earners such as teachers and bureaucrats in the area and the greater access of local people to markets and urban centres.

Side by side with the observed changes in class relations were changes in the relations between men and women. Lawson remarks that the separate economies of men and women within a household meant that the differences in the sources and periodicity of male and female incomes were important. This was also related to the social division of reproductive responsibilities between men and women. Thus men's more seasonal incomes were bulked enough to be applied to capital expenditure while women's incomes trickled in for use in day to day consumption. By 1964, however, the separation between men and women's purchases was becoming blurred, partly because of the wider range of goods women bought. However, it was still possible to distinguish between men and women's expenditures (Lawson, 1972).

Christianity had a much more vigorous presence in the 60s, a situation helped by the educational activities of churches. However, the shrines continued to have a place in the life of people in the Lower Volta. The education of children was increasingly seen as a source of future security with the result that more people sent their children to school. Informants mentioned the importance of clam picking incomes for financing education. It was in this situation of incremental socio-economic changes that the Volta River Project's dramatic impacts were experienced.

6. *The Post-Akosombo Dam Situation: Impacts of the Volta River Project*

The Volta Lake and the establishment of the Lake fisheries

As predicted, the Akosombo Dam created a vast water body, the Volta Lake,[37] which inundated the villages, farmlands, sacred groves and other religious grounds, burial sites and public institutions and infrastructure such as roads, health centres, telephones, markets and schools of 80,000 people (Yeboah, 1999). The majority of these

---

[37] 8,500 sq. kilometres (3,275 sq. miles) at a maximum height of 276 ft above sea level when it was finally filled in 1968.

persons were resettled. The substantial fisheries and the spontaneous and unplanned settling of fishermen along the Lake's considerable shoreline also came to pass. During the period of Lake formation, some fish species became extinct while others such as tilapia flourished beyond their known pre-dam levels in the Lake (Petr, 1966; Lawson, G. et al., 1968, 1969; Denyoh, 1969; Obeng, 1975).

Lakeside fishing established itself as an important economic activity, providing work and sustenance to large numbers of people. The Lake's fish stocks were estimated at 60,000 tons in 1968, having risen from only 3,000 tons in 1964 and decreasing and then stabilising at a figure of 40,000 tons by the mid 1970s (Obeng, 1975; Chisholm, p. 30; Braimah, 1999). The annual catch was estimated in 1971 at 42,000 metric tons, 1977 at 40,000 metric tons and in 1980 at 38,000 tonnes compared with estimated 10,000 tons from the Volta Basin before Akosombo (Obeng, 1975; Coppola and Agadzi, 1977; Hart, 1980).[38] There were 2,000 fishermen before the Lake formed. In the early post-dam period, 12,000 were estimated to work on the Lake, a figure which grew to 20,000 in 1969 (Obeng, 1975). They and their families (about 60,000 persons in all) lived in about 1,000 villages scattered around the lake and used an estimated 13,000 canoes (Devambez, 1970; Kumi, 1973; Coppola and Agadzi, 1977). The fish catch was estimated at 9.5 million cedis, a significant amount if compared with the 28 million cedis total revenue from electricity from Akosombo. This represented 20% of the demand for fish in Ghana.[39]

The conditions created by the Lake, coupled with the migration of already infected fishermen to the Lake were considered key to the high incidence of some diseases around the Lake. Paperna, for example, writes that *bilharzia* was introduced to the Lake by Ewe

---

[38] Gordon has argued recently that the 40,000-ton figure, which has become "enshrined" in the literature, is open to question because it has not been updated in over two decades when there have been significant increases in the numbers of fishermen and various changes around the Lake (Gordon, 1999).

[39] These gains of course have to be balanced against the loss of clam and creek fishing estimated at £25,000 and £65,000 a year by the Preparatory Commission and even less conservatively by Lawson. Another loss against which this has to be balanced is the food and other yields of the land which was now submerged (Titiati and Gilbert, 1969). The general absence of computations of gains and losses and differences in currency and time-frame where there have been computations make the issue of gains and losses hard to resolve. However, mentioning them signals an important qualification of the gains in fish catches around the Lake.

fishermen from the Lower Volta where *schistosomiasis haematobium* infections were prevalent (1969). The first snails, the *bulinus rohlfsi*, had been found in the Lake in late 1966.[40] By 1967, when there was an explosion of snails and a particular kind of aquatic weed, *ceratophyllum*,[41] there were already many cases of *schistosomiasis haematobium* in many sections of the Lake (Paperna, 1969).[42]

The Lake produced one positive effect on disease by flooding the part of the Volta that had provided good breeding grounds for the *simulum damnosum* (black fly). However, they continued to breed below the dam around the Kpong rapids until the 1980s when the Kpong Dam was built (Obeng, 1975). By 1999, it was reported that the *simulum* had been eliminated from the whole of the Volta Basin as a result of the flooding of the Kpong Rapids by the Kpong Dam (Kalitsi, 1999). The prevalence of *trypanosomiasis* too reduced drastically because large areas of tsetse-infested forests were drowned. Since 1973, no new cases have been recorded around the Lake (Derban, 1999). The establishment of the Volta Lake and fisheries went hand in hand with drastic environmental changes in the Lower Volta. It is to these we now turn.

Dam impacts on the Lower Volta

The great floods of 1963
There is now general agreement in the VRP literature that the Akosombo and Kpong Dams devastated the environment and livelihoods in the Lower Volta. For example, most of the authors of the

---

[40] The *bulinus rohlfsi* was at this time the only existing snail vector in the Lake (Odei, 1965b; Klumpp and Chu, 1977).

[41] It was found that the submerged forests in the Lake, which acted as wave breaks, were implicated in the explosion of the aquatic weed ceratophyllum (Klumpp and Chu, 1977).

[42] Studies of school children around the Lake showed average infection rates of 80% and in a few cases, 100% in 1968. In communities such as Ampaem and Amete, prevalence among school children shot up from 35–38% and 7–8% respectively in January 1967 to 99% prevalence in both communities by January 1968 (Paperna, 1969, p. 497). Laboratory studies of the snails harvested from these areas found them highly vulnerable to the strains of schistosomiasis found in these communities. Later studies confirmed these patterns. For example, Klumpp and Chu studied the infection rates of *bulinus rohlfsi* snails as well as the patterns of schistosomiasis infections in 26 villages in the Afram branch of the Volta Lake in the 70s and found infection rates ranging from 31.7% to 100% among humans (Klumpp and Chu, Bulletin of the World Health Organisation, 1977, 55 (6), pp. 731–737).

published proceedings of a 1996 seminar on the integrated development of the Volta Basin stated this in more or less detail (Gordon and Amatekpor (eds.), 1999). They included officials of the VRA (Derban, 1999; Kalitsi, 1999; Yeboah, 1999), officials from the Ministry of Agriculture (Asafo, 1999), and researchers of the VBRP (Amatekpor, 1999; Gordon, 1999; de Graft-Johnson, 1999; Geker, 1999). In the words of Geker, who is also the paramount chief of Mepe, Togbe Kwao Anipati IV, "the Tongu District can be singled out to date as having made the greatest sacrifice towards Ghana's development of the Akosombo and Kpong Hydro Electric Projects" (1999, p. 121).

The most dramatic occurrence in the Lower Volta soon after the Volta River Project began was the big floods of 1963. Lives, houses, tools of trade (such as boats and nets), livestock, crops at different stages of maturation, and cloth and clothes, bedding and furniture were lost. There was also the inconvenience, disorganisation and loss of productivity of having to move to other towns and villages or to higher ground until the floods had receded. The floods were considered by people in the Lower Volta to be the result of ongoing engineering works on the Dam. As we shall see in Chapter four, the Volta River Authority disputed this. At the time of the floods though, the river had been diverted to facilitate dam construction and it is not clear what this contributed to what has been described as the severest floods for decades. The floods were significant in destroying the accumulation of many decades. Coming as they did only a few years before dam-related changes in the Lower Volta, people who were not able to turn the changes to their advantage never recovered from their losses. Others did and went on to accumulate the resources to build cement block houses as a response either to the danger of future floods or to the prediction that the seasonal floods would cease. Discussions with respondents and informants about the VRP invariably led to the great floods. One informant described her experience of the floods as follows:

> As we went about our lives before the dam was finished, we suffered such a big flood that all our houses were submerged. We removed our valuables to be ferried to Dadome and Fakpoe since they were on higher ground on the other side of the river. We first took the children and the trunks to the place, by the time we returned to pick the rest of our things, the water had swept all our property away. I went to Fakpoe and the situation lasted two months. After the floods, we ferried our things back. I constructed a wooden structure here and we put our things in it. We started life all over again by the grace of God (MS, Mepe).

The belief that VRA was responsible remains strong today. Informants attributed this to the severity of the floods and official responses at the time:

> The VRA released the water before closing the dam. They wanted to see the level of the water before damming it. They are telling lies when they say they did not open the dam to spill the water. Because, since the time of my parents and grandparents we were always having floods but none ever got near our house let alone flooding this hill. They were seen all the time marking the level of the water at various stages and also after the flood too they came marking again. And we who suffered the effects, the government has ignored us (MA, Mepe).

One result of the floods was that many houses in the Lower Volta today were constructed post 1963. Lawson attributed the housing boom between 1964 and 1967 to the fact that the houses destroyed by the floods had to be rebuilt. Incomes from the fishing boom up the new Lake as well as "large amounts of savings made in the economy" in the decade before 1964 were used to finance this.[43] The building boom coincided with the period when the Lake enhanced men's livelihood activities while women lost the clams. This constituted a reversal of the pre-dam situation when women had earned much of the money in the area. Lawson argues that in taking the resources away from productive investments, the building boom was not conducive to the sustained growth of the economy. As we shall come to see, Lakeside migrants in the days of the fishing boom did not invest much in the Lower Volta.

Socio-economic impacts of the Volta River Project
As early as in 1965, the less dramatic but no less serious effects of the Akosombo Dam were being experienced in the Lower Volta. The combination of environmental and socio-economic changes resulted in the decline of key livelihood activities and problems such as the deterioration in the quality of drinking water, health problems, population decline and poor education and communication services. These changes included the cessation of the seasonal floods,

---

[43] Lawson has argued that these savings hid the rate of growth of the Lower Volta economy because indicators such as consumption and property inventories which had shown significant growth, still could not account for all the growth which this housing boom brought to light (Lawson, 1968, p. 60).

changes in the flow and character of the Volta, land degradation and the loss of tree cover.[44]

In the long-term, the cessation of the floods of the Volta River meant that patterns of livelihoods constructed around the cycle of seasonal flooding were compromised. For example, river transport between Tongu villages, described then as "cheap and reliable", was compromised once the Volta became a wider river with a more constant flow the whole year round at about 28,000 cusecs,[45] far above the dry season levels of 1,000 cusecs, but far below the between 125,000–390,000 cusecs which had once watered the creeks, ponds and the surrounding farmlands (Geker, 1999; Yeboah, 1999). Before the Akosombo Dam, it had been possible to cross parts of the Lower Volta on foot in the dry season (Yeboah, 1999). Since the mid 60s, people with farms across the river had to either own canoes or find money to pay to be transported across the river (informant interviews, Mepe).

Another problem created by the cessation of the seasonal floods was the proliferation of aquatic vegetation. If the explosion of aquatic weeds in the Volta Lake was entirely expected, the same could not be said for the river below the Dam. Research in 1966 found two new species of aquatic plants in the river at Battor. In 1967, another study at Vume found a "dramatic and explosive development" (Hall and Pople, 1968, p. 24) of the two plants—*vallisneria aethiopica* and *potamogeton octandrus*. Local fishermen confirmed that the latter was entirely new, while the former had increased dramatically. Further research revealed that about 30% of the riverbed between the depths of 1 and 2 metres, i.e. the surface parts, had been taken over by the plants. Also, between 70–100% of the bottom of the river had been covered by submerged weeds (*ceratophyllum, vallisneria* and *potamogeton*) (Hall and Pople, 1968; deGraft Johnson, 1999). The increase in aquatic plants was not seen as a wholly negative development at this stage, as certain types of fish would do better under these new conditions. However, even then, there was concern that the aquatic vegetation should not become so prolific as to interfere with the clam picking industry (Hall and Pople, 1968; Lawson, G. et al., 1968).

---

[44] In 1996, a study found that many localities were stripped of their trees creating shortages in wood fuel (Gyasi and Enu Kwesi, 1997).

[45] Cubic feet per second.

Fishing in the main river, which in the pre-dam period was seen as largely for subsistence, went into decline soon after the post-dam boom. Obeng reports that for a period, even the herring fisheries offshore were affected because the amount of freshwater going into the estuary changed (Obeng, 1975). Some fishing has continued in the main river stream up till now, but under difficult conditions and is increasingly a minority activity in all but a few communities. There is also a reduction in the quantities and varieties of fish (Geker, 1999) with the tilapia species becoming the most common.

The more spectacular casualties of the Volta River Project, however, were creek and clam fishing. Beyond even the most pessimistic predictions, most of the creeks dried up by 1965 (Lawson, 1968).[46] As Moxon (1984) noted, "undoubtedly, creek fishing has had its heyday" (p. 190; see also Petition of Tongu District Council to the Volta Regional Administration and the VRA, 1976; Geker, 1999). Mepe villages such as Degorme and Lukunu, which were named for creeks, now found themselves without these water bodies.[47]

In the short term, communities in the Lower Volta benefited from a very long season of clam picking and creek fishing before the decline set in. However, contrary to the Preparatory Commission and Lawson's optimism, clams gradually disappeared from their traditional breeding grounds, a development attributed to the shifting of a critical water salinity boundary.[48] Moxon, writing a few years after the Akosombo Dam, was not so optimistic about the chances of the clam industry. He argued that of the three types of fishing in the Lower Volta, the clam industry was possibly the one with the least chances of survival under the new conditions (p. 190; see also Obeng, 1975). By the 1980s, there was general agreement that

---

[46] Not surprisingly, the incidence of litigation with respect to land around creeks and the creeks themselves reduced drastically.

[47] The Preparatory Commission had reported that Deh at Degorme, the most valuable of the group of creeks in its neighbourhood, yielded £300 a season. The Aklamador, which was not far from Lukunu, could yield about £2,000 in a good year. Luku at Lukunu was also mentioned as a principal creek (Appendix VII, paragraph 153, p. 165). Of the three, only the Aklamador retained its vitality as a water course and even then was covered extensively by aquatic vegetation making fishing in it difficult (personal observation and informant interviews, Mepe). Deh, which was now a small pond, provided neither drinking water nor fish.

[48] It is thought that even if they had remained, they could not be collected due to the thick growth of the aquatic weeds over the river (Chisholm, 1982).

clam picking had ceased to be an economic activity of any consequence in all of the Lower Volta (Geker, 1999).

The demise of the clam industry was described in terms of the
loss of the jewel in the livelihood portfolio. More than the income,
the loss of the clams also heralded a change in the way of life which
involved travel to the clam sites and to markets as far as in Accra.
This had allowed the women to participate if only as traders and
consumers in the momentous changes that were taking place in the
capital of Ghana at the time. At the height of the clam industry,
women were able to contribute to the construction of family houses
or build their own cement block houses. The short boom in women's
building activities after the 1963 floods was to be ended by the collapse of the clam industry. As one informant explained:

> Women did not build much in those days, but after the floods that
> destroyed all our houses, women became the main builders. At Degorme,
> for example, most of the houses belong to women. These are cement
> houses. Because we already had the clamshells, we did not have to
> buy them. They were used in the concrete work for the foundation.
> So many women could build in those days. We started building cement
> block houses with the aim that if there should be future floods, and
> we moved out, we could come back into our block houses when the
> floods subsided. The collapse of the clam business brought an end to
> everything. These days, the ex-clam pickers who remained in the com-
> munity have had to settle for less prestigious projects (MS, Mepe).

After the clams, the more sedentary livelihoods that were fashioned
did not have the same economic and social possibilities. Some of
the obligations assumed by women in the clam-picking era were now
impossible.

Agriculture in the Lower Volta also declined. The Preparatory
Commission, as already indicated, had not anticipated this. Two
trends in agriculture—labour shortages and the increasing use of
marginal lands for farming—have been cited as indicators of decline.
The benefits of flood-plain agriculture in the Lower Volta—permanent cultivation, multiple cropping, the natural rejuvenation of soils
which made tilling and weeding unnecessary and the high crop
yields—were lost to the Lower Volta (Moxon 1984; Lawson, 1972;
Gyasi and Enu-Kwesi, 1997). Farming continued on the lands that
used to be flooded, but without the advantages of seasonal flooding.
It was soon extended to marginal and fragile lands on which more
effort and labour was needed. Farmers travelled longer distances in
search of new plots.

All these efforts notwithstanding, post-dam agriculture failed to match pre-dam productivity. Cassava and maize, whether grown on ex-creek land or upland, did not have creek-land's advantages of size and quick maturation. Crops, which used to thrive on creek-land—especially oil palm, groundnuts and sweet potatoes, plantain, banana, water-yam and cocoyam—declined sharply. Cassava became a preferred crop because of its drought resistance (Gyasi and Enu-Kwesi, 1997).

Lawson noted that the trend towards agriculture, which had been visible in the early 60s, was completely reversed when almost all the economically active males in the Lower Volta left to fish in the new Lake (1968). At Mepe and Battor, the Dam was blamed for labour shortages, which had resulted in reductions in the acreages cultivated annually and yields per acre (Chisholm, 1982, p. 31). In addition to crops, animal husbandry also declined partly because of the long distances that needed to be travelled to find water. This affected the quality and quantity of the animals being reared. Some farmers relocated their cattle and other animals to the Lakeside where conditions for fodder and water were considered better (Tongu District Council Petition, 1976; Geker, 1999).

In 1976, it was observed that agriculture in the Lower Volta relied solely on poor rainfall, an average of 39 inches (975 mm).[49] The Lower Volta Environmental Impact Studies (Volta Basin Research Project, 1997) noted that since the Akosombo Dam, rainfall in the area had reduced in quantity and reliability, with figures[50] "suggestive of a trend towards a more arid climate since the time of the Dam" (Gyasi and Enu-Kwesi, 1997). A trend towards the increased incidence of tenancies, litigation, shortened fallows and wood depletion observed in several Lower Volta communities, was described as "symptoms of ecological stress" all related to the seizure of the seasonal floods (Gyasi and Enu-Kwesi, 1997, p. 17).

The decline in sources of livelihood also affected health and nutrition. The Preparatory Commission's predictions about the health situation in the Lower Volta were not borne out by events. The changes in river flow and volume had an adverse effect on the availability

[49] Rainfall was concentrated in 5 months of the year, thus leaving long periods of drought (Tongu District Council Petition, 1976).
[50] Instead of two rainy seasons, there was now one. Recordings at Akuse showed a decline from pre-dam figures of 1183 mm between 1961–1964 to 1,116 mm between 1965–90 and 1,031 mm to 838 mm at Ada within the same periods.

and quality of drinking water in the Lower Volta. In 1976, it was noted that the upland villages lacked water because of the drying up of creeks and wells while the ones by the river had problems with the quality of their water supply. By 1989, pathogenic organisms were found in clams and prawns harvested in the Lower Volta. This was said to be the first time these bacteria, whose presence also signalled the deterioration in water quality, had been found in shellfish in Ghana (Amoah, 1999, pp. 36–37). The removal of the cleansing effects of the seasonal floods had been compounded by the discharge of effluents from industrial and commercial activities of organisations such as the Akosombo Textiles Ltd., the Asutuare Sugar Factory and the Akosombo Sewage treatment plant (Amoah, 1999). Other factors implicated in the increasing turbidity and bacteriological pollution of the river were the reduction of oxygen and the increase in suspended solids (Amoah, 1999).

The impacts of the relentless growth of aquatic weeds on disease soon became serious, creating the conditions for the thriving of the snail vector of *schistosomiasis* (bilharzia) as well as the mosquitoes, which caused malaria. The two diseases were believed to have increased dramatically (de Graft Johnson, 1999). Intestinal schistosomiasis, which, as has been indicated, had a very low incidence in the Volta Basin before the dam, began to infect large numbers of people especially in the Lower Volta.[51] Other diseases reported to have increased in the Lower Volta since the Volta River Projects were intestinal and stomach infections, eye and skin diseases. Guinea-worm infections, also associated with poor water sources, were also on the increase and the aquatic vegetation was harbouring dangerous snakes and other reptiles (Geker, 1999).

As Lawson noted, like in other rural areas in Ghana, there were seasonal variations in nutrition in the Lower Volta. Before the Akosombo Dam, the flood period was a time of shortages of fish and clams. In the early post-dam years, the seasonal variations in nutrition had become insignificant, especially in the case of fish, which could no longer be obtained in large quantities seasonally, but was available in small quantities throughout the year. At this stage, however, it was observed that nutrition was not a serious problem

---

[51] The now high incidence of schistosomiasis has also been associated with the low standard of living in the area because it afflicts communities without decent infrastructure and water facilities (Derban, 1999, p. 31; Kpikpi et al., 1999).

generally and had improved in the ten-year period between 1954 and 1964 (Lawson, 1967). By 1965, Lawson reported that canned fish consumption in the Lower Volta had increased since the Dam because of the reduction in catches from the creeks (Lawson, 1967). The protein content of the Lower Volta diet changed. Clams disappeared from the menu and the consumption of fresh river fish reduced drastically because there were much fewer fishermen and many more people had to buy their fish. The prices of fresh water fish were beyond the reach of many households. Households generally had to purchase more of their foodstuffs than they used to. Occasional supplements of sun-dried cassava (*kokonte*) and smoked fish from the Lakeside alleviated the deficits for some households for years, but these were under threat with the changing conditions around the Lake.

One of the main responses to the changes in the Lower Volta was upstream migration whose features were quite different from the seasonal migration which had long been practised in the Tongu area. As the economic activities in the Lower Volta continued to decline after the Dam, the clear advantages of higher Lakeside income resulted in many more permanent settlements upstream, but this time, along the new Lake. The effects of this scale of out-migration on the Lower Volta have been felt in many areas—downstream economic activities, local revenue generation, education and family relationships, among others (Geker, 1999). In the early years after dam construction, some of the socio-economic effects of ecological change were cushioned by the flow of resources from the Lake. Much of this was spent on the construction of family houses. The significance of these flows has reduced drastically since then. Even more significantly, the exodus of the 60s and the continuing out-migration over three decades have had an impact on the population statistics in the Lower Volta. It was only recently that the Lower Volta began to show signs of recovery from over three decades of depopulation. As tables 3.1(a) and (b) below show, between 1960 and 1970 the population of Mepe increased by 73% while that for Sokpoe decreased by 41.3%. In 1970 and 1984, Mepe's population declined by 36.5% while Sokpoe's declined by 4.5%.[52] In addition, the sex ratio calculated

---

[52] This was in the context of Tongu District average increases of 14.5% for the period between 1960 and 1970 and 17.4% for between 1970 and 1984.

at the number of males to 100 females showed that the Lower Volta
had many more women than men. The sex ratio of the population
was 82.5 for South Tongu and 90.4 for North Tongu. They were
both lower than the Volta Region ratio of 94.1.[53] The South Tongu
District's male-female ratio was the lowest for the Volta Region while
the North Tongu was the 5th lowest of the 12 Districts.[54] The age
structure of the population was also telling.

In the survey, it was found that 43.5% of household heads interviewed at Mepe and Sokpoe were 60 years and above, while in
migrant settlements, the figure was 9.6%. Conversely, 55.9% of household heads interviewed in migrant settlements were under 40 years
old. At Mepe and Sokpoe, this figure was 16.3%. The percentage
of household heads between 40 and 59 was more similar for the
two categories of settlement—40.6% for Mepe and Sokpoe and 34.6%
for the migrant settlements. As we shall see in the chapters on livelihoods, out-migration and the population structure were important
factors in the economy of the Lower Volta.

Other impacts of the Volta River Project on the Lower Volta
were the loss of forests and bio-diversity. Informants observed that
because of environmental changes, the big forests and various species
of trees and birds had disappeared. The remaining species such as
the silk-cotton tree, which had supported a kapok[55] trade in the pre-
dam period, had reduced drastically in number over the years. Palm
trees were also much depleted and those remaining so puny that
they could be cut and carried home before being tapped. The adverse
changes in environmental and socio-economic conditions of the Lower
Volta have overshadowed whatever positive changes followed the
Akosombo Dam.

---

[53] These sex ratios are also considered low by the provisional figures of the Ghana
2000 Population Census indicators for which any figure lower than 93 is classified
as low.
[54] South Tongu's population was 4% and North Tongu was 8% of the Volta
Region population. The total population of the Volta Region is 1,630,254, with
790,184 male and 840,070 female and is 8.7% of the national total of 18,845,265,
of which 9,320,794 is male and 9,524,471 is female.
[55] A fluffy-cotton like material for stuffing pillows and mattresses.

7. *Summary and Conclusions*

This chapter has examined conditions in the Lower Volta in the fifteen years before the construction of the Akosombo Dam in 1964. The economy and society of the Lower Volta was discussed in the context of the wider colonial and post-colonial political economy. It was argued that although the Lower Volta was an integral part of the colonial economy, it was not at its core. Thus it developed into an area of out-migration to the upper reaches of the Volta and to the cocoa-growing and mining areas. The Lower Volta at that time was an agricultural society with farming, fishing and clam picking as the major sources of livelihood. Trading in food crops and other consumer goods as well as artisanal and waged work was becoming increasingly important by then. The dominance of the Volta River and its rhythms in the life of the area was discussed. Of particular interest was its variability, specifically its seasonal flooding which was implicated in the organisation of seasonal out-migration, farming, fishing and clam picking. The autonomous and co-operative relations between men and women's livelihoods and the labour relations in the organisation of livelihoods were also discussed.

The changes observed in the political economy of the Lower Volta by the 1960s were outlined. There were indications of growing differentiation within different economic activities and within the society as a whole. The chapter highlighted the processes of intensification in farming, fishing and trading and the increasing specialisation within the clam picking industry. The political and social institutions implicated in the ability to access resources and in the organisation of livelihoods such as chieftaincy, land relations, kinship, marriage and households were examined. The chapter demonstrated that in spite of colonial administrative, political and economic control, the day to day running of communities and maintenance of law and order were left to the chiefs and clan elders. Tongu societies were patrilineal and male-dominated with the result that women had less access to and control over land and labour. Men were the juridical and ritual heads of conjugal unions, households and other primary arrangements. In spite of this, women were able to engage in making livelihoods independently of men. There were indications that decades of clam picking and long-distance trading by women was producing changes in gender relations. The continuities within the Lower Volta and the organisation of its rhythms around a particular set of envi-

Table 3.1(a): Population of selected lower Volta settlements (1948–2000)

Towns	1948 Total	1960 Male	1960 Female	1960 Total	1960 % Increase	1970 Male	1970 Female	1970 Total	1970 % Increase
Mepe	1,258	744	908	1,652	31.3	1,333	1,526	2,859	73
Battor	520	303	358	661	27.1	511	676	1,187	79.5
Sogakope	365	908	882	1,790	390.4	1,561	1,538	3,099	73.1
Sokpoe	290	584	692	1,276	340	321	427	748	-41.3
Adidome	874	959	991	1,950	123.1	1,402	1,858	3,260	67.1
Tefle	727	697	772	1,469	102	630	772	1,402	-4.5

Table 3.1(a) continued

Towns	1984 Male	1984 Female	1984 Total	1984 % Increase	2000 Male	2000 Female	2000 Total	2000 % Increase
Mepe	820	993	1,813	-36.5	2,140	2,584	4,724	160.5
Battor	624	864	1,506	26.8	2,828	3,215	6,043	301.2
Sogakope	2,157	2,113	4,270	37.7	3,336	4,005	7,341	71.9
Sokpoe	280	434	714	-4.5	1,276	1,622	2,889	304.6
Adidome	1,798	2,168	3,966	21.6	2,848	3,499	6,347	60
Tefle	645	908	1,553	10.7	1,594	2,002	3,596	131.5

Source: Gold Coast and Ghana Census Data: 1948–2000.

Table 3.2(b): Population in percentage increases

Towns	1948	1960				1970			
	Total	Male % increase	Female % increase	Total	% increase	Male % increase	Female % increase	Total	% increase
Mepe	1,258	744	908	1,652	31.3	79.1	68.0	2,859	73
Battor	520	303	358	661	27.1	68.6	88.8	1,187	79.5
Sogakope	365	908	882	1,790	390.4	71.9	74.3	3,099	73.1
Sokpoe	290	584	692	1,276	340	−45.0	−38.2	748	−41.3
Adidome	874	959	991	1,950	123.1	46.1	87.4	3,260	67.1
Tefle	727	697	772	1,469	102	−9.6	—	1,402	−4.5

Table 3.2(b) continued

Towns	1984				2000			
	Male % increase	Female % increase	Total	% increase	Male % increase	Female % increase	Total	% increase
Mepe	−38.4	−34.9	1,813	−36.5	160.9	160.2	4,724	160.5
Battor	25.6	27.8	1,506	26.8	353.2	272.1	6,043	301.2
Sogakope	38.1	37.3	4,270	37.7	54.6	89.5	7,341	71.9
Sokpoe	−12.7	1.6	714	−4.5	355.7	273.7	2,889	304.6
Adidome	28.2	16.6	3,966	21.6	58.3	61.3	6,347	60
Tefle	2.3	17.6	1,553	10.7	147.1	120.4	3,596	131.5

ronmental and social conditions were to end quite abruptly with the Volta River Project.

The discussion about the pre-dam situation was followed by an account of dam impacts in the Lower Volta. Events such as the formation of the Volta Lake and the establishment of its fisheries which surpassed conservative estimates were linked with the environmental changes in the Lower Volta which fuelled mass out-migration from the Lower Volta and the establishment of many villages along the Volta Lake. Aquatic weeds became a serious problem, not only on the Lake as predicted, but also in the Lower Volta. Also in the Lower Volta, the Dam devastated the environments and its resources causing a decline in livelihood activities and in other aspects of life. In the next chapter, state policy and community responses to dam impacts are examined in more detail.

CHAPTER FOUR

STATE POLICY AND COMMUNITY RESPONSES:
THE POLITICS OF RELUCTANT SELECTIVE ACTION
AND INEFFECTUAL ACTIVISM

1. *Introduction*

"We deem the VRA's action in 1996 to be a reluctant reaction to the persistent pressure from various interest groups in the area over the last forty years" (Concerned citizens of the Tongu Area, Accra, 30/8/2001).[1]

In the last chapter, the ways in which the Lower Volta communities were affected by the VRP was discussed. In this chapter, state policies towards three categories of dam-affected communities—communities that had to be resettled, migrant fisher-folk around the lake and downstream communities are examined. As well, community activism in downstream communities on a range of dam impacts is discussed. The chapter lays the bases for the subsequent chapters, which examine household level responses of downstream communities to dam impacts and state responses.

An important vehicle of state policy, which also showed up its limits and orientation, was the Volta River Authority (VRA), the institution established to oversee the construction of the dams and their administration. The failure to establish a separate institution with the resources and the mandate to address the problems of dam-affected communities left the VRA with this task for which, as we shall see, it was ill equipped. Thus, government policy towards affected communities has been shaped, influenced and conveyed by the VRA for over three decades. For this reason, the discussion of government policy towards affected communities has centred on the VRA.

---

[1] Press Statement read at a national conference organised by the VRA and VBRP to discuss the findings of the Lower Volta Environmental Impact Studies (LVEIS) by Joe Gidisu, MP for North Tongu, 30/8/2001. The action being alluded to was the decision to undertake the studies.

While such an approach has the danger of conflating the government and the Authority (and this is not the intention), it conveys the VRA's central role in shaping and implementing state policy towards affected communities. Wherever it has been possible to identify other players within the State, their views and actions are discussed. As we shall find, there have been disagreements among the various state agencies about how to address dam impacts.

The chapter begins with a discussion of the VRA's institutional and legal character, functions, priorities and preoccupations. VRA policies towards affected communities are then considered. What then follows is a discussion of community and district level activism to seek redress for the impacts of the Volta River Project on the Lower Volta. This is followed by a summary and conclusions.

2. *The Institutional Framework for Addressing Dam Impacts: The VRA Legal and Institutional Character*

The antecedents of the Volta River Authority (VRA), the institution in charge of the affairs of the Volta River Project, lay in the Development Commission where the Volta River Project's planning phase began. This institution was responsible for long-term economic development planning in Ghana. Headed by Sir Robert Jackson, the chair of the Volta River Project Preparatory Commission, the Development Commission's main business was the Volta River Project, the number one development project of its day (KK, Accra). The Commission was later broken into two separate entities, the Development Secretariat and the Volta Secretariat. The Development Secretariat became the Ministry of Economic Affairs while the Volta Secretariat took charge of the Volta River Project. The Volta Secretariat evolved into the Volta River Authority (VRA), a statutory public utility corporation established by the Volta River Development Act, 1961 (Act 46) to plan, execute and manage the Volta River Project. The Act placed the Akosombo Dam, the Volta Lake and its environs and the Akosombo Township under the jurisdiction of the VRA. The health and safety of VRA workers, the inhabitants of its townships and Lakeside residents were also made the responsibility of the VRA (Sections 10 (1) (d), 10 (2), 13, 14 and 15). The only mention of the downstream area in the VRA Act was in relation to flooding and salinity of the Volta River. The Authority was to control the dam to prevent flooding downstream and the harmful penetration of salt water up the River Volta to levels higher than pre-dam conditions (Section 11).

The VRA was composed of a number of departments, which executed its mandates and accounted to the Chief Executive. Originally, there were five departments—finance, engineering, administration, resettlement and accounts (Futa, 1963). Over the years, various amendments of the Volta River Development Act and a series of corporate organisational restructuring programmes resulted in changes. In 1989, a Real Estate Department was established in the Authority with responsibility for "the acquisition, maintenance, development, disposal and general management of the Authority's real estate, excluding the management of the transformer and generating stations" (VRA, 1992). This department took charge of VRA's townships, the resettlements as well as immovable property all over Ghana acquired as a result of the forty or so sub-stations owned by VRA. In recent years, an environment section has been created within the Real Estate Department. This section, located at Akosombo, was in charge of the VRA's residual responsibilities for the resettlement and environmental impacts issues.

At the end of 2000, the VRA as structured had a Chief Executive with three deputies in charge of engineering and operations, finance and corporate planning and resources and services. Each deputy chief executive had directors, who headed departments, working under them. The departments were made up of sub-structures run by managers and their staff. In 1998, the VRA had 2,724 employees as against 2,642 in 1997 representing an increase of 3%. It was VRA policy to keep employee numbers down.

Futa has argued that because its main function, power production, was a commercial undertaking the VRA had to operate on sound financial principles, show profit and plan ahead for future expansion. That this view was a firm part of the VRA's ethos was reflected in several of its Annual Reports in which the organisation also posted its profit situation (VRA, 1987, 1992). The VRA was also a state-owned enterprise and the government of Ghana as its owner guaranteed its financial transactions with others against default in addition to having a small investment in its business.[2] The VRA's

---

[2] In one year, for example, the government's investment in VRA was 374 million cedis out of thirty-eight (38) billion cedis (VRA Annual Report, 1988).

major sources of funds included what it earned from the sale of electricity and loans from a number of bilateral and multilateral sources to finance its major projects.[3] In spite of the VRA's good record of debt repayment, these loans had to be supported by Ghana government guarantees.

The VRA until the early 1990s considered itself commercially successful. Since the Akosombo Dam, the organisation has raised the money to expand Akosombo from four to six units, extend power to Togo and Benin, construct the Kpong Dam and extend transmission lines to Northern Ghana and many rural areas. In addition, it built the Takoradi Thermal Plant and successfully undertook major maintenance operations. In a situation where many state-owned commercial ventures have performed poorly, the VRA's relative successes were significant (KK, Accra). As will become clear in the discussion of policy towards affected communities, these achievements were only part of the story of the Volta River Project.

Policy-making processes

The VRA's relations with government, the lending institutions and its block of major consumers were important in its policy processes. This could be seen in the composition of its eight-member government appointed Board which was in charge of organisational policy. In addition to the Chief Executive of the organisation, the VRA Act also stipulated that one board member should have experience in financial management and two should be representatives of major consumers of electricity. In practice, the two were always VALCO and the Electricity Corporation of Ghana. No provision was made for representatives of affected communities to be represented on the Board. It was only from the mid-90s that chiefs from communities affected by the dams began to serve on the VRA Board as a discretionary practice. These arrangements ensured that government and the block consumers of electricity were the most powerful interests on the board, while the dam-affected communities were the weakest.

---

[3] Originally, the bulk of funding from Akosombo came from the World Bank, USAID Exim Bank, and the Export Credit Guarantee Department of the Board of Trade of the USA. Subsequently, its projects were financed by loans from bilateral governmental and non-governmental sources in several European and Middle Eastern countries.

The close and special relationship between the VRA and the First Republic Government (1957–1966), established from the days when President Nkrumah himself was the chair of the Board, was most critical at the start. According to Kalitsi, Nkrumah's close relationship with the organisation insulated it from political interference from other governmental officials and institutions. Similar organisations did not have the VRA's combination of strong governmental support and autonomy. The Electricity Corporation, for example, was under the jurisdiction of a Minister of State and did not have the same freedom to enter into loan arrangements and fix the price of electricity.[4] With the overthrow of the Nkrumah Regime, the VRA had to establish a more "normal" relationship with central government. Under the Second Republican Constitution, the Prime Minister could not be the chair of a Board. The VRA Act was therefore amended to enable the government to appoint a chair. These changes influenced the VRA's governance and policy processes. More importantly, the new political climate required a reorientation and serious strategizing to enable the VRA navigate a new and more uncertain environment in which the organisation stood out as privileged and well-endowed.[5]

While the lending institutions were not on the board, their relations with the VRA influenced its policy-making. As Kalitsi points out, fulfilling the various conditionalities and obligations such as taking out insurance cover on loans and regular debt servicing was key to continued good relations with creditors. Beyond obligations, the VRA maintained good relations and regular contacts with its financiers as good business practice. That way, the financiers were apprised of the changes in the organisation's circumstances, particularly those that had implications for their loans (KK, Accra). Affected populations were most certainly not considered to be in this category of influential players in the VRA's affairs.

---

[4] The flipside of the VRA's autonomy is the control exerted over it because of its heavy borrowing from multilateral and bilateral financing institutions. The Government of Ghana, as guarantor of VRA loans, had to ensure that the organisation was managed in a manner to enable it to meet all its obligations.

[5] Anecdotal accounts have it that the Busia Regime, Ghana's government between 1969 and 1972, wanted to take over the VRA's relatively well-appointed offices for the Prime Minister's offices. The instructions were reversed only after the VRA put its powers of persuasion into effect. Again, a three-member committee was established to review the Authority's affairs in this period. No adverse findings were made against the organisation.

Functions, responsibilities and activities of VRA

The Authority's primary function was power generation and supply.[6] Secondary functions were the development of the Volta Lake for fishing and transport, the administration of the Akosombo Township, and periodic research and development work in the areas of fisheries, hydrobiology of the lake, public health, shoreline agriculture and resettlements.[7] Ventures such as the Kpong Farms Limited[8] and the Volta Lake Transport Company Ltd. (VLTC)[9] were to fulfil some of the mandates of the organisation. Every year, over 20,000 local and foreign visitors including several foreign heads of state visited the dam (VRA, 1987, 1988). The VRA reported in 1990 that it had renovated a three-star, thirty-five-room Volta Hotel. In 1992, the hotel was up and running with plans to construct facilities to retain its three-star status (VRA, 1990, 1992). From the foregoing, it is clear that generating power efficiently, getting commercial returns, anticipating, and supplying increasing demands for electricity have remained the core functions of the VRA.

However, other issues periodically demanded the VRA's attention and it has approached them with varying levels of enthusiasm and attention. An early example was the issue of resettlements, which originally was not to be the VRA's responsibility. Other examples were what the VRA described as environmental problems and much more recently, the issue of the Lower Volta. It is to these issues,

---

[6] It supplied power directly to VALCO, the Electricity Corporation, the mines, Akosombo Textiles Ltd. and the Akosombo and Kpong Townships. Since 1987 it was also directly taking power to consumers in the Brong Ahafo, the Northern and Upper East and West Regions of Ghana. Outside Ghana, the VRA supplied power to Togo and Benin and until recently, Côte d'Ivoire. In recent years, these exports and exchanges have been affected by supply and demand problems in Ghana leading to imports from Côte d'Ivoire to supplement supply in Ghana.

[7] Until 1971, the VRA was in charge of the resettlement townships. At the request of government, it transferred its oversight function to other government agencies. However, some questions pertaining to resettlements continued to engage its attention.

[8] Kpong Farms consisted of 100 hectares of irrigated land mostly devoted to rice but also cowpeas, soya beans and maize on a smaller scale because of clayey soils. The farm is highly mechanised, with a labour force of 45 with equipment such as a combine harvester, grain dryer, rice mill, tractors and accessories, a workshop, stores, etc. The farm provided training for technology transfer (VRA, 1987).

[9] The Volta Lake Transport Company Ltd, a subsidiary of the VRA, was established in 1970 to promote Lake Transport. It is engaged in the transportation of cargo and passengers on a north-south route between Akosombo and Buipe with stops in between. Its cargo includes diesel oil, kerosene, petrol as well as cattle and dry cargo (VRA, 1988). By 1999, it had 13 river craft and a carrying capacity of 4,000 tons. Its craft include dry and wet cargo barges (Kalitsi, 1999).

which pertain to affected communities—the resettlements, lakeside and downstream communities—that we now turn.

3. *The VRA as Resettler*

The 1956 Preparatory Commission Report on the Akosombo Dam devoted one of its three volumes to the issue of resettlement. Originally, the Commission had recommended cash compensation to enable people to resettle themselves to maintain their self-reliance. This idea was rejected because of experiences of self-resettlement in India, the serious time constraints facing the project and the large number of persons to be resettled. In fact, dam-building had been underway for nine months before resettlement began to receive serious consideration. The Commission had considered resettlement to be an integral part of the Volta River Project. This was reversed by the decision to drop project components not directly related to power generation. Thus, resettlement became the responsibility solely of the Ghana Government, which the VRA inherited when it was established.

An amount of £4.5 million, £4 million of which was to come out of the VRA's coffers, was estimated as a reasonable figure to address the issues of affected communities. Any expense beyond this amount was to be borne by the Ghana Government. In practice, VRA spent about £8 million, the bulk of which went into compensation and resettlement. Even this amount was to prove inadequate.[10] The Lower Volta did not receive any of this expenditure. Kalitsi argues that while the exigencies of the period made resettlement an urgent problem, it was not the intention to completely ignore the downstream.

In all, 64,000 persons from over 700 communities were resettled in 52 new communities in the Volta Basin because of the Akosombo Dam. While the communities were provided with various facilities— dwelling houses, potable water, sanitary facilities and schools[11]—they

---

[10] A VRA document puts this figure at £10 million and compares this with the £65 million spent on the project as a whole (VRA, undated but written in or after 1999).

[11] According to Yeboah, 1,300 houses, 82 school blocks, 46 markets, 146 public toilets, 52 boreholes, 6 wells, 34 mechanical and 23 handpumps, 500 miles of road and 100,000 hectares of farmlands were provided for the resettlements (1999, p. 126).

did not enjoy electricity until over three decades after their resettlement. The absence of electricity in the resettlement townships was defended on economic grounds. The earliest connections to the grid, which involved large towns such as Tema, Accra, Sekondi-Takoradi and Kumasi, were to generate the revenue to meet the VRA's obligations.

There have been a number of studies which have assessed this first resettlement experience (Chambers, 1970; Diaw & Schmidt-Kallert, 1990). Many of the problems of resettlement were attributed to the modernisation approach which led to the uncritical adoption of mechanised farming to replace shifting cultivation, the lack of adequate resources and poor planning (Graham, 1986; World Bank, 1993). By the end of the resettlement exercise, costs had escalated to three times the original estimate of $10 million. This was notwithstanding the fact that the Government had reneged on undertakings to provide government buildings, recreation facilities and a river transport scheme to cut costs. Compensation was paid on housing and crops only if their value exceeded £330, the stated value of a resettlement house. Given the low value put on traditional houses, this was a rare occurrence. Butcher, who was connected to the resettlement team, noted that "a deduction of 780 new cedis was made from the compensation for flooded crops of each settler to pay for his house. This was not in keeping with the declared policy of compensating crops in full and replacing flooded houses in kind" (Butcher, quoted in Hart, p. 80).

In 1974, the government formally acquired the land submerged by the Volta Lake by an Executive Instrument. The land included the areas around the Lake where draw-down agriculture was now practised. There were two kinds of land owner to be compensated; those whose two million acres (800,000 hectares) of land were submerged, and those who owned the 430,000 acres (172,000 hectares) required for resettlement townships and agriculture. As at 2003, these compensation cases were still pending for various reasons. Some progress has been made in respect of compensation for land acquired for resettlement. By 1976, no compensation had been paid for flooded land. VRA handled compensation until 1973 when it was handed over to the Lands Department. Hart noted that VRA policy on compensating such land was unclear. It seems to have been the view that the resettled were being compensated by receiving land in return for the land they had lost. However, resettlement acreages were on the average only a fraction of the land people were farming before the dams. In addition, the intensive agriculture that was to make up for smaller land sizes was not very successful.

It was fashionable then and well into the 80s to claim that the land was of little value. However, the loss of bio-diversity and the future value of such land were not considered in such assessments. More recent valuations estimated that 22,680 hectares of farming land which was used for staples such as cassava, maize, guinea corn, rice, yam and cash crops such as cocoa by numerous small farmers, was flooded. In addition, large tracts of forests and forest reserves with important economic trees such as mahogany, *wawa* and rarer species such as ebony were also submerged (Amatekpor, 1999; Yeboah, 1999).

The compensation paid for the loss of land, crops, houses and other assets did not take account of the fact that the resettlers had to establish new livelihoods which required a stronger resource base to reproduce. For example, resettlement housing, the facilities provided and indeed, the whole of the "modern" life being prescribed to resettlers required a much higher outlay of resources than their old lives did. The situation was not helped by the failures of resettlement agriculture. That programme has been harshly criticised for making a hash of a planned programme of mechanised farming, which was then abandoned midstream in favour of manual land clearing with food aid which also did not achieve its goals. In the original plan, several small plots, totalling about 5 hectares were to be given to individual farmers. All of them were expected to adopt mechanisation. VRA was to own the tractors, sell fertiliser and buy the agricultural produce. Also, the farmers were to be assigned to particular types of agriculture by the VRA—40% were to be arable farmers, another 40% tree crop farmers, 15% livestock and 5% pastoralists (Hart, 1980, quoting Chambers, 1970).

There were delays in the preparation of land. Only 15,000 acres of the 54,000 targeted had been cleared by the time of resettlement partly because the clearing of land for agriculture had to be abandoned to construct houses. Only a portion of the land was cleared and of that, only a third was cultivated mechanically. The crops were produced at a loss and resettlers had to be supported with food aid. The plan shifted to manual clearing and that too did not work. As Hart notes, at each resettlement, the amount of land that could be allocated per farmer was a little over one hectare and this was simply not sufficient for subsistence either by manual or mechanised farming techniques (Hart, p. 85).

There were also problems between those resettled and the communities whose lands they were being settled on, a situation fuelled by the failure to pay compensation to the owners of such land (Kalitsi, 1970; Graham, 1986). One result of all these problems was that few farmers made the transition to mechanised farming or even grew any crops in the first years after their resettlement in spite of pressure from the Project (Graham, 1986). Farmers resisted mechanised farming because they did not have the resources to purchase inputs (Graham, 1986).

Resettlement housing also had its problems. Those who had lived in rented premises before resettlement were not among those provided with resettlement housing. The houses provided were based on the core house concept. Irrespective of the number of rooms a family used before resettlement, they were provided with a single room with the foundation for three additional rooms. Building materials and technical advice was provided for the completion of the house. This approach, according to the VRA, was to ensure a roof over the heads of resettled families before the quickly-rising waters of the Lake had submerged their homes and also to promote the spirit of self-reliance. Many of these core houses were not expanded beyond the initial one-room core (Yeboah, 1999) and were considered by those who had lost many more rooms to be grossly unfair. More importantly, resettlers complained that the houses were of poor quality, overcrowded and failed to take account of the hot climate and the needs of polygynous households. Health experts worried that this created conditions for the spread of communicable diseases such as yaws, measles and smallpox (Derban, 1999).

The health situation was not helped by the sanitation and water problems of the resettlements. Communal latrines broke down very quickly and the disposal of sewage, refuse and other waste became difficult. The water pumps soon broke down and could not be repaired mainly because of the lack of resources (Derban, 1999). The VRA gave up its responsibility for supplying water in 1972 and many communities therefore had to turn to the Volta Lake for water. This contributed to an increase in the incidence of diseases; particularly schistosomiasis and other prevalent diseases—malaria, dysentery, typhoid fever, hookworm and other intestinal worm diseases—were associated with these environmental problems. During the early years of resettlement, yellow fever and dengue were very prevalent and resulted in high mortality rates (Derban, 1999).

The resettled were generally dissatisfied and considered that their living standards had been adversely affected. At Kete Krachi, the population was "unhappy and dispirited four years after being resettled" (Graham, 1986), while at New Mpamu, people were "demoralised, apathetic and bitter about their experiences" (Tamakloe, 1968). Schram diagnosed the inhabitants of New Ntewusa as suffering from a state of "advanced anomie" as a result of their inability to adapt to their new circumstances (Schram, 1967). Summing up the experience of resettlement agriculture, Derban has argued that it contributed to "economic hardship, starvation and malnutrition in children" (Derban, 1999, p. 28). Perhaps the most eloquent statement of dissatisfaction with the resettlement programme was that 20% of those displaced immediately opted for cash and left the area. Of those who actually moved to the new villages only 40% remained in 1970, five years after resettlement (Kalitsi, 1973; Graham, 1986). According to Graham, many of those who moved were men who left wives and young children behind (Graham, 1986).

The Kpong Resettlement, a much smaller project implemented from 1980, some 15 years later, explicitly aimed to avoid the problems of the Akosombo Resettlement Project (Futa, 1983; Yeboah, 1999). Fifty five (55) small villages and one (1) suburban community displaced by the Kpong Dam were resettled in six new communities—Torgome, Fodzoku, South Senchi, Old Akrade, Natriku and West Kpong. The resettled were grouped into these communities based on ethnicity, proximity to their original communities and their status as rural or suburban. The six sites were chosen to ensure some distance from the Volta River to prevent schistosomiasis. In terms of housing, the core house concept used for the Akosombo resettlements was abandoned. Instead, houses were constructed for each family, their size based on what they had before the Dam. Other improvements include improved infrastructure and social services as well as innovations such as landing ramps for resettlement townships with large fishing populations (Yeboah, 1999).

Studies of the Kpong Dam Resettlement Project have suggested that while it was an improvement on the Akosombo Resettlement, some of the problems of Akosombo were reproduced (Taylor, 1973; Yeboah, 1977; Derban, 1985; Futa, 1983). A World Bank Evaluation Report confirmed that there were improvements in social services.

The majority of households considered the health facilities, schools
and agricultural extension services to be better than in their old villages (World Bank, 1993). Resettlement housing received a mixed
verdict, and transport, markets and water supply were not up to
expectation. Urinary schistosomiasis increased, especially in the resettlements closest to the river. The World Bank Report noted that
80% of the resettled considered themselves worse off in respect of
incomes and employment opportunities. The main problems settlers
reported in relation to livelihoods were the lack of agricultural equipment, land and capital.

As was the case of the Akosombo Dam Resettlement Project, the
timing of land clearing and the amount of land cleared were not
according to plan and irrigation plans were abandoned for financial
reasons. There were also land disputes in at least four of six planned
resettlements. The land available was inadequate, particularly when
farmers were expected to continue with their traditional methods of
agriculture. Average farm size declined from 3.4 hectares before resettlement to 0.8 hectares after resettlement and was even worse in
some communities where average holdings were down from 4.8 to
0.6 hectares. Land availability was a critical issue since for the majority of households, agriculture remained an important component of
the livelihood portfolio (World Bank, 1993).[12]

The resettlers' lack of legal title to housing and farmlands under
both the Akosombo and Kpong resettlement projects has been criticised. Graham noted that the government was considered the owner
of the land given to members of the communities resettled in 1965
on a 33-year lease. The land had to be inherited without being
divided and farmers could be ejected for refusing to adopt the recommended farming practices (1986). Yeboah thought this was a factor
in the "considerable litigation on agricultural plots" (1999, p. 132).
There was not much litigation on housing plots. The Authority was
working on giving legal titles for all housing plots within all its 58
resettlement townships. It hoped to tackle the problem of title to
farmlands in the future although it was expected to be a more difficult
process (Yeboah, 1999). The decision to tackle title to housing before
the problem of title to farmlands was a curious inversion of priorities. If there was little litigation on title to housing, why was that

---

[12] Some households had adapted to this situation by continuing to practise bush
fallowing with shorter fallow periods. This had implications for current and future
productivity of the land and for land relations.

being tackled before the more serious problem of title to farmlands?

By the early 70s, the VRA, under instructions from the government of the Second Republic, transferred responsibility for the Akosombo Dam resettlements to other government agencies, mainly the Ministry of Agriculture and the Ministry of Social Welfare. The former took responsibility for resettlement agriculture while the latter was in charge of the general welfare of the resettlers. Kalitsi felt that this was the right approach but had reservations about the timing of this decision. As he explained;

> We too were interested to see the local authorities extend their services and coverage to the settlements we had built. We could not imagine ourselves perpetually saddled by the settlements we had to administer. Our thinking was that they should develop as normal towns. They should learn to draw upon services of local, district, regional and national authorities and develop like any other communities in Ghana. However, some of us felt that they were not quite ready to be handed over at the time, but the question would be when would you have considered them ready? (Interview with K.K., Accra).

The transfer entailed the handover of substantial resources belonging to the VRA to the two Ministries. Kalitsi felt that this could have been a reason for the interest of the institutions in taking over the management of the resettlements. Because of the manner of the transfer, the VRA did not maintain a monitoring and advocacy role in relation to the resettlers (Interview with K.K., Accra). Events which followed the transfer showed that the two institutions were ill-equipped to address the particular problems of the resettled communities. The establishment of a specialised organisation would have been a more effective approach. Instead, these mainstream state agencies had to add this new assignment to their pre-existing responsibilities. Even more problematic was the lack of coordination between the two institutions and the central government. Kalitsi conceded that the VRA could have made a more strenuous effort to pay some attention to the resettlements, if its engineering focus had not been so overwhelming. However, in relation to the VRA townships, the engineering focus did not appear to get in the way. The minimalism in relation to resettlements was in sharp contrast to the elaborate provisions the VRA made for its own townships and workers over the years.[13]

---

[13] In one year, the Management committee for Akosombo met six times and discussed issues affecting the "orderly development of the township." In that same

While the VRA was happy to divest itself of responsibility towards the resettlements, it reported that by an executive instrument dated 30th May, 1989, issued by the Head of State, VRA was made the local authority of the Akosombo Township.[14] That the resettlements were not a priority was also expressed in the structure of the VRA's expenditures. Health and safety, under which affected communities' health issues were addressed, was only 1.1% of power sales. Only a fraction of this figure was devoted to affected populations around the Lake and in the resettlements. The VRA spent much more on administration (5.3%), Akosombo (1.2%) and Akuse (.24%) than on health and safety in 1987 (VRA, 1987).

As a response to the continuing problems of resettlement, the organisation established the VRA Resettlement Trust Fund to which it contributed half a million US dollars annually. As at 1999, the Trust Fund Deed was still being executed and, therefore, the money already paid into the Fund was yet to be disbursed (Yeboah, 1999).

4. The VRA and Migrant Fisher-Folk and their Communities: From Promoting Fisheries to Environmental Protection

Establishing the Volta Lake fisheries

From the start, the various initiatives around the Volta Lake concerned the establishment of the fisheries (Kalitsi, 1999; Yeboah, 1999). A number of problems were identified and tackled under the auspices of the Volta Lake Research and Development Project (VLRDP) established in 1968 by the Ghana government and UNDP.[15] These included the unsuitability of the canoes in use for fishing and Lake Transport (Devambez, 1970). The canoes were unstable in the new

---

year, some activities for the improvement of the township included new water works designed to serve the projected increase of the town's population to the year 2000 and a major slum and squatter clearing project. An afforestation programme and a programme of institutional housing were implemented at Akosombo from the 60s and extended to Akuse, Tema, Tamale, Techiman, Kumasi, Sunyani, Tamale and Bolgatanga over the years (VRA, 1987, 1989, 1991).

[14] Under the instrument, "VRA performs the functions of the District Assemblies in respect of Akosombo including development, rating, licensing and the regulation and control of specified activities". The executive instrument replaced the one issued in 1963, E.I. 106, by the first president of the Republic (VRA, 1989, p. 12).

[15] After a number of phased interventions, it was finally wound up between 1982 and 1983.

more open, windier and unpredictable environment of the Lake and fishermen had trouble visiting their nets in rough weather. The capsizing of canoes, the loss of equipment and drowning were common occurrences around the Lake in the early years (Devambez, 1970). Fishing in the deeper parts of the Lake was avoided by fishermen although its economic potential had been recognised and confirmed by experiments because of the canoe problem. For the same reason, fishermen tended to attend those markets closest to them as opposed to those where their fish would fetch the best prices and where they could access a wider range of supplies (Devambez, 1970).

The canoe problem was exacerbated by the presence of both emergent and submerged dead trees (Addo-Ashong, 1969; Devambez, 1970; Yeboah, 1999). The flooded trees provided the medium for the development of algae on which fish such as the *tilapia* species feed and were therefore a factor in the Volta Lake fish landings being over ten times those recorded from Lake Kariba (Petr, 1971), providing the unexpected added advantage of preventing the "sweeping of fish using illegal fishing methods" (VRA, undated). In spite of these advantages, the standing trees proved to be a long-term hazard and many fatal accidents on the Lake were attributed to them. Unsuitable fishing methods and equipment were also a constraining factor (Titiati and Gilbert, 1969a, 1969b).

In 1969, a decision was taken to develop a stronger type of canoe, assist fishermen all along the Lake with fishing gear at reasonable prices and train them in new fishing techniques and new technologies (Titiati and Gilbert, 1969a). The United Nations Food and Agricultural Organisation (FAO) began work on the modified canoe in mid 1970 (Coppola and Agadzi, 1977). Mono-filament nets, which caught more fish than the traditional multi-filament nets, canoes fitted with outboard motors for fishing and improved transport boats for carrying fish and food crops to markets, were introduced. Fish-smoking techniques which dramatically increased the shelf life of smoked fish from a few to at least 30 days were introduced (Kalitsi, 1999). The VRA also cleared some of the trees within the Lake to improve safety on routes to major markets around the Lake (Yeboah, 1999). While the use of mono-filament nets caught on, the introduction of safer fishing and transport vessels was not very successful in spite of legislative backing (Yeboah, 1999).[16]

---

[16] The VRA in 1973 passed a Legislative Instrument, L.I. 862 to regulate traffic

In addition to these measures, a Master Plan was prepared for Lake Fisheries. An important component of the plan was the establishment of a number of Fishery Complexes around the Lake. The Kpando Torkor Complex, built in 1975, was the first of these to be implemented. Others in the plan included Yeji, Buipe, Kwamikrom, Dambai and Ampem. Of these, only the Yeji Complex, established in 1993 by the VRA and the Fisheries Department with United Nations Development Programme (UNDP) support, has so far been established (Kalitsi, 1999; Yeboah, 1999).[17] Each complex was to have fish landing, processing and marketing, boat-building and training facilities where fishermen could purchase the inputs they needed and learn about new techniques.

The Lake Fisheries in general and the Kpando Torkor Complex were originally run by the VRA. However, in 1983, the VRA handed over management of the Lake fisheries to the Fisheries Department. Kalitsi (1999) has argued that the handover was possible because the goals of developing efficient methods of fishing, improved canoes and nets as well as more effective fish processing and preservation techniques had been achieved. Gordon (1999), on the other hand, has argued that the VRA withdrew from Lake Fisheries because of falling revenues from power generation, leaving its responsibilities to the Fisheries Department which has been unable to carry out its statutory functions and provide leadership because of serious resource constraints. This problem was exacerbated by the lack of co-operation and communication among the various organisations involved in the Volta Lake and an outdated legal and policy framework. Added to this, in the last decade, the VRA's priorities have shifted from fishing as it became more focused on the protection of the Dam and Lake, environmental degradation and the health of communities around the Lake. The next section focuses on this cluster of interests.

---

on the Lake. While the instrument made provisions for the registration and licensing of boats and the regulation of the types of vessels in use on the Lake, the machinery for enforcing these regulations was too weak to do the job (Yeboah, 1999).

[17] An innovation in the case of this complex was the development of woodlots for fish processing because of concerns about deforestation.

Defining and addressing environmental problems

The VRA's environmental management programme around the Volta Lake consisted of a number of measures including afforestation, minimising tree cover depletion and allowing the natural regeneration of depleted tree cover.[18] Others were the provision of healthcare for neighbouring and affected communities, dealing with tree stumps in the Lake and tackling aquatic weeds in the Volta Lake, the Kpong Headpond and the Volta River itself (VRA, undated). The VRA Annual Reports detailed some of these ongoing strategies and their results.

Safeguarding the health of communities

The Akosombo Hospital and a Health and Safety Department were in charge of sanitation and public health and for ensuring that the VRP caused as little adverse effect on the surrounding population as possible (VRA, 1989, p. 7). However, in reports about infectious disease outbreaks, there was always the underlying implication that the control of diseases in neighbouring communities was ultimately to protect the inhabitants of Akosombo from such diseases.[19] One of the earliest concrete references to the health of Lakeside settlements was in the 1991 Annual Report. It said that the VRA's medical boat "*Onipa Nua*"[20] had provided health education and medical services to the Lakeside population throughout that year (VRA, 1991; see also 1992). In 1992, the boat made ten voyages covering 47 Lakeside communities. Around the resettlements and villages along the Kpong Headpond, about 7,738 inhabitants were treated.[21] The

---

[18] Undated VRA document written in or later than 1999.

[19] Public health services typically include sanitation services, pest control, environmental sanitation and special programmes to control schistosomiasis and malaria (VRA, 1988, 1989).

[20] The hospital boat purchased and fitted at the cost of 500 million cedis in 1990 (VRA, 1992, p. 10). The boat, which travels from village to village along the Lake, brings medical services to inaccessible communities. It is run at an estimated annual cost of 1 billion cedis (Yeboah, 1999, p. 129).

[21] The statistics for clinical cases was revealing. In 1992, 11,046 persons with various diseases and 11,890 schistosomiasis cases were treated, i.e. there were more such cases than all other diseases put together (1992, p. 31). Other services rendered that year include maternal and child health services to 16,424 children and 8,987 mothers and the construction of 80 improved pit latrines (1992).

growing incidence of schistosomiasis was a matter of concern to the VRA for decades. As the Annual Report of 1992 indicated, "snail prospecting results revealed high populations of schistosomiasis vector snails in the Lake and Lower Volta area. The surveillance of aquatic weeds also revealed high densities of submerged weeds which are noted for accelerating the siltation which reduces the volume of water for power generation" (1992, p. 32). The weeds were of concern to both the VRA and the inhabitants, but for different reasons. For the VRA, it was their threat to power generation. Therefore, the organisation's focus was the Volta Lake and the Kpong Headpond.[22]

For over three decades, the VRA sought to tackle schistosomiasis, a diseases it believed was best controlled by the avoidance or reduction of water contact, even while acknowledging that changing human behaviour was difficult. It, therefore, discussed its control in terms of an integrated strategy of chemotherapy, the control of weeds and snails by manual and mechanical clearing and health education. It also involved the provision of sanitary facilities such as urinals and toilets as well as the provision of the medical boat especially for communities that could only be reached by boat. There was explicit policy to avoid chemical control of the snail population for ecological reasons (Kalitsi, 1999; Yeboah, 1999). From the point of view of affected communities though, a more fundamental approach to the problem of aquatic weeds and the snail vectors was necessary to eradicate schistosomiasis which has remained a serious problem in spite of all the efforts.

Safeguarding the Dams, the Volta Gorge and the Volta Lake

The VRA's position is that agriculture and other land-use activities around the Volta Lake and the Volta's tributaries contribute to the sedimentation of the Lake, ultimately affecting the power production capacity of the VRP.[23] Such activities include unplanned human

---

[22] Thus the VRA reported that in 1988 there was effective surveillance at the Kpong generation intake to remove aquatic weeds "which threatened the power plant" (1988, p. 25; see also 1989).

[23] By the 90s, both the intake area of the Akosombo powerhouse and the cooling pipes of the generators were showing evidence of sedimentation. This was said to have an adverse effect on the cooling system of the generators (VRA, undated).

settlement along the Lake, farming on high slopes, land clearing practices and the cutting down of trees for firewood and charcoal (VRA, undated; Yeboah, 1999; see also Amatekpor, 1999). The VRA commissioned two studies in 1994 to address the problem of land-slides, shoreline erosion around the Volta Lake and sedimentation in the Lake and in the neighbourhood of the powerhouse.[24] In 1998, the VBRP was also tasked to provide information on the magnitude of deforestation, erosion and siltation in the 138 sq. kilometre gorge, an area of 1.5 kilometres on each side of the Lake and 30 kilometres upstream from the dam at Akosombo.[25] All three studies took a serious view of the threat to the health of the Lake and ultimately the hydroelectric power generation potential of the dams represented by landslides, erosion and sedimentation. The first two studies recommended afforestation and further studies on sedimentation. The VBRP study recommended an integrated approach of mitigation measures and management of the gorge and other sectors of the Volta Basin. The study also recommended the prohibition, restriction, protection or reservation of all communities within 1.5 kilometres of the lakeshore, the degree of restriction depending on the environmental sensitivity of the area and the actual level of degradation. Other recommendations were the extension of tree planting in the gorge area to the entire protection zone and the protection of reforested areas from bush fires. To arrest major rock slippage, it was recommended that the steep slopes around the Lake be planted with stronger trees. The promotion of communal and individual woodlots, alternative domestic energy sources such as LPG and sawmill dust and fuel saving technology were recommended to reduce the human factor in tree depletion. In addition, intensive farming methods were recommended to replace the extensive migratory systems and fishing methods such as bamboo traps were to be banned (VBRP, 1998). The VRA also asked the Water Research Institute (WRI) to carry out pollution studies in May 1997 to acquire baseline data on the hydrobiology of the Lake as a basis for assessing future pollution and mitigation measures. The study found the lake water reasonably good for drinking and recommended the provision

---

[24] The studies were conducted by Conterra Ltd., a Ghanaian company and Bidex Consult, respectively.
[25] The VBRP study provided the basis for a document produced by the Ministry of Environment, Science and Technology (MEST).

of sanitary facilities to reduce levels of bacterial contamination. The study also found that the use of fertiliser in the area had supported the proliferation of aquatic weeds and algae. It also confirmed the high prevalence of malaria, diarrhoea and schistosomiasis.

In 1994, farming along the slopes of the gorge area of the Lake was banned by the Ministry of Environment, Science and Technology (MEST) as a response to the findings of the two studies. Non-farm economic activities such as beekeeping were introduced in 1999. Following the VBRP study, the Ministry went even further, proposing a ban on settlement in the most critical areas of the gorge area, from the hilltops to the shores of the Lake. This was an area of 94 sq. kilometres. The settlement ban was to be accompanied by the prohibition of bush burning, farming, wood harvesting and all other forms of economic activity that would adversely affect the environment. Fishing was the only economic activity not affected by the ban (VRA, undated).

Populations affected by the ban were to be resettled in more sparsely populated places in the area. Phrases such as "humane" and "socio-economically better off than before", were used in the literature with regard to this group of people. They were to be spared under-compensation and socio-economic deprivations, which have been the hallmark of resettlement in the past. Fisher-folk would continue to enjoy fishing rights in the gorge area even after resettlement (VRA, undated). A programme of afforestation was also introduced. The Volta Gorge Afforestation Project was started in May 1994 to protect and grow forests in an estimated 7,000 hectares on both banks of the Volta Lake.[26] Another effort, the Tree Cover Depletion Minimisation (TCDM) Project, also initiated in 1994 at Yeji, a low slope area in the northern part of the Volta Lake, under the direction of the Fisheries Department. The Authority provided funds to the tune of one hundred and thirty thousand, seven hundred and seventy five dollars (US$132,775) for this Project.[27]

---

[26] By the end of 1997, the Volta Gorge Area Protection programme had planted a total of 1,100 hectares with 2,750,000 seedlings. In addition, more than 72.5 kilometres of a one metre wide fire belt was constructed to protect the afforestation area from bush fires. Forty eight settler communities in the protected area were sensitised to prevent farming along the slopes of the gorge area.

[27] It was to restore over a thousand acres of lost tree-cover and minimise tree depletion through the promotion of fuel efficient and energy saving devices for fish processing and household use within a hundred and fifty two (152) villages. According

From the foregoing, it can be argued that the search for coinciding interests permeated VRA's relationship with Lakeside communities. In this connection, concerns about the health of the dam were critical in determining policies towards Lakeside communities. The changing policy on draw-down[28] agriculture was a good example of this. As Kalitsi noted, there had been something of a U-turn on this issue anchored in new thinking about the protection of reservoirs and ultimately dams. Draw-down agriculture which had been encouraged up until the mid 90s was banned because afforestation was now preferred to agriculture and human settlement as it protected the life of the dam and the explosion of diseases around the Lake (KK, Accra).

No process of consultation and negotiation took place over this change in policy. Instead, instructions were handed down to Lakeside communities and some public education undertaken by the VRA. Subsequently, forestry employees were mandated to destroy the farms of persons who persisted in farming on the hillsides and the draw-down area. The Military was called in to police the Volta Gorge to ensure that the slopes were not farmed. The decision to ban draw-down agriculture was a continuing source of tensions in the Lakeside communities affected by the ban.

5. Downstream Communities

In relation to downstream communities, the VRA always maintained that except for issues of flooding and salinity clearly set out in the Volta River Development Act, 1961, it did not have the mandate to address their VRP related problems.[29] This position, derived from

---

to the VRA, one thousand, two hundred and eighty two (1,282) acres of tree-cover were restored on the banks of the Volta River and fifty nine (59) rural integrated fish processing facilities were established by the end of the first phase of the project in December 1998. This was calculated to have contributed to 60% minimisation of tree resources depletion (VRA, 1997; VRA, undated).

[28] The draw-down area has been defined as "all the land bordering the Volta Lake, which is alternately flooded and then exposed as a result of the seasonal fluctuations in the level of water in the Lake" (Amatekpor, 1970; see also Ahn, 1970). The size of the draw-down is estimated at 211,000 acres (85,455 hectares) assuming a ten-foot fall in the water level in the Lake between seasons (Amatekpor, 1970). Ahn has noted that its importance for agriculture is significant.

[29] As has been indicated, Article 11 of the Act enjoins the Authority to control

the Act setting up the VRA was buttressed by government policy that long-term issues of affected communities would be taken up by the Ministries of Social Welfare and Agriculture. However, these institutions did not have the resources, institutional arrangements or the support to execute this informal mandate. The VRA often argued that it had gone beyond the call of duty in spending about three times what it was expected to on environmental impacts. This view, which externalised the costs of damming the Volta, was paradoxically defended in terms of the commercial calculations around the Project:

> VRA tended to look to the government to implement some of the recommendations. This the VRA had to do to prevent its expenditures from escalating and putting pressure on the price of electricity (KK, Accra).

Community leaders in the Lower Volta did not agree with this interpretation of the VRA Act. In a recent statement (30/8/2001) community leaders, while conceding the Act's silence about the Lower Volta, argued that under article 17, the VRA had incidental powers to carry out any activity in relation to the discharge of its functions. The implication here was that studies and actions in the Lower Volta were legal under this clause.[30] However, the only functions related to the Lower Volta in the Act were with respect to water flow and flooding (Article 11). It therefore required a very broad interpretation of the Act to come to this conclusion, something the VRA was not equipped nor inclined to do. This section examines the VRA's record in the areas of acknowledged responsibility as well as its performance in relation to the other issues raised by the people of the Lower Volta such as transport, river pollution, health and livelihoods.

Areas of acknowledged responsibility: Flooding and salinity
Between 1963 and 1968, the flooding of the Volta River was one of the most contentious issues between the people and businesses in

---

the Dam to prevent the harmful penetration of salt water up the river, the rising of the Lake to a height greater than 280 ft above mean sea level and the flooding of the downstream beyond pre-dam levels.

[30] The article in question says "The Authority may carry on any activity which is reasonably requisite or convenient for or in connection with the discharge of its functions under this Act" (Article 17, Volta River Development Act, 1961).

the Lower Volta and the Volta River Authority. Although the Lower Volta had always experienced annual floods, in 1963, the heaviest floods of the Volta River in living memory occurred. The VRA put this down to high levels of rainfall in the West African Region. However, the waters of the river had been diverted into a 200 foot channel so dam construction could continue during the floods (Moxon, 1984, p. 129). Therefore, the information circulating in the Lower Volta at this time was that the VRA was responsible for the floods. In 1967, areas in the Lower Volta were again flooded, this time because of spillage from the Dam by the VRA. Property consisting of canoes, clam beds, houses and firewood was destroyed downstream.[31] This time, VRA admitted that it should have notified the people downstream of the impending spillage so they could prepare, although the organisation declined to compensate the people for their losses.[32] Again in 1968, there was flooding because more water than usual had to be released from the Dam. The Ministry of Agriculture wrote to VRA complaining about the destruction of its water pumps.[33] A private citizen wrote a strong letter about the same issue[34] as did some farming enterprises.[35]

The VRA argued that it had released that amount of water because of the heavy rainfall in Ghana as a whole. It also stated that but for the Dam, the situation would have been worse downstream.[36] However, the affected companies and irrigation projects were there in the first place as the non-power benefits of the Dam and had been given assurances that the VRA flood control programme would protect their interests. In the Lower Volta, property would not have been built in areas traditionally affected by the floods if there was not the perception and expectation generated by Government of Ghana and VRA publicity that there would be no more floods. In 1969, the Tongu Youth Association requested that the VRA time

---

[31] Letter from Evangelical Presbyterian Church Hospital, Adidome 14/2/1967; Letter from chief of Volo, a centre of heavy clam farming in the Lower Volta—13/2/1967.

[32] VRA letter to Volo chief 13/3/1967; VRA letter to Evangelical Presbyterian Church Adidome—11/3/1967.

[33] Letter from Ministry of Agriculture to VRA—13/11/1968.

[34] Letter to VRA, 14/9/1968.

[35] Mentiase Farming Enterprises to VRA—11/9/1968; Volta River District Co-operative Sugar Cane Growers Union Ltd. to VRA—12/9/1968.

[36] VRA to Mentiase Enterprises—19/9/1969; VRA to Nana Idan Owuodai VIII of Ayeldu—16/10/1968.

its future annual spillage to coincide with the traditional flooding
season to avoid the destruction of crops as occurred in 1968 and
allow floodplain agriculture to continue.[37] The VRA's response was
that its timing was dictated by the need to create space for the next
flood in order to avoid the high discharges which were so harmful
to downstream property. According to the VRA letter, the minor
spillage it was planning would not cause hardship.[38]

The Ministry of Agriculture wrote to the VRA arguing that the
Dam was multi-purpose and, therefore, all aspects of its operations
had to be kept in mind by the VRA in its decisions about spillage.[39]
The VRA wrote back saying that the purpose of continuous power
supply was paramount and all other purposes were subject to this.[40]
A UNDP team was commissioned to look into the problem of flooding
in the Lower Volta and Keta areas. In its preliminary notes, the
team argued that "the exceptional discharge in September 1968 was
a consequence of the strict application of purely theoretical recommendations" (UNDP, 1968). It urged the VRA to acquire additional
information for the whole of the area before making decisions about
spillage. It also recommended that in the future, in the interest of
agricultural development, exceptional discharges had to be avoided.[41]
These views were in sharp contrast to the VRA's insistence on the
correctness and inevitability of the timing and quantities of its spillage
programme and the pre-eminence of power supply considerations.[42]
The flood control issue resolved itself when from the 1980s spillages
were no longer necessary because water levels in the dam became
almost permanently low. The concern then shifted from how much
water was going into the Lower Volta to how little water was enter-
ing it.

The drinking water problem, which was almost as old as the flood-
control issue, was however more intransigent. An important aspect
of the problem was the level of salinity of the river. During the construction of the dam, the low levels of the river created conditions

---

[37] Tongu Youth Association to VRA—8/2/1969.
[38] VRA to Tongu Youth Association—12/2/1969.
[39] Ministry of Agriculture to VRA—13/11/1968.
[40] VRA to Ministry of Agriculture—2/12/1968.
[41] UNDP, Preliminary Findings—19/12/1968.
[42] The Preparatory Commission had called for flexibility in spillage after the construction of the Akosombo Dam, to safeguard the wellbeing of the communities
downstream, while not wasting water, power and money (Paragraph 357, p. 139).

where seawater travelled further up the river than usually occurred before the Project.[43] In 1954, the Preparatory Commission found that most of the riverine communities in the Lower Volta were within easy reach of the Volta or one of its permanent connections from which good quality water could be acquired. The Preparatory Commission had recommended that in order to safeguard the water supply, up to 5,000 cusecs be released for whatever period was required in order to prevent undue penetration of salt water. This would prevent damage to drinking water with secondary effects on fishing and agriculture.[44] The VRA was unable to follow the recommendation of 5,000 cusecs and maintained water flow at 1,200 cusecs during the dam construction period. The result of this was that the traditional period of salt water penetration (February to March) began much earlier, in November, and was expected to last even longer than April.[45] In 1964, the level of the water fell even lower to 800 cusecs, contrary to assurances by the VRA that the 1,200 cusecs level was not likely to change before September 1965 when it was likely to go up to 6,000 cusecs and be maintained at that level.[46] This rendered the water unfit for human consumption from the Delta up to Sogakope in the mid section of the Lower Volta, threatening water supply to the Kpong Water Works, which supplied water to Tema.[47] The MP for South Tongu, B.A. Konu, wrote to the VRA stating that the failure to provide drinking water to the riparian communities in the Lower Volta was a serious omission in the compensatory measures proposed for affected communities. This was because the longer post-dam duration of saltwater penetration was having an adverse impact not only on drinking water, but also on fishing and agriculture. The MP, therefore, demanded that the VRA provide drinking water to all the villages affected, pay

---

[43] The Sogakope Secondary School, for example, claimed expenses from the VRA for the supply of fresh water to the school between January and March 1965. Although a cheque was sent to the School to cover the claim, the VRA made clear that it was not accepting liability for the high level of salinity of the water in the area (Sogakope Secondary School to VRA—13/3/1967; VRA to Sogakope Secondary School—22/5/1967).

[44] Paragraph 357; Appendix VII, p. 139.

[45] Letter from South Tongu MP, Mr. B.A. Konu to the VRA—11/1/1965.

[46] VRA to the Ministry of Works and Housing—22/10/1964.

[47] Memo from Ministry of Works and Housing to VRA dated 25/11/1964 with covering letter dated 1/12/1964.

for the hiring of water tankers by the regional organisation and the Sogakope Secondary School. The MP's letter took the opportunity to ask the VRA to disclose what compensatory provisions it had made for the people of the Lower Volta with respect to the fishing industry and agriculture.[48]

The VRA, while acknowledging the reduction in the flow of water to the Lower Volta due to technical problems, argued that based on its scientific investigations, the problem existed before the Volta River Project. It also requested proof of differences between past and the current levels of salinity, raising the question of how local communities acquired good drinking water during periods of high salinity in the past and why these sources were not being used to deal with the crisis.

Similarly, in response to a letter from Agave (which is immediately upstream from the estuary) requesting that pipe-borne water be provided to the area since the river had become too salty for human consumption, the Authority argued that water supply was a matter for the Water Supplies Division and, therefore, the Regional Commissioner, and not the VRA. As was already becoming its normal practice, the VRA argued that the salinity problem of the lower reaches of the Volta could not be blamed entirely on the Dam.[49] Nearly two decades after the debates of the 1960s about salinity during the construction of the dam, the VRA continued to deny any linkage between the dam and salinity.[50] However, part of the scientific evidence the VRA was relying on, had specifically made a connection between the Akosombo Dam and the problem. The VRA Hydrologist's Report had stated specifically:

> from January to July, the volume of fresh water flowing downstream into the sea averages about 15 times the magnitude if the Dam had not been there. This eliminates salt water intrusion, which would normally occur during the dry months.[51]

---

[48] What is interesting is that the letter based its demands on the Preparatory Commission provisions and the Volta River Development Act, clause 11 (a) (Letter from Konu, MP, South Tongu to the Chief Executive of VRA, 11/1/1965).
[49] Volta Regional House of Chiefs to VRA—8/5/1965; VRA to Volta Regional House of Chiefs—25/10/1965.
[50] Citizen to VRA, May 1979. VRA to Citizen—11/10/1979.
[51] Hydrologist Report, VRA—11/10/1979.

In addition to the salinity issue, there was a growing problem of river pollution. Industrial waste from the industries situated along the Volta River, which were established after the Akosombo dam, has been an additional source of stress on the river. In the 1970s, there were indications of growing public concern about industrial waste in the Volta and its implications for the health of communities that depended on the river for water supply and their livelihood.[52] The Ministry of Health was of the view that, even if the communities were provided with alternative sources of drinking water, the pollution of the river would still affect aquatic life and, therefore, have economic and social consequences. In a letter to the then Ghana Water and Sewerage Corporation, the Ministry wrote that "there can be no doubt that a serious threat to public health is inevitable if dangerous levels of pollution have not already been reached" (1973).[53] The VRA responded, "as the local authority responsible for the township of Akosombo" by writing to the Akosombo Textiles Corporation about the pollution of the Volta River by the factory's activities.[54] In 1976, a petition to the VRA from the Tongu District Executive referred to pollution from the industrial waste of the textile and sugar factories and the sewage system of Akosombo and other townships.[55]

By the 1980s, the problem of aquatic vegetation had become serious. Again, the VRA declined to take responsibility for this problem. In 1981, the Tongu District Council wrote to VRA complaining about the growing density of aquatic weeds in the Volta and requesting that the river be flooded periodically to clear them.[56] The VRA responded by asking the Council to contact the Environmental Protection Council and the Institute of Aquatic Biology for chemicals to control the problem.[57]

---

[52] The Environmental Health Division of the Ministry of Health wrote to the Ghana Water and Sewerage Corporation (GWSC) to this effect—18/5/1973.

[53] The Ministry, therefore, proposed that the GWSC liaise with the relevant institutions and agencies to monitor and address the issue. Specifically, it was to identify the pollutants, the levels of pollution of the river and aquatic life, changes in the ecosystem and their implications for health and welfare of riverine communities. The outcome of this process was to be the formulation of measures to solve the problems (Ministry of Health to GWSC—18/5/1973).

[54] VRA to Akosombo Textiles—3/9/1973.

[55] Tongu District Executive to VRA—26/5/1976.

[56] Tongu District Council to VRA—1/12/1981.

[57] VRA to Tongu District Council—3/2/1982.

Problems outside the mandate: Communications, river pollution and livelihoods

Communications

Both Lawson and the Preparatory Commission observed that the Lower Volta prior to the dams had poor land and river communications. There was only one motor boat on the river at the time (Lawson, 1967; Preparatory Commission, paragraph 230). The Commission attributed this to the high fluctuations in water levels during the flood and off-flood seasons (paragraph 230) and predicted that the dam would result in a more regular flow of the Volta, which would increase its use as a means of communication. This view was to prove optimistic. In January 1965, Mr. Kalitsi, then Resettlement Officer, wrote an internal memo to the Chief Engineer reporting that the VRA had been asked to pay for the construction of a road between Kpodoi and Volo to serve communities on the eastern bank of the Lower Volta. The road was needed because the serious fall in the level of the river downstream had disabled the launch, the major means of communication in this area from operating.[58] The memo, which stated that the problem was temporary, recommended temporary road works funded by the VRA, to assure access to the area.[59]

The Design Engineer of VRA in an internal memorandum to the Chief Engineer established the relationship between the dam and the problem of river transport. He also stated that the problem would be permanent because of the lower levels of river-flow after the dam and the problem of siltation. Therefore, he recommended the dredging of the river in its lower reaches and the sale of the gravel obtained to building contractors in the area to offset the cost of the operation. However, he criticised the idea of road construction as uneconomical.[60] The VRA however disputed the link established in the memo, blaming the high floods of 1963 instead for the problems of river transport. The organisation also denied any obligation to finance road works or the dredging of the river.[61] The Ministry of Works,

---

[58] Mr. Kalitsi to Chief Engineer—11/1/1965. The importance of the launch to the Lower Volta was because of the poor state of other forms of transport (Lawson, 1972).

[59] VRA Internal Memo—11/1/1965.

[60] Internal Memo from Design Engineer to Chief Engineer—1/4//1965.

[61] Internal Memo from Chief Engineer to Chief Executive—1/4/1965.

however, insisted that the dam was responsible of the shallowness of the riverbed and problems with water transport. It therefore requested the VRA to release a promised grant of 24,000 cedis as contribution to a road estimated at 144,000 cedis.[62]

Road and river transport in the Lower Volta Basin remained quite poor. The launch service from Akuse to Ada has been operating intermittently. A number of feeder and first class roads had been built in the area, but not by the VRA. In 1999, the Volta Basin Research Project (VBRP) study found that roads in the Lower Volta Basin remained very poor, impeding the movement of goods and people and, therefore, economic and social development. River transport, represented mainly by the launch service from Akuse to Ada, was described as very slow, requiring from eight to twelve hours of travel to the final destination. Much of the travel, which employed small canoes, was hazardous because of the proliferation of aquatic vegetation and the quality of vessels. The study described the area as an enclave in most parts, recommending the clearing of aquatic weeds, the provision of outboard motors, improvements in the launch service as well as a major road rehabilitation programme (VBRP, 1999, pp. 38–39).

The problem of livelihoods: From silence to impact studies

Livelihoods had long been a contentious issue between the VRA and downstream communities. For decades, the VRA would not be drawn on this issue. Most of the VRA's annual budgetary allocation of $2 million (about 2–5% of its recurrent budget) for affected communities had hitherto been spent establishing a Resettlement Trust Fund, studies on the Keta Lagoon and on dredging the Estuary. However, in response to pressure from local communities and from influential persons within past and present governments, the VRA decided to investigate this persisting problem.

In 1996, the VRA commissioned the Volta Basin Research Project (VBRP) of the University of Ghana to study the environmental impact assessment of the dams on the Lower Volta Basin. In 1997, the first phase of the research was carried out. The study was to generate recommendations for addressing some of the adverse effects of the dams and promote the effective management of the environment

---

[62] VRA to Ministry of Works—29/10/1965. Ministry of Works to VRA—23/12/1965.

and resources of the Lower Volta Basin.[63] Some of the preliminary
findings were presented to VRA officials, government officials, chiefs,
MPs, District Chief Executives, NGOs and community representatives in 2000. The study, completed in January 2000, confirmed
many of the complaints about livelihoods which people in the Lower
Volta had been making for decades. The VBRP together with the
VRA organised a National Conference in August 2001 to discuss
the findings with the view to seeking support for implementing the
recommendations. These and other recommendations are discussed
in the concluding chapter of the book. Even before the study was
completed, the VRA was in consultation with the Ghana Water
Company Ltd. (GWCL), to provide water for 20 communities estimated at £2,960,000.00 and looking for external funding for the
project. During the 2001 National Conference on the Lower Volta,
a group of concerned citizens issued a statement saying they had
"reservations about some of the conclusions and recommendations."
The statement said the recommendations were not comprehensive
and fell short of the expectations and aspirations of the people. Thus
far, there have been no signs of a systematic and comprehensive
response to the problems confirmed by the studies.

6. Responses to Dam Impacts and State and VRA Policies: The Politics of Compensation and Development Projects

The politics of compensation

From the discussion above, there are clear indications that communities in the Lower Volta have tried in various ways to draw the
attention of the government and the VRA to their VRP-related problems. This section of the chapter discusses community responses in
some detail to draw attention to these efforts and their outcomes.
Of particular interest here are the factors shaping community responses

---

[63] The area has 403 communities in four districts—North and South Tongu in
the Volta Region, and East and West Dangme in the Greater Accra Region with
156, 154, 49 and 44 communities respectively (VRA Document, undated). The
VRA was more specific. It hoped that the research would lead to the revival of
the creek fishing and clam picking industries, improve agriculture along the banks
of the Lower Volta and control schistosomiasis specifically and improve health in
general (Yeboah, 1999).

and why, like other dam-affected groups, communities in the Lower Volta have generally not been able to secure satisfactory redress for their problems. Community responses are those initiatives and measures which have taken place in different communities, settlements and Districts to demand some form of redress for the problems of the Lower Volta. Designating them as community responses is not to convey the idea of a strict separation between community and household level responses or to argue that there is necessarily community mobilisation and decision making around these issues. The term is used to denote the fact that those who speak and act on these issues, claim to do so as community leaders working for the benefit of the community as a whole or some groups within it.

Community responses in the Lower Volta and at Sokpoe and Mepe in particular, have had two broad strands. In the period soon after the VRP started, there were demands for compensation for the loss of property during the floods in 1963 and during the unannounced release of large quantities of water by the VRA in 1969. Other demands were for the restoration of the Lower stretch of the Volta to its pre-dam vitality and usefulness,[64] compensation for the loss of clams and other sources of livelihood. These demands were made through petitions directed to the VRA by different levels of leadership—the Members of Parliament for the area, chiefs, town development and youth associations and the Tongu District Council.

A number of entries in the Minutes Book of the Tongu District Council, for example, give a window into how the Council approached the issue. At its third meeting of 10th December 1953, the Chairman of the then Tongu District Council,[65] Rev. S.A. Dzirasa, was reported to have "disclosed the near future problems in Tongu when the Volta River Project (Dam) is in its full operation."[66] A Councillor

---

[64] It was recommended that this be done by dredging the riverbed and by regular and judicious releases of water from the Dam.

[65] In the 1950s, the Tongu District was divided into four sections—Upper, Central, Lower and East Tongu. Sokpoe was in Lower Tongu while Mepe was in Upper Tongu. The Council has gone through several changes over the years. It was dissolved and reconstituted after the 1966 coup d'état. An interim management committee ran its affairs during the dissolution. In 1992, however, a major change took place when the District was divided into two—North and South Tongu. After this, the minutes book continued to be used to record the affairs of the South Tongu District Assembly.

[66] Among the problems he mentioned were the scarcity of good water supply, shortages of fish and food resulting in famine, and the migration of local people.

moved a resolution which was unanimously adopted that a memorandum be prepared and sent to the Prime Minister of the Gold
Coast for a joint discussion with him and the chiefs, local council-
lors and associations in Tongu.

On 29th June 1965, after the Volta Lake had formed, the Council
agreed that "in view of the heavy emigration of fishermen from the
Tongu District to the Volta Lake, the revenue realisable from rates
should be drastically reduced". It was estimated that if the present
rate of emigration continued, the Council might lose about half its
present rateable population (Minutes Book of the Tongu District
Council, 1953 to 1998). After the overthrow of the Nkrumah Regime,
in 1966, the Tongu District authorities again put their grievances
before the new government of the National Liberation Council (NLC).
On 31st March 1969, the 27th Emergency meeting of the Tongu
Local Council Management Committee resolved to send a delegation to meet with the Chairman of the NLC for a special grant for
re-housing schools in the Tongu District and an "Equalisation Grant"
for the Council.[67] On 5th October 1969, the Council meeting was
given a report of the visit. The delegation met with the welfare
officers of the VRA[68] in Accra on 16th September 1969 and discussed "in detail how the Volta River project damaged many schools
and private properties and contributed to the loss of sources of income
to the people of the Tongu District." The Welfare Officers had
promised to offer some resolution to the problems outlined by the
delegates (Minutes Book of the Tongu District Council).[69]

---

[67] The rationale for this request was a) the deplorable condition of school buildings due to the ravage caused by the 1963 Volta Floods and b) that most of the
rate-payers in the Council area had migrated to the Akosombo Dam site because
of the lack of industries in the area (Minutes Book, 1969). Another entry in the
Minutes Book said the Clerk of the Council was instructed to arrange an appointment with the chief executive of the VRA in Accra on Friday, 15th August 1968.
The matter for discussion was "How the Volta River Project Affects the Tongu
District" (Minutes of 23/7/69).

[68] Note the gradual downgrading of the meeting, most likely by the Government.
It had started as a desire to meet the Head of Government, became a planned
meeting with the head of the VRA, and finally what took place was a meeting with
the welfare officers of the VRA.

[69] This matter of flood damage to schools came up again in 1968 (18/9/1968)
and was still an issue in 1973 (13th September 1973; Minutes of the 6th Ordinary
meeting of the Interim Tongu Local Council Management Committee).

During the second meeting of the Reconstituted Tongu District Council (20th and 21st August 1975),[70] the second day was devoted to a discussion of the "effects of the Akosombo Dam on the people living around the Volta River".[71] The Council decided that an ad hoc committee be appointed to visit the towns and villages along the Volta Basin to find out any problems that might have arisen as a result of the Volta Dam. At the 4th ordinary meeting of the Tongu District Council on 21st May 1976, the chairman stated that a report on the effects of the Akosombo Dam on life and property of the people of the Tongu District had been sent to the various bodies concerned with the Dam.[72] The strategy of statements and petitions emanating from District level continued through changes in government and changes in the District level structures without any substantial results.

In 1993, the District Assembly decided to apply to the government for compensation. This was based on information from the then MP for North Tongu that the government "wanted" to compensate all those who had suffered losses in the floods. Forms were sent out to be filled by people who had lost property in the floods of both 1963 and 1968/69 and sent to the Volta Regional Administration at Ho. The Regional Administration said that they were forwarding the names to the VRA (Interview with Assemblyman, Sokpoe). The MP for South Tongu also followed up on the claims and received assurances from the Regional Administration that some action was being taken. Claimants contributed money to process their claims at the Volta Regional Administration at Ho.

The then MP of North Tongu was reported around 1996 to be saying that VRA's policy had changed. Kalitsi confirms that there was indeed a change in VRA policy. While the organisation was willing to give money for development projects based on the priorities of communities, it would not pay individuals compensation. This was mainly because of the difficulties with verifying actual losses after

[70] The new Council was inaugurated in June 1974 but it had held its first meeting on 16th May 1975.
[71] The Council listed the following problems—schistosomiasis among school children, the disappearance of oyster from the water, and the growth of weeds in the riverbed arising from the slowing of the river's current due to the Dam.
[72] Because of gaps in the Minutes Book, there is no record of what further actions were taken in this matter.

so much time had elapsed (KK, Accra). The VRA's policy change, notwithstanding, the issue of compensation for flood losses and more general dam impacts was still very alive in the Lower Volta. In 2001, a statement issued by the "Concerned Citizens of the Tongu Area" during the VRA National Conference on the Lower Volta mentioned dam impacts and compensation for flood losses (Concerned Citizens, 2001).[73]

Compensation demands had been made with regard to both flood losses and the general loss of livelihoods. However, the narrower agenda of flood losses was more vigorously pursued. Perhaps it was felt that pursuing compensation for tangible losses such as houses, livestock and farms would be easier than for the less easily quantifiable losses of a wider and more diffuse range of victims.

In accordance with its new policy on compensation and as an outcome of negotiations with them, the VRA delivered 400 electric poles to the Tongu MPs, which were then distributed in consultation with the District Chief Executive (DCE). The Sokpoe chiefs disagreed with this new approach to flood losses because it was not the outcome of negotiations involving them. Secondly, they considered the electricity wholly inadequate especially since consumers from dam-affected communities were expected to pay the full cost of electricity and water. Moreover, since communities that had not suffered flood losses were deriving similar benefits, it was not clear how the electricity poles could be seen as compensation.

There was a strong perception at Sokpoe that the distribution of the electric poles had been caught up in multi-party politics in that more populous parts of the Lower Volta had benefited disproportionately from the electric poles. The sense of frustration was understandable. If electrification was to be compensation for flood damage, then the areas which suffered had to receive priority attention. On the other hand, the failure to secure adequate compensation and redress and to clarify failures had resulted in high levels of suspicion

---

[73] The issues of compensation for losses arising from the Volta River Project are not particular to Tongu. The chiefs of the Akwamu traditional area whose lands were submerged by the Volta Lake recently demanded that the government repeal Act 46 of 1961, which gave the VRA jurisdiction over the Lake and its environs. This was to enable the Asuogyaman District Assembly to collect revenue from those areas presently under the VRA. This demand was said to be in frustration at the non-compensation following the submersion of "the greater proportion of their lands" (The Ghanaian Chronicle, Monday August 13th 2001).

and cynicism about government interventions in the Lower Volta. This was exacerbated by a sense, right or wrong, that community leaders were promoting their own personal interests instead of focusing on obtaining redress for the people. The point is not the truth or otherwise of these views, but that the experience of state neglect had made them a regular feature of life.

The politics of development projects

Within community leadership structures, with the failure of the compensation option, more attention was being focused on making appeals for "development", specifically the provision of employment avenues, good drinking water, electricity and roads. An important strategy in this approach was the use of the annual festivals to appeal to government officials and representatives of foreign development agencies for assistance.[74] This was supplemented by what was collected from visiting migrants and their associations, town and youth development associations and clans and lineages. An informant has argued that this strategy of appealing to various agencies for support was problematic. This was because the entitlements of communities in relation to the Volta River Project could not be asserted with development agencies who applied their own conditionalities without taking into account the special circumstances of the Lower Volta. Thus, for example, it was felt that had it been the VRA rather than a development agency, which had provided pipe-borne water in the Lower Volta, people might not be paying such high prices for clean water.[75]

From the point of view of community leaders, however, there was logic to this shift in strategy from demanding compensation to appealing for development assistance. After three decades of petitions with minimal achievements, a shift in strategy was warranted. In spite of

---

[74] For example, an informant at Sokpoe spoke of the appeal made to the Indian Ambassador for scholarships for young people from Sokpoe to go and learn trades in India. Even the District Assembly seemed to have shifted its orientation. At the 3rd ordinary meeting of the 4th session of the South Tongu District Assembly between 13–15th January 1998, the issue of aquatic weeds which were spreading beyond the banks of the Volta along the District came up for discussion. It was decided that the District Administration would contact the American Embassy on ways and means of stopping the weeds (Tongu District Minutes Book).
[75] During the research period, a bucket of water was being sold for 50 cedis.

the outlined limitations of the appeals strategy, it has yielded some results. DANIDA has financed several KVIP toilets and boreholes at Mepe and pipe-borne water at Sokpoe. Both Mepe and Sokpoe have had electricity since the mid-1990s, bringing some significant changes in nightlife, within homes and to commerce. These electricity-related changes are discussed in more detail in the chapters on livelihoods. However, the position that electricity would somehow compensate for the loss of livelihoods was not popular in the Lower Volta, partly because its costs have put it beyond the reach of the majority of people and also because its full potential had still not been realised and was not likely to be in the near future.

Why was community level action so ineffectual?

A number of factors hampered community action on dam impacts. These included the power relations between communities and the state, the lack of a properly designated state institution to address grievances, the less than committed role of the VRA and the culture of leadership within the communities themselves. Communities and their leaders were from the start ranged against more powerful and organised forces, which had access to State power. The Ghanaian post-colonial state in that period was led by a government with unassailable confidence in its particular vision of development, particularly in relation to the Volta River Project. By contrast, rural communities were distant from the State and lacked the political, economic and social currency to make their case. The issue of where to direct complaints and who had responsibility to tackle dam impacts was never and is still not clear. One informant, J. Kaleku, argued that complaints should have been directed at the government and not the VRA "because the VRA is not an entity of itself". However, in the absence of an institution designated for this purpose, the VRA became the default recipient and processor of complaints. The VRA meanwhile gradually eased itself from the position of being the target of demands for compensation to becoming an intermediary between communities and the aid agencies. This strategy has allowed the VRA to choose how to respond to demands without having to negotiate with affected communities.

Community leaders for their part have had an ambiguous attitude to the VRA's role as broker. At one level, there was acceptance of the VRA's facilitation role, on grounds that the institution could open some doors and in any case did not have the requisite resources in its coffers. At another level, they continued to press the VRA, although less persistently. The current strategy, though unarticulated, seemed to be to use whatever channel was on offer to secure redress.

Beyond specific disagreements, the pattern of communication between the VRA and the people in the Lower Volta was a problem. On the issues of flood control and salinity, for which the VRA acknowledged its legal responsibility, the organisation took a high scientific tone that could not be successfully countered. As the dispatches showed, locals tried to give the VRA common sense advice about the timing and quantity of its water releases, but did not get a hearing. The VRA generally paid more attention to the views of industrial concerns around the Lower Volta. In 1966, the VRA wrote to the Asutuare Sugar Corporation commiserating with it about unofficial reports of damage caused to the corporation's property because of an unannounced spillage by the VRA. It invited the corporation for a discussion with VRA officials about another imminent spillage.[76] This courtesy was never accorded to the people of the Lower Volta. A request from the Volo chief to the VRA to travel to inspect damage done to property, was considered unnecessary by the Authority.[77]

Thus, while the VRA engaged with institutions and industries along the Volta on issues of flood control, communities in the Lower Volta were never represented in the various meetings on issues of concern to them. Their interests had to be represented by government agencies. While in the beginning these institutions made an effort, their exertions were not sustained. The concerns of affected communities were further marginalised by the VRA's practice of either denying that the problems were dam related, or not taking responsibility for acknowledged dam-related problems. In spite of its ambivalence and minimalism, the VRA always held itself out as very concerned with the welfare of affected communities as the following statement in one of its annual reports shows.

[76] VRA to Asutuare Sugar Corporation—9/12/1966.
[77] Letter from Chief of Volo to VRA—13/2/1967; VRA to Chief of Volo—13/3/1967. VRA officials did finally visit the Lower Volta decades later to see things for themselves (Interview with KK, Accra).

I wish to emphasise that the Volta River Authority is committed to seeking the economic and social welfare of all communities affected by the construction of the Akosombo and Kpong Dams and will continue to pursue this policy within its financial capabilities. In this connection, I am happy to announce that the Authority has earmarked, in its ten-year investment programme beginning in 1993, an amount of US$ 2 million (about 1 billion cedis) each year to cater for the environmental protection and welfare activities in the Volta basin. In addition, the VRA intends to look for off-shore funding to supplement its own resources in the implementation of projects and activities identified as necessary to ameliorate hardships caused to the people in the Volta Basin" (VRA Annual Report, 1992).

The continuity implied in the above announcement was not an accurate rendition of VRA policy. A closer examination of its record shows a poor record of achievements. In relation to the above statement, the resources to be devoted to the problems, the equivalent of the cost of one dredger, were too modest to make a difference. Until 1996 when the VRA commissioned the Lower Volta Environmental Impact Studies (LVEIS), much of that money had to have been spent around the Volta Lake and dredging the estuary of the Volta River. There was no indication of how the amount was arrived at and what percentage of the VRA budget it represented.[78] As will become clear, to get the VRA's attention for any issue, it either had to coincide with the organisation's identified self-interest or involve an influential constituency. The VRA's decision to dredge the Volta River's Estuary was a case in point.[79] Following decades of neglect of the Lower Volta Basin as a whole, the VRA in the 1990s took a decision to dredge the Volta Estuary, which ordinarily the Authority would have deemed to be outside its jurisdiction. Studies had shown that because of the Dams, the Volta Estuary was being blocked by a silt bar, which was partially preventing the flow of saline water into the river channel during high tides. This had resulted in the growth of freshwater vegetation and the incidence of bilharzia at the

---

[78] In 1992, when the announcement was made, the amount can be measured against various figures in the Annual Reports. For example, the income from electricity sales was 58 billion cedis, operating and general expenses were 14 billion cedis, and operating profit was 30 billion cedis and capital work in progress 78 billion cedis.

[79] One of the explanations given by Kalitsi for the Authority's ability to ignore the Lower Volta was that there was no activity directly related to the production of electricity there (KK, Accra).

estuary, developments which were threatening tourism in the area. Dredging the channel to the sea would aid the flow of river water to the sea and prevent the build-up of silt in the river below the Dams. The seawater would then continue to enter the river channel thus increasing salinity and helping to reduce the incidence of bilharzia. In this way, the VRA would also safeguard its freedom to discharge excess water into the Lower Volta without fear of flooding riverside communities.

In 1990, the VRA purchased a dredger and began dredging activities in the estuary. A 1997 survey commissioned by the VRA found that although bilharzia was still prevalent, the dredging combined with education and public health initiatives had improved the situation in the estuary (VRA, undated; Kalitsi, 1999; Yeboah, 1999). According to Kalitsi, the dredging also revived tourism at Ada (KK, Accra). The response to the problems around the Delta was noteworthy. Simply put, it seemed that the VRA itself had to see a connection between a particular problem and the health and safety of the dams and therefore power generation before organisational time and resources could be committed to its solution. Secondly, complainants had to be able to show that "modern investments" such as hotels and other infrastructure were under threat. It was never enough to prove that rural livelihoods have been endangered, or that ordinary citizens were in distress. This was because for this class of problems, the VRA had to rely on its moral obligation as a good corporate citizen. It was never a strong enough reason to spend the amounts required to salvage some of the more intractable problems of the Lower Volta Basin.

In spite of this, Kalitsi suggests that pressure from affected communities has managed to effect some changes in the organisation's policies. This was to stem negative and damaging publicity. It has been suggested that the changes in policies towards affected communities were influenced by the appointment of an economist (i.e. a non-engineer) as chief executive of the organisation. While Kalitsi was uncomfortable about taking credit for this change, he accepts the critique that the outlook of the engineers at the head and in important positions in the organisation had been critical for the neglect of affected communities.

The organisation and political cultures of rural communities such as those of the Lower Volta which had a strong "chiefs and people" ethos contributed to a weak culture of citizenship and a sense of entitlement among rural people. The subject culture meant that the accountability of chiefs to their people was limited. This has not been helpful for a difficult undertaking such as making and sustaining demands of the State. The relationship between the chieftaincy institution and the colonial and post-colonial States in Ghana has been an added complication. The reliance of chiefs on the State as the ultimate referee and legitimiser of their authority puts them in a weak position and tempers their actions with the reality of their self-interest. As a result, the chiefs did try but never acquired the muscle for struggle. The changing character of chieftaincy from which the Lower Volta was not immune, was also a factor. As an informant noted, political leaders such as chiefs no longer lived permanently in many communities. At Mepe, for example, several important chiefs lived outside the community and, therefore, experienced a different daily reality from the locals.

The sense of entitlement of communities in the Lower Volta was also severely weakened by the initial response of the wholesale migration of the most active sections of the population. This took the core and resilience out of the Lower Volta. Those left behind did not form the critical stable mass to articulate the issues. Forty years on, the Lower Volta was seething with resentment and suspicions about who had misappropriated compensation money and who was misusing compensation for political ends. The cynicism generated by this situation has to be distinguished from community apathy. The limited achievements of community efforts in securing compensation for flood losses and the more general and increasingly pressing problems of livelihoods, had the result of strengthening the belief in personal salvation. Many people were, therefore, devoting their energies to their own survival and those of their dependants.

7. Summary and Conclusions

This chapter has sought to discuss state policy towards three interrelated categories of affected community—communities that had to be resettled, migrant fisher-folk and communities in the Lower Volta. This was to lay the foundations for subsequent chapters of the book which focus on the livelihoods of downstream and lakeside communities and their members. The discussion of state policy has concentrated on the Volta River Authority (VRA) as the institution most

connected with the VRP, and which also assumed some responsibility for affected communities. The chapter sought to demonstrate
that the VRA as an institution established primarily to produce power
and convey it to its largest consumers, was not equipped to address
the questions of affected communities. In the absence of a designated and equipped institution for this challenging task, the VRA
selectively took up some of these problems within the constraints of
its establishment law, its institutional culture and preoccupations. This
it did while formally denying responsibility for the problems.

It was argued that the failure to set aside adequate resources to
deal with dam impacts in the Lower Volta and around the Lake
resulted in long term environmental and socio-economic problems.
The communities in the Lower Volta petitioned the VRA on issues
such as water salinity, the quality of drinking water, flood control,
the amount of water flowing into the Lower Volta and river transport. The organisation responded by either questioning the link
between the Dam and the problems or arguing that responsibility
lay elsewhere. Until 1996, the VRA ignored issues concerning the
loss of livelihoods in the Lower Volta. The VBRP's Lower Volta
Environmental Impact Studies, which were commissioned by the
VRA, sought to explore ways of addressing the socio-economic decline
of the area. Their recommendations had not been implemented by
the end of 2002 and there was little indication of plans to do so.

In relation to Lakeside communities, their issues became hostage
to the VRA's concerns about the health of the Dams and the Lake.
The problem of water-borne diseases and aquatic vegetation received
some attention because VRA was interested in containing these diseases. The resettlements, which received the most attention, were
handed over to mainstream government institutions as part of a
process to normalise them. Only residual aspects of their issues have
continued to be the responsibility of the VRA.

The chapter also discussed out-migration and its implications for
the Lower Volta where the impacts of wholesale out-migration of
the 60s were still being felt. Migration and its attendant cultures had
resulted in different categories of ex-migrants (retired, economically
active and children) whose livelihoods were linked in specific ways
to the Lake. This was because they had been organised in ways
which took advantage of the migration history of the individuals
concerned and the migration culture of their communities. These
included the use of old connections for long-distance trading, receiving

remittances from children as well as rent and profits from resources left around the Lake. As well, a proportion of the foodstuffs and fish sold at markets in the Lower Volta were from the Lake. However, there was a clear shift from seeing the Lakeside as a place with good livelihood possibilities to seeing it as a location with suffering fellow Tongu people who could be encouraged to return home if the situation in the Lower Volta improved. Young people both around in the Lower Volta were responding to the migration culture and the changing relationship between migrant settlements and the Lower Volta with urban migration.

One clear conclusion of the chapter is that community level attempts to seek redress for the adverse effects of the Dam in the Lower Volta were largely unsuccessful. This was because of the unequal power relations between communities and the VRA as well as the lack of mobilisation within communities to insist on government action.

In response to the failure of community action, households and their members have had to devise their own strategies for survival. These strategies as they have been organised and executed around the Volta Lake and in the Lower Volta, are the subject of the rest of the book.

CHAPTER FIVE

LIVELIHOODS IN TIMES OF STRESS: LONG TERM
RESPONSES TO ENVIRONMENTAL CHANGE AT
MEPE AND SOKPOE

Ne etsi vɔ le dɛ me hā, asiklɔtsi mevɔ o.

Even when the water pot is empty, water for
washing the hands is never finished (Ewe Proverb).

1. *Introduction*

This chapter discusses responses to the environmental and socio-economic impacts of the Volta River Project at Mepe and Sokpoe. The
research findings are examined in the light of concepts in the livelihoods literature such as adaptation and diversification. We argue
that while multiple livelihood activities were the norm in the Lower
Volta before the Volta River Project, the post-dam practice of multiple livelihood activities within a dwindling resource base has contributed to the impoverishment of households and their members.
Also, while multiple livelihoods had different implications for different households, for the majority it was more a coping strategy than
one of accumulation and savings in recognition that few, if any, of
the existing activities could, on their own, guarantee survival. In any
case, not all households were able to engage in multiple livelihood
activities and their differences depended on factors such as their composition, life-cycle stage, capital and resource base, their array of
skills and training and access to resources at other locations. Therefore,
peoples' responses to change and changing conditions was not adaptation as understood in the livelihoods literature.

In response to environmental change and the decline in the resource
base, households and their members adopted several strategies to
intensify their exploitation of the river and the land, or failing that,
downgraded activities involving these resources in their livelihoods
portfolio. In addition to these strategies of intensification, the practice

of multiple livelihood activities was continued but with modifications in both the activities combined as well as their organisation.

The chapter has two main parts. In the first, the main livelihood activities are examined in some detail to show the different strategies being pursued in relation to each of them. The second part of the chapter explores the practice of multiple livelihood activities through the examination of five cases, three from Sokpoe and two from Mepe involving the households of three women and two men. These cases illustrate different strategies including the practice of multi-spatial livelihoods, multiple livelihood activities that included farming, those which did not, multiple livelihood activities at the level of individuals and/or their households and cases of specialisation. They are discussed within the framework of the debates on multiple livelihood activities or diversification.

Owing to their similarities, examples are drawn from both Mepe and Sokpoe. Where possible, the two settlements are compared and contrasted. In the light of the commonalities in their pre-dam and post-dam conditions, their differences were considered to be of interest. The Volta River and its tributaries were and are still important in the economic and ritual life of Mepe and Sokpoe and the rest of the Lower Volta. As downstream communities, both Mepe and Sokpoe experienced the Akosombo and Kpong Dams in similar ways. Both communities were now characterised by a dry monotonous landscape dotted with stunted neem trees. However, Mepe and Sokpoe had important spatial differences. One of these was the Lower Volta Bridge. Constructed in 1965 across the Volta at Sokpoe and Sogakope, the bridge links a first class road, which is the most direct route between Accra and the capitals of the Republics of Togo, Benin and Nigeria. The road and the bridge were an important factor in livelihood activities such as trading and fishing at Sokpoe, allowing traders access to consumers travelling the road to and from places further a field.

The chapter is structured as follows. It begins with a background to the two main communities—characteristics, population and facilities. This is followed by an examination of migration as a factor in livelihoods. A discussion of the intensification and re-organisation of livelihood activities follow this. The practice of multiple livelihood activities is tackled and the chapter ends with a summary and conclusions.

2. Background to the Research Communities: Mepe and Sokpoe

Mepe

According to the 2000 Population Census, Mepe had a population of 4,724 (2,140 male and 2,584 female) making it a rural area in demographic terms (Ghana Statistical Service, 2002). More important though, the figures represented a reversal of decades of population decline. The main settlement of the Mepe Traditional Area, Mepe, our research settlement, was on the Western Bank of the Volta River as were Mepe villages such as Degorme. Much of the lands of the Mepe State, though, were on the eastern banks of the Volta, stretching as far as Abutia and Adaklu towards the mid-Volta. The Mepe State's numerous villages were run by Headmen, who were responsible to particular Division chiefs. There were also the District Assembly's local structures, the Unit Committees (UC), which were sometimes shared by several settlements.[1]

Mepe, like many settlements of its kind, had a clearly defined residential structure at its core, becoming looser around its edges. The core was composed of contiguous compounds (*afemewo*) of the maximal lineages of the five Divisions. There was a section beyond this core, but now also central, where the early Christians settled, known as Salem. The Presbyterian Church and its schools were in a large compound in this part of Mepe. Then there were the newly-settled areas where people of various divisions had purchased land and built houses. These newer areas did not usually have the elaborate lineage compounds found at the centre of the settlement. As kinship was the basis of compounds, there were many connections between households within a compound.

A tarred road ran through Mepe and the houses were on both sides of the street. In addition, there was a grid of untarred paths, which created some symmetry in its layout. A little beyond Mepe southwards, the tarred road ended at a fork, one part winding its way to Degorme, a Mepe village and the other to join the main

---

[1] Each unit committee had 10 elected and 5 appointed members. Like the chiefs, they were involved in the settlement of small disputes such as fights and debt collection. Their decisions could be appealed at the level of the Assemblyman of the community.

Accra-Lome road near Kpotame. The side of the Mepe settlement closer to the Volta was the more built-up area, suggesting that the community was expanding outwards away from the river. Shops trading in a varied range of goods were lined up along the road. Behind the shop fronts were the built-up areas with several enclosed courtyards created by the rooms opening into them.

The road running through the town was a good footpath as it was empty of vehicular traffic much of the time. Infrastructure was poor at Mepe. Housing covered a wide spectrum—from large three storey cement block houses with aluminium roofs, plastered and painted, to smaller bungalows and then to laterite block houses plastered with cement or laterite with either thatch or aluminium roofs. The mix of elaborate and very basic housing at Mepe and Sokpoe was in keeping with the situation of many small towns and larger villages in southern Ghana.

Toilet facilities were very basic with a few public toilets dotted around the community. Some houses had private KVIPs, but these were in the minority. Water was a problem because the most important source of drinking, bathing and washing water was the Volta which, all agreed was polluted. There were a few boreholes, but these were not as widely used. Cooking was mostly done under sheds within the compounds and the most popular cooking equipment was the earthen tripod fireplace constructed under a shed. A number of people also had coal-pots, which used charcoal produced by some households in the community. Mepe was relatively well located in relation to health facilities. The mission hospital at Battor was only a few kilometres away and many people at Mepe patronised its services, the main complaint being the cost of treatment. There were also a number of chemists selling basic medicines as well as some traditional healers and midwives.

Less than 40% of households in the sample had electricity which they mostly used for lighting at night. There was no pipe-borne water at Mepe and 7% of households had access to a borehole. No household in our sample had access to private toilets.

There were several Christian churches in Mepe. On weekday nights and on Sundays, several church services were held to the sound of drumming and music. Shrine activity around the Mepe gods was said to be on the decrease because fewer people were willing to patronise them. Some of the Christian churches, the Presbyterian

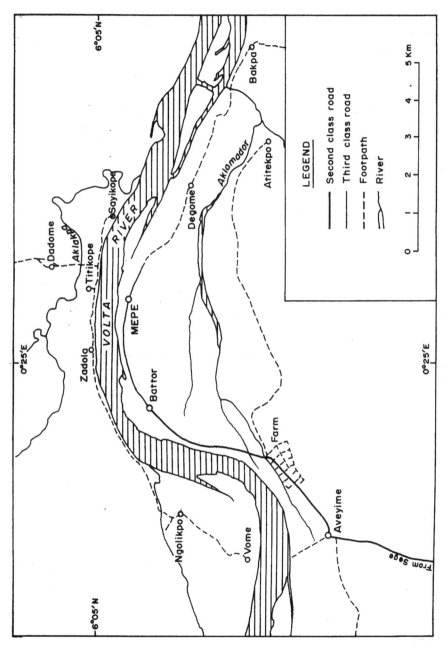

Figure 6: Map of the Mepe Area

and Catholic churches for example, had primary and junior secondary schools.

Sokpoe

Sokpoe's population was 2,889 (1,276 male and 1,622 female) according to the 2000 population census. A significant feature of Sokpoe as already indicated was the major first class road cutting through it. Both old and new sections of Sokpoe were found on either side of the road. The roadside was now prime land, the subject of several disputes. 20.2% of male-headed households and 19% of female-headed households in the sample had electricity. There were both private and communal toilet facilities. 2.1% of male-headed households and 0.8% of female-headed households had private toilets. Since 1998, Sokpoe has had pipe-borne water in public stands and also in a few homes. 3.2% of male-household heads and 4.8% of female-headed households had private taps. 2.1% of male headed households and 1.6% of female-headed households used boreholes. However, river water was widely used for domestic activities although some households purchased tap water for drinking at 50 cedis a bucket. Young men using push trucks could fetch river water in drums for a fee.

Two of the four schools in the Sokpoe traditional were at Sokpoe (the remaining two at Anaosukope and Morkodze). These were two primary schools—one mission and one local authority, one of which had a junior secondary school (JSS) with two streams. Across the Lower Volta Bridge at Sogakope, there was a senior secondary and also vocational and technical schools.[2] There were several churches—one Presbyterian and the others Pentecostal, including the ARS which had a church by the roadside. Health facilities included one maternity home at the roadside, the Sogakope Government Hospital and the Comboni Clinic, a Catholic mission facility at Sogakope. Serious ailments were taken to either Battor Catholic Mission Hospital or the Evangelical Presbyterian Mission Hospital at Adidome, or another hospital at Akatsi.

---

[2] Literacy rates in the South Tongu District were 39%, lower than the national average of 67%.

Residence in Sokpoe originally was according to clan affiliation and this was still reflected at the core of the settlement. Over the years the edges of the settlement, which were now quite substantial, had been settled by people irrespective of their clans. Housing at Sokpoe was largely similar to that found at Mepe in terms of quality and distribution.

3. *Migration and Livelihoods at Mepe and Sokpoe*

In chapter three, the massive out-migration from the Lower Volta was discussed as one of the more dramatic and immediate responses to the formation of the Volta Lake. In chapter four, we argued that it affected the strength and effectiveness of community struggles to get redress for dam impacts on the environment and on livelihoods. This section considers the implications of out-migration for livelihoods within the Lower Volta. The scale of out-migration had a deep impact on the Lower Volta and its inhabitants, including those who had never migrated before.

Not only was the population in a constant state of flux, but it also had a large proportion of ex-migrants (retirees, war refugees, economic returnees, temporary returnees) and the children of migrants who had come to the Lower Volta to learn a trade or to study. There was also a significant minority of men and women who had never established themselves as migrants on account of various factors such as gender, age and their situation at the time of the exodus. Some of the women had not migrated because their husbands either did not go or went with another wife or because they had young children who were in school. Some people pleaded old age or a dislike for the strange lifestyles of the migrant world. Some people who had some education or artisanal training either migrated to an urban area or stayed in the Lower Volta pursuing their trade or engaged in wage work such as teaching or administrative work.

Remaining in the Lower Volta allowed some people access to lineage resources that otherwise they would have had to share with others. A number of male chiefs and family heads were able to access substantial lineage resources for their private use, and were among a minority with larger than average farms. Similarly, young men and women who were farming with either parent expected to inherit their farmlands because all other siblings were away. While it was

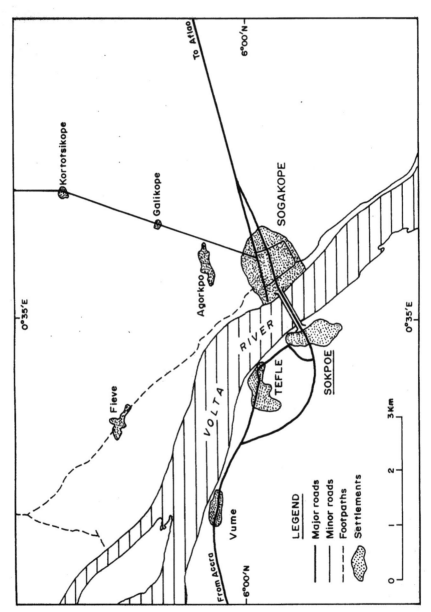

Figure 7: Map of Sogakope area Showing Sokpoe

not clear whether this factor played a role in the decision not to migrate or whether it was an advantage that came to accrue to non-migrants after the fact, it was an important aspect of the logic of remaining in one's hometown.

The survey of Mepe and Sokpoe found that returned migrants were back for a variety of reasons, the most important being ill health 29.4% (26.4% of male respondents and 31.8% of female respondents) and old age (13.2% male and 6.7% female returned migrants). 27.2% (30.8% male and 22.8% female respondents) returned because their livelihood activities were not going well. 9.5% of female respondents returned because of marital breakdown while another 6.7% returned because their husbands asked them to. 3% of male respondents and 10.4% of female respondents were back in the Lower Volta to enable their children to attend school. 3% of males and 2.5% of females were back because of armed conflicts among their hosts, harassment by landowners or expulsions by state agencies. Other reasons for returning included those who just wanted to come back home (13.2% male and 6.7% female). Others had returned on account of family problems (6% of male respondents and 4.5% of female respondents). The rest returned because of problems of housing, to attend school and to help relations with their work.[3] 1.4% male respondents and 3.9% female respondents were back only temporarily.

Migration had a bearing on livelihoods in the Lower Volta. Several ex-migrants continued to have links with their communities of migration after their return. In some cases, these links were important for the livelihoods they came to fashion in the Lower Volta. The retirees who had returned to the Lower Volta in their old age after decades away had left children and grandchildren in these places. It was from them they received foodstuffs, money and other forms of support. Some of them, especially the men, were receiving money and food because they had assigned their cocoa farms or fishing nets and boats to their children to look after. For those of them who were

---

[3] Those returned migrants who are still economically active are referred to as returnees to distinguish them from those who have returned for reasons of old age and ill health. This is a somewhat arbitrary distinction because old people continue to be economically active until they become blind, bedridden or too disabled to work.

no longer able to work, these links with migrant communities became even more critical for their ability to survive.

The economically active ex-migrants also continued to retain strong and weak links with migrant communities. Where possible, they continued with their livelihood activities of their days as migrants within the constraints of the Lower Volta. For example, some women traded in consumer goods they acquired from Accra, which they sold in migrant villages, and brought back smoked and dried fish, groundnuts and maize purchased from around the Lake to be sold in Accra and the Lower Volta. For others, the main link might be the funds they returned with to begin economic activities in the Lower Volta or the remittances they continued to receive from spouses or other kin in migrant communities. Those who were temporary returnees were back for fixed or indeterminate periods for a variety of reasons. These included having a baby, to look after children in school, care for a sick or old parent or close relative, or to look after some resources acquired in the home village. In one household made up of 21 persons, there were two sisters who had been back at Mepe for three months, one because she had come to give birth and the other because she had eye problems. They were farming and trading around the Lake and were regular visitors to Mepe.

This regular in-flow of individuals had implications for the composition of households. It was also important for establishing a pervasive culture of migration. Many young men and women had plans to migrate and considered formal education or learning a trade to be part of the preparatory process. Given the lack of employment and income generation opportunities in the Lower Volta, it was mainly the expectation that they would leave once they finished studying that made training a viable option in the first place. In cases where parents and guardians could not afford to pay for apprenticeships, several young women and men still migrated to find work in Accra and its environs while a significant number still continued to head for the Volta Lake. This was usually preceded by several efforts to find work to pay for their training. Respondents suggested that boys had a wider range of opportunities to find such work in the building, fishing and farming sectors than girls.

Those young people who had family either around the Lake or in Accra, Tema or at Ashaiman also spent holidays with them in the hope of earning money to pay school fees and other expenses. This also allowed them a taste of migrant life, perhaps in preparation for staying on a more long-term basis. By the year 2000, there was a major shift from migration to the Volta Lake to migrating to urban areas and the majority of young persons who were interviewed were headed for urban rather than rural areas. This change was in keeping with the changing perceptions about the Lake. From being seen in the mid 60s as a place with good livelihood possibilities, it was now a location with suffering fellow Tongu Ewe people who could be encouraged to return home if the situation in the Lower Volta improved. Geker (1999) for example, mentions the loss of dignity and insecurity arising from having to live with hostile hosts as well as tensions and conflicts over the use of land and other resources as some of the problems suffered by Tongu Ewe migrants around the Lake. The harassment of migrants was a regular subject of the speeches at the durbars of chiefs and people during the annual festivals. Geker (1999) recalls that the Tongu Union wrote to the VRA in 1987 on the subject of its relations with migrant fishermen and farmers. The letter alleged that Tongu citizens living upstream were being harassed by local people and the police as a result of unclear policies on fishing gear created by conflicts between the directives from the Ministry of Agriculture and the Fisheries co-coordinator and the Fisheries Regulations of the Ministry. These incidents had resulted in the deaths of some Tongu fishermen.

Migration as a factor in livelihood activities

Migrants gave various forms of support to their relations in the Lower Volta. Almost all respondents had close kin—siblings, children and parents—in Tema, Accra, at Ashaiman, or around the Volta Lake and the expectations people had of migrants varied. While parents and children expected maintenance in the form of foodstuffs, smoked fish and money, others had looser expectations of migrants, which they continued to fulfil with more or less enthusiasm. Migration has long been seen as a factor in the loosening of kinship ties. Routinely, people said that kin who lived up the Volta Lake no longer visited home regularly and had also lost any close connections with their kinsfolk. As one informant put it, "I have a brother in Kwamikrom whom I have not seen for at least 5 years" (HB, Mepe). In spite of this, remittances from migrants continued to make a contribution to some livelihoods at both Mepe and Sokpoe. Migrant support was regular, occasional, or mainly in times of crisis. Children returning from holidays with their parents around the Lake usually brought foodstuffs. In between holidays, lorry drivers plying the routes between particular Lower Volta communities and Lakeside destinations delivered foodstuffs to Mepe and Sokpoe from the relations around the Lake. In times of sickness, locals could call on their migrant children and other close kin in different places to pay for treatment. During visits, migrants also gave small gifts to close kin.

A significant number of respondents, including some of the ones looking after the children of migrant kin (47.6% male- and 41.9% female-headed households) said they were not receiving any support from outside the community (Table 5.1 below). The number of respondents around the Lake who said they were not looking after anyone outside their communities (58% male-household heads and 69% female-household heads) supported this (Table 5.2 below). In addition, few received significant amounts of money and food to make a difference to their livelihoods, the value of such remittances sometimes being more symbolic than substantive. The sums mentioned by respondents as the support they received from migrants tended to be quite small with the money being sent 1–6 times a year, with an average of 3 times a year.[4] In spite of the dwindling support over the years however, those who could call on such assistance were in the position of having one more possible source of scarce resources.

A number of factors accounted for the dwindling support from migrants. In the almost four decades since the construction of the Akosombo Dam, there have been changes in the relationship between migrants and the Lower Volta. Many persons who left very close kin such as spouses, children and parents behind no longer have these ties with the Lower Volta. This has drastically reduced the numbers of persons to whom migrants felt a sense of direct responsibility. In turn, adults within the Lower Volta spoke of migrants, particularly those around the Lake, as people whom they barely knew and some people found migrant cultures as they were displayed during visits home, strange. The distances between some migrant

---

[4] 10,000 cedis each time or more or less was quite common. Respondents mentioned sums such as 4,000 and 5,000 while others mentioned that they were given money leftover from transporting food to them, such as 1,000 cedis and sometimes even nothing.

villages and natal communities made the business of maintaining strong links difficult, a situation exacerbated by the dwindling of migrants' fortunes. Increasingly, discussions of Tongu Ewe migrants around the Volta Lake had been focused on their treatment at the hands of locals, which was causing suffering, pain and occasionally, death (Anipati III, undated; Geker, 1999).

Table 5.1: Number of households receiving remittances by gender of household head

| | Absolutes | | | | | | | Percentages | | | | | | |
| | Mepe | | Sokpoe | | Mepe and Sokpoe | | | Mepe | | Sokpoe | | Mepe and Sokpoe | | |
	M	F	M	F	M	F	T	M	F	M	F	M	F	T
Yes	72	83	36	53	108	136	244	76.6	65.9	32.1	49.1	52.4	58.1	55.4
No	22	43	76	55	98	98	196	23.4	34.1	67.9	50.9	47.6	41.9	44.5
Total	94	126	112	108	206	234	440	100	100	100	100	100	100	100

Table 5.2: Number of households remitting people outside the community by gender of household head (migrant settlements)

| | Absolutes | | | Percentages | | |
	Male	Female	Total	Male	Female	Total
NS	8	2	10	4.9	3.4	4.5
Remittance	58	16	74	35.8	27.6	33.6
No remittance	94	40	134	58	69	60.9
NA	2	–	2	1.2	–	.9
Total	162	58	220	100	100	100

Rent-free housing took one important item off the expenditure of households. The majority of respondents and indeed the inhabitants of Sokpoe and Mepe lived in houses that were built by more successful family members or themselves when they were more economically active (64.9%–53% for male heads and 75.2% for female heads). Very few household heads were tenants at Mepe and Sokpoe (3.1%). The more recently constructed homes of migrants were outside the clan compounds and were mostly empty except for a caretaker who was either a family member of the owner or a wage employee who was a stranger in the community. They were either tenants or living rent-free in return for paying for electricity or just keeping the house clean for when the owner visited.

While the houses built by migrants were not mainly constructed with their more unfortunate relations in mind, they came to be very useful as a source of free accommodation for persons who would otherwise have to rent housing. This has challenged the view that hometown houses did not have much economic value. Even if in conception and implementation they were meant for prestige purposes, they came to be used for normal occupation and a range of people took advantage of this source of housing. Not all houses made this transition from monument to dwelling place, partly because those who initiated them could not complete some of them. There were also some completed ones that had been locked up by their owners.

Apart from houses, migrants also bought furnishings, mattresses and electrical appliances, which they either kept locked up for when they visited or allowed their relations to use in their absence. The ownership structure of housing in the Lower Volta meant that it was not a reliable indicator of the circumstances of respondents. Several very poor people lived in rooms in elaborate structures put up by relations who had long since become ancestors or who were living outside the community. There were others who "owned" or were "part-owners" of the homes in which they currently lived which had been put up during their years of active working life. However, in so far as housing was a basic necessity, the ability to secure rooms from whatever source was significant. In any case, it was observed that many people who lived in very basic housing were also among the poorest and some did not appear to be able to access the many unoccupied and locked-up rooms of absent relations referred to above.

Other indirect benefits of having relations living around the Volta Lake and in Accra included the facilitation of long-distance trade and the role of Lakeside markets at Dzemini, Kpandu Torkor and Marine as an important source of food crops and smoked and dried fish for the Lower Volta. As was indicated in previous chapters, prospective migrants from the Lower Volta expected to be hosted by their migrant relations on arrival. Migrant settlements around the Volta Lake continued to be potential rural destinations for new migrants. Urban destinations were becoming more significant recipients of Tongu migrants from both the Lower Volta and the Lake and this change in the character of migration was visible during the festival periods.

The changing conditions around the Lakeside have raised the possibility of different scenarios in future relations between migrants and the Lower Volta. This is more so because of the contradictory elements of existing relations. On the one hand, the deteriorating conditions around the Lake have reduced the ability of Lakeside migrants to contribute directly to livelihoods in the Lower Volta through remittances or the establishment of multi-spatial livelihoods. At the same time, the growing insecurity and persistent troubles with locals were making some older migrants return or contemplate returning home. The Lower Volta's role as a source of cheap labour for the fishing industry was also part of the equation. Thus migrants maintained relations of different levels and intensity with the Lower Volta and its inhabitants.

In relation to young people, there was a clear shift in relations. Their broader access to education and artisanal training and their more vicarious links with the Lower Volta as already indicated, was leading them into more urban livelihoods and away from the Lower Volta. In the survey, in response to a question about the locations of at least three ex-household members of migrants, only 12.9% of ex-household members were now residing in the Lower Volta. 32.3% of them were still living around the Lake and around 36% were living in an urban area. The responses from the Lower Volta was slightly different in that 57% of ex-household members lived around the Volta Lake, 20.2% were in Accra and another almost 10% were in other urban areas. The figures do confirm a broadening of migration location options but suggest that for people leaving the Lower Volta, the Lake was still one of several options.

4. Squeezing Water Out of Stone?

Intensification and restructuring of pre-dam livelihoods

At Mepe and Sokpoe, the major livelihood resources were still the land and the river. Farming, fishing, livestock rearing, charcoal burning, trading of all kinds, palm-wine tapping and *akpeteshie* (local gin) distilling, the mining of clam shells, sand and stone quarrying were all related in one form or the other to the land and the Volta. Resources were largely similar at Mepe and Sokpoe, but with some variations. In the Sokpoe area, there was no mention of clamshells and fewer people were engaged in akpeteshie distillation. Bread baking and selling cooked food around the Lower Volta Bridge were important activities for Sokpoe women, while at Mepe, no one baked bread, although a few women sold bread procured from nearby communities on the main Accra-Lome road. Selling of cooked food was a more common activity at Sokpoe than at Mepe.

To continue to exploit the land and river under the changing environmental conditions described earlier, strategies were adopted which could be broadly described as the restructuring of livelihood portfolios.

They included in different combinations the following elements:

• Making changes to the methods and intensity of exploitation of particular resources (e.g. fishing at Sokpoe).
• Continuing to exploit resources as before but with much poorer results, thus downgrading their purpose and significance in the livelihoods portfolio (e.g. fishing at Mepe and farming in both communities).
• Intensifying the exploitation of hitherto economically marginal resources, raising questions about sustainability because of their ecological marginality (e.g. charcoal burning and stone quarrying on farmlands).
• Wholesale adoption of activities without regard to the market (e.g. baking at Sokpoe).
• Putting old resources to new uses (e.g. using the river as a route to assist smuggling at Sokpoe).

We examine these changes in more detail through a discussion of the different activities—fishing, farming, trading, artisanal activities, stone quarrying and charcoal burning.

Fishing at Sokpoe

Fishing at Sokpoe was a good example of the strategy of intensification. In the pre-dam days, fishermen set their nets, went home to sleep and returned the next day to inspect them, a practice known as *ɖogbleɖi* (literally, set and leave in Ewe). Fishing at Sokpoe no longer followed this practice. In response to the changes in the Volta described in earlier chapters, Sokpoe fishermen established a practice of fishing more intensively. Days and nights were spent on the river and the process of setting the net and harvesting it was now done many times in one night. Night-time was considered the best time for fishing. The use of ice blocks to preserve the catch allowed

Table 5.3: Location of ex-household members living outside the community by gender of respondent* (The Lower Volta)

Locations	Absolutes							Percentages						
	Mepe		Sokpoe		Mepe and Sokpoe			Mepe		Sokpoe		Mepe and Sokpoe		
	M	F	M	F	M	F	T	M	F	M	F	M	F	T
Around the Lake	122	173	44	84	166	257	423	55.7	55.4	53.7	65.1	55.1	58.3	57
Juapong	1	2	0	0	1	2	3	.5	.6	0	0	.3	.5	.4
Ashiaman/Tema	19	15	4	4	23	19	42	8.7	4.8	4.9	3.1	7.6	4.3	5.7
Accra	44	66	20	20	64	86	150	20.1	21.1	24.4	15.5	21.3	19.5	20.2
Urban Area in the Volta Region	5	13	3	8	8	21	29	2.3	4.2	3.7	6.2	2.7	4.8	3.9
Urban Area outside Volta Region	9	11	4	4	13	15	28	4.1	3.5	4.9	3.1	4.3	3.4	3.8
Rural area in the Volta Region	11	15	5	6	16	21	37	.5	4.8	6.1	4.7	5.3	4.8	5
Rural Area outside the Volta Region	3	4	2	0	5	4	9	1.4	1.3	2.4	0	1.7	.9	1.2
The Lower Volta	2	2	0	1	2	3	5	.9	.6	0	.8	.7	.7	.7
Outside Ghana	3	11	0	2	3	13	16	1.4	3.5	0	1.6	1	2.9	2.2
Total	219	312	82	129	301	441	742	100	100	100	100	100	100	100

* Cumulative total of first three on the list of relations.

fishermen to spend days on the river, but this created its own pressures to stay longer because of the need to maximise the ice blocks.

There were a number of young men involved in the fishing industry and this suggested that fishing was likely to continue to be an important activity at Sokpoe for years to come barring any dramatic new developments. However, fishing was also becoming a minority activity in the sense that many more young men expressed a lack of interest in it and even those who were fishing were in many cases involved in other activities they considered more important. This is because the catch was small when compared with Lakeside catch even allowing for the fact that some of the fish had been sold along the river. For those who did not have their own fishing equipment and had to hire nets and canoes, the situation was even more unfavourable because the owners of the net and canoe were waiting ashore to take their share of the earnings.

It was estimated that Sokpoe had about 200 fishermen and only a fraction of them had their own canoes and nets. Some fishermen had two or more nets and some had nets, but no canoes and had to hire them from others.[5] Fishermen from Sokpoe operated all along the Lower Volta in either direction from Sokpoe, although they preferred to go upstream than towards the estuary where salinity levels were higher. They travelled in groups that could be as large as twenty, four persons to a boat and fishing in pairs for 2–3 days at a time. These were flexible arrangements which enabled fishermen to work longer hours if they so desired, but their ability to do so also depended on their relations with the canoe and nets. Before the Dam, fishermen did not organise their Lower Volta fishing in bands as they were doing now. The main innovation they introduced was two bamboo sticks (about 8 yards long). After the net had been set, the river was agitated by the fishermen using the bamboo sticks to hit the top of the water (horizontally) or thrust into the river vertically at rhythmic close intervals to bring the fish out of hiding and into the net. This was done for a few minutes and then the net was

---

[5] A canoe could be hired for 1000 cedis a day, 2000 cedis overnight. Canoes were quite easy to hire because some of their owners were not in the fishing business. Some who owned nets and boats were able to rent their equipment for 1/3 of the catch when they did not go fishing or they earned 2/3 of the proceeds when they did.

collected, i.e. the fish was harvested and placed on ice. Then the net was laid again around the same spot or moved to another part of the river to begin the process, which was 20 minutes between laying the net and harvesting it, again. This was done until the fishermen were hungry or until the fish container was full. The fishermen then returned to the riverbank to sell their fish and to rest.

Some fishermen went to the river more regularly than others. Average sales were 40,000–50,000 cedis a day and expenses were about 5,000 in 2000. However, there were seasonal variations in the amounts and species of fish caught and therefore earnings. There was no agreement among those interviewed about the best times for fishing in terms of earnings. Part of the reason for the differences was that some seasons were better for some species of fish than others. As well, it reflected the overall decline in fishing. Good seasons could be disappointing and annual variations in the catch made predictions difficult. Variations depended on rainfall, which was variable. To compound matters, some fish species had disappeared completely.

To be successful, it was also important to choose the right net for a fishing expedition. This implied that fishermen needed to have more than one net. Fishermen shared information about fishing grounds and took decisions about which net to use by also looking at the catches of their colleagues. In spite of all the skill and effort, their earnings did not allow fishermen to fish full time, many of them combining fishing with other activities. These included artisanal occupations such as masonry and carpentry and also farming.[6] Sokpoe fishermen were at a disadvantage in this regard because their itinerant life and year-long involvement did not allow for multiple livelihood activities.

Fishermen and fish sellers confirmed that most ordinary people could not afford river fish although the situation at Sokpoe was better than at Mepe probably because there were more fishermen. The

---

[6] For some, artisanal activities were for the periods when fishing was not going well, because for all its limitations, fishing meant protein and money on a daily basis. For example, one fisherman who was also a mason said building was a more uncertain job so he stopped fishing only when the terms of a building job were better than his fishing earnings in a particular period. However, several respondents also considered artisanship to be an escape from the poor rewards of fishing and farming which were considered not commensurate with their rigours.

high price of fish was blamed on traders wanting to make 100% profits on the fish. In addition, the heavy mantle of aquatic weeds caused frequent losses of nets and canoes (Sokpoe fishermen, Mepe). The loss of equipment was often disastrous because of the capital outlays needed for procuring equipment.

The fishing practices of Sokpoe fishermen contrasted sharply with the conduct of fishing at Mepe and other places along the Lower Volta. At Mepe, there were few fishermen left and they continued with pre-dam fishing practices. Those who had nets still set them, went home to sleep and returned the next morning to harvest the fish. Mepe fishermen now mainly used prawn traps and hook and line technology. While fishing at Mepe was not doing well, fishermen there had more space to engage in other activities and thus down-grade it to a supplementary activity within their livelihood portfolio.

There were tensions arising from the differences in the Sokpoe and Mepe responses to the changes in the Volta. Some Mepe fishermen complained that their nets, prawn traps and *efe* (hooks) were often disturbed and sometimes destroyed by the Sokpoe fishermen because of poor visibility at night. They also felt that the prawns and fish were being driven underground by the noise on the river created by bamboo-assisted fishing. Sokpoe fishermen disputed those claims, arguing that they were not obstructing any individual or group's livelihood activities as there were very few communities fishing as intensively as they were doing. For example, they counted only 3 fishermen at Mepe who were in any case using prawn traps, which were a danger to nets and not the other way round. Also they were not facing such problems at Agave where fishermen were also using prawn traps because all the parties were present at the same time on the River.

Interestingly, all the parties blamed the weeds in the river, the deep layers of mud and the disappearance of a shoreline of firm land for their new fishing practices and the disappearance of old fishing methods. In the past, prawn traps were put in shallow water near the shoreline and clearly marked with sticks to protect them. With the disappearance of the shoreline, which had now been replaced by a floating island of aquatic weeds, it was not possible to set traps in shallow water. Secondly, the prawns were now to be found under-neath one of the species of aquatic plants proliferating in the Lower Volta River. Therefore, prawn traps now had to be carried by canoe

into deep water.[7] Because of the concern about the security of equipment and the catch, fishermen now preferred not to mark the location of their traps.

One result of the tensions was that some of those who felt aggrieved
by the Sokpoe fishing method were beginning to question the right
of Sokpoe fishermen to leave their part of the river and travel all
the way upstream to fish. The "boundary—less" river was now being
demarcated by implication. While the Sokpoe fishermen had never
received a formal complaint, they were aware of plans to prevent
them from coming to fish in North Tongu waters.[8] They were
confident that they could not be excluded from any part of the river
because it was not owned by any group of persons, not even the
portions bordering particular villages. They wanted a government
statement to this effect and were confident of governmental support
on grounds that their fishing yielded more than the mainly subsistence fishing activities of others around the Lower Volta.[9]

This developing dispute had not yet reached crisis proportions.
However, the emotions it was generating raised questions about the
river, which did not arise in the days when its use patterns were
largely similar across the Lower Volta. While the oblique talk about
stopping the Sokpoe fishermen had an unclear basis given the river's
open status, the different users of the river each had interests wor-
thy of the sensitivities of all. Fishing in the Lower Volta was undergoing a transformation, which was threatening subsistence fishing of
the type going on in Mepe.

Farming at Mepe and Sokpoe

"Even if your farm does not do well, you will still get something out
of it" (respondent, Dadome, Mepe).

---

[7] The particular weed has been christened as the prawn weed "ebɔ gbe" by locals.
[8] Not all fishermen at Mepe interviewed had such strong feelings about the issue.
One Mepe fisherman observed that the equipment used by the Sokpoe fishermen
was more suited to conditions in the Lower Volta. Their nets were larger and
weighted down with lead pieces and, therefore, could reach the bottom of the river
and catch fish there.
[9] In the 80s when a night-time curfew was imposed nationally for years in response
to political instability, they had been given curfew passes by the authorities to enable
them to fish at night.

"You always have to plant just in case. No matter how bad the last season is, you still plant" (respondent, Toklokpo, Sokpoe).

"Our farmlands have become so barren and the land is so infertile that we can't say that we are farmers because we cannot do any meaningful farming on the land. And this is due to the construction of the dam" (respondent, Mepe).

"The land is dead" (respondent, Sokpoe).

The two contrasting views of farming represented by the above quotations sum up the ambivalence about farming in the Lower Volta. Many survey respondents and informants argued that farming had become unviable as a basis for livelihoods in the Lower Volta. At the same time, they would not contemplate not farming at all. There was still a commonsensical and ideological attachment to farming as the foundation of food security, although the many seasonal failures had taken their toll. Thus farming was still the most common livelihood activity at Mepe and Sokpoe, providing some foodstuffs for both consumption and exchange, with a much larger number of practitioners than fishing. 78.9% of households (81.6% male-headed and 76.3% female-headed) had someone farming even if it was not the household head.

The commitment to farming had clear generational demarcations. Older women and men continued to farm even when they had given up on other activities on account of their age and health as did some more economically active men and women. However, many households often had to purchase a significant proportion of the food they consumed because of cyclical failures of the rains. Younger people, especially those with some schooling, were less likely to have farming in their own livelihood portfolio although they helped their parents on their farms and a few of them expected to inherit farms.

Although it seemed to have a "way of life" status much more fundamental than its value for income generation and food security, farming was in a state of long-term crisis in the Lower Volta. In spite of the decades that had passed since the seasonal floods stopped, ex-creek and other floodplain land was still intensively farmed without long enough fallow periods partly because of its scarcity and fragmentation which was a result of inheritance practices and food security considerations. According to respondents, each piece of land farmed by a deceased parent was divided among all the children so each beneficiary had a number of dispersed smaller pieces rather than one large piece. It was considered equitable because it enabled all heirs to inherit creek land as well as land on higher ground, thus sharing risks across the beneficiaries. Tenancy arrangements also contributed to the state of land fragmentation. More people were involved in tenancy arrangements because of a growing shortage of lineage farmland close to settlements. At both Sokpoe and Mepe, people rented farming land for reasons of proximity. Thus in some cases, the same persons were both tenants and landlords. Land was rented for cash[10] and also on a sharecropping mainly *abusa* (1/3 of harvest) but in a few cases, also *abunu* (1/2 of harvest) basis. Those renting out land sometimes said it was because they lacked the time to farm or were pulling out of farming because of bad harvests.

Large-scale out-migration had ameliorated the fragmentation problem somewhat. However, the practice of farming a number of small, dispersed plots of land continued. The Agricultural Extension Officer confirmed local perceptions about the depletion of soils and argued that farms were too small for rain-fed mostly hoe and cutlass agriculture. Most farmers at Mepe and Sokpoe did not use fertiliser because apart from the cost, they believed it resulted in even poorer yields than normal during the drought period.[11]

In the dry spells, one of the most serious problems was the termites. They could destroy 90% of the maize crop and posed a danger to newly planted cassava sticks as well. The small size of farms and low yields made farmers loathe to invest in recommended pesticides and drought resistant improved seeds. The latter was also unpopular because their cereals were believed to have poor flour yields. From the point of view of farmers, because the main problem was the loss of water and alluvial resources, which had not cost money to acquire, a switch to expensive inputs such as fertiliser, which could not address the water problem, was not attractive. It would take much more than extension advice to address this issue.

One major change in farming since the Akosombo Dam was the farming timetable. People waited for the rains before planting on

---

[10] For example, people reported paying rent of 12,000 cedis a year or 20,000 cedis for three years.
[11] The Agricultural Extension Officer at Mepe explained that fertiliser absorbed what little moisture there was in the soil leaving the plants high and dry in times of drought (Interview with Agricultural Extension Officer, Mepe).

Table 5.4: Households who have someone farming

| | Absolutes | | | | | | |
| | Mepe | | Sokpoe | | Mepe and Sokpoe | | |
	M	F	M	F	M	F	T
No one farming	19	19	19	36	38	55	93
Someone farming	75	107	93	71	168	178	346
Total	94	126	112	107	206	233	439

| | Percentages | | | | | | |
| | Mepe | | Sokpoe | | Mepe and Sokpoe | | |
	M	F	M	F	M	F	T
No one farming	20.2	15.1	17	33.6	18.4	23.7	21.1
Someone farming	79.8	84.9	83	66.4	81.6	76.3	78.9
Total	100	100	100	100	100	100	100

prepared land instead of waiting for the floods to subside and farming now had a major and minor season. The crops had also contracted in variety and sweet potatoes and Bambara beans were now cultivated by only a minority. In the major season, farmers generally grew a combination of cassava, groundnuts, pepper and beans while in the minor season, they tended to grow cassava and maize.

Another change was the rise in the incidence of farming across the river or in neighbouring villages. There were larger tracts of land across the river and in the outlying villages which allowed the possibility of larger scale cultivation. Average farm size within Mepe and Sokpoe was 1/2 an acre while across the river and in the villages, it was one (1) acre. Farmlands close to or on the beds of streams which had either dried up completely, shrunk in size or were dry during parts of the year, were favoured because of their higher moisture content. Apart from its relative abundance, land across the Volta River and in some outlying villages was considered better than that around Mepe and Sokpoe. Farming across the river was however both more time consuming and expensive. At Mepe, those who owned canoes, now a minority at Mepe, could visit their farms at their own convenience. Others had to take the schedule of canoe owners into account or go by the privately owned canoes, which ferried people and goods across the river throughout the day.[12] Another change was the increasing incidence of the sale of farm produce, not because of increases in yields,[13] but to find the money to pay for other needs.

Animal rearing, where it was possible, was good for the livelihood portfolio. In some of the outlying villages goats and sheep were reared alongside farming and were an indication that some savings were being made by households. However, overall agriculture was in a state of decline, a finding which confirmed the conclusions of the

---

[12] It cost 200 cedis each person for a return trip. Farm produce and firewood also cost 200 cedis or more to transport. In the case of the firewood, this depended on the size of the bundle. Those who had to cross the Aklakpa had to pay an additional 100 cedis for a return trip. People who could not pay had to wait until someone in a hurry hired a boat or until the boatman decided to do them a favour.

[13] The study found that for most farming households, crops rarely lasted until the next harvest. For several months in the year, farming households were having to either purchase food or rely on the ever dwindling food remittances from the Volta Lake-side. Food imports were an important part of what was sold and consumed in the Lower Volta.

Lower Volta Environmental Impact Studies (Volta Basin Research Project, 1997).

Wholesale adoption of activities: Trading at Sokpoe and Mepe

Sokpoe women have a history of long-distance trading. In the period before and during formal colonisation, they carried smoked fish, pepper, groundnuts, cowpeas, bambara beans and maize (all produced in the Lower Volta) to Accra and beyond for sale. In addition, they were also involved in more sedentary trading activities around a ferry crossing at Sokpoe. The construction of the Lower Volta Bridge brought the ferry crossing service to an end and shifted the centre of the trade to the roadside on either side of the bridge. Those who serviced the patrons of the ferry crossing now had to reorient themselves to chase vehicles by the roadside.

Trading in the Lower Volta has also been influenced by post dam conditions. Informants at Mepe and Sokpoe reported an increase in small scale trading over the years with many persons, especially women, introducing some buying and selling into their livelihood activities. At Mepe for example, it was observed that ex-migrants were among those opening shops and selling consumer goods. This increase in trading activities was in the context of widespread complaints about the lack of markets, the poverty of people and poor levels of production in the area. It was a function of the decline in the primary livelihoods of fishing and farming and the lack of ready easy entry alternatives. Trading took many forms and was on different scales. While the majority of traders were female, the trade in drinks, drugs and general goods had a significant male presence.

The largest number of people trading at Mepe and Sokpoe were engaged in selling foodstuffs. Not all women involved in trading were traders. At its most basic, on market days, women would sell surplus farm produce in markets in and around their communities and buy necessities such as fish, soup ingredients and soap to take back home. Some women had expanded this to buying foodstuffs from other farmers and combining this with their own harvests to sell. In some cases, they would in turn buy some necessities for sale in their home villages. Then there were the more professional traders who travelled from village to village buying farm produce for sale in the different markets around the area. A few travelled further afield to the Volta Lake to buy food items for sale in local markets. A more elaborate triangular trade consisted of people who purchased a range of consumer goods from Accra and elsewhere which they sold around the Volta Lake, purchased fish and other foodstuffs from there, which they then sold in the Lower Volta or in markets in Accra.

At Mepe and Sokpoe, there were three types of localised trading practices. Women patronised the various local markets, sold small items on tables and in small stalls in front of their homes or engaged in itinerant trading, carrying their wares on their heads and walking around their own and neighbouring communities calling out to potential customers. Many cooked food and raw foodstuff sellers were engaged in more than one of these types of trading. In addition to the trade in foodstuffs, there were small- and medium-scale traders who had shops and stalls of various sizes who stocked a mixture of food and non-food items—canned food, sugar, biscuits, sweets, soap, mosquito repellent sprays and coils and batteries. Also present were a few shops which stocked crockery, electrical fittings, school uniforms and books. Shops devoted to particular goods and services e.g. drugs, ice cream, drinks of various kinds, fish and meat, sewing, hair dressing, vehicle tyre repairs and telephone services could be found on the main streets of both settlements.

The markets were important not only because they were the most used sites of exchange, but also because the goods sold in them were a window on the character and state of the local economies. In the Lower Volta, the markets were an important source of revenue for the District Assemblies. The low levels of economic activities and tax income, identified as the number one problem of the District Assemblies, was remedied with tax revenue from the markets.[14] North Tongu, which was generally better off because of its larger population, also had three large markets—Juapong, Adidome and Mafi Kumasi, the smallest of which was bigger than the Dabala market. At Mepe, there was a small market, but people also patronised the Battor and Aveyime markets next door as well as two of the major markets already mentioned, Mafi-Kumasi and Adidome and the

---

[14] For the South Tongu District, the Dabala Market in the Agave area yielded 60% to 70% of the Assembly's revenue. The collection of personal rates was difficult because people complained that they could not afford to pay. There were as yet unimplemented plans to tax groups such as fishermen in South Tongu and plans to establish a landing stage and fish market for revenue purposes. It was not clear if the yields would make this viable. South Tongu was one of the three districts in the Volta Region classified as deprived.

Agormanya market in a contiguous district. At Sokpoe, where the only market was the roadside, women patronised larger neighbouring markets such as Sogakope, Ada Junction, Dabala, Mafi-Kumasi and Akatsi to both buy and sell. The daily roadside markets, which mainly sold cooked food, drinks and small consumer items to travellers, was similar to roadside markets dotted strategically along the road from Accra to Aflao in communities such as Sege, Ada Junction, Sogakope and Akatsi. Mostly younger women but a few younger men peddled cooked food and water to passing vehicles.

Sales could be low with the daily sales of the smallest traders estimated at between 3,000 to 15,000 cedis a day. Some traders said their sales were even lower than this. The earnings of the more professional traders were estimated at between 20,000 to 40,000 cedis a market day. Transport costs were about 1,000 cedis per market day, making it much more expensive for small operators. The range of goods sold in the Mepe market was considered inadequate by both buyers and sellers. It was regular practice for traders after they had sold their wares to go to the nearby market at Battor to buy smoked fish and other goods.

There was a strong presence of various species of sea fish of the small variety, purchased from Ada Junction or from neighbouring coastal people such as Ningo and Akplabanya women, who had come and sold it to the retailers at the market earlier in the day. Few traders sold smoked and sun-dried river fish which was procured from Accra, specifically from the Adabraka market, an important depot for Volta Lake fish. The Mepe market, a more informal affair, was two times a week on Tuesdays and Fridays. Other markets in this part of South Eastern Ghana were organised every fourth day.

A system of informal credit was an important element of trading at both Mepe and Sokpoe. While many of the traders were involved, the rules of engagement were varied and complex. What was posed as a rationale for granting credit in one case did not apply across the board. At the Mepe market, some of the traders sold on credit, but differentiated what could be the subject of credit arrangements. In one case, a trader explained that she would extend credit for the *garri* she was selling, but not the palm fruit because the palm fruit was not much, while her stocks of *garri* were substantial. One woman who had brought cassava from her own farm, who did not come often but needed the money that day, had no plans to extend credit to her buyers and was prepared to take her cassava back home if not bought. As she explained, she was not a trader. On the other hand, a woman from Fakpoe who had brought maize from her own farm and who was not a regular at the market, still extended credit for a week to enable her to sell everything, although she said that sometimes people would refuse to pay. At the Sogakope market, some people exchanged cassava, but mostly charcoal for fish, foodstuffs and other needs without the medium of money. Barter arrangements also existed at markets such as Ada junction which were much larger. People from villages who brought small quantities of their harvest in turn purchased tomatoes, okro, soap, other provisions, kerosene, palm oil and fish for consumption. The use of credit created difficulties for most traders because their capital base was quite low. The social relations of credit will be discussed in more detail in chapter six.

In addition to the shops at Sokpoe, not less than thirty girls, young women and a few boys and young men hawked cooked foods and cooled water to passing vehicles which had to slow down as they approached the Lower Volta Bridge. Their wares included bread, fried fish, shrimps, turkey-tail and clams, abolo and kenkey (made from maize meal), cassava biscuits and oranges. Several bread sellers had tables along the road although they also approached the vehicles with a few loaves in polythene bags. The fresh fish sellers had also established a small market at the edge of the Lower Volta Bridge. A number of people had established small water purification concerns within Sokpoe and were bagging the water for sale by the roadside.

The poor development of markets around the Lower Volta in terms of infrastructure, goods and personnel was mentioned by a number of respondents. If the Mepe, Battor and Sogakope markets and shops were an indication of the character of the Lower Volta economy, then it was clear that most farmers produced barely enough for subsistence. Except for charcoal and preserved red peppers, the Mepe, Battor and Sogakope markets did not have stocks on a scale suggesting that foodstuffs were being produced in large quantities. Cassava, cassava dough and dried cassava, which were staples, were sold in quantities suggesting that they were part of the stocks meant for household consumption. Those who sold in large quantities were often long distance traders who had purchased these goods from outside the area. The main imports—cereals, pulses, dried cassava, second-hand goods, smoked and preserved sea fish—suggested that consumption levels of consumer goods in the area was very basic.

The market was dominated by charcoal and second hand-clothing. The character of non-market trading at the Mepe and Sokpoe supported these impressions. With regard to the shops, the range of goods sold was quite narrow. Also, the opening and closing down of shops in quick succession was significant. During the research period at Mepe, about five shops remained closed. Francis has argued that the appearance of vibrant markets was not necessarily a sign of prosperity as all their goods might be imports (see Francis, 2000). In this case, it can be argued that the converse, the absence of vibrant markets and the narrow range of goods sold in shops, were a sign of low levels of production, exchange and consumption. This was even granting that some exchanges and transactions were by-passing markets (Whitehead and Kabeer, 2001).

The wholesale adoption of a livelihood activity: Baking at Sokpoe

> Women in Sokpoe do more baking than farming. Some people only bake and a few combine it with farming (Head of the Bakers' Association, Sokpoe).

Bread baking and retailing were major livelihood activities for women at Sokpoe. Established by virtue of the community's location on the major road, much of the bread made at Sokpoe was now sold by the roadside on either end of the Lower Volta Bridge and at markets such as Dabala, Mafi-Kumasi, Mafi-Vedo, Battor (in the Tongu area) Akatsi and Agbozome (in the Avenor area to the east of Tongu), Ada Junction (in the Dangme District to the West of Tongu) and at Dzemini and Krachi (along the Volta Lake). For the distribution of bread around the Lower Volta and further afield, bakers had one or two women with whom they usually had loose or close kinship ties, who sold the bread in the markets or by the roadside. In some cases, members of the head baker's household did the distribution. Some bakers sold their own bread and these tended to produce smaller quantities at a time than those with distributors. For example, one baker who sold her own bread produced half a bag of flour worth of bread at a time.[15]

---

[15] Each half bag of flour was worth 60,000 cedis of bread at the time of the study. Those who sold it kept 10,000 cedis as their commission. Therefore those who sold their own bread got to keep the commission as well.

Baking had its peaks and troughs. August to October was not a good period for the industry because food was relatively plentiful. November to March was good because farmers would have sold their produce and would have money to buy bread. Apart from problems of seasonality of sales, bakers had health concerns because of the heat generated by the baking process. A combination of factors such as the size of the bread-baking households, their dependency ratios, the low capital base of bakers and the complicated economics of bread baking[16] raised doubts about the profitability of the industry. However, the most serious problem was the large numbers of bakers at Sokpoe. Only a few bakers appeared to have done well and diversified into other activities to supplement and support their bread making enterprises. As an activity which pre-dated the Akosombo Dam, but flowered in the post-dam period in response to the decline of other options, bread making at Sokpoe involved large numbers of women—bakers, apprentices, hired labour and informal help.[17] This resulted in overproduction and a regular glut in the bread market. Respondents said it took twice as long to sell the same amount of bread as it did some years ago. As well, several respondents had had to give up baking and the membership of the Bakers Association had halved from the figures of the 80s.

Intensifying the exploitation of marginal activities: Charcoal burning, buying and selling

The growing importance of hitherto marginal activities[18] was an added dimension of the strategy of putting pre-dam resources to different uses. While some activities of this nature were common to both Mepe and Sokpoe and other Lower Volta communities, e.g. charcoal burning and small scale trading, some were specific to particular communities, e.g. stone quarrying at Toklokpo, a Sokpoe village. As already indicated, charcoal burning was now a major activity

---

[16] The head of the Sokpoe Bakers' Association has argued that because many members were illiterate, their grasp of the economics of the business was weak and, therefore, they are unable to make profits.

[17] Relations within the bread baking industry will be discussed more fully in the next chapter on the organisation of livelihoods in the Lower Volta.

[18] Marginal in the sense of their economic importance in the pre-dam days and their environmental implications in the post-dam situation.

at Mepe and Sokpoe, particularly in the outlying villages, involving
people of all ages and gender. The scale of charcoal burning within
an environment with depleted vegetation cover posed clear medium-
term risks to the environment and to livelihoods. Already, many
respondents were complaining about the dwindling supplies of wood
suitable for charcoal burning or for use as firewood. The charcoal
was burned in small lots and then bagged for sale, each 50 kilo-
gram bag sold for 6,000 to 8,000 cedis in 2000. Respondents reported
different levels of charcoal production from a few bags a year to
quantities that were a significant, but by no means adequate, for
livelihood.[19] There was a potentially large market for charcoal and
traders came from Accra and beyond to purchase supplies from local
women who produced and also purchased charcoal from other
producers.

Apart from charcoal burning, there were more localised examples
of the increased use of marginal resources. Stone quarrying mostly
by young men at Toklokpo was one such activity. While it yielded
more than farming, its devastating effects on the topsoil and the
rapidly shrinking farmlands around Toklokpo raised questions about
its sustainability. This, not surprisingly, was creating tensions between
those quarrying and those who had complaints about encroachment
on their farmlands. Quarrying at Toklokpo shared some of the features and issues of other mining activities in the Lower Volta such
as the extraction of large deposits of clam shells[20] in certain communities in the North Tongu District including Mepe and the mining of clay deposits at Vume.[21]

[19] For example, one young man reported that he and his siblings had produced
30 bags of charcoal last year. This was a large amount of charcoal, given the
amounts reported by most respondents, but with total earnings not more than
200,000 cedis (an amount the equivalent of less than US$ 20), charcoal burning
was useful but inadequate as an anchor activity.
[20] The clam shells were a source of lime in the building industry for terrazzo
chippings, whitewash paint or simply as a strengthening ingredient for foundations
of buildings. Animal feed industries also used it as a source of calcium for poultry.
At Mepe, the development of a small clam shells industry had been stalled by
litigation.
[21] At Vume, the clay deposit had generated a visible pottery industry whose value
for women's livelihoods was beyond the scope of this study.

Expansion in training but not in practice: Artisanal activities

> There are a few new professions—sewing and hair-dressing. But you need money to sew. People learn and go back to chop-bar work (TJKA, Tsiamiga of Sokpoe Traditional Area).

Artisanal activities have been growing in importance all over Ghana, and the Lower Volta Basin was no exception to this. In the Lower Volta, however, artisanal activities also reflected the growing crisis of livelihoods. Traditional crafts such as mat-weaving, basket-weaving, the making of fish traps and wooden needles for repairing nets, which continued to be common activities in the off-farming season, particularly in the outlying villages but also in the main settlements, were supplementary in terms of time use. However, the newer artisanal activities such as sewing and hairdressing for women, masonry, carpentry, vehicle repairs and corn and flour milling for men, were growing in importance because the majority of young people were going into one or other of these professions. At Mepe for example, the few seamstresses plying their trade also had scores of apprentices they were training. The possibility of taking on apprentices seemed to offer a supplement to the generally low patronage of artisanal services. Apart from paying for their training, apprentices could provide labour for the farming and reproductive activities of their masters and mistresses. This aspect of the artisanal business would be discussed in more detail in the section on social relations. However, artisanal activities did not offer a way out of the livelihood crisis. There was a glut in some of the services they provided. The lack of electricity in a number of villages made some services impossible to establish fully. As a result, they continued to be minority activities in most communities in the Lower Volta with the exception of the more urbanised and many young people in training were planning to use their skills elsewhere after training.

5. *Multiple Livelihood Activities at Mepe and Sokpoe*

In the preceding section, we focused on a series of responses to the threats to pre-dam livelihoods posed by the long-term environmental changes which involved people continuing to put pre-dam resources to work, described broadly as a strategy of intensification and restructuring of the use of pre-dam resources. This strategy was often

combined with having two to three livelihood activities at the same
time. In this section, this practice is examined in some detail. Multiple
livelihood activities at the level of the household and for its individual members were common at both Mepe and Sokpoe. Tables
5.5 and 5.6 below give an indication of the prevalence of multiple
livelihood activities among heads of households. 51% of male and
52.5% of female household heads in the two communities had more
than one livelihood activity and of this figure, about 11% had three
activities. Farming was the anchor livelihood activity for a large number of respondents (46.6% of men and 42.9% women). Trading was
the anchor activity for 7.8% of men and 33.6% of women. Trading
and farming remained the most important second livelihood activities (16.9% men and 13.7% of women for farming and 4.4% of men
and 16.2% of women were trading—Table 5.5). This suggested that
while people were involved in multiple activities, the range of their
undertakings was narrow in terms of the resource base. The involvement in fishing was significant at Sokpoe (15.1%) but negligible at
Mepe (4.3%). Participation in traditional artisanship, the newer artisanal activities and wage labour, was also quite small for first activities at both Mepe and Sokpoe. There was also a difference in male
and female involvement in these activities (7.3% male and 2.1%
female for wage work and 11.2% male and 4.3% female for artisanship). Differences between men and women were larger at Mepe
than at Sokpoe. Another difference between Mepe and Sokpoe was
that when the first and second activities were taken together, far
more Mepe women were more involved in farming than Sokpoe
women were (64.6% to 41.6%). This was entirely in keeping with
the differences in the livelihood traditions of the two communities.
What was surprising was the findings about involvement in trading.
While for first activities there were slightly more Sokpoe women than
Mepe women (38% to 30%), once the first and second activities
were combined the difference disappeared and Mepe women had a
slight edge over Sokpoe women (60.9% Mepe women and 58.4%
Sokpoe women—Tables 5.5 and 5.6).

In terms of the ongoing debate about the significance of multiple
activities, the findings of our study suggested that the practice of
multiple activities represented different things—coping, accumulation
and not coping—to different people and households. Therefore, we
examined the multiple livelihoods observed in the Lower Volta in
the light of these debates. Our observation in both the Lower Volta

and around the Volta Lake was that livelihood outcomes could be differentiated in terms of coping, accumulation and not coping. In addition, there were community wide patterns which were significant. Therefore, these household and community level differences are examined in more detail through the case material. The following cases illustrate some of the livelihood trajectories of respondents.

CASE 5.1: Katherine, female, 50, late migrant, baker, long-distance trader and cooked food seller (Sokpoe)

> Katherine first left Sokpoe in 1979. When Rawlings first came to power after the June 4th Uprising in 1979, her mother was farming at a village near Yeji, a Lakeside settlement. Katherine was a long distance trader buying consumer goods in Accra and selling them at the village. The soldiers began to harass traders who took goods there.[22] On the advice of her mother she stopped trading, but decided to remain in the Lakeside settlement. Her three children were at Sokpoe with their father. She lived around the Lake for thirteen years farming and making kenkey; she grew sugarcane on one acre of land and later started a cassava farm. Both farms together were a little less than two acres. Later, she also bought nets and a canoe and took her two sons to the Lake to fish for her. They did this for four years and then returned to school and so the work went down. Her mother fell ill so she had to sell everything and bring her back home. Her mother died a year later in 1993.
>
> When Katherine returned to Sokpoe with her sick mother, she took up baking which she did for a few years, incurred debts and gave it up. She was able to build the house she lived in with earnings from her baking (a three-room house, laterite blocks, plastered with cement and painted, with an aluminium roof). When she gave up the baking, she returned to long-distance trading. She would go to Yeji taking cloth, torch batteries and cigarettes and such goods worth about 300,000 cedis, which she purchased from Accra. She would travel by road to Yeji in one day and sell her wares around the Lake, stay for a week to buy salted tilapia (*dzenkpe* or *akpatogui*) and smoked fish. She bought about 200,000 cedis or sometimes all the money she had. She would then sell the fish at Sokpoe. Her two sons who lived with her would carry the items round Sokpoe selling them. In a week the fish

---

[22] 1979 was a very uncertain and dangerous time for traders all over the country because they were identified as a target of the coup d'état government's anti corruption drive and many were flogged, prosecuted or suffered general harassment. Markets were burnt down and many women were driven out of the trade in consumer items (Manuh, 1993; Tsikata, 1997).

Table 5.5: 1st livelihood activity of household heads in Mepe and Sokpoe

| | Absolutes | | | | | | | Percentages | | | | | | | |
| | Mepe | | Sokpoe | | Mepe and Sokpoe | | | Mepe | | Sokpoe | | Mepe and Sokpoe | | |
	M	F	M	F	M	F	T	M	F	M	F	M	F	T
Wage work	7	1	8	4	15	5	20	7.7	.9	7.1	3.8	7.3	2.1	4.5
Artisanship	12	5	11	5	23	10	33	13	4	9.9	4.7	11.2	4.3	7.6
Trading	7	16	7	17	14	33	47	7.7	13	6.2	15.8	6.9	14.2	10.6
Food trading	–	21	2	24	2	45	47	–	17	1.8	22.2	.9	19.4	10.6
Farming	35	54	60	39	95	99	194	38	44	53.6	36.1	46.6	42.9	44.6
Fishing	4	1	17	2	21	3	24	4.3	.9	15.1	1.8	10.2	1.2	5.6
Retired/ Pensioner/ Disabled	15	16	4	9	19	25	44	16.3	13	3.6	8.3	9.3	10.9	10.1
Traditional Artisanship	5	–	–	1	5	1	6	5.4	–	–	.9	2.4	.4	1.3
Other	3	6	–	3	3	9	12	3.2	4.9	–	2.8	1.4	3.9	2.7
Unemployed	3	3	3	4	6	7	13	3.2	2.4	2.7	3.8	3	3	3
Total	92	123	112	108	204	231	435	100	100	100	100	100	100	100

Table 5.6: 2nd livelihood activity of household heads

| | Absolutes | | | | | | | Percentages | | | | | | |
| | Mepe | | Sokpoe | | Mepe and Sokpoe | | | Mepe | | Sokpoe | | Mepe and Sokpoe | | |
	M	F	M	F	M	F	T	M	F	M	F	M	F	T
Wage work	1	–	–	1	1	1	2	1	–	–	.9	.4	.4	.4
Artisanship	1	–	4	–	5	–	5	1	–	3.6	–	2.4	–	1.1
Trading	1	31	5	14	6	45	51	1	24.6	4.4	13	3	19.3	11.5
Food trading	1	8	2	8	3	16	19	1	6.3	1.8	7.4	1.4	6.9	4.2
Farming	17	26	18	6	35	32	67	18	20.6	16.1	5.5	16.9	13.7	15
Fishing	7	–	17	–	24	–	24	7.4	–	15.1	–	11.7	–	5.4
Traditional Artisanship	–	–	2	–	2	–	2	–	–	1.8	–	.9	–	.4
Other	–	1	–	1	–	2	2	–	.8	–	.9	–	.8	.4
NA	66	60	64	78	130	138	268	70.2	47.6	57.1	72.2	63.1	58.9	60.9
Total	94	126	112	108	206	234	440	100	100	100	100	100	100	100

would be finished and then she would buy new goods and return. Her profits at Yeji for each trip were in the region of 50,000 cedis before subtracting her transport costs of 20,000. At Sokpoe, she could make 40–60,000 cedis profit on the fish. She would leave Sokpoe on Saturday and return on the second Tuesday after that (10 days) and this she did throughout the year.

Once her children went to Secondary school and their father died five years ago, she had to stop. In the last five years, she had been selling and cooking beans and *garri*. She was now planning to start her long-distance trading again with the help of her children.

CASE 5.2: Godwill, individual and household level multiple livelihood activities (Sokpoe)

Godwill (50), a Sokpoe man, was engaged in farming and fishing. He was educated with a middle school-leaving certificate. He sold locally brewed gin, *akpeteshie*, in a small bar complete with an open-air hut for sitting down. His wife was a baker. Apart from visiting Yeji during school holidays, he had never migrated. His household was made up of seven persons—five adult and two children. Two of the adults had dropped out of school and were helping out selling bread; three persons, Godwill, his wife and a son who was a carpenter, were engaged in independent production activities but co-operated in the production of food for common consumption. The house, comprising three rooms, was made with laterite blocks, roofed with thatch roof and painted black. There was a separate kitchen, which was also a thatch and laterite-block structure.

Godwill had farmlands totalling 3¾ acres in two places. One was a three-acre plot at Dendo across the Volta, but quite easily reached by road transport. Both lands had been rented to him by uncles—a paternal uncle rented him the three-acre plot while his maternal uncle rented him the ¾ of an acre plot. This was in spite of the fact that his lineage owned vast tracts of land. He had only 1¾ of an acre under cultivation. He planted maize and cassava on one plot and only maize on the smaller one. His wife was too busy to help him farm so she paid for the labour he hired. His children also helped with the harvesting. In 1998 when the harvest was good, he sold about 60,000 cedis worth of maize and consumed ⅔ of the crop.

He considered fishing to be his main activity in terms of income, time use and its status in his life. His fishing assistant was usually his uncle Kobla who belonged to a different household and who also had his own farm. They did the net fishing together while Godwill did prawn fishing by himself. He set the prawn traps in the evening and harvested them in the morning, between 5.00 and 6.00 am. Then he got the traps ready for resetting. He fished prawns six days a week. Three to four times a week, he went fishing with a net at 5.00 pm, returning at 6.00 am in the morning. He did not spend days at a time on the river sleeping in other villages along the Volta as other fishermen did.

He owned a net, prawn traps and canoes. The net was a 1½ inch mesh type, which was used for catching smaller fish. He had fished tilapia before but no longer did so because he found net repairing too time-consuming. His net and boat were rented about five times a month by people who did not have their own equipment and they paid him ⅓ of the catch whenever this happened.[23]

He sold most of his catch leaving a little for household use. He earned between 10–25,000 cedis a day depending on how the fishing was going and this represented ⅔ of the catch, a third for the equipment and another third for his labour. He also earned 24,000 cedis profit on a container of local gin, which cost 112,000 cedis, which he sold in a month. However, much of the drink was sold and bought on credit.

Godwill and his wife were responsible for the major expenditures of the household. They had electricity which they shared with other households around. They listened to the radio and had the use of a fridge.

CASE 5.3: Gladys, multiple activities at the individual level (Sokpoe)

Gladys, who was 56, was living at Toklokpo. She grew up in the Kumasi area where she had been taken by her mother's sister and worked for several people as house-help. When she was 26 she met and married a Sokpoe man who took her to the cocoa growing areas where he was an *abusa* labourer. After the Akosombo Dam, they went to Yeji where they lived for twenty years, her husband fishing and she preserving his fish and selling it. She also purchased fish from other fishermen. She decided in the mid-1990s to return to her hometown Toklokpo because the earnings from the fish business were no longer good. Three years after she left, her husband died and he had been dead for twenty months at the time of the interview. He had supported the idea of returning home and since he had the younger children with him, he planned to return when she had established a farm. After his death and burial at Yeji, she returned with the younger children and the older ones remained there.

Gladys, five years on, was farming, rearing animals and engaged in petty trading. She was the only member of her seven-member household who had independent livelihood activities. She lived with three children—a daughter and two sons between 22 and 12 and three

---

[23] A net could last for three years if nothing went wrong while a boat could go for 6 years before needing replacement. The prawn traps lasted for only three months. Things like the ropes and lead pieces and cork lasted forever and could be taken from an old net and used on a new one.

grandchildren. Gladys lived in a two-bedroom and one living room house belonging to her mother, who used to be a pepper farmer. The house was built from laterite blocks and had an aluminium roof and a separate kitchen.

She farmed four pieces of land, a total of three acres, and was an *abusa* farmer for all except one acre, which was her mother's land. None of her farms was more than twenty minutes' walk away from where she was living. She grew cassava, maize and pepper in different permutations on the land depending on its quality. She sold the pepper but kept the cassava and maize for consumption. The whole pepper crop could yield something in the neighbourhood of 240,000 cedis for about six sacks of pepper. She also grew a few tomatoes. She hired a tractor to prepare the land and planted two seasons. The clearing and preparation of the land was expensive (between 40–50,000 cedis an acre) and she sometimes sold one of her animals to pay for the clearing. She had 11 sheep and 5 goats. The animals were penned because farming was being done all around the village. One male sheep was sold for 100,000 while a female sheep went for 30,000 cedis. Her income from the one or two animals she sold was about 200,000 cedis a year. Her 12-year old son in primary school class 5 was the one who looked after the animals.

Gladys's petty trading involved smoked and preserved fish which she bought from Ada Junction every Tuesday with a capital of 60,000 cedis. She said her profits were about 12,000 cedis every week, i.e. on every consignment. Some of the fish went towards their own consumption. The same son who helped with the animals helped her to sell the fish, which they sold at home. Most people purchased the fish on credit, usually buying anything between 500 and 2,000 cedis worth of fish. She bought soap, kerosene and everyday needs from the trading income, paid school fees from the sale of sheep and pepper from her farming. Her children contributed by helping with the farm before and after school during the planting season.

Gladys did not usually spend too much money on foodstuffs. Last year though, she had to buy cassava and maize from December to May. It was the school fees which were difficult to pay regularly, now that she no longer had support from her husband. Occasionally relations helped with gifts of money and school uniforms for the children. Gladys owned a house in one of the migrant villages—a four-room laterite-block house in which one of her children was staying. In spite of her relatively better off status, she did not enjoy electricity and her source of water was a hole in the stone quarry and a well, same as for everyone else at Toklokpo.

CASE 5.4: Ayorkor, whose husband had sent her home from the Lakeside. Rural-Rural multi-spatial livelihoods (Dadome, Mepe)

Ayorkor was in her mid forties. She was born at Dadome to parents who farmed, and grew up there. One of her older sisters took her to Accra and hired her out to a trader who sold bags. When she was in her late teens, she left Accra and went to visit her brothers at Yeji. She stayed and began to sell enamelware. She met and married a Dadome man within a year of her arrival and they moved to a place called Kafaba and then to Buipe. Three years into the marriage, he took a second wife. A third wife joined them after a while.

She sold her pans for two more years after the marriage. Her trading did not go well and she lost her capital. Her husband, then a fisherman, refused to give her money to recapitalise her trade. He also preferred to sell his fish to other women traders rather than his wives. Ayorkor and her co-wives, having no capital of their own to buy from other fishermen, preserved their husband's fish before it was sold. At the end of the fishing season when it was time to go home to Mepe for the annual festival, he gave them some money for their work. They also worked on a farm acquired by their husband. They sold the farm products for him and he gave them some of the earnings on a regular basis, separate from the household maintenance money. The husband's business did well and he moved into boat transportation and trading in nets and fuel.

Five years before the interview, armed conflict broke out in the Buipe area between two local groups. The migrants felt insecure and Ayorkor's husband decided that she should return to Dadome with all their children of school-going age. She came with seven children, three of her own and four belonging to her co-wives. Three of the children were 15, two were 13 and the last two were 8 and 7. Her household also included a young cowherd, about 14 years old, who was hired to look after her husband's cattle. She and the children did much of the housework—sweeping, cooking, washing clothes and picking firewood. Her own children washed her things and theirs and the others did theirs separately.

She was farming with the help of the children for their food. Food was also sent from Buipe. In the last six months, they had received three parcels of kokonte and garri, each parcel lasting for about three weeks. They farmed cassava, maize and groundnuts. The groundnuts were sold to supplement the money from Buipe, which she said was not enough and dwindling in regularity. She also made some charcoal, an average of 4 bags in three weeks. A bag of charcoal was sold for 5,000 cedis to buyers who came to Dadome. This was work she only did three months a year (10–12th months).

She received about 25,000 cedis every two months for food items and other sundries. School fees were paid separately by her husband. They did not sell the cassava and maize they produced because of the size of the household. When things became desperate, a letter was sent to Buipe written by one of the children in school. In the meantime, they would buy food items and soap on credit up to 40,000 cedis. Ayorkor was creditworthy because when the money came she repaid all her debts.

When she first came to stay from Buipe, things were much better. Her husband came more regularly and they did not want. Things were now very hard at Buipe. Fishing was not going well because the water levels were low. This had affected all his businesses adversely, curtailed his visits home and reduced the amounts of money they were getting. He used to come about ten times a year but he had not been for five months. Ayorkor was, therefore, experiencing material deprivation. She could not buy cloth and other needs with the regularity and ease with which she made purchases during the Lakeside days because the money she earned and what her husband sent was never enough. She had no capital to trade with and now she could not look to Buipe for that kind of money. Her household was classified as poor.

CASE 5.5: Kpeglo, an artisan whose livelihood was not diversified (Mepe)

Kpeglo, a mason born at Klikor, lived at Mepe with his wife who was a farmer. They were married in 1986. He was an Anlo-Ewe, one of the few non-Tongu residents of Mepe. His wife farmed near a creek, Avilonu, and had two separate plots which together came up to less than one acre. She was a share crop tenant and they took a third of her cassava. The maize was subjected to the share crop arrangements only when the harvest was good. She grew cassava, maize, ground-nuts, tomatoes and garden eggs. She dried her cassava and sold some but kept most of it because she believed that if you sold too much cassava, you were in danger of starving. She farmed alone with no support from Kpeglo.

Kpeglo had studied masonry as an apprentice to a relation at Adidome, the capital of the North Tongu District, for four years and helped his master to work for two years after that. He then became a wage worker on a poultry farm at Adidome for 11 years. He returned to building while he was still at Adidome and then he moved to Kpong. He had came to Mepe to build a house for someone for five months, and decided to settle there. He liked the peace and the river. He was now working as a mason around Mepe and its environs. The year before, he had built three houses. The owners bought their own material and he built for them in stages and was paid for each stage, i.e. the foundation, the walls and the gables. At this stage, he handed over to a carpenter to do the roofing. He hired five labourers to assist him at 4,000 cedis a day each. He charged an average of 80,000 cedis for each room he constructed and on average, people built houses of 4–6 rooms.

He was renting a room for which he was paying 1,000 cedis a month from a farmer who farmed across the river. The house had laterite blocks and an aluminium roof. They lived there with another household of tenants. Between him and his wife they had ten adult children living around the lake working as fishermen and farmers. Some of the children sent them food once a year during the festival. The food did not last beyond the festival period when there were a lot of visitors. The household was not relying on anyone for maintenance. They had no electricity and had no visible resources.

According to his wife, her children did not go to school and had been "hired" to people around the Volta Lake to go and work for them. Kpeglo's children, who were born at Adidome, had also been taken to Yeji when they were young to stay with people and work until they were old enough and then they became independent. He said that these days, they could be paid as much as 120,000 to 140,000 cedis a year and they paid their own transport costs to come home. Kpeglo was one of the few respondents living in rented premises apart from other households.

Elements of practice

The five cases set out above illustrate various elements of the practice of multiple livelihood activities as well as the similarities and differences in practices within the research communities. While some people combined different activities simultaneously or within a seasonal or cyclical structure, others moved from one activity to another over the years, returning to old activities and starting new ones depending on various environmental factors and their personal circumstances. The latter were not always involved in multiple engagements at any point in time, but over several years had been involved in several activities and therefore did not benefit from multiple sources simultaneously. Katherine (Case 5.1) was an example of those who had this serial approach to multiple livelihood activities. At each point in time, she concentrated on one activity even though she deployed the training and other resources from past activities. Her livelihood activities had been multi-spatial, involving and selling in the Lower Volta and around the Lake until she settled around the Lake and farmed and fished with the support of her sons. Years later, her trading experience and connections during her years as a migrant were used in her long-distance trading. She had returned to Sokpoe with her sick mother after fourteen years as a migrant. To be able to look after her mother, she had chosen a more sedentary approach to making a living, focusing on baking. When that did not work out and her mother died, she went back to long-distance trading between the Lakeside and the Lower Volta. She had had to give this up again on account of her children and had sold cooked food and was now planning to start long-distance trading again. If diversification as defined meant the pursuit of multiple activities, then people like Katherine were not diversifying their livelihoods. In contrast, Godwill (Case 5.2) and Gladys (Case 5.3) were each involved in three different pursuits at the same time.

Within a household, each individual could have two or more activities geared to generating the resources on which to live, but in many cases, different members of the household each had one activity. In such a case, the practice of multiple livelihood activities was in relation to the household and not to individuals within it. Ellis has suggested that people in that kind of position were usually better off than situations where each member was engaged in multiple activities. This argument has merit, especially in the case of people engaged in high capital entry activities such as bakers at Sokpoe who no longer did any farming, preferring to concentrate on their baking. However, it did not always apply and a number of contradictory factors accounted for the levels of specialisation of households and their members.

While people dealt with the uncertainties of farming by planting smaller acreages or not planting at all for a few years, only a few people had given up farming completely. For these, their history of farming was pertinent in that those who had not been farming for long, for whatever reason found it easier to give it up. As well, household size and composition was a factor. For bakers with small households with very few adults and, therefore, smaller food needs but also labour constraints, dropping farming was a sensible option. Baking yielded higher returns and on a more regular and predictable basis than farming. For large households with many dependants, giving up farming was not an option because the food bill was a matter of concern. Godwill (5.2), whose household was involved in several activities at both the individual and household levels, continued to have farming in their portfolio, but it was done by Godwill, who combined it with fishing and selling local gin. His wife baked full time and paid for hired labour to do her portion of farm work. They were each able to pursue their livelihood activities with the support of three adult and two minor children who provided unpaid labour.

Apart from bakers, artisans such as Kpeglo (Case 5.5), a carpenter, sometimes specialised in one activity. Even here, some of them took in apprentices and had farms. In Kpeglo's case, his wife farmed and sold a little of the produce, but without his support.

There were also some households whose heads were involved in more than one livelihood activity but who were the only ones with independent activities within their households. Other household members would then provide labour for production and reproductive activities. Gladys (Case 5.3) who was engaged in farming, selling fish and keeping livestock was in this position. Her animals were largely the responsibility of her young son who also assisted her with her trading. Several of the households headed by quite old people and composed of themselves and their grandchildren were also in this situation. In some cases, they were engaged in only farming, supplemented by remittances in return for looking after grandchildren. As the household heads became old and frail, their dependence on remittances increased until it became their only source of sustenance. While arguably, their care of grandchildren strengthened their call on the resources of their children, the intermittent character of the support and the demands of bringing up young people placed additional stresses on such households. Not all retired persons were in this situation. Some had left resources which included cattle, goats and sheep and fishing equipment around the Lake in the care of their children; they also left behind goodwill, which they continued to draw on.

Multiple livelihood activities were usually not structured in the neat and coherent ways described in the case studies. There were cases of a more experimental approach to livelihoods whose patterns were difficult to understand except in the sense that people were trying out different things using old forms of knowledge and practices, but which were not working well under the new conditions. In some cases, people appeared to be chasing down every economic activity which appeared to have possibilities, but failing to find the balance between how each activity fitted in the portfolio, its viability at present and its long-term prospects. Salt winning and clam picking at Mepe were examples of this problem which raised a more general question of the synergies between different activities. For example, some activities could augment or reinforce each other, while others did not necessarily have a relationship except that they produced cumulative value or in some cases, one replaced the other in importance. Thus, for example, growing food crops and keeping livestock might provide some synergies as would farming and charcoal-burning in the sense that people tended to collect firewood around their farms for charcoal making and charcoal sales provided money for sustenance in between harvests. However, in relation to farming and charcoal, given their common resource base, the same problems which have made farming difficult have resulted in the depletion of wood sources. Furthermore, Kinsey's (2002) argument that a rapid expansion of non-farm activities could reduce the returns on each activity even if total incomes increase, is relevant here. Rarely did households have enough capital and labour to make the kinds of investments that would bring adequate returns on each of their activities. Therefore, more was not necessarily better in this situation of a depleting resource base. Godwill's household (5.2), which was combining fishing, farming, selling local gin, carpentry and baking was doing better than many. However, the low capital base of their various operations, poor earnings from their farming especially, but also the drinks and the fact that two of their children had dropped out of school, raised questions about the future of the livelihood prospects of this household.

Factors influencing the multiplication of livelihood activities in the Lower Volta

The cases above support the findings of earlier studies that factors such as spatial advantage, education and socio-cultural factors influence the form and character of the practice of multiple livelihoods (Francis, 2000). The study found that in addition to the above, the ability to straddle rural and urban locations, the skills and technological advantages of individuals and their households were helpful. As well, the household's developmental cycle, size, composition and access to resources were implicated in livelihood trajectories in general and in the practice of multiple livelihood activities in particular.

Multiple livelihood activities and spatial advantage
Natural resource endowments and location specificities illustrate the influence of spatial factors in livelihoods. This issue was raised earlier in the chapter to draw attention to how Sokpoe's location on a highway and at a bridge crossing and differences in natural resource endowments have made particular activities and, therefore, combinations of undertakings possible. Mepe's clam shell deposits in which several young men were interested but which were not yet being

fully exploited because of a dispute over ownership, were a good example of an activity which was specific to Mepe and possibly other communities in the upper sections of the Lower Volta.[24] In any one traditional area in the Lower Volta, those in the outlying villages did more charcoal burning and had larger farms than those who lived in the main settlements. At Toklokpo, a Sokpoe village, livestock rearing had been organised in harmony with farming. Animals had to be penned during the farming season and released only after the maize harvest. Thus, several households were able to boost their agriculture-anchored livelihoods by combining farming, livestock and trading.

Another aspect of spatial advantage was the establishment of multi-spatial livelihoods. This was defined as a situation where members of a household lived in two different locations and used both locations for making their livelihoods. In the Lower Volta, the practice of operating in two locations had been present from the early stages of wholesale out-migration of the 1960s. It had traditionally involved two rural areas—the Lower Volta and the Volta Lakeside—but increasingly involved one rural and one urban area. Several Lakeside migrants in response to the deteriorating conditions there, had sent home some members of their polygynous households to settle in their hometowns. For others, it was a retirement strategy. Older men and women came to spend the last years of their active working lives in their hometowns buoyed by savings and investments from their Lakeside years.

Ayorkor (Case 5.4) was an example of a rural-rural multi-spatial livelihood strategy which was rare in studies of its practice elsewhere (Francis, 2000; Foeken, 1997). After decades of living around the Volta Lake, she was back in the Lower Volta as a result of decisions made by her husband in response to their deteriorating livelihood conditions around the Lake. While her husband was around the Lake operating a Lake transport business and farming with the help of his other wives, she was back at Mepe, farming, making charcoal and overseeing the rearing of cattle with the support of

---

[24] Elsewhere in the Lower Volta towards the Estuary, mangroves were now an important source of fuelwood and reeds for making mats and various receptacles for storage were also important.

some of her children and those of her co-wives. She was receiving foodstuffs and money from the Lake to supplement her efforts. However, her husband's dwindling visits and remittances were now making life very difficult. In any case, he could not participate in the household's livelihood activities and decision-making processes on a day to day basis. There were other cases of multi-spatial livelihoods in both research communities which involved husbands who were urban-based wage employees. In one case, this wife of a man with another wife lived at Sokpoe almost from the start of her marriage because her husband wanted to have a strong presence in his hometown which he visited very regularly. Typically, the urban-based husbands were able to contribute more money to their rural households and they also visited more often, in some cases, they were reported to come at least every fortnight. Thus they also could participate more actively in the life of this branch of their households in the Lower Volta. Although Ayorkor had the advantage of returning to her own hometown, having lived around the Lakeside for years and not been involved in any trading, she did not have the capital or experience to engage in trading. In contrast, several of those women whose husbands were urban migrants had the capital and some urban trading experience and were involved actively in trading.

A dimension of this issue related to returned migrants, many of whom had established multiple livelihood activities around the Lakeside and other communities and who, on their return, were finding their ability to continue with these multiple activities constricted. Gladys (Case 5.3) was in the unusual position of successfully establishing a livelihood similar to what she had around the Lake and this had been made possible by conditions at Toklokpo. Thus, while multi-spatial livelihoods could improve livelihood outcomes, they did not insulate people from the hardships of living in a precarious environment.

Multiple livelihood activities, skills and technologies
Many of the multiple activities in which people were engaged in the Lower Volta occurred within a common resource base—the land and the river. Farming was often combined with fishing, charcoal burning or quarrying, or trading in foodstuffs some of which were locally produced. As Bagachwa found elsewhere, the seasonality of farming was a factor which made it possible to combine with non-

farm activities (1997, p. 141). Furthermore, farm sizes in the Lower Volta allowed time for other undertakings. The most important reason, however, for the attraction to certain activities was ease of entry. People did not have the resources to start new activities which needed large capital outlays. Additionally, to be able to diversify beyond farming, charcoal burning and fishing, it was necessary to have some training, skills and the technologies, and all this in an economy with people too poor or too few to give adequate patronage to such services. As Bryceson has argued, many non-agricultural activities are unviable in rural areas where purchasing power, infrastructure and the availability of natural resources are all limited. This is notwithstanding the value of their surplus labour absorption and training functions (1997; pp. 253–254). This was also true of the Lower Volta and had a bearing on the range and intensity of artisanal activities in the Lower Volta. There were also examples of livelihoods which had been diversified within an agricultural natural resource base and which appeared to be relatively successful especially when combined with some trading in foodstuffs. In one case, a respondent was vigorously pursuing both farming and fishing with money he had brought from a short stint in Accra and five continuous acres of lineage land he had secured through his father, one of the leaders of the lineage. He was a member of a small household with two independent incomes as his wife was trading. Gladys (Case 5.3) was another example of this approach. Although her farming was critical to her livelihood portfolio, capital as well as skill and experience from the Lakeside had proved very useful. While she did not have access to rent-free lineage land, she was not paying for a third of the land she farmed and much of the rest of her farm land had been rented from relations on reasonable and flexible terms.

These examples notwithstanding, those who were able to include artisanal activities in their portfolios tended to do better than those who had to rely solely on activities related directly to the land and the river. The cases generally supported the view that artisanal and other forms of training were important for the strategy of multiple livelihood activities. Some of those who had never migrated before or who had lived around the Volta Lake for only short periods were those with some artisanal training which they continued to use in the Lower Volta. Formal education allowed people to access the few avenues of wage employment within the Lower Volta. These when combined with fishing, trading, baking and other more traditional

activities improved livelihood outcomes. Few persons at Mepe and
Sokpoe were able to secure wage work, the most commonly available being teaching which required some level of training. Teachers,
particularly the women, often combined teaching with small scale
trading. Their long years of wage work was often positive for their
livelihood outcomes. They typically had smaller households, children
in higher education and in some cases owned the house in which
they lived.

In relation to technologies, activities such as trading and fishing
had derived some benefits from electricity. As well, some farmers
were using tractors to supplement more traditional farming technologies. Artisanal training went hand in hand with the introduction of new technologies such as sewing machines, irons, hair-dryers
and welding machines. As already indicated, there was a growing
number of artisans and service providers at both Mepe and Sokpoe
particularly with the introduction of electricity. A number of artisans no longer or had never farmed independently, even though
many had grown up in households which had farms. For this group,
artisanal training had resulted in a shift from a natural resource-
based livelihood to one depending on training and service delivery.
This was the case even with artisans who still did some farming with
the assistance of apprentices. For many of them, farming and fishing
had become supplementary undertakings.

The outcomes of diversification: Adaptation or coping with long-term crisis

> Even though we are farmers and fishermen, we now have to buy
> foodstuffs and fish to survive (Azanu Wadza, Morkodze, Sokpoe).

The above cases broadly supported the argument that having multiple activities could improve livelihood outcomes if they were the
right mix of agriculture and natural resource-based activities, services and wage employment. Adopting more than one activity could
also be useful depending on the availability of adequate capital and
labour inputs. Thus, not all households with multiple livelihood activities were able generate what was needed to secure their survival,
the welfare of all and long-term security. A number of factors made
livelihood outcomes unfavourable even in situations of multiple activities. The generally poor environmental resource base of the Lower
Volta, the fragmentation of the available lands and the specific prob-

lems of the various activities reduced the benefits of multiple engagements. Secondly, while training and technology were helpful to the practice of multiple livelihoods, they could not guarantee success because of the poor patronage of services. Thus, several artisans found specialisation difficult and tended to include farming and the training of apprentices in their livelihood portfolios. Those who did not have conditions to combine artisanal services with these other activities were usually among some of the poor households.

One condition which appeared uncontroversial for successful livelihood outcomes was access to different types of resources and locations. Some of the most successful households were those which had relatively larger farmlands, labour and capital in abundance—even if in only one location. Also, households in which some members operated in a different location from the rest, thus allowing the household to deploy resources from two different kinds of environment, also had a stronger survival base. The ability to gain reasonable outcomes from each undertaking was vital to successful practice of multiple livelihood activities. In situations where only one or none of an individual or a household's livelihood activities produced particularly strong results, the household usually did not do too well. For example, in the Lower Volta, the poor prognosis for fishing, farming and charcoal burning meant that even when combined, households still found themselves in difficulties unless in exceptional situations of access to relatively large acreages of land. Where synergies existed between the multiple activities, livelihood outcomes improved. This included situations where earnings from one activity went to finance another, as for example a man at Sokpoe who used his earnings from his trade in flour, his wages and some other resources to buy a flour mill. Or people whose farming and livestock rearing yielded enough to support their trading activities. It was also helpful when differences in seasons allowed different activities to be successfully undertaken (farming, animal rearing and trading) or where proximity made a number of activities convenient (farming, palm-wine tapping and *akpeteshie* distilling).

Household characteristics, which influenced the resources it could command and the ability of its members to straddle different locations, were an important factor in livelihood strategies and trajectories. However, the wider context were even more critical in livelihood outcomes. This context in the Lower Volta included the declining resource base and the continued dependence of most households on the land and the river for their livelihoods. Unlike in other places where the practice of multiple livelihood activities might have contributed to the transformation of rural households (Bryceson, 1997), they continued to be locked within agrarian livelihoods partly because of the lack of alternatives.

From the foregoing, it is clear that the practice of multiple livelihood activities in the Lower Volta did not represent adaptation to the long-term impacts of the Volta River Project. Within the livelihoods literature, adaptation was considered to be a potential outcome of diversification or the practice of multiple livelihood activities. However, the definitions of adaptation suggest that it has taken place only when livelihood outcomes are positive. As we indicated in the conceptual framework, a distinction has been made between negative and positive adaptation, the former necessary, irreversible and failing to reduce vulnerability and the latter by choice, reversible and increasing security (Ellis, 1998, p. 14). This account of multiple livelihood activities at Mepe and Sokpoe suggest that for most people, it did not reduce insecurities. This assessment is supported by a comparison with the findings of another study in which adaptation was found to have taken place (Thomas and Adams, 1999). The particular relevance of this study was its focus on communities similar to those of the Lower Volta as well as the finding that there had been adaptation to dam impacts in the long-term. This is in spite of stated limitations in the scope of the study[25] and the contestation of its conclusion that adaptation had occurred.[26] There are differences between the study area, the Hadejia-Jama'are Floodplain and the Lower Volta. For example, seasonal flooding did not completely cease in the Hadejia Jama'are Floodplain as it did in the Lower Volta. In spite of these differences, the impacts of the dam as reported in the lit-

---

[25] The study was limited to farming. Fishing, pastoralism and forestry, which were also critical for livelihoods in the area, were not considered (Thomas and Adams, 1999).

[26] For example, Hoover argues that the wetland downstream at the confluence of the Hadejia-Jama'are rivers had now shrunk drastically and the conflicts over the land had intensified between its traditional users such as pastoralists and more recent users such as sugarcane and wheat growers (Hoover, 2001). According to Hoover, this situation had been exacerbated by the absence of a holistic approach to the water resources which take account of all users—large-scale irrigation, fishermen, farmers and pastoralists.

erature on the Hadejia-Jama'are were similar to what occurred in the Lower Volta.[27]

Thomas and Adams themselves did qualify their success story, raising some specific problems as well as more general issues of sustainability and the question of the counterfactual.[28] In spite of all the caveats and qualifications, the sum of which do weaken the case being made for adaptation, the study set out some useful criteria for assessing the presence of adaptation and the factors which made it possible in the Hadejia-Jama'are Floodplain case. These criteria, for example the higher than national average population growth, the widespread adoption of technological innovations and increased production in agriculture, were absent in the Lower Volta. While there were more waged workers at Mepe and Sokpoe than in the pre-dam days, their presence was more a result of government decentralisation policies and their impact on agriculture did not appear to be significant. On the contrary, there was evidence that the problems identified from the late 60s had festered and become even more intractable. For example, while population decline in the Lower Volta had been arrested, its growth continued to be lower than regional and national averages. Other manifestations of the population problem,

---

[27] These, as already mentioned in earlier chapters, included reductions in crop production and in some cases crop failure and a decline in fishing and cattle rearing. Secondary activities such as trading and crafts were also adversely affected by the decline in local incomes and growing out-migration in an area which had formerly experienced in-migration (Stock, quoted in Thomas and Adams, 1999).

[28] They noted the ecological impacts of the technologies being introduced in the long-term as well as intractable land conflicts related to scarcity and different uses for land. They also argued that the heavy dependence of villagers on small-scale irrigation whose technical sustainability was not clearly established was likely to become problematic. Another problem was the persistence of seasonal out-migration which was expected to bring into question the viability of shops, schools and other socio-economic services in the long-term (Thomas and Adams, 1999). As well, they raised the question of what would have happened within the floodplain without the dam. This was on account of the poor record of large-scale irrigation and the fact that even before the dam, the area was already undergoing agricultural intensification. Also important in this regard was the resulting loss of the floodplain's ecological functions of recharging the water table, maintaining water quality and stabilising the climate (ibid., 1999). Thomas and Adams made clear that their conclusions were to be understood as meaning that in some situations adaptation could soften socio-economic impacts and even improve the productivity of downstream environments. However, they stress that this does not justify the neglect of short-term impacts although short-term impacts do not necessarily foretell long-term impacts.

as already mentioned, were the large presence of migration-affected household structures and abnormally high dependency ratios.

None of the recent studies of the Lower Volta have suggested that there have been improvements in livelihoods. They have instead confirmed continuing environmental and socio-economic problems with adverse impacts on livelihoods (Yeboah, 1999; Geker, 1999; Volta Basin Research Project, 1999). Indeed, one of the aims of the Lower Volta Environmental Impact studies conducted by the Volta Basin Research Project was to identify measures that would lead to a revival of the creek fisheries, clam industry, agriculture and health (Yeboah, 1999, p. 131). While farming at Mepe and Sokpoe changed from being flood-based to being rain-fed, it had not recovered from its post-dam decline because of the unreliability of rainfall[29] and the decline in soil fertility. The proportion of imported food in the markets, its high costs as well as the fact that households consumed more dried sea fish than river fish were all indications that fishing and farming had not recovered. Related to this, the widespread and socially accepted use of short-term credit to secure food was problematic and debilitating for the trade in foodstuffs, creating social tensions in a situation where debtors were often unable to pay on the agreed date. Also, some of the most popular livelihood activities such as charcoal burning and bread-baking as well as the less popular such as quarrying and assisting smugglers to cross the Volta, raised questions of sustainability. Emerging and re-emerging activities such as salt winning and clam picking had questionable promise because they required spending periods away and, therefore, were not easily combined with reproductive and other livelihood activities in these new conditions.

Incipient and actual conflicts such as the one between Sokpoe fishermen and others, land disputes as well as everyday tensions over credit were also suggestive of some of the continuing challenges of making a living in the Lower Volta. The survival problems of young persons, particularly those whose parents were far away in migrant villages along the Lake, as well as the lack of future prospects for young people in the study settlements were also indications that adaptation had not taken place.

---

[29] As a 1976 petition written by the Tongu District Council stated, agriculture in the Lower Volta was having to rely solely on poor rainfall, an annual average of 39 inches.

At both Mepe and Sokpoe, respondents discussed their livelihoods in terms of attending to present needs (for themselves and their dependants), being able to sustain themselves into old age and also being able to leave something to posterity.[30] What signified that a person was well on the way to fulfilling these goals included the ownership of some of the cattle which were consolidated in kraals in the Tongu hinterlands and around the Volta Lake. Very few people owned cattle in the numbers that would realistically fulfil the above goals.[31] For the majority of people, cattle were mainly used to feed mourners during funerals of loved ones considered important enough to merit the killing of one or two cows and sold to purchase equipment for work. Cattle were, therefore, in the category of savings. Goats and sheep did not have the status of cattle, but were also considered useful because they were more easily and more conveniently acquired, liquidated and kept locally within the communities by their owners and were, therefore, more secure as savings. Other such resources, which were mostly owned by retired men, were cocoa farms in the Akan areas, other tree crops such as palm, nets and canoes and cement block houses put up in district and regional capitals such as Sogakope and Ho for rentals. Interestingly, houses built in hometown communities were not considered to be such a resource unless they were rented, a relatively rare practice. They were more an indicator of success and a resource to deploy in cementing clan and lineage relations than a tool for the narrow pursuit of profits. In the long-term, they were also a potential home for retirees.

The Hadejia-Jama'are Floodplain's success story even with all its qualifications had not been replicated in the Lower Volta because some of the policy factors present there were absent in the Lower Volta. These included the introduction of new technologies, the availability of credit, improvements in communications and access to the area. Much of the technology came through World Bank and government projects with the political, organisational, technical and

---

[30] The importance of having resources that could be bequeathed to children was underlined by a few informants as a way of guaranteeing that a person would be cared for in old age (TA, Morkordze).

[31] Moreover, cattle were not the most secure of assets. The poor conditions under which they were kept meant that losses were high, a problem exacerbated, according to the people who kept their animals with others, by dishonesty in reporting births and deaths of cattle.

financial support this implied (Thomas and Adams, 1999).[32] The Lower Volta on the other hand, has suffered massive State neglect.

6. *Summary and Conclusions*

In this chapter, we discussed the pervasive impacts of out-migration on livelihoods in the Lower Volta. The chapter considered how livelihoods were organised in ways which took advantage of the migration history of the individuals concerned and the migration culture of their communities. These included the use of old connections for long distance trading, receiving remittances from children as well as rent and profits from resources left around the Lake. As well, a proportion of the foodstuffs and fish sold at markets in the Lower Volta were from the Lake. However, there was a clear shift from seeing the Lakeside as a place with good livelihood possibilities to seeing it as a location with suffering fellow Tongu people who could be encouraged to return home if the situation in the Lower Volta improved.

Two interrelated strategies to making livelihoods in the Lower Volta—intensifying the use of pre-dam resources and practising multiple livelihood activities, were discussed. The study found that intensification of the use of pre-dam resources was a widespread response to the drastic environmental changes. It took several forms which included changes in the method of exploitation of particular resources in order to improve yields, continuing to exploit them as was done in the pre-dam environment but downgrading their significance in the livelihood portfolio and promoting new activities instead. Other forms were the intensification of the exploitation of hitherto little-used resources, the wholesale adoption of activities leading to saturation and the deployment of old resources for new uses. The chapter pointed out that several cases of intensification raised the issue of further environmental degradation and sustainability.

The discussion noted that in many cases intensification went hand in hand with the adoption of multiple livelihood activities. Secondly, that while the practice of multiple livelihood activities pre-dated the

---

[32] But see also Francis, 2000 for cases suggesting that while government intervention has been critical for changes in agriculture in East Africa, its interventions have not necessarily been successful, for example, the attempt to create small-holder agriculture in Kenya.

Volta River Project, the post VRP era was different in terms of the activities combined, their organisation and their outcomes. Some activities were completely dropped from the portfolio while some anchor activities became supplementary and vice versa. For example, artisanal services and other waged work tended to replace farming as an anchor livelihood activity. On the other hand, much fewer of those engaged in extractive activities such as charcoal, firewood and mining saw these as a replacement for farming. In the case of trading, the ease of entry into petty trading was partly because it did not require specialised training or a heavy capital outlay.[33] While some forms of trading were easily combined with and in some cases had a basis in farming, i.e. the sale of farm produce, the establishment of a shop or long-distance trading sometimes signalled a shift from agriculture to these services. At the same time, the low capital ease-of-entry trading activities also tended to deliver low returns.

Beyond household level livelihood strategies and trajectories was the question of the overall state of livelihoods in the Lower Volta with regard to the continuing environmental and socio-economic problems. The study explored whether adaptation had taken place in the Lower Volta and if not what conditions were responsible. The chapter concluded that adaptation had not occurred in the Lower Volta. On the contrary, conditions there continued to deteriorate due to the absence of governmental intervention to arrest environmental deterioration, promote technological innovation and provide communications and other infrastructure and credit. Because the bases of livelihoods had generally been undermined, many people were not doing more than surviving in spite of their best efforts. However, a small minority did better than the rest and the factors that accounted for their relative successes were examined. The study found that the differences between them and the poorest households were about the resources they were able to command, their ability to organise multi-spatial livelihoods, preferably from a combination of urban and rural resources and their ability to secure successful outcomes for each of their pursuits. A critical issue skirted in the

---

[33] In communities with strong trading traditions such as Sokpoe, trading in the pre-dam days was not considered to be unskilled and had been learned by younger women from older more experienced women. The arrival of artisanal training with its more formal processes relegated trading to the realms of intuitive knowledge.

chapter was that of social relations in livelihoods and their organisation. These issues will be tackled in the next chapter which together with this and the preceding chapter, provide an account of responses to the problems of livelihoods in the Lower Volta. In short, they explain the business of keeping hand-washing water in an otherwise empty water pot.

Plate 1: The Akosombo Dam

Plate 2: Children repairing fishing nets at the Volta lakeside at Surveyor Line. The submerged trees are very visible in this part of the Lake

Plate 3: Processing cassava at Surveyor Line

Plate 4: The fish market at the Kpando Torkor fishing complex

Plate 5: Travelling across the Volta at Mepe

Plate 6: Vendors chasing passing vehicles at the Lower Volta bridge at Sokpoe

Plate 7: Weaving baskets at Dadome, Mepe

Plate 8: Charcoal burning at Mepe

CHAPTER SIX

THE SOCIAL RELATIONS OF LIVELIHOODS
AT MEPE AND SOKPOE

1. *Introduction*

This chapter explores the social relations underpinning livelihoods in the Lower Volta. Why social relations? The focus on social relations allows the examination of the organisation of livelihoods, thereby deepening our understanding of an important element of differentiation in a context of generalised crisis. Social relations are explored in four areas: labour relations, conjugal and intra-household relations, relations with other kin and formal and informal social networks. These are also the social relations of class, gender, kinship and inter-generational relations. As is well established in the literature, they are structured and legitimised through institutions such as marriage, the household and the workplace and determine access to and control of resources (Whitehead, 1981, 1985; Kabeer, 1994; Risseeuw and Palriwala, 1996; Imam, Mama and Sow, 1997; Agarwal, 1997). We argue that in a situation of generalised hardship and insecurity, social relations have become even more critical in the difference between those who are comparatively better off and the almost destitute.

Through the use of cases, we illustrate how social relations enabled people to access the labour of their fellow household members and others outside their households, lineage resources and formal and informal networks for their livelihoods. The cases also show that for others, these same relations represented a constraint in an already difficult situation. Some conflicts resulting from the increased competition over critical resources such as land are also examined on grounds that they are one indication of which social relations might be under stress or in the process of transformation now or in the future. We also argued that these conflicts, some quite quickly resolved and others more intractable and requiring arbitration or the intervention of religious and secular courts, were indicative of some of the anxieties of those trying to make a livelihood in the Lower Volta. The particular situation of young people is discussed in the context of inter-generational relations, but also in terms of the future of the Lower Volta.

The social relations we examine in this chapter operate at various sites—the household, the lineage compound, the community and beyond. All or some of the social relations considered in this chapter which were manifested in unpaid family labour, paid and paying labour, were deployed together, sometimes simultaneously and in cross-cutting ways. For the sake of simplicity, each of these is considered separately. However, we hope that the cases demonstrate the messier and complicated reality of how they were manifested in practice.

2. *Household Relations and Livelihoods*

Household characteristics such as size, developmental cycle and composition were important in their ability to deploy certain livelihood strategies such as taking up multiple activities and achieving and maintaining successful outcomes. The interaction between household characteristics and particular livelihood activities and their organisation was also critical. Some studies have suggested that larger households were better able to organise multiple activities and secure better outcomes (Whitehead, 2002). In the Lower Volta, while the large households were often the ones with a number of livelihood activities, they were also in some cases organised around one activity. For example, the households of the older and more established bakers at Sokpoe were among the largest. However, even when certain members were engaged in some other activities, e.g. the young male members rearing livestock purchased with funds from the baking, the household was organised around the baking. Some kenkey-making households at Mepe and Sokpoe were in the same situation. Apart from being a regular source of money for day to day expenditures, both kenkey-making and bread-baking were more time and labour consuming than other activities. Households which were large enough to deploy appreciable amounts of labour for their livelihood activities had good outcomes, as some of the cases of the kenkey and bread-baking households suggested.

Thus while household size was important, its composition, dependency ratio and stage in developmental cycle could be even more critical than size. Households which had more independent producers did better, as did those that had many generations of family members assembled. Those with many minor dependants or those with a single, widowed or divorced head tended to find the adoption of multiple activities difficult. In addition, those households whose heads were still economically active also had some advantages, as did those households with retired heads who were still able to call on resources created during their economically active years or the support of adult children. Some household heads that were either young or old, for various reasons found it hard to secure and sustain good livelihood outcomes.

There were interconnections among the character of the household, its livelihood activities and their organisation. In some households, independent producers contributed to organise some kinds of consumption in common. In others, production, exchange and consumption involved the whole household. In some, there were clear differences in the organisation of productive and reproductive activities. In the situations where a household had a conjugal core, spouses and children participated in differing levels of unpaid labour.

In the last chapter, it was established that households at Sokpoe and Mepe had features common to areas of large-scale out-migration, an important one being the varied and changing configurations of households. Other features were the significantly large numbers of female-headed households and the substantial number of households not organised around conjugal unions. This was, however, not fully reflected in the statistics because in all cases we accepted the respondent's identification of household head for the sake of consistency. There were instances of de facto female headship for example, when women identified someone other than themselves as household heads when it was clear that they were the pivotal persons within their households. In practice, whenever men were present or in some cases, even when they were absent, they were identified as household heads. The exceptions were in cases where they were young or were a sibling or son as opposed to the spouse of the most economically active person in the house. Some of the old men who said they were heads of households appeared to be grafted onto pre-existing households of their sisters. Since the pattern was for grown-up siblings to have households independent of each other, then it was assumed that these persons were household heads mainly on the basis of ideology. In some situations, old men lived apart from the households which were doing their cooking. On the other hand, when the old man in question was a husband and not a sibling, his status was less clear-cut. Several men lived apart from some of their wives while living with others. Some also lived apart from all their wives. Wives also had their own complicated households. They might be living in their family compounds with and caring for their own and other children. In one case, the man contributed a fixed sum every month and ate meals at his wife's house. Some decisions were made by husband and wife, but the woman lived with her mother, sister, children and siblings' children and they helped her produce and sell kenkey (which was her work, not theirs) and they ate together. Thus for that household, there was a different configuration for different activities—production, consumption and decision-making. In some cases, some members slept in different compounds because of lack of space or the desire for more privacy, but spent the whole day in a parent's compound, worked together doing household chores and ate together. In one case, a young couple seemed to have been reabsorbed into the husband's natal family because the man was in school and his wife was young, unemployed and pregnant. The man had been a teacher and was now in training college.

The high dependency ratios of many households were also very striking. Households had large numbers of unemployed or apprenticed young adults and school-going children who assisted with reproductive activities such as fetching water, sweeping, cooking and child minding. In addition, they were involved in farming, fishing, charcoal-burning, trading and other household-based productive activities. The contribution of children to the production of food and to other productive and reproductive activities was important. Both men and women worked with their children and grandchildren, but in keeping with the gendered nature of livelihood activities such as fishing, baking and aspects of housework. Thus, some fishermen at Mepe and Sokpoe mentioned their sons as fishing partners while some bakers were working mostly with their daughters and other female kin. In the case of farming, both male and female children and grandchildren were useful to whichever parent or grandparent needed their services. Schooling was mentioned as having reduced the frequency and length of children's labour in productive activities.

Some adult children continued to play important roles in their natal households even as they themselves were establishing their own households. A young photographer at Mepe was a case in point. He lived with his wife in a single-room house he had built. They were in their twenties and had no children yet. When I interviewed him, his wife had gone to wash for his mother. His relations with his mother's household were extensive. He helped her on her farm at least twice a week during the planting season. His mother reared goats, ducks and chicken and he helped out with that too. This he did together with his sisters who lived with his mother. As he explained, "I am the man here. My older brother is in Tema and so all things face me". He ate at his mother's house when his wife travelled. When his mother was sick he paid for her treatment, and took her to hospital. He justified this in terms of her past and current financial support for him, "My mother gave me money to rent accommodation at Ashaiman. She used to give me money when I was not working. Even now she lends me money. For example she gives me 50,000 cedis when I have to pre-finance photographs. I pay her back now that I am working." (male head of a young household, Mepe).

Husbands and wives, on the other hand, rarely provided labour for each other's productive activities with the exception of farming. This was in keeping with pre-dam practices. While some women were unhappy about being excluded from the fish trade by the husbands, it was not as large an issue of marital conflict in the Lower Volta as it was around the Volta Lake. This was partly because the structure of the fishing industry in the Lower Volta promoted a division of labour that cut wives out of the fishing industry. The itinerant character of fishing, the fact that the fish was mostly sold fresh and the general paucity of the catch meant that it was not worthwhile to rope the whole household into this activity.

In relation to farming, women and children made important labour contributions to men's farms. This kind of co-operation around food production was so enshrined in conjugal and household relations that some women who could not physically fulfil this obligation paid for the hired labour to do their share. While this demonstrated the continued vitality of the labour obligations of wives, it raised some questions about its future. The paucity of farm harvests, which had resulted in increased food purchases, was also likely to be a contributory undermining factor of this practice.

Studies of household relations elsewhere have suggested that women's contribution of labour to their husband's farms, especially in situations where men did not have the resources to hire labour, allowed them some leverage within the household with regard to the distribution of resources. In situations where the division between cash and food crops was clearer, women were better able to negotiate the use of their labour for their own benefit (Mbilinyi, 1989; Manuh, Songsore and Mackenzie, 1997; Mikell, 1989; Whitehead, 1981; Francis, 2000). In the Lower Volta, there was not a strict demarcation between food and cash crops although some respondents mentioned groundnuts as the main cash crop. This might account for what Francis (2000) has observed in relation to similar situations to be a more covert approach to bargaining which also occurred mainly around the time of consumption.

Beyond co-operation around food production, husbands and wives, even when they lived together, tended to pursue livelihood activities separately. In some households however, particularly those for which farming was the main livelihood activity and represented more than a food security device, women sometimes did not pursue their own account farming. In households where women pursued their own account livelihood activities, men were expected to provide the capital for such ventures. In turn, women contributed to particular aspects of household expenditure. The division of labour around expenditures was also interesting in its variations, but followed a basic pattern. Typically, "modern" and visible expenditures such as electricity, school fees and hospital fees were said by men to be what they took responsibility for. Also, in a number of cases, it appeared that women paid for the upkeep and training of daughters while men paid for sons.

Much of marital co-operation was around the division of labour and responsibilities in the production of food crops, in the cooking of food and other reproductive activities and in expenditure on school fees, clothes and other needs. In some cases, these conjugal "understandings" had been breached by the implications of physical separation of spouses, an issue discussed in the last chapter, specifically in relation to multi-spatial livelihoods and the decline in Lakeside conditions. Whatever the reasons for such separations, their impacts on women's livelihoods were similar. The study found that these constant movements, while they might have been useful for managing households kept the women involved off balance and unable to establish continuity in some of their pursuits. In the Lower Volta, they were disadvantaged by having been away for a long time and therefore often had weaker claims on family farmlands. In cases where their husbands had access to family land, wives could use that for growing food. They often became heads of economically disadvantaged households or attached themselves to the households of better-off siblings or other kin in a position neither of dependence nor autonomy. The study found that although it was mostly women in these situations, a few men had also returned home as a result of marital breakdown. For the latter though, marital breakdown might be a signal that their livelihoods were also in difficulty as around the Volta Lake, the ability to contract more marriages conveyed the impression of success and losing wives gave the opposite signal. Men discussed women's contributions to the livelihoods and general welfare of their households mainly in nostalgic terms in relation to the past when the clam pickers were central to the maintenance and education of children.[1] Even though women's contributions continued to be critical to livelihoods as the cases in the last chapter show, men were often dismissive of these contributions. There might be no contradiction in this because in underlining the contributions of clam pickers, many men were talking about their mothers while for the current situation, the discussions centred on spouses and partners. Conversely, women in the Lower Volta complained regularly about the failure of men to take responsibility for the maintenance of children. At Sokpoe for example, the discussion of male irresponsibility among the young women selling by the roadside was couched in terms of community character, i.e. they spoke in terms of the men of the community not looking after women.

While it was common practice all over Ghana for grandparents to have a role in the upbringing of children, at Mepe and Sokpoe, it was of a different order. As we found in the discussion of migration and household composition in previous chapters, in most households headed by older persons, especially women, there were a clutch of grandchildren, some quite young. Some of these households also included between one and three adult children of the head of household, but it was not always the case. While the grandchildren were generally said to help with productive and reproductive activities, their enthusiasm for such activities could not always be taken for granted. Moreover, given that most of them were in school and had actually been sent to the Lower Volta for this purpose, there was a limit to how helpful they could be. The older children who had the physical capacity to be most helpful in some cases did not accept

---

[1] Some clam pickers were reputed to have sponsored the education of children, male lovers and husbands who are today prominent Tongu citizens.

the jurisdiction of the grandmothers. The cases below illustrate elements of the interaction between household characteristics and livelihood activities and their organisation.

CASE 6.1: Millicent: Multiple livelihood activities and remittances. More than one household member using a multi-spatial livelihood strategy (Mepe)

Millicent was in her 60s, a kenkey maker, farmer and a trainer of traditional birth attendants. She was the head of a household, which included two sons, both traders—one described as a businessman—and five young persons who were all in school, the eldest in senior secondary school and the youngest in primary school. Three of these five were the children of one of the two sons and the other two were a grandniece and nephew (children of her younger brother's son and daughter). Both sons operated between Accra and Mepe. The older son bought and sold goods in a shop in Accra. The second one was in the timber business; he bought wood from the forest regions and sold it in the Timber Market in Accra. In spite of this, both sons spent a lot of time at Mepe, the younger even participating in the family farm along with Millicent and the children of the household, who were mostly in their teens; four of them between 16 and 13 years and the last 8 years old. Both sons also had children (seven in all) living with their mothers in different quarters of Mepe. According to Millicent, those children ate regularly in her house during school hours. The household lived in a six-room house built by Millicent's father who had been a boat builder in the pre-dam days. It was a cement blockhouse, plastered, painted, with an aluminium roof and walled.

Millicent was a primary health worker and traditional birth attendant. The Mepe State sponsored part of her training at the Battor Hospital. After her training, she was set up in hired premises to practice and her salary paid with state funds, but these premises were destroyed to give way to the new road running through Mepe. Now she was working from home, delivering babies, training other traditional birth attendants and keeping records of births in the area. Her activities also included assisting the community health nurses in their immunisation programmes and treating fevers. She travelled to about fifteen other Mepe communities across the river, treating people and educating them about family planning and immunisation and reporting outbreaks of diseases such as measles to the health authorities. She was supplied medicines such as paracetamol, chloroquine, multivitamin and cough syrup by the Battor Hospital for her work and she repaid them when the drugs had been sold. For this work she earned about 50,000 cedis a month. People paid her 10,000 cedis to deliver their babies. She did not earn more—not for lack of clients, but because they were often too poor to pay for her services.

She was farming two plots of lineage land at two different Mepe villages. While she was not paying rent, she was expected to pay a contribution to litigation expenses as and when needed. She grew maize, cassava and groundnuts with the help of several household members and sold some of the produce. A female relation helped Millicent with the kenkey-making which was not doing too well because it was often bought on credit and could be unsold for days until the children ate it. The household had electricity, the cost of which was borne by all the working persons in the household.

Millicent was receiving some support from seven children in Accra and Kumasi, four males and three females, who were each working either selling nets, trading, teaching or sewing. They sent food and money to the tune of about 100,000 a year. She in turn assisted some children outside the household by giving them food and paying their school fees when needed.

CASE 6.2: Esinam, head of a large household dominated by a baking enterprise (Sokpoe)

Esinam had lived in the cocoa areas as an abusa labourer with her husband for years. She then came to live at Sokpoe as a kenkey maker in the days of the ferry crossing at Sokpoe. After the Lower Volta Bridge was completed, her mother decided to try baking and Esinam went to work with her. In those days, there were not many bakers at Sokpoe. Esinam at 65 was still presiding over a baking business, though not involved in the physical preparations of the bread. She was head of a large household of eighteen members, nine children and nine adults. Two of her adult daughters were mainly doing the baking now and she described herself as retired although she still had some over-sight functions. Other workers in the house were her brother's son who was a fisherman, a daughter who was trading to and from Lome, Togo, a granddaughter who was a seamstress and an uncle's son who was unemployed but weaving baskets. There was one unemployed adult son. The nine children were her grandchildren, some of whose parents were not part of her household. They were mostly in school except one grandson who had just finished secondary school. In spite of these many other independent producers, the bakery dominated the house and its rhythms.

The household lived in an eight-room house with one sitting room. It was a cement blockhouse with aluminium roofing. Esinam and her mother built it in the 1960s from their baking. Esinam did the cook-ing, but the children and grandchildren did all the other household chores. They purchased firewood for the bakery and used some for their domestic cooking. The two women who baked worked jointly. They baked once a week and it took two days to mill and bake the bread. One day was market day and the remaining four days were spent cleaning up, preparing the tins and procuring ingredients. They took the bread to Akatsi market (in a neighbouring district on the same road running through Sokpoe) themselves. Other people came and bought the bread to resell in villages in the Akatsi area. They gave out the bread on credit and were paid the next week when they took a new consignment. They made three flour bags worth of bread denominated in 200, 100 and 50 cedis portions. The current glut in the bread market had forced them to reduce their production from 5 to 3 bags a week.

The school children in the house assisted with the bread. The earnings from the bread were used for all household expenses. Accounts were made to Esinam who then kept the money. Some of it was given to the two women for their particular expenses. Esinam also received money every month from her son, an electrician in Koforidua, for the upkeep of his children who were living with her. There were two large ovens being used for the business and a large number of bread pans, bowls, baskets and tables. The house had electricity but used river water because they considered the tap water to be too far away. The household was classified as poor.

CASE 6.3: Nayra, female-headed large household: Multiple livelihood activities within an agricultural base (7/2/99, Mepe)

Nayra was in her 60s, a Mepe woman and head of a household made up of 14 persons—herself, two adult children, a son and daughter, the wife of a son who was living around the Lake and ten children and grandchildren of her children, absent and present. The children were all in school except the youngest who was five. The son who was in the house had been a fisherman around the Lake but was now suffering from a serious illness. There were, therefore, three independent workers and eleven dependants in this household. Two members of the household, two teenage boys, originally lived with their mother's mother in a different compound but had no one caring for them and therefore had joined this household while continuing to sleep in that compound in a room belonging to their mother's father.

Nayra farmed and sold kenkey, her daughter-in-law sold cooked rice and sauce and farmed and her daughter sold consumer items such as garri, sugar and soap and also farmed. Mother and daughter farmed together on four plots, which were about two acres in total, growing cassava inter-cropped with groundnuts and beans. As well, they cultivated some pepper and okra for sale. They burned their own charcoal and collected firewood. Some of the charcoal was sold to buy fish, according to Nayra. The kenkey was to ensure that there was always food in the house. The groundnuts were their main source of income when the harvest was good and could buy cloth and other more substantial needs.

The children in the house assisted with farming over weekends and during their holidays if they did not travel to the Afram Plains. The younger women and children did the household chores. Their efforts were supplemented by occasional and small contributions of food and money from Nayra's children around the Lake. The money was not more than 50,000 cedis a year in all and it came in amounts between 2,000 and 10,000 cedis three or four times a year. The foodstuffs were more substantial, sacks of maize and dried cassava and fish came regularly. These were sent through other migrants who were visiting and children returning from holidays would also bring their school fees. The food typically lasted between two weeks and a month.

The house they lived in, a cement block and aluminium sheet-roofed house with 6 bedrooms, was owned by Nayra's husband who had built it when he was fishing and farming around the Lake. While the roof was in disrepair, there were bundles of new roofing sheets waiting to be used at the time of the interview. Nayra had stocks of palm kernel oil for frying pepper and fish to support her kenkey making.

CASE 6.4: Kobla, a pre-dam migrant with artisanal training who did not migrate after the dam. He worked with sons, combining artisanal activities with farming (Sokpoe)

Kobla was a 65-year-old carpenter who also did some farming. He was widowed and lived with three children and two grandchildren. One son, a fisherman who did not own any fishing equipment of his own, had just gone to a place near Accra to help a widowed cousin whose husband died leaving some nets. Of the two children remaining, a son who was 17 was a carpenter while a daughter was a baker's assistant. Another son worked with his father as a carpenter. He sometimes had his meals with the household, but had his own house where he lived with his wife and one child.

The household lived in a house constructed entirely with aluminium sheets. Four other rooms were being constructed, three from cement blocks and one from laterite, but they were not complete. They had an open-air kitchen with low laterite walls and an aluminium roof where they used firewood as their main fuel for cooking. Kobla's daughter, the baking assistant, did most the reproductive work assisted by one grandson who did the washing up. Kobla gathered the firewood and she carried it home.

The carpentry work which he ranked as his first activity in terms of earnings, time use and status was done by Kobla and two of his sons and consisted of making boats, roofing houses, making doors, windows and furniture. Their customers pre-financed the wood and other items and paid them for their labour. In good years in the past, when some of the few still existing creeks filled, he had made an average of thirty boats a year. However, he made only seven boats and roofed one house the year before and by July of the year he was interviewed, he had made five boats and roofed one house. It took them four days of work to make a boat, which earned them 50,000 cedis. A roof was between 40,000 and 200,000 cedis depending on the size of the house. When he and his sons worked they shared the money into three. The tools "took" one part, he took another part and the particular son he worked with earned the last third. He used to have apprentices but was no longer accepting them because there was not enough work these days and the workshop was not big enough.

Only he and his grandson who was 9 did any farming. The farm was 10 minutes' walk away on land leased because their own family lands were too far away for farming on them to be combined with carpentry. He had a three-year lease for 20,000 cedis. He had been farming the land for 16 years and when he started the rent had been 12,000. In turn, he had two tenants on inherited land 3 miles away and they were abusa farmers. He also had control over land scattered in seven other places. He did not sell the 1/3 share of produce he received from them because it was too small. They ate it instead. He was growing maize and cassava on the rented land which he said was 50 sq. feet and this was for consumption, although now and again he sold some produce to supplement his resources. Sometimes, he stopped going to the farm to do a carpentry job.

They drank pipe-borne water but used the river for other needs. They did not have electricity because according to him he did not have the money. His major resources were his carpentry workshop, the tables and tools. He was a member of three funeral organisations to which he paid dues monthly. Kobla's household was not doing very well judging by their living conditions and they were classified as very poor.

CASE 6.5: Nukunya, farmer, single livelihood activity, support with charcoal; household members able to help with farming (Mepe)

Nukunya was 57 and a farmer living at Mepe. He and his wife who also farmed presided over a household made up of four of their adult children in various stages of training, two said to be unemployed and two grandchildren. They farmed on about ten scattered plots, a total of two acres in all. Nukunya and his wife farmed separately and both used their produce for home consumption. The wife helped the husband on his farm and the children helped their mother. They grew maize, cassava, groundnuts and pepper. The land was his father's inherited plot so they were not paying rent. His father had been an important chief in the town before he died. Nukunya's wife and daughters produced charcoal for sale and sometimes sold firewood. They did it in small lots to buy fish and clothes and drugs. They also sold small amounts of cassava. Large expenses like the hospital were a problem to finance.

They lived in a four-room house owned by the elder brother of Nukunya, a Kumasi-based lawyer. The house was cement block, plastered and painted, and roofed with aluminium sheets. It was very well built. The owner of the house had had electricity connected, but the bill was being paid by one of Nukunya's sons. They had children around the Lake who supported them with fish and foodstuffs. This did not happen often because they had their own responsibilities and sometimes even if they had food, they could not find the money to finance its transportation. As a rule, they did not send money. They in turn gave some cassava and maize to others—kin and friends in need. In addition, they fetched water and firewood for others when there was an illness or when a new baby had been born.

Nukunya and his wife had been Lakeside migrants, fishing, farming and trading in smoked fish for years. They had left their four children at Mepe in school and they looked after themselves although his mother looked out for them until they finished school. They stayed for a long time until Nukunya fell ill and decided to return home for treatment. They had since farmed and burnt charcoal to support themselves without much support form outside. They were classified as poor.

The above cases illustrate the issues raised in the discussion of household characteristics and livelihoods, specifically questions of structure, size and composition, livelihood activities and their organisation. In relation to size, while the tendency of the more successful bakers to have very large households might be a function of the demands of bread-baking, it was not clear whether it was the household size which made baking an attractive option in the first place. Esinam (Case 6.2) was one of several such households at Sokpoe. Another one had 27 people (11 adults and 16 children). Typically, some of the adults, the males especially, were still in school while some of the minors were listed as bakers. The households also tended to include non-family members. Another feature was that a significant proportion of those listed as household members were involved in baking activities even when it was not the only livelihood activity, as in one case where the boys reared pigs, goats and sheep. While male household members were not always involved, females within bakers' households helped out with whatever else they did.

In their composition, the large multi-generation female-headed households of bakers were a microcosm of the range of social relations around production within the Lower Volta. Bakers had different categories of labour—daughters and other close kin, apprentices, employees and casual labourers. Daughters, who were being trained to inherit the business, were not paid directly for their services. They were given increasing responsibility for the business until they took it over when their mother retired. When they retailed bread, they earned some money for that. In some of the bakers' households, joint kitty arrangements had been established between mothers and adult daughters. They bought food and necessities from their earnings. It was not entirely clear how individual items of expenditure were financed.

There were other kin who assisted with baking activities for a fee. They were like the non-kin waged employees, the bakers' assistants, in that their terms were defined by conventions in the industry. Some adult kin assisting a baker might be able to make their own bread for sale at times when the ovens were free. Apprentices paid to be taught the trade and did not receive payment for their services except being fed and clothed if they lived within the household of the baker. Persons employed as bakers' assistants, on the other hand, were paid between 1,000 to 2,000 cedis for every bag of flour baked. If the baking schedule was consistent, for example, five bags a week, which was a good average for medium-size bakers, they earned between 10,000 and 20,000 cedis every two weeks. This was very poor remuneration indeed, lower than the national minimum wage of 2,900 cedis a day.[2] The assistant's work was to take the flour to the mill to be mixed with sugar, fat and spices. The dough was then carried on a trolley home for cutting, shaping and raising by trolley pushers who provided casual labour for the baking industry. Kenkey producers were similar to bread makers with regard to household sizes and the fact that several household members were involved in the production of the kenkey. However, they did not have the range of social relations of the bread industry.

Some other large households that were not involved in baking also had a more unified production base particularly when their dependency ratio was high. Nayra's household (Case 6.3), which had fourteen members, only three of whom had independent activities, was similar to the large bakers' households. She and her daughters' joint farming, charcoal-burning and kenkey-making kept the household together. Millicent's (Case 6.1) household, which was not formally large had to take account of seven children of her two sons living

---

[2] In 1997–98, the minimum wage was 2,000 cedis, 2,900 in 1999–2000 and 5,500 cedis in 2001–2002 (source, the Trades Union Congress of Ghana). In 2003, the Government of Ghana pegged it at 9,000 cedis.

with their mothers at Mepe. Although she made kenkey, her primary activity was her role as a community health worker. Her sons were trading in Accra but actively participating in the household's activities. The minors within the household who were her grandchildren helped her with the farming.

The developmental cycle of households was a factor in their livelihoods and a source of differentiation because it determined the ability of members to contribute their own account activities to the livelihood portfolio of the household and therefore determining its capacity for multiple activities. The developmental cycle of households was however complicated in the Lower Volta as in other places, by the sometimes large age gap between retired household heads and their spouses as well as the numbers of young people staying with grandparents. What stage would such households be in? Would it be with reference to the more economically vigorous wife or the older husband? And what would this imply for the welfare and security of the household? In some of the cases, the household head's livelihood history continued to work in the household's favour long after he or she had retired.

3. Kinship and Livelihoods

Kinship and labour relations

Scott (1978) has identified reciprocity, forced generosity, work-sharing and the use of communal land as arrangements which help people to survive. In the Lower Volta, some of these strategies such as the use of lineage land and reciprocity were deployed through kinship relations. Outside the household, in lineage compound interactions and relations between kin who did not live in the same compound, there were ways in which kinship had a bearing on livelihoods. Kinship was also implicated in access to resources such as land and credit and in some of the labour relations underpinning livelihoods.

Lineage compound relations

Households, particularly those located in larger compounds, had many connections on account of kinship and the configuration of the physical space. There were many compounds whose households

were made up of persons with varying degrees of kinship at both
Mepe and Sokpoe. Rooms within a compound opened into one large
space and fireplaces of different households were often found under
one central shed. There were some activities which were planned
and executed at the level of the compound, but their nature, intensity and regularity depended on how closely related compound members were and whether they were on good terms. For example, within
compounds there were households that had emerged from an older
household with the result that their continued inter-linkages were
very strong. For example, in a compound at Mepe, one respondent
had a household of herself, her son and the children of various children. In the same compound, her daughter and a niece she had
brought up lived and ate separately most of the time. However, they
often ate together and also supported our respondent and their overlapping transactions were important for the survival of both households. This was not the level of intercourse between the majority of
households in our sample, however. People generally conducted their
livelihoods, including reproductive activities such as cooking, separately within compounds and ate together occasionally. Food was
offered to neighbours mainly when it was something special. This
was a change from the pre-dam days when compounds had a much
more collective approach to the different aspects of their livelihoods.
As a retired migrant recalled with nostalgia:

> The old women knew when you had a stomach ache without you
> telling then. When they saw you passing, they asked you if you had
> a stomach ache. If you said yes, they would go into their rooms, pour
> a little drink in a glass, drop some herbs in it, drink a little and give
> you the rest. Almost immediately, your stomach ache disappeared. The
> akple[3] came from about ten different sources and sometimes you did
> not even know which one was your own mother's. You and all your
> uncles ate together messing each other's hands in the process (male
> informant, Mepe).

It was, however, still common practice for compounds to organise
certain ritual activities such as funeral donations and financial obligations to the lineage and clan collectively. Varying combinations of

---

[3] *Akple* is a mixture of the maize and cassava dough in particular proportions
made into a watery paste and cooked by stirring in hot water over the fire until
it is thick enough to shape into balls. It is eaten with a range of soups and stews.
A staple of the area, its use here refers to the evening meal.

reproductive activities, particularly those involving children, were also organised collectively. For example, the children fetched water from the river and this was stored in large pots and used collectively. The sweeping and cleaning of the compound was also done by all or a designated group of children. Thus older members of the compound and those who had no children within their households could benefit from the services of the children of the compound. Such benefits could extend to even those activities which were traditionally household-based such as cooking, washing up and washing.

There were, however, changes taking place in the organisation of some reproductive activities arising from their commercialisation or the introduction of new technologies and other socio-economic developments. At Sokpoe for example, the introduction of pipe-borne water and young men with trucks fetching water for households was changing the acquisition and use of water from a compound level to a household-level activity. This process was deepened by the extension of the services of truck pushers from pipe-borne to river water.

Compound-level co-operation sometimes included the collective socialisation of children within the compound. Older persons, including those living outside a compound could discipline children with whose parents they had some form of real or fictive kinship relations. At Mepe during an interview with a fisherman, a male relation came from another compound and subjected the fisherman's small son to a beating for missing school. There were other children involved and he indicated his intention to punish all of them. My respondent appeared to have no objection to his son being disciplined in this way, probably in deference to the fact that the issue concerned education, which the other man appeared to know more about. Some of these observations were supported by the findings of the survey. 58.4% of households were not in lineage compounds (Table 6.1). The most often mentioned compound-level activity was the contribution to funeral donations (19.8%). 7% of respondents did some eating together while 4.3% described themselves as doing everything together. 2.6% mentioned the sweeping of the compound and keeping its environment clean while 2.2% contributed financially to the care of sick members of the compound. 1.6% were involved in joint water procurement and use arrangements.

Beyond the statistics, the survey's findings are useful in the list of possible compound-level activities. Some activities, which were not statistically significant, however, raised interesting questions. These included farming together, settling conflicts, celebrating the festival together, meetings and discussions and wearing the same clothing (Table 6.1). It would have been even more interesting to make such a list from the point of view of different social groups within the compound—the children, the women, the heads of households and so on.

There were also kin who did not live in the same compound that helped each other in times of trouble or stress. For example, when a baby was born, a looser network might render services such as bathing the baby, donating firewood and water in the first few weeks after the birth. They might also give loans or pre-finance the treatment of relations who were expecting money from migrant children or parents as the case may be. The issue of loans will be discussed in more detail in the section on credit and kinship arrangements. In this connection, Apt's (1992) observation that adult children were the primary supporters of their parents needs to be kept in mind as a balance for this discussion of kinship and livelihoods.

Kinship and access to resources

Land relations
Household, conjugal family and compound relations were situated within wider kinship relations such as those of lineage, clan and community. The far-reaching socio-economic changes and pervasive hardships had affected these relations in various ways. However, kinship remained an important basis for access to critical resources. At a very basic level, the inherited farm or farmland, *"nudufe"* allowed both men and women to farm without having to pay rent or enter into share-cropping arrangements. Those who could secure unused lineage land for farming were also assured of rent-free farming and were only obligated to pay a contribution to litigation and related land protection activities.

Large-scale migration from the Lower Volta had freed up family land for cultivation by those who remained behind. In spite of this, more and more people had to rent some or all of their farmlands when the family farm or lineage land was too far off or fragmented as a result of inheritance practices.

In chapter three, we discussed the contested nature of women's access to lineage land. However, the study found many women working on land which had been used by their mothers and fathers. Both men and women were also mentioned as landlords and rent payments such as 1/3 of yields or a fixed sum of money for a particular piece of land were made to men and women. However, as more men than women were farming on their own account and men on the average had much larger tracts of land, it was reasonable to assume that male landlords had larger tracts of land to rent than females.

Quite distinct from directly inherited farmlands were corporate resources belonging to lineages and clans. Members of such collectives could ask for and be given small pieces of such land. However, a few people, mostly men, as heads and elders of families, lineages and clans were able to control and benefit from substantial collective resources such as vast tracts of land, clam-shell and stone deposits. It was for this small elite group that these resources were most beneficial whether directly as used in own account farms and other ventures, allocated to children and close relations or rented out for large-scale enterprises.

At both Mepe and Sokpoe, there were land disputes within and between lineages and clans (division), some of which were the subjects of formal litigation. Members of lineages and clans were expected to contribute in various ways to protecting collective resources in times of disputes. Several respondents had varying degrees of involvement in the land disputes—from those who simply made monetary contributions to finance litigation to those who were attending court hearings as lineage representatives. One respondent who was farming on both his mother and father's family lands was contributing money to land litigation within his division at Mepe. He had already contributed 60,000 cedis and expected to pay more. The case was on account of an intra-division dispute. The descendants of two lineages or compounds were fighting over the right to dispose of farmland, sand and clam-shell deposits. Two other compounds had come together to sue the litigants at the Denu High Court for not involving them in a matter in which they also had an interest. This first intra-division dispute of its kind had halted the commercial exploitation of clam-shell deposits pending the determination of the suit.[4]

---

[4] In the past, disputes had been boundary disputes involving the division and other land-owning clans in neighbouring communities such as Mafi.

Table 6.1: Activities taking place at the compound by gender of household head

Activities taking place	Absolutes — Mepe M	Mepe F	Sokpoe M	Sokpoe F	Mepe and Sokpoe M	F	T	Percentages — Mepe M	Mepe F	Sokpoe M	Sokpoe F	Mepe and Sokpoe M	F	T
Eat together	8	15	2	6	10	21	31	9.4	11.1	2.3	4.5	6	7.8	7
Pay funeral donations	26	34	10	17	36	51	87	30.6	25.2	12	12.6	21.3	18.9	19.8
Farm together/share proceeds	1	1	2	1	3	2	5	1.2	.7	2.3	.7	1.8	.7	1.1
Fetch water/drink from same barrel	1	4	–	2	1	6	7	1.2	3.	–	1.4	.5	2.2	1.6
Contribute financially to help sick members	1	7	–	2	1	9	10	1.2	5.2	–	1.4	.5	3.3	2.2
Settlements of issues/conflicts	2	–	1	1	3	1	4	2.4	–	1.1	.7	1.8	.3	.9
Sweep compound/clean environment	3	1	5	2	8	3	11	3.5	.7	6	1.4	4.8	1.1	2.6
Celebrate festivals together	–	2	–	–	–	2	2	–	1.5	–	–	–	.7	.4
Meetings/discussions	1	1	–	1	1	2	3	1.2	.7	–	.7	.5	.7	.6
Do everything together	1	2	7	9	8	11	19	1.2	1.5	8.4	6.8	4.8	4	4.3
Share electricity bills	2	–	–	–	2	–	2	2.4	–	–	–	1.1	–	.4
Washing/cleaning utensils	–	–	–	1	–	1	1	–	–	–	.7	–	.3	.2
Wear same clothing	–	1	–	–	–	1	1	–	.7	–	–	–	.3	.2
N.A.	39	67	57	94	96	161	257	45.9	49.6	67.9	69.1	56.9	59.4	58.4
Total	85	135	84	136	169	271	440	100	100	100	100	100	100	100

There were also tensions and disputes around lands now being used for building privately-owned houses. The land by the Sokpoe roadside was now prime building land with a quite well-developed informal land market. People were paying from between 1.2 million cedis and 2 million cedis, the higher end of the scale, for plots abutting the roadside for land of 70 by 100 feet. At Mepe, it was 72 by 72 feet at 1.5 million cedis. The phenomenon of multiple sales of the same piece of land, ownership and boundary disputes were some of the issues of contention.

In relation to clan and lineage land, there were several disputes. An example was the longstanding conflict over the sale of almost 800 hectares (2327 acres; 13.5 sq. miles) of land to the Government of Ghana for an agricultural project known as the Angaw River Basin Project which began in 1985 as a joint venture between the Libya and Ghana governments.[5] There were a number of unresolved issues with respect to the land. They included who to compensate and the adequacy of compensation, the loss of farmlands, the interests of other land users such as pastoralists, and the use of kinship for the acquisition of collective resources for private use. As the land given to the Project represented much of the main farmlands in the Morkodze area, local farmers had to use more marginal, clayey, flood-prone land, which was different from the Project land, a mixture of sandy and clayey soil. The Headman at Morkodze therefore made regular appeals to the management of the Project over the years to be granted some of the acquired land for farming. Correspondence between the Headman and the Company show that in certain periods they were allowed to use small portions of the land but subject to the needs of the Project and restricted to short-term maturing crops, specifically maize, groundnuts and pepper.[6] In other cases they were asked to stop farming or move to plots farther away as the Company needed the land (letter from the Company, 25/9/91; letters from the Morkodze Headman to the Project, 12/5/1993; 13/6/1994; 29/5/1997). The Morkodze Headman's responses to Project demands,

---

[5] The Ghana Libya Arab Agricultural Company (GLAACO) had managerial oversight for the project. The Project has experienced several stops and starts and since 1997, it has been revived under the management of the V.A. Agricultural Development and Holding Company Ltd.

[6] Letters from V.A. Agricultural Development Holding Company Ltd., 8/5/1997; 9/3/1998.

suggested that the problem of using the Company's land was intractable:

> The only problem we are facing is that, we do not have any proper land apart from what we have given to you. That is the reason why we are still using part of the Company farms (Morkodze Headman to V.A. Agriculture Development Holding Company Ltd., 29/5/1997).[7]

These problems were exacerbated by the unfulfilled expectation that such a venture would bring much needed employment for many of the young men.[8] Other users of the land such as cattle owners lost their grazing land as a result of the acquisition. There were about 20 kraals in the area, their owners from Sokpoe, Tefle and Ada who were using the land for grazing their cattle before the Angaw River Project.[9] As the grass on the marshy land was not suitable for the cows, they had no clear options and this became a source of tension between herders and the project. Another area of tension between Morkodze and the Project was the accusation of theft of grain levelled against the locals by the Company. The Headman strongly denied it, charging in turn that it was the management of the Project who were stealing the grain and selling it to people from neighbouring villages and even further afield across the Angaw River.

---

[7] While the Morkodze Headman had the possibility of enjoying some favours from the Project, other members of his clan did not. His communications with the Project were full of requests. For example, the company ploughed a new piece of land for him to use in 1984 on account of four acres of cassava he lost when the land was acquired. (Interview with Morkodze Headman). A letter from the Headman to the Company requested 3–4 plots to farm cassava. According to the Headman, one plot was 30 acres of land.

[8] There were now eight (8) permanent employees (4 farm supervisors and 4 watchmen) and twelve (12) casual employees, all male. Every three months, the casuals were laid off and re-employed. There were also contract labourers employed for fixed periods, sometimes as short as for one week, for weeding and the application of fertilisers for periods. The catchment area for labourers was Sokpoe, Tefle and Sogakope. The farm manager maintained that this labour regime was because in the past, lazy full-time employees could not be laid off and were a drain on the project's resources. Since the farm had only just restarted, there was concern to keep the wage bill down. Casual workers were paid 3,500 cedis a day and they worked 5–6 days a week. Permanent employees were paid monthly. The farm manager, for example, was paid 382,000 a month and had a room on the farm. The company officials said there were difficulties with getting labour on time and in the quantities needed at any point in time partly because of the too high expectations of local potential employees who were mostly JSS and SSS graduates.

[9] A few of the kraals had over 100 cows but most of them had between 20 and 30 cows.

Kinship and credit

One of the ways in which kin and non-kin neighbours supported each other at Mepe and Sokpoe was the extension of credit by traders to their customers. The particular features of credit relations at Mepe and Sokpoe were an indication of the difficulties of survival in the Lower Volta. Credit was usually short-term, from just a week (until the next market day), to a month (until the next salary) and involved very small amounts of money and could, therefore, be time-consuming to administer. While credit was critical to households in the sense that it made activities that would otherwise not be possible happen and, therefore, was an important component of household livelihood strategies, it raised questions of the security of the capital base of traders and the sustainability of their enterprises. It also had implications for the kinship relations that got caught up in a credit nexus.

Credit was especially useful to the young people with parents outside the community because it enabled them to survive in between remittances. A cluster of households of young people interviewed would borrow amounts between 2,000 to 4,000 cedis each time from an older brother of one of them who sold drinks and was a tailor. There was also another person they went to when they were sick and he would buy them medicine from one of the several chemists or pay for their hospital treatment at the Battor Hospital. They then sent a letter to their parents through the drivers who came to Mepe once a week. A trader who sold oil, rice, beans, tomatoes and other cooking items gave credit up to 35,000 cedis to several teachers who paid back at the end of the month. Others paid back within days. While the majority of persons were buying goods for consumption, a few bought food items meant for producing cooked food for sale on credit. A woman who made a fried sweet corn-flour cake (*jolly kaklo*) bought the maize, oil and sugar on credit for periods between three days and two weeks depending on how quickly people paid for the *kaklo* they also bought on credit. A petty trader in food items found that four out of ten of her customers bought things on credit of up to about 5,000 cedis a day.

A system of informal credit was the bedrock of the market. While many of the traders were involved, the rules of engagement were varied and complex. What was stated as a rationale for granting credit in one case did not apply across the board. Some of the traders sold on credit, but differentiated what could be the subject of credit arrangements. In one case, a trader explained that she would extend credit for the garri she was selling, but not the palm-fruit because the palm-fruit was not much, while her stocks of garri were substantial. Another would not extend credit for the cassava from her own farm because she was not a professional trader and was in the market because she needed the money that day. On the other hand, others who did not identify themselves as traders were extending credit to enable them sell all their stocks especially when they travelled long distances to get to the market.

Traders also relied on even larger amounts of credit extended by those they bought goods from in the large markets such as Ada Junction and Agormanya in the Eastern Region. One woman bought oil on credit to the tune of 100,000 cedis. Credit was not on offer across the board. It depended on the circumstances of the people selling the goods, the situation and attitude of their suppliers and the credit ratings of their customers. For example, a respondent reported that maize was not sold on credit at Agormanya market because it was purchased from rural people who could not afford it. Those who did not honour their obligations were refused credit in the future. One group who could access credit was wageworkers because the regularity of their wages promoted the belief that they were more likely to pay their debts. However, there was some dis-illusionment with this category of persons owing to instances of debt default.

The widespread use of credit for the most basic needs signalled that livelihoods for most people were not delivering adequately. That the credit was not being used for production but mainly for short-term consumption needs was problematic. It created uncertainty among traders and other service providers because their capital base was always in danger of being frittered away by the terms of repay-ment. Those who had to purchase their stocks on credit were caught up in a nexus which challenged the meaning of the market place. They were forced to buy goods from their creditors and not from those offering the best prices or the best quality products. And if their customers at home did not pay up as expected, then their abil-ity to buy new stocks was threatened. Credit was thus a source of interpersonal conflict in situations where people were too poor to honour their credit repayments or were too persistent consumers of credit.

4. *Labour Relations Outside the Household: Using the Labour of Others*

Labour relations involving people who were not members of the same household were important in the organisation of livelihoods at Mepe and Sokpoe. Such labour relations tended to be activity specific and, therefore, gendered. They involved people who owned some capital items—canoes, nets, land, mills, shops, ovens, flour and other inputs—and who, therefore, could get other people to work for them. This enhanced their livelihoods and their ability to engage in multiple activities. For example, men who had boats and nets not only used such equipment with the help of household labour, but also that of others whom they paid a share of the catch for their efforts. In addition, on days when they did not use the equipment themselves, they rented it out to people for a third of the catch. We have already discussed the labour relations of the baking industry involving apprentices, casual labourers and retailers of bread. In relation to farming, there were sharecropping arrangements and labourers could be hired for specific tasks such as land clearing and preparation and weeding for a fixed amount per acre. In trading and service activities, there were persons employed to sell goods or operate some machinery such as a corn or flour-mill on behalf of the shop owner.

Labour relations were often complicated by the idiom of kinship even in cases where those involved were not close kin. This extended relations beyond their normal remit. Particularly with household-based enterprises such as baking and kenkey-making, different categories of labour also had close or loose kinship connections with the household head. This sometimes resulted in household heads assuming some reproductive responsibilities for these persons, but at the same time creating open-ended relationships, which could be even more exploitative than formal labour relations.

There were gender dimensions of the ability to use other peoples' labour. For example, while men who had nets and canoes owned them, women who financed such equipment did not have ownership. Instead, they were considered to have loaned money to the fishermen who owned the equipment. The transaction gave the women privileged access to the catch on very good terms. As already indicated, this did not happen much at Mepe and Sokpoe because of the economic conditions and was considered by some fishermen to impede the growth of their activities.

Relations between artisans and their apprentices were part of the labour relations in the Lower Volta. As pertained in much of Ghana, female apprentices were engaged largely in sewing and hairdressing while males were involved in masonry, carpentry, driving and vehicle repairs. Owners of these ventures were training younger persons of their own sex. In a few cases though, male tailors had women among their trainees. In the last chapter, we noted that because of poor markets, artisans increasingly had to supplement their livelihoods by taking on apprentices. Apprentices were thus both a source of additional income and once they learned the basics of the trade, a valuable source of cheap labour. Apprentices were regularly sent out to render minor services such basic carpentry work and in the building industry they helped to lay bricks, mix concrete, carry water, sand, stones and cement to building sites. In tailoring shops, hairdressing salons and bakeries, apprentices helped to produce and deliver services. Apprentices, particularly those working with female artisans, were also involved in a variety of reproductive activities thus freeing the artisan from time-consuming tasks such as sweeping, fetching water and washing clothes. As well, they worked on farms belonging to their masters and mistresses.

Apprenticeships were becoming more and more expensive across the board as apprentices also had to bring their own tools. While artisans were generally aware of the conditions under which apprentices were living and acknowledged that many apprentices were dropping out of their training for financial reasons, they needed the services and payments of apprentices to supplement their earnings. Some artisans such as masons and fitters took responsibility for the daily maintenance of their apprentices in recognition of their labour services while others such as the seamstresses and tailors did not. The situation from the point of view of apprentices will be discussed in the section on young people and the future of livelihoods in the Lower Volta.

5. *Acquiring Support Through the Membership of Formal and Informal Associations and Networks*

Many respondents at Sokpoe and Mepe were members of either a church association or a funeral society. Church groups were organised by age and gender for moral education, socialising, solidarity, mutual support and entertainment. The funeral societies provided assistance to surviving relations of deceased members. Such support included a coffin, a fixed sum of money and drumming and dancing to entertain mourners. Some associations also supported members when they were bereaved or ill. The low membership dues were in recognition of the general situation of people, but it had implications for the levels of financial support that were possible. However, the solidarity and the entertainment value of drumming and dancing were highly appreciated.

For the majority of respondents, the networks that were important for their livelihoods were the informal ones. It was through these that credit and other forms of support could be accessed. Thus, neighbours could get foodstuffs on credit and also extend credit when needed by others. Informal networks were also a source of solidarity and support for people engaged in the same activities or having to cope with similar difficulties. The groups of women who travelled outside Mepe together to try their hands at salt-winning or clam picking were good examples of the informal mutual support networks. They provided the kind of support which made it possible for those who would otherwise not venture out on their own to attempt certain kinds of activities and be among trusted friends and relations in a similar position as themselves. The informal group also allowed a collective discussion of strategies even as each member worked independently and some were more successful than others.

Another kind of grouping which was more structured but still informal was the association of people working at a particular location. The Toklokpo stone winners were an example of this sort of network. Originally established as a mechanism for the settlement of disputes among members, it had grown into a more regular self-help association of workers.[10] Now the organisation was also supporting members in times of bereavement through a collection of contributions and the donation of some of the fines collected. If someone was injured at work the group would contribute to send the person

---

[10] Disputes included inter-group disagreements over the boundaries of each group's "concession" and intra-group tensions over the amount of work each group member was putting in. In the past these conflicts had resulted in violence and police involvement. The landowners had responded by asking the stone winners to organise themselves to deal with these problems. All grievances now had a proper forum for settlement and any member who got into a fight had to pay a fine of ten thousand cedis and two bottles of schnapps.

to hospital. While these informal and semi-formal associations were very useful, they were not organised to secure outside support for their activities.

More established operators such as the bakers and the fishermen at Sokpoe and the *akpeteshie* distillers at both Mepe and Sokpoe and other parts of the Lower Volta, had formal dues-collecting registered Associations through which they addressed their welfare issues. These Associations also facilitated dealings with institutions such as the District Assembly and the Banks. Through them, fishermen and bakers at Sokpoe secured credit from Rural Banks.[11] The Banks preferred to lend money to established groups without collateral if they had guarantors, preferably workers whose salaries were paid through them. Individual members were still accountable for the loans they had procured through the group.[12]

Not all fishermen and bakers were able to sustain their membership of these Associations. Loan defaulters could not continue to enjoy membership benefits. The Sokpoe Bakers Associations had recorded a more than 50% decrease in membership since its establishment as a result of indebtedness.[13] On the other hand, members of good standing who no longer baked continued to collect their share of flour and sugar to sell to other members and non-members who needed more than they received. At Mepe, no economic groupings were successful enough to organise in this way. Indeed, it appeared that less money was circulating at Mepe although it had a Rural Bank, which had a consumer credit outlet for various electrical appliances, luggage and cement. The difference in the strategies of the two associations was interesting. While the fishermen's

---

[11] The Agave Rural Bank branch office at Sogakope (the main bank was at Dabala) had customers such as the Sokpoe Bakers Association, the Agbakofe Okra Farmers, Hikpo Okra farmers, Agbogbla Distillers Association, the Vume Ceramics Group and the Kpotame/Tademe Fishermen's Association. Opening an account was usually a prelude to applying for a loan.

[12] Interview with Official of Agave Rural Bank, Sogakope. The Sokpoe Bakers Association, the Vume Ceramics Group, Distillers Associations from Adutor and Hikpo and the Torsukpo Distillers Association had been lent money by the Bank. However, most of the Bank's customers were salaried workers, a few, building contractors, farmers and traders. They were usually from the larger towns in the area such as Sogakope, Anloga and Agbozome. Less than 20% of them were from Sokpoe and surrounding villages.

[13] One of the leaders of the Baking Association at Sokpoe claimed that membership had halved because the debt defaulters had migrated to "Krachi" (representing communities around the Volta Lake) to work to pay off their debts.

co-operative had benefited from the implementation of international agreement to designate fragile wetlands as Ramsar sites, the bakers had had to rely on more private commercial channels. Interestingly, the fishermen had applied for District Assembly support, something that had not come up with the Bakers Association which had to exclude potential and actual members to protect it from loan defaults. It was not established whether these differences constituted a pattern of behaviour. This issue which has policy implications could be taken up in future studies. In spite of professional associations and the possibilities of District Assembly and Rural Bank support, livelihoods in the Lower Volta were largely carried out without support from the State and other institutions.

The long-standing unresolved wrangles over compensation for and mitigation of dam impacts had resulted in a distance from and distrust of the State and its officials even at the level of the District. As already noted, there was cynicism borne out of experience of the inability of the District Assembly and the MPs to resolve these problems. The Poverty Alleviation Fund of the District Assembly was seen by the few respondents who knew about it as a tool for political patronage and therefore relevant only to those who already had resources. Thus, the Fishermen's Co-operative Society leadership had doubts about their ability to secure resources from the Fund. However, all communities in the Lower Volta had to contend with the increasing tax demands of the District Assemblies. The markets were the single largest source of revenue for many Districts in Ghana and the Tongu Districts were no exception. Thus women made up the bulk of those whose taxes financed District Assembly activities, but were not those benefiting the most from the revenue in terms of market facilities and other livelihood support. In any case, financing development projects was a problem in the two Districts because of people's inability and in some cases, reluctance, to pay taxes and there were signs of tensions between groups and the District Assembly. More broadly, District level taxation raised a range of issues, which were not tackled in the study. For example, Ellis and Freeman's account of the District level taxation regimes of several Southern and Eastern African countries raised concerns about the impoverishment of rural dwellers through the privatisation of tax collection (Ellis and Freeman, 2002). This suggests that the District and Sub-district levels' tax systems were likely to have implications for livelihoods now and in the future as decentralisation processes deepened in the Lower Volta and elsewhere in Ghana.

6. *Livelihoods and Inter-Generational Relations:*
The Situation of Young People

This discussion of the specific problems of young persons and their
experience of the contraction in livelihoods in the Lower Volta
addresses a number of issues. They include questions of how kinship and inter-generational relations played out in conditions of crisis, the use of young people's labour, the livelihood options open to
them, and their likely trajectories and the future of the Lower Volta.
It is based on interviews with young persons belonging to a range
of household types in the Lower Volta and involved in both household and non-kin labour relations. The discussion focuses on two
broad issues. One is the Lower Volta's contribution to the socialisation of the children of migrants and the role of young people in
the organisation of livelihoods.

The Lower Volta and the socialisation of children of migrants

One of the areas in which migration had had a direct impact on
the Lower Volta was through the support people in the Lower Volta
gave to the children of migrants who had been sent there to receive
training. Several households had children and young people born in
migrant communities and sent to hometowns to acquire formal education or learn trades.[14] Some of these young persons saw their stay
as temporary while others did not intend to return to where their
parents were, but expected to go on to other places which had some
use for their skills. While this practice of people sending children to
relations in the Lower Volta was old, it was in some decline because
of the changing conditions in both locations. There was now recognition that it was easier economically to maintain children in migrant
settlements because you could get a large enough piece of land and
also some fish. In some cases, the people caring for children had
become old, exhausted and quite frail themselves. On the other hand,
the support from the Lakeside had become intermittent because of

---

[14] The children stayed anything from 8–12 years to complete Junior and Senior
Secondary School depending on the age at which they were sent. Things did not
always go according to plan and respondents spoke of children who returned to
their parents after 2–3 years for a variety of reasons.

the hardships there. Therefore, many old people had to continue with their farming and other livelihood activities, not for themselves alone, but also to cater for the needs of their charges, some of whom were too young to be of much assistance. The suggestion that being sent children from the Lakeside was an opportunity for old people to secure some maintenance for themselves was strongly rejected by some respondents.

When the children were older and in a position to travel themselves to their parents to bring food and money, tensions often arose because they wanted to keep the food for themselves in order to stretch its use. In a number of cases, young persons had set up separate eating arrangements while continuing to live with guardians. While households listed such children as members in important respects, some of the children, especially when they were a group and were quite young, seemed to be nesting within the larger households until such time as they could gain their independence.

The practice of sending children to hometowns to attend school as a strategy of socialisation had not worked very well in some cases largely because of the poor material conditions of the Lower Volta. The often poor economic circumstances of guardians, the increasingly parlous state of schools in the Lower Volta and the differences in age and culture between the children and their hosts were all factors that undermined the practice. Others have argued that the wholesale migration of elders and the upholders of tradition and discipline were at the root of social problems such as juvenile delinquency, poor school attendance and a general decline in moral standards (Geker, 1999). Thus, the very conditions which made sending children back home to be socialised had rendered what was left of Tongu society in the Lower Volta unsuited to this task. The old community that saw children as collective property has been under strain all over Ghana for decades. This resulted in the makeshift character of some of the households that played host to the children of migrants. In the past, younger children were sent to grandparents. As they grew and became more independent, they often ended up on the fringes of households, not quite in the care of any one person. More recently, groups of parents with kinship relations cobbled together households of young persons. Such households were found at both Mepe and Sokpoe, and in one case, four identifiable but close-knit units were living in one house. In another, a 17 year old male was in charge of two other boys. Only a year before, this last household had not existed in this form and its life-span depended on the arrangements working well.

This growing incidence of households effectively headed by persons who had either just become adults themselves or were still minors was a crisis response to the problem of the lack of adult figures willing and able to take charge of the children of migrants. Their strivings and their relationships with more regular households were illustrative of the erosion as well as the continuing strength of the co-operative community ethos. Although the primary source of support were absent parents, there were several adult relations who helped with money in times of crisis—illness, when they ran out of money or any other serious problem. The problem was that many such persons had their own financial difficulties. Fellow children of migrants also supported each other. While it was possible for them to keep body and soul together with the help of all these support networks, on questions of socialisation and nurturing, the situation was more difficult. The household heads who kept the discipline and corrected younger children were themselves minors or young adults who ordinarily would not have the responsibility to socialise and nurture younger minors (some as young as six years) for another few years. Several adults expressed disapproval of the teenage children of migrants, particularly the girls. They were perceived as not under anyone's authority even when they were part of households and respondents complained about their morals. It was not clear if they behaved differently from other young women whose parents were within the communities, but it would seem that a certain brash individualism associated with them irked people who had their own prejudices about the alien life, values and culture of Lakeside.[15] While there was an appearance of disjunction between the cultures of children of migrants and those of the communities they had been sent to, the latter were also in a state of flux and many of the cherished customary practices were under stress. For example, the

---

[15] During the research period, the Parent Teacher Association (PTA) of the Presbyterian School at Mepe at its meeting discussed the problem of girls left to their own devices because their parents could not send them money regularly. There was concern that they were accepting sums as small as 500 and 1,000 cedis for sex. The amounts being mentioned underlined the parlous situation of the young people, but also the general poverty in these communities where money transactions, except in relation to the sale of land for housing and food items such as river fish, tended to be in small amounts.

practice of sharing food gifts with neighbours and friends worked well only when there was some level of reciprocity. In a situation of periodic food shortages and the lack of guarantees that one could expect some food gifts in return, giving out food gifts sent from the Lake for the upkeep of children was one source of tension between wards and the children of migrants in their care.

The livelihoods of young people

In the following discussion, young people were categorised into school goers, apprentices and young workers in order to address the specificities of their livelihoods problems. All the young persons interviewed identified the lack of viable livelihood options for themselves, their parents and other elders as a serious problem in the Lower Volta. Others put it in terms of financial problems, the poverty of parents and their inability to cope with the needs of their children such as school fees and the problem of children having to look after themselves. Other related problems were poor rainfall, lack of access to education, disrespect for elders and immorality of youth—teenage pregnancy and stealing by boys. A few mentioned problems with the quality of education on offer, the maltreatment of apprentices by their masters and the amount of work outside their training they had to do. The study found that because of the poor resource situation of most households and the absence of many parents, young persons, whether in school, learning a trade or just working, tried to earn some money either to supplement remittances or look after themselves.

Several young people dropped out off school before the end of primary or Junior Secondary School. The majority of school dropouts encountered during the study were girls and they stopped for financial reasons or because of pregnancy. After finishing or dropping out of a stage of primary or secondary school, many young persons became apprentices. The girls were being apprenticed into traditional female professions—mostly sewing but also hairdressing and some were helping chop bar keepers. Male apprentices were not so visible, partly because the masons were not set up with workshops like the seamstresses. The carpenters did but did not have the apprentices assembled as though they were in school. While artisanal training was possible, the money to enter into training was hard to find. Moreover, some young persons who had learned trades could not practise their professions.

When not in school either because they had finished one stage or had dropped out, and when not learning a trade or practising a profession, Mepe young persons were engaged in charcoal burning, traditional artisanship such as basket weaving, casual labour and petty trading. At Sokpoe, girls and young women sold food and other consumer items by the roadside while the boys assisted fishermen and farmers, did some trading and also ferried smuggled goods across the river. A Sokpoe resident observed that many more young men were involved in assisting smugglers and a number of them had been arrested and imprisoned. Thus, young people were facing serious challenges in their livelihoods. Too many of them had to take charge of themselves from an early age and also look after even younger siblings without parental supervision.[16] As livelihood activities were often gendered, young males had a wider range of options for survival than females. As well, their difficulties were manifested in the gendered nature of their anti-social behaviour. Boys were accused of turning to crime and the girls of getting involved in early sex, teenage motherhood and abortions.[17]

CASE 6.6: Agbenyega, a school boy working to finance his education (Mepe)

> Agbenyega was 15, in JSS 3. He lived at Nuwuloi, at Mepe's border with Mafi, another Tongu group. He was born and grew up there. His father, a teacher, was at the moment at the University of Education, Winneba, while his mother was trading. Since his father went to school two years ago, he had stopped contributing to the maintenance of the house. Even before he left, Agbenyega's mother did more for them. He now had a new wife and as a result his mother had moved out three years ago with some of the children to live in her grandfather's house. Agbenyega and another sibling remained in their father's house for a year before moving out to join their mother. Agbenyega was the 6th of ten children of his parents and all of them were still living at Nuwuloi. The first, at 28 was a fisherman, charcoal burner and farmer having finished SSS some years before. Although he was married and had a child, his wife lived at her mother's and he continued to live in his natal household. All the others were fishing or trading or in school. Agbenyega was paying his own school fees and had been doing

---

[16] One informant, an RC Primary School teacher, speculated that about half of the school children were looking after themselves (HB, Mepe).

[17] Respondents who, as grandmothers, had to look after such children complained routinely about their behaviour, but were especially critical of the girls.

this since JSS 2. Before this, his father had been paying, but he had stopped without explanation. He would promise to pay but the money would not come. Agbenyega was working as a farm labourer, farming and burning charcoal. In one term, he and one of his brothers helped to clear land at a farm near the Aklamador River and he was paid 6,000 cedis for this. He fished a total of ten times and produced one and half bags of charcoal in one term. Apart from paying his fees, he was also buying clothing. His school uniform had been given to him by one of his brothers.

Agbenyega still had hopes of going to senior secondary school at Mepe and training college in a nearby District. He wanted to become a teacher at Afiadenyigba in a neighbouring District, the only place he had visited outside the Mepe area in the last two years. As a child, his parents had taken him and all his siblings who were born then to the Volta Lakeside in 1983 when there was a food crisis in Ghana. His father fished there while his mother farmed. They returned 2 years later when the food crisis passed and also because the schools there were not very good.

CASE 6.7: Valerie, the Sokpoe student maintained by her mother (Sokpoe)

Valerie was 17, single and in the first year of Senior Secondary School. She was born and grew up at Sogakope, the South Tongu District Capital. A year before the interview she and her mother went to live at Toklokpo. They had been living in her grand-aunt's room and she wanted the room back. Now they were in her mother's brother's house. Her father died when she was six and her mother married again and was now divorced. At the time her mother remarried, her sister came and took her to Anexo and she spent a year as house help to a woman from Nigeria. Her mother came for her because she was not satisfied with her situation. She had lived with her mother since and attended various schools in the Sogakope area—L.A. Primary, JSS at Agorkpo, a nearby Sokpoe village and Sogakope Secondary School. Her mother was sponsoring her education through her farming and trading activities. The farms were mainly for food. Valerie herself was not working and helped her mother to farm during weekends and holidays. To finance her education, she and her mother used to cook for a certain man who then helped them throughout her Junior Secondary School years and in the first year of her Senior Secondary education. The arrangement had broken down when they moved to Toklokpo and in any case, the man was under pressure from his wife about his own children's school fees.

Valerie's ambition was to study weaving or tie-dye making, an outgrowth of her current studies in visual arts. She did not know where she could pursue those studies but felt it would become clear when the time came. Her mother preferred that she go to a polytechnic to her going to a university, for financial reasons. Valerie was in agreement with this decision. She was a day student to save money on school fees and complained that she did not have enough time to study because once she came home, she had to help with farming and other household activities.

Valerie's mother herself had left school in middle form four but was interested that her daughter should further her education. The school fees could be carried forward so she was hoping to finish paying when she completed school. Valerie said if her mother did not find the money for further education, she would find some money to go and study sewing at Sogakope. After her training, she was thinking of living with her sisters in Accra or Kumasi because they both had promised to support her future training.

CASE 6.8: Jemima, the apprentice who came from the Lakeside (Mepe)

Jemima was 29, married and in the second year of her apprenticeship. She grew up with her mother's mother at Mepe where she went to school and finished middle school. This was after her parent's marriage broke down and they went their separate ways, her mother to Sunyani in the Brong Ahafo Region with a new husband. She met her husband and married him in 1986. In 1989, she joined him at a settlement around the Lake and they lived there for six years. He was a fisherman and she bought his fish and sold it in the market and even travelled to Accra to sell sometimes. She also sold garri. Two years ago, she left and came to Mepe to learn a trade. While she had chosen sewing, her mother had had to ask her husband and he had agreed that she could come and learn. Part of her reason for leaving was that they were having marital problems. He had met and married another woman and was having affairs. She left her only child with her husband.

Her husband was sending her 40,000 cedis and a bag of maize every month as maintenance. She was not engaged in any economic activities herself and lived in her sister's room and, therefore, was not paying any rent. Whenever she ran out of money, her mother's sister advanced her some until she could repay. She was planning to set up a workshop at Mepe after her training and wanted to take on apprentices. She had no desire to go back to the Lakeside because things were getting difficult there. If things did not work out for her at Mepe, she would go to her mother who was still a cocoa farmer in the Brong Ahafo Region.

The three cases were selected to illustrate the conditions of young people at different stages of their training. Agbenyega was in JSS, Valerie in SSS and Jemima a middle school leaver who was training to become a seamstress after several years of migrant life. The underlying commonality of their conditions was that they were each facing challenges of survival but coping in different ways. Agbenyega was supporting himself, Valerie was being supported by her mother and Jemima by her estranged husband. All three were also facing the issue of their future and each of them had plans which involved leaving the Lower Volta at some stage. In the following discussion, the findings of interviews with several young people on their conditions, the issues of survival facing them and their future are presented. Because of the small size of the sample, only absolute figures are presented here.

School goers

Twenty-seven persons (15 male and 12 female) in Junior and Senior Secondary School were interviewed at Mepe and Sokpoe. They were chosen randomly from various schools at Mepe and Sokpoe and outlying villages. Sixteen of them were in JSS while eleven were in SSS. They were living with various persons. Eight of them (4 male, 4 female) lived with their mothers, three (1 male, 2 female) with their fathers, while six (5 male and 1 female), lived with both parents. Six of them (3 male, 3 female) lived with their grandmothers while one male lived with his grandparents. One (male) lived with his brother while one female lived with her mother's brother. There was only one person (female) living on her own but with support of a relation living nearby. The group was evenly divided between those who had to work to supplement their upkeep or looked after themselves completely (13) and those who did not have independent means of survival (14). Of the males in the sample, eight worked while seven did not. Of the seven, another two helped their parents/guardians to farm after school. Among the females, seven were not engaged in any economic activities while five were. Of the seven, one was helping with farm work. The activities of those working included petty trading—bread and fruit, pushing trucks, running errands, casual labour—farming, fishing, basket weaving and making pestles, mat weaving, burning charcoal, collecting firewood. A few went to the Lakeside on holidays and brought money back and one person mentioned support from her boyfriend. One person was helping his father in his tailoring shop while four were helping with family farms.

The majority of the sample was interested in further education (10 boys and 8 girls) while four boys and five girls were interested in learning a trade. However, at this stage, they already had to do various things to maintain themselves. The findings were confirmed in interviews with teacher informants (HB, R.C. Primary Teacher, Mepe).

Apprentices

> We apprentices are suffering. Even those who do not plan to be bad are getting spoilt. They find a man who has money and give themselves to him. They get some money for today and move to the next person the next day. Some get pregnant and then they have problems. If you get pregnant, the madam will fine you. You will pay her 400,000 instead of the 200,000. She will take your machine if you cannot pay. Those it happens to have an abortion so the madam never finds out (Jemima, Sewing Apprentice, Mepe).

Seventeen apprentices were interviewed at Mepe and Sokpoe. The vast majority of them (13) were women and they were all learning how to sew. All the four men were studying masonry. Most of the apprentices were in their 20s (12-nine female and three male), 3 in their teens (all female) and one in her 30s (female) and one in his 40s (male). A range of persons sponsored apprentices: themselves (5) grandmothers (2), mothers (3), parents (1), aunts (2), master/brother (1), boyfriends (2) and husbands (3). Thus, the largest single sponsor was the apprentices. Most of the sponsors were farming (8) and fishing (5). The rest were artisans and traders (4) and wage employees (2). Apprentices responded in kind by helping with farming (10), housework (5), helping with the upkeep of younger siblings (1) and assisting with artisanal work (1).

A number of reasons were advanced for going into particular apprenticeships. The most common was a love or admiration for the profession among the various options on offer (7), wanting to learn a trade (4), guaranteeing daily bread or good wages (2) and having to stop formal education because parents could no longer afford it or pregnancy (4). In one case, a female apprentice had been enrolled in gratitude for long years of domestic service (1) while for another it was that fishing was no longer lucrative (1). Some respondents had more than one reason for taking up an apprenticeship and an underlying reason in most cases was that it was the best option under the circumstances. The majority of respondents said that they had come to the decision themselves (9) while others said it was their mother by herself or with an uncle or the respondent (4). Others mentioned an aunt (2), a father (1) and a brother who himself was the master they came to learn the trade from (1).

Most apprentices were working to support themselves or contributing to their upkeep. Five were farming on their own account, one was helping on a farm while two were helping a master builder. A number of the women were selling oranges and banana and kokonte (2), making brooms for sale (1) and picking mangoes for sale (1). Only three persons were not engaged in any income generation activities. Twelve apprentices planned to set up workshops after their training, two were interested in waged work while another three did not know. Nine were going to remain at Mepe, Sokpoe and surrounding areas, one of these mentioned Sogakope. One was planning to go to the Volta Lakeside, two to Accra and four did not know. Of the people planning to stay in the area, five of them wanted to remain at home while three said they wanted to train others. One said the migrant communities were no longer good places for work while another one wanted to help her mother. One woman was planning to settle in her husband's hometown while the rest wanted to leave because there was no custom in their villages. Three did not advance reasons for their choices.

The school dropout rates and the growing attraction and proliferation of artisanal training without a commensurate increase in patronage of such services were especially problematic for the future of the individuals involved as well as that of the Lower Volta. For girls especially, artisanal livelihood options were even more limited, comprising mainly of sewing and hairdressing while for boys, it was carpentry, masonry, driving and mechanics.[18] After training, artisans were less likely to find work in the Lower Volta than those without any education at all because of their different expectations. It was not surprising, therefore, that several thought that they could make successful livelihoods only outside the Lower Volta and were planning to migrate.

Young workers
The Sokpoe roadside was full of young traders chasing vehicles. There were a few who had their own small shops. An example was

---

[18] The building industry, which used both carpenters and masons, had some possibilities because it was patronised by people with resources from outside the Lower Volta economy.

Christiana. At 24, a JSS graduate and single, she was a member of a household made up of nine persons. She had dropped out of school because she was not doing well. She had decided to go into trading and had been selling drinks for six months at the time of the interview.

Besides the traders, the Sokpoe roadside was full of young persons sitting around shop fronts especially those that had music systems where loud music issued from. While on first appearance they seemed to be unemployed, they were all trying their hands at various things but were dissatisfied with what they were doing for a living and considered it temporary. Kingsley for example, was 30 years with middle school education, single and had no children. He used to farm with his mother but was now fishing three days a week with his own canoe and net. He was earning about 10,000 cedis on each day of fishing. Dickson was a barber and a driver's mate. At 23 years old, he was a JSS graduate and married with a child. He worked daily as a mate in a cargo van which travelled between Sogakope, Aflao and Akatsi. He was paid 6,000 cedis a day. He cut hair when he closed from work. Victor was 26, also a JSS graduate, single, no children and a truck pusher. He transported bread from Sokpoe to Sogakofe market for the bakers. He charged 1,000 cedis for each trip from Sokpoe to Sogakope. Nestor was 30 years, with primary school education and was married with three children. He fished sometimes and helped to unload cargo such as cement from trucks into shops for a fee. He did not have a net or canoe and earned an average of 6,500 cedis on each fishing trip. He went fishing about three times a week. He also earned about 6,000 cedis for each cargo he unloaded and did unloading jobs two or three times a week. Nestor was interested in a factory or an agro-industrial job because it would pay more regularly and he could advance in that. Kingsley wanted to learn a trade such as welding, mechanics or carpentry but did not have anyone to pay for his training and maintenance during the training period. Dickson found the unloading of vehicles very difficult and strenuous but had no other options.

Some of the young men in this position at Sokpoe had recently taken to assisting smugglers. The illegality of smuggling meant that no respondent mentioned it as an occupation. However, a number of respondents mentioned its growing importance in the context of the lack of satisfactory livelihood activities for young people and therefore there was no serious community disapproval of this activity.

During a discussion with the Sokpoe chief, two angry young men came to see him about a complaint they had already laid before him. A former courier now turned a Ghana Customs, Excise and Preventive Service informant was obstructing their work of ferrying smuggled goods across the river in a hired boat. They were particularly agitated because two vehicles had been seized that day and they believed it was on the information of this person. The chief expressed sympathy and promised to summon the informant and speak to him. One of the arguments the complainants made to support their demands was that smuggling was the only option left to young men in the community.

Part of the reason for the tolerant attitude to couriers was that they were able to offer support in times of crisis because they had some money. In one case when a vehicle hit someone, it was one of the couriers who had provided money to send the man to the Battor Hospital. An overwhelming number of young persons thought that outside intervention in the form of job opportunities such as agro-industries, other kinds of factories and credit was needed to address the problems of livelihoods in the Lower Volta. Interestingly, they were not referring to improvements in fishing and farming.

7. *Summary and Conclusions*

In this chapter, we focused on the social relations of livelihoods in the context of long-term adverse environmental and socio-economic change and responses. We examined some specificities of social relations of class, gender, kinship and intergenerational relations, which as we argued, had been shaped by the Lower Volta's history of large-scale out-migration. We observed the proliferation of and changing configurations of different kinds of households including some very large households, some with high dependency ratios and mostly headed by women and organised around one livelihood activity such as farming, baking or kenkey-making.

We also found that while households with many children had problems of survival, children were critical for the organisation of reproductive and some productive activities. In situations where households lived within lineage compounds, the collective organisation of children for some reproductive activities allowed those with no children within their households to benefit from these relationships. The use of children for both productive and reproductive activities was undergoing change in the Lower Volta for a variety of reasons. These included the changing nature of the economy, the growing importance of formal education for livelihoods and the changing residential patterns at Sokpoe and Mepe. Other factors were the changing composition of households and the commercialisation of some activities such as procuring water and fuel, which had resulted in the reduction in children's contributions to productive and reproductive activities.

The role of conjugal relations in livelihoods was examined through a discussion of marital co-operation around food crop production as well as the division of labour in production and expenditure. We argued that as a result of the large-scale migration, the nuclear family structured by a conjugal union at its core was far from the norm at Sokpoe and Mepe. This was important as household characteristics such as size, composition and point in the developmental cycle were important for its ability to engage in multiple activities and also to secure good outcomes. Household characteristics such as points in the developmental cycle were complicated by the composition of households. However, the research concluded that households with the best livelihood outcomes were reasonably large, had several adults with independent livelihood activities with broad, sometimes, multi-spatial bases and including artisanal activities and wage work. Many of the households headed by women did not fit this bill, as the larger ones were often organised around one main activity and supporting a host of people with varied and complicated relations with its head.

Outside households, various degrees of kin relations were implicated in the organisation of livelihoods, from the basic advantages of rent-free accommodation, remittances from migrant relations to access to land and labour. We found that just as it was in the pre-dam period, access to lineage resources such as land was gendered and men had larger plots of land to farm and to rent out than women did. However, few male clan and lineage members had been able to benefit from alienating vast tracts of land. Instead, the competition and conflict over lineage resources arising from these transactions had been detrimental to the livelihoods of many members of these collectives, both male and female.

Labour relations within and outside the context of kinship allowed those with capital and equipment to secure the labour of others, including their children, other kin, hired labour and apprentices.

These relations were less visible in the Lower Volta where the returns on exertions were small, but their existence had even more import for those providing the labour in these relationships. The poor rewards consigned many to a life of labour without the resources to establish their own independent livelihoods unless they could inject capital from outside the Lower Volta and access substantial amounts of lineage resources. The particular benefit derived by the financiers of equipment was gendered for activities such as fishing. The minority of women who financed nets were not in the same position as men who did, their absence from fishing expeditions making it more difficult for them to realise their investments.

Relations between artisans and their apprentices were an important dimension of labour relations. Apprentices were able to learn a trade, which allowed them the possibility not only of multiple livelihood activities, but also an escape from the limits of natural resource-based livelihoods. However, the conditions of apprenticeships made them an important source of free labour for productive and reproductive activities. For apprentices, the period of training was extremely difficult and uncertain and not all apprentices were able to stay the course and thus benefit fully from their investment of time and labour.

Formal and informal networks and associations in the organisation of livelihoods were examined. The research found that the presence of formal organisations signalled a higher level of production and outcomes and also allowed members to access resources such as credit from outside their economies. Very few people at Mepe and Sokpoe, but especially at Mepe, had the benefit of these associations. Instead, the majority of people were involved in funeral associations, church and other drumming and dancing groups, which provided a little relief, solidarity and entertainment in times of trouble. The benefits of membership of these groups, while open to a wide range of people because of the relatively easy to fulfil requirements for membership, were limited by the low resource bases of the organisations.

The role of credit in the organisation of livelihoods was discussed. We observed that both close and loose kinship ties smoothed credit transactions and allowed people a way out of immediate crises. However, those who could benefit from credit in the long term were those who could honour their obligations. Also, the widespread use of credit not for productive activities but for very basic consumption and reproduction was an indication of poor livelihood outcomes. The character of credit also had adverse impacts on traders whose capital base was usually very low and put pressure on the very kinship and friendship ties that made it possible in the first place. We also discussed certain conflicts over resources such as land as a manifestation of stresses on livelihoods.

The chapter focused on young people in the context of inter-generational relations, kinship and gender. We examined the trajectories of young people in various situations. The study found that because of the generalised character of formal education, the majority of young persons were opting for artisanal training or higher education if their parents could afford it. For those who completed their training, out-migration was an important strategy for realising this investment. The research found that most young people in training were either having to contribute to their upkeep or doing it by themselves with great difficulty and this resulted in high dropout rates. The situation of young people and their sense that there was no way of surviving without migration pointed to the long-term reproduction of the livelihood crises facing the Lower Volta and the fact that social relations were enabling for too few people.

CHAPTER SEVEN

RESPONSES TO THE VOLTA RIVER PROJECT:
VOLUNTARY MIGRATION AND THE ESTABLISHMENT
OF LAKESIDE SETTLEMENTS

1. *Introduction*

About two kilometres before the end of the badly eroded road to
Surveyor Line[1] stood a stone sculpture of a white cockerel, the totem
of the Akorvie Division of Mepe. Having spent time at Mepe some
months before, it was immediately apparent to me that its sudden
appearance by the roadside was significant. It was meant to signal
that the settlement we were about to enter was home to members
of the Akorvie Division of Mepe.[2] This desire to mark their dis-
tinctiveness as a group was a function of their migrant status. This
chapter examines how this sense of difference was played out in the
lives of migrants around the Lake. The chapter is the first of two
which focus on the people involved in the mass migration from the
Lower Volta in the 1960s and the communities and livelihoods they
established along the Lake. Also of interest are their relations with
local communities, state agencies and other migrant settlements. We
argue that these interlocking multiple relationships were deployed,
some in tandem with or against others in the establishment of migrant
livelihoods.

---

[1] Surveyor Line, a migrant settlement along the Volta Lake, is a small village of
huts constructed from laterite and thatch with a population of 557 (309 male and
248 female) [2000 Ghana Population Census]. It is just beyond Gyakiti in the
Asuogyaman District of the Eastern Region of Ghana, which is home to the Akwamu,
an Akan group.
[2] Interestingly, the Akorvie believed that they originally came from Asante-Mampong
and settled in Akwamu until wars drove them down the Volta River to become a
founding Division of Mepe. The Division's name Akorvie is said to be a corruption
of Akwamuviawo i.e. the Akwamu people. Like all other Mepe people, the Akorvie
speak Ewe. However, many of their family and stool names are Akan in origin.

In migrating to the Lake, the Tongu Ewe fishermen were continuing in their pre-dam traditions of migration upstream. However, there was a significant change, marked by a shift from multi-spatial to mono-spatial livelihoods in that most of them no longer participated in economic activities in the Lower Volta. As the Volta Lake was central to the livelihoods they were about to fashion, the migrants established hundreds of settlements along its shores. Settlement names were in some cases inspired by the new strange surroundings, the enormity of the task of domesticating the Lake, religious fervour or the desire of founders to immortalise themselves, their old settlements or their hometowns.[3]

The chapter is based on a study of three settlements established by or populated predominantly by Tongu Ewe migrants along the Volta Lake—Surveyor Line, Kudikope (known officially as Asedja)[4] and Kpando Torkor. The chapter is organised in seven parts. The first is a discussion of the changing context of migrant communities from the early period of migration and the establishment of communities and livelihoods. The themes of this section include procedures and processes for early and subsequent settlement and the itinerant traditions established by Lakeside migrants to deal with uncertainties arising from their incomplete knowledge of the Lake and its character and possibilities. The section also discusses the specificities of the study settlements, their similarities and differences in size and composition, and their common legacy as unplanned settlements with poor infrastructure and institutions. The political, judicial, social and economic institutions are the subject of the third section of the chapter. In the fourth section, community relations in migrant settlements are tackled. We argue that while community differences appeared minor to outside observers, they were sometimes significant in the organisation of livelihoods and were felt intensely. The relations between migrant communities and the various players within

---

[3] A study of those names—Hyenwuhudin, Asempanaye, Nketepa, Kutuso, Etsi Amanfro, Sempoa, Sendeme, John Holt, Dedeso, Abotoase, Surveyor Line, Kudikope, Gbitikope, Amenekefi, Konkordeka, Wulorxe, Adumease, Dzemeni, Aklusu, Duaduase, etc.—would make fascinating reading, but is beyond the scope of this book.

[4] In the official census reports (1984 and 2000), the name Kudikope does not appear. While its founders and inhabitants call it Kudikope, the landlords have named it Asedja and its primary school is also called Asedja L.A. Primary School. The name of the settlement is a point of contention between migrants and their landlords. We have retained the usage Kudikope to reflect the name used by the migrants themselves.

their environment—local host communities, state agencies, particularly the VRA and the District Assemblies—are the subject of section five of the chapter. We argue that each of these relations had a bearing on livelihoods and together created a complicated and contradictory matrix of support and hampering factors for livelihoods. This is because they affected the terms of access to land, the use of the Lake, what kinds of livelihoods were possible and their outcomes. Section six discusses the changing relation between migrants and their hometowns as an important factor in migrant livelihoods. The section argues that migrants considered themselves as strangers after over four decades, but had moved from seeing their hometowns as the places to educate their children to places where they might still be buried. The chapter concludes with a summary of the main issues raised.

2. The Early Period of Migration and the Establisment of Settlements

Two interrelated processes in the early period of large-scale migration to the new Volta Lake were the establishment of the fishing industry and the fashioning of relationships with local communities, state institutions and fellow migrants. As already indicated, many of the Tongu Ewe migrants who settled around the Lake had been pre-dam migrants and were upstream when the Lake began to fill. The Volta River Authority resettled some of them. Others established new settlements, their locations determined by proximity to the Lake. To grow, settlements relied on new migration, which over the years, reduced from the levels of the sixties and seventies to a trickle by the end of the nineties.

Settlements such as Surveyor Line,[5] Kudikope[6] and Kpando Torkor were established in the mid-sixties when the great migrations took place. Their founders were Tongu Ewe fishermen and their families. Both Surveyor Line and Kudikope were around the South-western tip of the Volta Lake while Kpando Torkor was on its Eastern

---

[5] Surveyor Line was founded on land which used to be a forest reserve, parts of which were submerged by the Lake. Just before the settlement was established, the land had been surveyed and a surveyor's demarcation made, giving the new settlement its name.

[6] Literally Kudi's village.

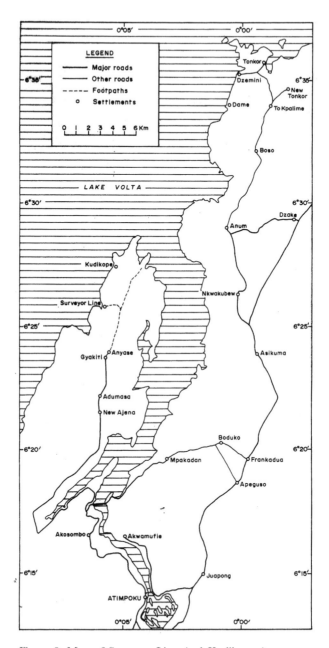

Figure 8: Map of Surveyor Line And Kudikope Area

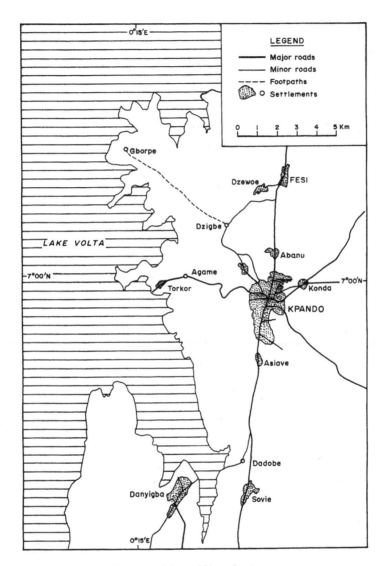

Figure 9: Map of Kpando Area

shores to the north of Surveyor Line and Kudikope. While all three were rural communities in demographic terms, Kpando Torkor was more urbanised in size, composition and infrastructure. It was a larger version of Kudikope in ethnic composition, but quite unlike Surveyor Line, which was made up mainly of migrants from the Akorvie Division of Mepe. Kudikope, which was about one and half times the size of Surveyor Line, had a number of communities—Tongu Ewe (mostly from Battor and Mepe), Dangme (from Ningo and Ada) and Fanti.[7]

Of the three settlements, Kpando Torkor was the only one whose residents included people from Kpando Dzigbe, the *Ewedome*[8] community on whose land Kpando Torkor was founded. A significant arrival at Kudikope in the late 70s was a group of Ningo fisherman who were accepted as guests by a Battor fisherman named Batakari after they had been refused permission to settle in neighbouring villages. After a few years, some Fanti fishermen arrived and Kudikope became larger than many of its more homogenous neighbours. The pattern of settlement at Kudikope was segregated with its Dangme community living closer to the Lake and the Ewe community further away. As a result, Kudikope appeared to be two communities in one.[9] Kpando Torkor grew over the years and now had its own *Torgodo* (literally "behind the Lake", referring to smaller communities across the Lake). These settlements considered Kpando Torkor to be their home and were in turn seen as the "hinterland" of Kpando Torkor.[10]

---

[7] Kudikope's non-Tongu Ewe groups together were a larger group than the Tongu, but the latter remained the largest single community.

[8] *Ewedome* literally means middle Ewe, and refers broadly to the Ewe groups who reside in the northern half of the Volta Region as well as the various dialects of Ewe spoken in this area. This description distinguishes them from the Anlo and Tongu Ewe who are found in the Southern parts of the Region.

[9] This appearance was strengthened by perceived differences between the two communities and the fact that the fishing communities (both Dangme and Akan) considered themselves as one and different from farming Ewe communities. The divisions were largely linguistic and related to current livelihood strategies. It is important to remember that all the communities gathered around the Lake, except for the locals, came from strong fishing traditions.

[10] The Tongu chief mentioned six such communities, which were established by their Tongu inhabitants. They considered themselves as part of Kpando Torkor and while they had informal leaders, disputes they could not resolve were brought to the Tongu chief (Togbe Adze, Tongu chief, Kpando Torkor).

Kpando Torkor's expansion in the 1980s has been attributed to the impacts of VRA fishing complex policy on its market and other infrastructure (Interviews with TKA and MAA, Kpando Torkor). It has since stagnated, a situation blamed on factors such as the long-running chieftaincy dispute among its landlords, competition from newer trading posts along the Lake, such as Dzemeni,[11] Amankwa Tornu and Donkorkrom (TKA and MAA, Kpando Torkor) and the limitations of the fishing complex policy.[12]

Processes and procedures of early and subsequent settlement

New arrivals at already established settlements had to seek permission from the Headman to settle. The procedure involved the presentation of a bottle or two of local gin, which the Headman had the discretion to refuse, with the result that a prospective migrant could not settle.[13] If the Headman was agreeable, he would either show the new migrant where to build or ask him or her to find a place and endorse their choice. If the identified place was someone else's farming land or an abandoned house, the person's consent had to be sought, but the Headman had the final authority over where buildings were constructed. A place given to a new settler eventually became a family compound as adult sons built their houses in or around the same compound. This often resulted in a pattern of settlement in which areas were informally designated as the compound of a family or the quarter of a linguistic group.

An informant suggested that only men had built houses at Surveyor Line. While there was no rule against women building their own homes, the small size and homogeneity of Surveyor Line might have

---

[11] Dzemeni had become a serious contender only in the nineties because of its now larger market and greater proximity to Accra, from where a significant proportion of buyers were coming. Indeed, the 2000 population census puts Dzemeni's population at 3403, higher than Kpando Torkor's population at 2,702. In both the 1970 and 1984 censuses, Kpando Torkor's population (738 in 1970 and 1537 in 1984) was much larger than Dzemeni's (353 in 1970 and 920 in 1984).

[12] Kpando Torkor's comparative advantage was further diminished when the Akosombo Queen and Yapei Queen, the lake vessels of the Volta Lake Transport Company, stopped calling there because of damage to its landing stage and have not returned since.

[13] The Headman of Surveyor Line cited instances where he had refused to allow new migrants to settle because their stories about why they wanted to settle were contradictory or they had shown bad behaviour such as excessive drinking.

accounted for the absence of independent female house owners. At
Kudikope but especially at Kpando Torkor, a number of women
owned houses although they were in the minority. Two of my Kpando
Torkor informants had rented rooms from Tongu women fish traders
at different times (VA, Kpando Torkor; MAA, Kpando Torkor). The
survey found that 57.8% of the men and 18.3% of the women interviewed owned houses. Of this number, 33.6% men and 9.6% women
owned houses in the settlements they were living in. Another 7.8%
men and 4.8% women owned houses in other parts of the Volta
Lake. 7.8% men and 0% women owned houses in their hometowns.
Given the status of hometown houses, the low figures are quite
significant and may signify some shifts in migrant relations with their
hometowns, an issue that will be discussed in more detail in the next
chapter. In terms of building materials, the vast majority of houses,
64.1% for men and 52.7% for women, were built with laterite blocks
while 28.4% men and 26.3% women had used cement blocks. This
was not surprising as most of the houses were around the Lake,
where cement block houses were a recent development.

Itinerant traditions around the lake

Migrants over the years established different itinerant traditions around
the Lake. One kind involved having one base and moving temporarily
from place to place around the Lake in search of the best fishing
grounds and this could be done in days, weeks and months. This
was known among the Tongu communities as *gbedɔdɔ* (sleeping away
from home in Ewe). There was also the more permanent movement
to new settlements in response to the perception that livelihoods were
better in those places or that they had some other clear advantages
over the present location. In some cases, what may have started out
as sleeping in the bush progressed to a more permanent move.

There were new migrants coming into all three study communities,
albeit in small numbers.[14] New migrants typically came from the
northern parts of the Volta Lake, from places such as Yeji, Nketepa,

---

[14] For example, about ten persons, men, women and children had come to
Kudikope in 1999. Surveyor Line had three new male migrants who had arrived
with wives and children. At Kpando Torkor, one such family was a woman and
her children.

Krachi and Dambai to settle with relations at Surveyor Line, Kudikope and Kpando Torkor. They were usually moving for a variety of reasons. These included the loss of land, conflicts involving their landlords, the education of children, proximity to hometown and the breakdown of relationships. A number of respondents had settled at Kpando Torkor so that their children could get a decent education. In some cases, the parents of school children had acquired property at Kpando Torkor for them, while the rest of the household continued to live across the Lake,[15] where the fishing was considered better. Should things not work out in the new location, migrants would keep on moving until they were satisfied. In some cases, they established multi-local livelihoods involving their old and current migrant settlements. In the space of over three decades, some migrants had lived in several places from periods ranging from one to twenty years. There were also people leaving all three settlements all the time. In particular, younger persons were going to neighbouring urban areas to study, for artisanal training and for employment. Accra, Ashiaman and Tema (all in the Greater Accra Region) and Juapong (the largest town in the North Tongu District) were popular as new locations for young migrants. A number of younger people were now organising their lively-hoods in both the Lakeside settlements and these urban areas. As we saw in earlier chapters, this changing pattern of migration had its counterpart in the Lower Volta and had implications for the relations between Lakeside migrants and their hometowns.

Many migrants both around the Lake and in urban areas had chosen particular locations on account of knowing some people or having relations there. However, some had simply arrived and then found relations and acquaintances on arrival. One such person argued, "You don't see a relation before you go to 'Akosombo'. You find them when you get there" (AA, Surveyor Line).

The itinerant traditions around the Lake were also helpful for evading the law, troublesome customers and creditors and this made the regulation of fishing and farming and the enforcement of judgement

---

[15] Some children were at Kpando Torkor by themselves and as one respondent noted, "They rent their own places and are not under anyone. When they grow a little, they get pregnant or impregnate others. They can influence other children". This was very similar to sentiments about the children of migrants who had been sent to the Lower Volta to attend school.

debts difficult. On such a vast Lake, the apprehension of wrongdo-
ers was a tall order.[16]

Infrastructural legacy of early independent settlement

One of the most striking aspects of migrant settlements was their
lack of basic facilities. This was because no planning authority was
involved in their establishment. This was not remedied, we have
argued earlier, because of government and VRA's policies towards
Lakeside migrants. The decentralisation policies of the 90s brought
some infrastructural improvements. However, most lakeside settlements continued to experience poor transport and communications
facilities and sub-standard educational, health, market, financial, regulatory and security institutions.[17] There were differences in the level
of the problem in the three research settlements. Kpando Torkor
was better served than Kudikope and Surveyor Line. It had health
centres and proximity to a large hospital, public and private toilets
and larger and better organised schools with most of the teachers
living in the settlement. Unlike Kudikope and Surveyor Line, which
had two shops—one chemical store and a bar selling drinks between
them—Kpando Torkor had about 47 shops delivering a range of
services.

Several studies have concluded that poor infrastructure, markets,
regulatory and other institutions result in the dissipation of resources
and livelihoods in rural communities (Whitehead and Kabeer, 2001;
Piesse and Thirtle, 1999; Devereux, 2001). In the early years of the
Lake, the poor state of these facilities and institutions had an adverse
impact on livelihood outcomes. The profits fishermen and traders
could have made with the record levels of fish stocks in the Lake
could not be realised. Many fishermen and women traders had to

---

[16] For example, the secretary of the Unit Committee of Surveyor Line wrote to
the convenor of the Dzemeni Unit Committee asking that he assist two men to
collect a judgement debt against a man found guilty of assault. He had paid only
20,000 cedis of the 60,000 cedi debt and failed to pay the rest on several demands.
Two attempts by the Ajena police to arrest him failed. The debtor was now believed
to have migrated from a neighbouring village to "somewhere near Dzemeni" (UC,
Surveyor Line).

[17] Road transportation was difficult and expensive because of the very poor state
of the roads. Postal facilities were absent from migrant settlements as were police
stations (MAA, Kpando Torkor).

travel long distances to the few markets along the Lake. Over the years, many more markets were established, creating the possibility of forum shopping, but this was hampered by the perennial problems of lake transport and non-existent roads.

Attempts by the Kpando District Assembly throughout the late 60s and 70s to establish a ferry service across the Lake from Kpando Torkor proved unsuccessful. The District Assembly, which saw the issue mainly in revenue terms, tried to discourage private operators, refusing them licences and requesting those operating anyway to stop. The private operators continued to ply the route and the Assembly's own vessel continued to operate at a loss (Minutes of the Kpando District Council, 30/11/67; 15/12/67).[18] We discussed the VRA's lake transport programme in the last chapter. Its limitations and those of the Kpando District Council's lake transport programme left the field open for small private local operators. Plans for a pontoon service between Kpando Torkor and Amankwa Tornu to carry people and road vehicles were yet to be implemented. While this was not necessarily a problem, the VRA's inability to regulate their activities[19] rendered lake transport dangerous and accident-prone.[20]

The fear of boating accidents had a depressing effect on lake transport traffic through Kpando Torkor. Several respondents preferred not to cross the Lake each time they had to go and market their fish and foodstuffs. However, for many residents in settlements

---

[18] By 1973, the Council had a new fund-raising scheme, i.e. acquisition of a Toyota Hiace bus being sold by the Volta Regional Administration on hire purchase to run a transport service between Kpando and Kpando Torkor. The stated rationale was that Kpando Torkor was set to become a commercial area with the construction of a fishing complex and a lake transport service (Minutes of the Kpando District Council, 29/5/73).

[19] The VRA's efforts at regulation consisted of the painting of the matter centre line on all boats, the requirement that they carry enough life jackets for all their passengers and that the boats be insured (TN, Kpando Torkor). The insurance, estimated at 34 million cedis ($5,000) was not a small sum and put the whole enterprise above the reach of new operators within migrant communities unless they simply ignored these demands.

[20] A report in Ghana's Daily Graphic, the largest circulation daily, mentioned a 2002 accident that claimed 99 lives, mostly school children and traders and an earlier one in 1999 which resulted in 76 fatalities. As the report noted, the last accident had raised serious concerns among communities along the Lake about the frequent accidents on the Lake that had resulted in "the heavy loss of lives". The Volta Region Minister was reported to be warning boat owners that those overloading their boats and thereby showing a lack of respect for life would be treated ruthlessly to deter others (Daily Graphic front page, Tuesday, 30th April 2002).

such as Kudikope, Surveyor Line and Dzemeni, which had a Thursday market across the Lake, remained the most important outlet for selling and buying. For markets such as Marine (Friday) and Akosombo (Monday and Thursday), there were difficulties with the regularity and quality of transportation both in terms of the vehicles and roads which turned travelling quite short distances into long painful and risky journeys (Unit Committee Convenor, Kudikope).

Other elements of institutional weaknesses related to the absence of credit. Traders had to resort to selling on credit to customers from a wide range of Lakeside settlements. This made it difficult to find them when they defaulted thus adding to the precariousness of trading.[21] At the same time, these relations were important especially in periods after the harvest when the glut in raw and processed food crops created much competition among sellers and drove prices down. The absence of savings facilities made certain kinds of accumulation more difficult. Even when harvests and prices were good, many Lakeside residents could not access banking facilities[22] and had to keep their earnings on themselves or with trusted relations in their hometowns, something which they could do only when they made visits there.[23] Reinvestment in other livelihood activities if environmental factors and settlement norms were favourable and there was the time, skill and inclination, did not resolve this problem, which affected the ability of Tongu fishermen to make the technological transition to outboard motors. It was also implicated in the persistence of the yearly accounting system which, for all its exploitative elements was, for fishing assistants, a device for saving some of their earnings to be used for projects back home. The current economic difficulties of many migrants have been exacerbated by their inability to save when times were better.

---

[21] During the research period, a woman came from one of the market settlements across the Lake to bring a case against a Surveyor Line resident for maize he owed her as repayment for a loan he had taken months before. The Unit Committee sat on the case and gave the woman judgement. The man then promised to convey the maize to her the next market day (Surveyor Line).

[22] A rural bank started at Kpando Torkor collapsed when employees embezzled the money leading to it being closed down.

[23] Interestingly, one man at Kudikope said his trading career had been established with money given to him by his mother that belonged to a relation around the Lake who had left the money in her care.

Migration did not only affect adults. From early on, it impinged on children's lives in various ways. For example, the lack of schools in migrant villages and the distances they had to travel to attend schools in neighbouring host settlements were fatal for many children's educational aspirations. This, together with the strong belief among Tongu migrants that schools in Tongu were of better quality than those around the Lake, established the practice of shipping children back to the Lower Volta to attend school in the period soon after the period of wholesale migration. The social problems created by what was still a common though diminishing practice in the 1990s were being experienced in the Lower Volta as we will see in subsequent chapters. While there was improvement in educational facilities at Kpando Torkor, but less so at Surveyor Line and Kudikope, the situation was not ideal when compared with the quality of teaching personnel and facilities in schools in neighbouring host communities. Some parents at Kpando Torkor preferred to send their children to school at Kpando, the nearest local settlement and capital of the Kpando District which had two well regarded senior secondary schools and several mission and local authority primary and junior secondary schools. The schools at Kpando Torkor had a significant percentage of children from across the Lake (Tɔgodo) where there were no schools. Several of the children, some of whom were young adults, were living on their own in premises owned or rented by their parents with whom they were in more or less regular contact.[24]

While both Kudikope and Surveyor Line had government-assisted primary schools, their facilities were very poor and teaching staff not fully trained. After primary school the children had to go to Gyakiti to attend junior secondary school. Some parents went into Gyakiti to find families who could host their children for the weekdays.

Health was not much better than education and the lack of health facilities and poor transportation and roads had even more dramatic implications in that accidents and other health emergencies could easily be fatal. This was an early problem that was not helpful to the sense of insecurity that was a backdrop to migrant life. While

---

[24] Especially on Kpando Torkor market days, some school children skipped school to assist their parents from Tɔgodo in the market. So established was this route of contact that some schools drove away pupils who had not paid fees, on market days (LKA, Kpando Torkor).

both Kudikope and Surveyor line had traditional birth attendants,[25] traditional healers and itinerant peddlers of pills and herbs, and in the case of Surveyor Line, a chemist,[26] they did not have health centres. Seriously sick people who could not walk were either carried by relations and friends to Gyakiti or Adjena[27] or transported across the Lake to Dzemeni and on to Peki hospital. Kpando Torkor was much better served with three chemists close to the market complex, a nurse midwife since the 1970s and more recently, a small clinic at the market complex. There was a catholic mission hospital at Kpando, but it required road transport to attend from Kpando Torkor. For residents of *Tɔgodo*, there was first a river crossing.

The poor health facilities were compounded by the presence of disease in the Lake. Bilharzia became and continued to be a problem with all three communities reporting some cases as well as recalling past treatment programmes organised by the VRA. Several people, men and women, old and young were either suffering or had suffered from bilharzia. The younger boys especially spoke about urinating blood. Bilharzia was listed as the second of four health conditions identified as the main water and sanitation related health problems at Kpando Torkor.[28] The proprietor of a private maternity home at Kpando Torkor, a government trained nurse-midwife, confirmed that bilharzia was a serious problem at Kpando Torkor, but infection rates were lower than in the 70s when about half of all patients she saw had bilharzia. This year, she had seen exactly one case.[29] In addition to bilharzia, the Lake suffered other forms of pollution which were dangerous given that it was the only source of water for thou-

---

[25] There were three at Surveyor Line, two women and a man and one of the women had formal training. If there was difficulty with the birth, women were taken to Akosombo, Atua or Agomenya hospitals (all in the Eastern Region) or across the Lake to Peki hospital.

[26] A chemist owned by a son of one of the early migrants. For many rural and urban people, a chemist or an itinerant seller of pills was the first line of treatment.

[27] People were treated at Gyakiti or Ajena health facilities, which were run by nurses, or if it was more serious, they were conveyed to Akosombo, Akuse and Battor hospitals.

[28] The other three were diarrhoea, malaria and intestinal and hook worms as first, third and fourth respectively (GWSC/DANIDA, 1995).

[29] She was of the view that part of the problem with bilharzia statistics was that it was considered an occupational hazard by many fishermen and it was only the pain accompanying urinary processes that drove them to seek help (MAA, Kpando

sands of Lakeside inhabitants. For both Kudikope and Kpando Torkor, there was no other source of water at that moment. A Project document written for Kpando Torkor described it as "the polluted Volta Lake" (GWSC/DANIDA, 1995).[30] Surveyor Line had a new borehole at the time of the research, but it was not yet in use because the community had not finished paying its contribution. In general, therefore, Lakeside inhabitants lived with high levels of deprivation at first in the hopes of returning to their hometowns one day to enjoy a higher standard of living but now it was their permanent reality. This was the result of a combination of government policies, policies of their landlords and their own rationalisations of their situation. As one Surveyor Line Resident remarked, "We live simple lives here because this is not home. Many of us sleep on *atsatsa* (reed mats) here. I have a vono[31] mattress at Mepe. I also keep a lot of my cloths there. We only buy expensive things that we can carry away" (A.Z., Surveyor Line).

3. *Political, Judicial and Social Institutions at Surveyor Line, Kudikope and Kpando Torkor*

In the first three decades of migration, political leadership and judicial authority in migrant settlements were provided by Headmen and their elders. Their peers from among the earliest arrivals chose Headmen when settlements matured to the point of needing formal

---

Torkor). The low statistic in this particular case was also due to the decline of patronage of her services as a result of competition from the clinic established at the fishing complex.

[30] Kpando Torkor had had one borehole fitted with "a submersible pump" provided by the Volta River Authority to supply water to both the fishing complex and the community (GWSC/DANIDA, 1995). The water system broke down barely two years later and after failed representations to the VRA and the District Assembly to restore it, an application to DANIDA a few years ago yielded two boreholes, only one of which was in use at the time of the research. The DANIDA project also provided private toilets in about fifty four houses in the community that have eased the demand for the two ten-seater public toilets provided by the District Assembly (LKA, Kpando Torkor). However, because of its size and complexity, Kpando Torkor appeared to have more problems with sanitation judging from its appearance and the preoccupations of its unit committee officers.

[31] Vono is a brand name of a spring mattress that has all but disappeared from Ghana now. It is now used to describe foam mattresses covered with cotton cloth produced in Accra and Kumasi.

leaders. There were no settled criteria for succession to the position
of Headman. However, headmanship resembled chieftaincy in that
the elders who put the Headman in place became his *zikpuitɔwo* (the
owners of his stool), in effect his key advisers.[32] After being chosen,
the Headman was introduced to the landowners who gave him formal recognition in the form of a gift and then began to treat him
as the representative of his settlement. A similar process pertained
in the case of community heads where there were several communities in one settlement.

At Kudikope, each community—the Dangme and other fishing
groups and the Tongu and other Ewe groups—had their own leaders who represented them in affairs of the settlement. At Kpando
Torkor, this practice had been taken to its logical conclusion and
there were now three "chiefs"[33] of the Tongu, Anlo and Ewedome
communities. Some informants suggested that there was no overall
chief of Kpando Torkor. Until 1993, there was a chief of Kpando
Torkor (Torkorfia), known as Togbe Adabra, appointed by the
Kpando Dzigbe stool. He died in 1993 and because of the chieftaincy dispute at Kpando Dzigbe, a successor had not been appointed.
Instead, both the Tongu and Anlo chiefs considered themselves to
be the chief of the settlement as a whole (Interviews with TA and
TN, Kpando Torkor). Togbe Adze, the Tongu Ewe chief, based his
claims on their history as the first settlers. The first *amedzrofia* (stranger
chief in Ewe, referring to the leaders of migrant communities) recognised by the landlords was a Tongu man from Sokpoe known as
Gbadagbali. He had been the only chief in his time and Togbe
Adze, who also called himself a regent (*fiatefeno*), had been one of

---

[32] At Kudikope, there were two such elders and they were expected to continue
to select future Headmen. The majority of the Headmen and community leaders
interviewed did not know who the Headman's successor would be. The Surveyor
Line Headman, though, said it would be one of his children or his brother's children
(TK, Surveyor Line). He was the only Headman the settlement had ever had and
his settlement was dominated by people not only from his hometown but also from
his division. He was also an important elder of his hometown's paramount stool,
regularly called home to attend to stool matters. This was another example of the
influences of the chieftaincy institution on the office of Headman.

[33] In keeping with its more elaborate institutions, each group also had a queen-
mother (*nyɔnufia*) at Kpando Torkor. This was different from Kudikope and Surveyor
Line, where women leaders had no formal title. They settled quarrels between
women, which were appealed at the chief's court. Like the chiefs, the queenmothers
at Kpando Torkor had formed a committee of three to solve cases.

his elders. Togbe Adze succeeded Gbadagbali and was the first of his contemporaries to be recognised by the landlords. In 1982, the Anlo chief was recognised. The *Ewedome* chief was yet to be formally recognised by the landlords.

The Anlo Ewe chief has used various strategies to stake his claim with the result that he now had a slight edge in the undeclared chieftaincy contest.[34] During the study, however, the Anlo chief said that the chiefs of all three communities were equals (TN, Kpando Torkor). Some informants confirmed this, one making the point that all three chiefs were voting members of the Kpando Traditional Area Council with equal powers. Others, usually depending on which community they belonged to, mentioned one of the two as settlement head. The one point of unanimity was that each community had its own leader.

The erosion of the Tongu chief's position was related to the fact that he was the only one among the three community leaders who had no formal schooling. Education also played a part in the growing prominence of Unit Committee leaders in migrant settlements. The majority of cases of interpersonal disputes still went to the Tongu chief and this was explained in terms of the fact that he was not actively pursuing his livelihood activities at the moment (JA, Kpando Torkor). At Kpando Torkor, there was also a *tɔ fia* (lake chief) who dealt with disputes arising from fishing on the Lake. These included the destruction of people's nets and traps by others, murders on the Lake and the maltreatment of fishing assistants (JA, RLA, Kpando Torkor).

In the early days, interpersonal disputes, therefore, went to either Headman or chief or the leaders of economic and social organisations to be solved. With the coming of the decentralised administration and the District Assembly, a new power centre was emerging in all three settlements in the form of Unit Committee (UC). Many of the individuals involved in this new structure were already involved in

---

[34] In 1995, a letter written to the Kpando police in the name of the chief and elders of Kpando Torkor concerning an assault case, was signed by the Anlo chief. While there was no particular designation under his name, that he signed the letter feeds the impression that he was the settlement chief being referred to. In a feasibility report for a water and sanitation project of the then Ghana Water and Sewerage Corporation (GWSC), he was described as the Head of the Community (GWSC/DANIDA, 1995, p. 1). The same document has the Tongu chief as the first on the list of opinion leaders (1995).

settlement and community leadership and judicial processes as part
of the Council of Elders of the Headmen and Chiefs. They were
usually younger and had some education. This, together with their
new offices, had resulted in the formalisation of the dispute settlement processes they presided over in the settlements. When asked
who ran the town, the Kudikope Headman mentioned himself and
the Unit Committee Convenor (UCC). A UC typically had jurisdiction over several settlements.[35]

While the UCs did not have a legal basis for the exercise of judicial functions, this had become an important and unchallenged part
of their role in rural communities around the country.[36] Their more
direct relationship with the District Administration gave UCs a gate-
keeping role and boosted their powers in relation to the Headmen,
who increasingly had many of their community leadership functions
taken over by the UCs. It was only in certain situations that the
District Administration communicated directly with Headmen.[37]

There was a rough division of labour between the UC and the
Headman. At Kudikope, for example, land cases were the province
of the Headman as were cases of death and interpersonal disputes
arising from adultery, or any occurrence serious enough to be called
"*dunya*" (an issue of settlement-wide concern because it is seen as
affecting its very health and survival). The Committees' most regular
activities in all three settlements were the organisation of communal
labour and resources for sanitation and development projects and
dispute settlement.[38]

---

[35] The Surveyor Line UC, for example, oversaw the affairs of five settlements—
Surveyor Line, Aponawu, Konkordeka, Todzi and Akwenor. Out of the 15 members of the Unit Committee, 8, including the chair, were at Surveyor Line alone.

[36] Both Ghana's 4th Republican Constitution of 1992 (Article 241(3)) and the
law setting up the District Assemblies (Local Government Act, 1993, Act 462,
Section 10 (1 & 2)) make clear that their powers are deliberative, legislative and
executive. Similarly the Legislative Instrument (Local Government—Urban, Zonal
and Town Councils and Unit Committees Establishment Instrument, 1994, L.I.
1589) did not give the UCs as sub-structures of the Assemblies judicial powers
(Paragraph 25, Fifth Schedule, L.I. 1589).

[37] For example, the District Chief executive of Asuogyaman in 1999 wrote to the
Surveyor Line Headman who was the head of a fledgling council of 16 Headmen
in the area asking him to stop their people from farming around the Lake. Also,
Headmen received invitations to meetings called by the District Assembly although
not all of them were members of the Unit Committees.

[38] As in judicial processes, communal labour was also an area of changing jurisdiction between the Headmen and the Unit Committees. It used to be that the

The division of jurisdiction between the UC and the Headman was not always neat, overlapping in some cases. This was partly because of the infancy of the Unit Committee, the overlapping membership of the two institutions in certain cases and the designation of roles to unit committees without reference to existing institutions. As at now, people were free to select the forum for addressing their grievances. Some preferences related to the desire for a more formal forum of record or wanting stiffer punishment for a culprit. It was acknowledged by all that the UC was more formal as its summons and proceedings were set out in writing. As well, it was more likely to institute and enforce a fine (CS, Surveyor Line).

At Kpando Torkor, it appeared that the question of jurisdiction was being resolved by designating the Unit Committee to be the court of first instance and the chiefs to be the appeal panel. As one informant said, "The Unit Committee settles quarrels first and collects the fines. If it is not settled, then the chiefs and ultimately the police are brought in" (TN, Kpando Torkor). Another informant went further, suggesting that the court was a unified Chieftaincy and Unit Committee tribunal, something in the nature of a community tribunal (LKA, Kpando Torkor). Several informants in the three settlements also suggested that the Unit Committee was under the overall jurisdiction of the chiefs, although in practice this did not appear to be the case.

Apart from these differences in perception about the relationship between community tribunals and the chiefs and the degree of separation between them, there were variations in the jurisdiction, composition and character of the Unit Committee's courts in the three settlements. This was on account of the interpretation that particular settlement leaders gave to their mandate to establish UCs and the nature and membership of already existing political and judicial institutions. Other institutions such as the churches had their own informal conflict resolution practices and people were said to prefer these to the police.

Because the UC's leadership was all male, some female respondents considered it a men's organisation. The 31st December Women's

---

Headman had the power to call communal labour sessions. Now it was under the leadership of the UC. Communal labour was essential; the building of roads, schools and general cleaning and sanitation had been achieved by communal labour at Surveyor Line, Kudikope and also Kpando Torkor.

Movement (DWM)[39] branch in the settlement was seen as the equivalent women's organisation (AA, Surveyor Line). The Unit Committees, which were barely a year old at Kudikope, Surveyor Line and Kpando Torkor at the time of the research, were growing in influence. They were allowing migrant settlements to convey their needs directly to state agencies. One informant also observed that the UC had improved their access to lawmakers and the police. For the first time at Kpando Torkor, the settlement had its own District Assembly representatives, an improvement on the past when someone from Kpando Dzigbe had represented Kpando Torkor. At Kudikope, the Unit Committee had been able to procure cement, roofing sheets and chairs for the school. In two out of the three settlements, the UC was enforcing a ban on certain farming and fishing practices on behalf of state agencies. The different trajectories in the development of these institutions in the three settlements, their complicated and sometimes competitive relationship with the Headmen and the concentration of powers represented by the overlapping membership of the two institutions were indications of possible future struggles and conflicts and institutional problems in migrant settlements.

Besides the political judicial structures, there were various economic organisations that facilitated and regulated livelihoods in the migrant settlements. Kpando Torkor had the largest number of such organisations. They included the Canoe Fishermen's Association, the Lake Transport Owners Society, the Irrigation Farmers Association and the Association of Fish Sellers. Surveyor Line used to have a Fisherman's Society established for acquiring nets cheaply from government agencies but it was now dormant because it was not able to deliver the nets.

The most important social organisations in all the migrant settlements were the funeral associations, ku habɔbɔ, also known as "company". Surveyor Line had one, Kudikope had a few and Kpando Torkor had several, more than seven, in keeping with its status as a multicultural central settlement with several outlying villages. While a particular community, be it ethnic, sub-ethnic or hometown based, dominated each company, they were generally open to all residents. In return for monthly dues, these associations provided financial

---

[39] The organisation led by the then first lady, Mrs Nana Konadu Agyeman-Rawlings.

support and solidarity in times of illness and death. When a member died, other members had to pay a fixed funeral donation some of which the Association then paid to the deceased member's family as death benefits. The Association would also organise drumming and dancing sessions. When a member was very sick and was being carried to his or her hometown to die, the death benefits were also paid. Failure to pay monthly dues for three consecutive months could result in expulsion from the Association. The offending member had to pay a fine of one bottle of drink and all arrears before being readmitted. The leaders of the Associations, known as *kufiawo* (funeral chiefs) kept membership records and accounts. If a member died, the organisation would go to his village and organise a wake. The funeral societies were much stronger than the branches of hometown associations devoted to the upliftment of hometowns.

There was a proliferation of Pentecostal charismatic churches with very active proselytising practices that sometimes converted sections of whole communities to one church. In all the three settlements around the Lake there were several churches. Surveyor Line and Kudikope had only Pentecostal churches while Kpando Torkor had the older more established Christian churches such as the Catholic and Presbyterian churches in addition.[40] There was evidence of indigenous religious activities. There was a small shrine for the protection of hunters at Kudikope and three more general shrines (none of which were brought from the Lower Volta) at Kpando Torkor. Several informants though maintained that shrines were in numerical decline as there were many more of them in the early days.

An overwhelming percentage, more than 80% of both men and women, mentioned Christianity as their religion as compared with only 5.2% male and 11.5 female who mentioned traditional religion. While those in the old established churches (described as orthodox) were in the majority (44.8% and 49% of male and female respondents respectively), membership of Pentecostal churches was almost as high (42.2% male and 31.7% female). Among the Tongu communities, rites of passage concerning birth, marriage and funerals continued to

---

[40] During the research, 12 different churches were counted at Kpando Torkor. They included the two factions of the Evangelical Presbyterian Church, the Catholic Church and various Pentecostal churches such as the Apostles Revelation Society (ARS), Church of Christ, the Brotherhood, New Apostolic, Apostolic Church, Aladura among others.

be conducted broadly according to Tongu customs, according to informants. However, migrant life had produced various variations. For example, one informant recalled that when they first settled around the Lake, those who died were buried without elaborate rites. It was with the growth of settlements that burials came to be organised according to the customs of the deceased. Burial rites had been modified to take account of the requirements and norms of the landlords, the Christian churches and the funeral companies.

Marriage rites were said to be similar to those at home. Interestingly, very few marriage and divorce ceremonies were taking place in the three settlements. It would appear that people preferred that marriage rites take place in their hometowns. The practice may have begun when parents and other important family members of migrants remained in hometowns in the early days of migration. However, informal and yet to be formalised unions were contracted regularly, and respondents differentiated between a formal and non-formal union only when asked, particularly when there were children between them. Parties to non-formal unions were able to change partners without serious consequences.

In spite of this appearance of a more flexible attitude towards marriage and multiple relationships, communities took such a serious view of adultery that it was the kind of case which went to the Headman's court. Attitudes to adultery were exemplified by two cases concerning one incident in an outgrowth of Surveyor Line. In the first, the "landlord" of a woman brought an action against another man for an "unnatural visit" he paid her. The defendant was fined after he pleaded guilty with explanation and gave an account of why he was visiting the woman at midnight. The panel members stated that they had weighed the gravity of the case in arriving at the size of the fine (Surveyor Line Case Entry, 2/10/98). Subsequently, the husband of the woman brought summons against the same man "to come and answer charges why you were with his wife in the dead of night" (4/10/98). There was no record of the outcome of that case. However, since the defendant had already pleaded guilty in the earlier case, the outcome was probably a foregone conclusion and was likely to attract a further fine.

4. *Community Relations in Migrant Settlements*

Community differences appeared minor to an outside observer. However, they were experienced intensely, and in some cases, differences had some significance. An example is the differences in labour practices of Tongu Ewe and Dangme fishermen. Tongu Ewe migrants appeared more settled with family-based households. The Dangme communities on the other hand had a disproportionately larger male population and their households often included a large proportion of hired labour. The few females were usually the wives of company leaders, their assistants and very young daughters of company heads. As a Dangme informant explained, "Young women do not come here. There is no work for them, so the few who come are wives. When a young girl grows, she goes to Accra to serve someone, washing plates or other work at a chop bar, running errands or doing housework" (TKK, Kudikope). A Tongu ex-fisherman argued that this difference accounted for dissimilarities in livelihood outcomes:

> The Ningos behave differently from us. They borrow other people's children and bring them here. The children repair the nets all day so it is possible for them to fish continuously. They also bring women to come and help. Some of them also have outboard motors with large boats. The Tongu are not able to do this and that is why the Ningos and Fantis make more money on the Lake than we do (Tongu ex-fisherman, Surveyor Line).

The above statement which emphasised differences between Tongu Ewe and Ningo (Dangme) labour practices was not entirely accurate as Tongu Ewe fishermen also had their fishing assistants. Few of them though, owned outboard motors or had fishing companies as large as those of the Dangme fishermen. These differences which were evident even from the early days of migration when both communities were engaged in fishing were now expressed as a distinction between fishing and farming communities.

The meeting of different migrant communities which had hitherto lived in more homogenous settlements heightened existing inter-community tensions, created new ones where none existed and brought prejudices into the open. The Headman of Kudikope said it was the deliberate policy of its leaders to create a heterogeneous settlement.

It enabled the creation of a relatively large settlement and also facilitated technology exchange.[41] This account appeared to be a ratio-
nalisation of the current situation. Granted that this was planned, it
had not been without difficulty. Indeed, some informants saw it as
a weakness, citing the more peaceful atmosphere of Surveyor Line
in support. As one respondent argued, "There is more peace at
Surveyor Line because they are one people. They understand each
other. A mixed community does not make progress. People from
Surveyor Line have been saying, that given my efforts, we would
have done better if we were all Mepe people" (UCC, Kudikope).
The peace and quiet of Surveyor Line had its limits. In addition to
interpersonal conflicts, it had proved difficult to collect levies to
acquire settlement-owned assets and facilities.[42]

In any case, the meaning of homogeneity and heterogeneity was
more complicated than appeared at first sight. Some respondents
argued that tensions within the Ewe community at Kudikope (attributed to differences between people from Mepe and Battor, contiguous settlements in the Lower Volta) in contrast to the peaceful
atmosphere within the Dangme community at Kudikope could be
attributed to the latter's unity. "The Ningo community is more united
than us and are not as envious of each other" (Ewe respondent,
Kudikope). As has already been indicated, what was being called the
Ningo community included other Dangme people and also Fanti
fishermen. Clearly, the notion of a multi-cultural settlement being
applied in this case was in some cases narrower and in other cases
broader than having the Ewe language in common. This was not
particular to Kudikope. Tongu residents at Kpando Torkor spoke
of their fellow Tongu fishermen across the Lake (*Tɔgodo*) as though
they were a strange species of humanity.

---

[41] For example, informants said that Tongu fishermen learned a particular way
of sewing two pieces of net to make a larger piece as well as new swimming techniques from the Ningo fishermen. The Ningos in turn learned maize cultivation
techniques suited to the new environment.

[42] For example, a subsidised bore-hole acquired by the community with the support of some outside organisation was not yet being used because the settlement
could not raise their contribution to the cost. Secondly, an outboard motor donated
by an aid agency was still not in use because the money could not be found to
buy wood to make a boat. A proposed collection of 30,000 cedis a person was
proving very difficult to implement.

These qualifications notwithstanding, the differences between the Ewe and Dangme communities at Kudikope were significant. These differences, some of which stemmed from the specificities of the livelihood strategies of the two communities, were expressed as cultural. For example, several Tongu Ewe respondents considered their communities to be different from those of the Dangme in matters of hygiene, attitude to communal labour[43] and their animal husbandry practices. Some informants at Kudikope charged that the fishing communities did not submit to rules operating in the Tongu quarter about roaming animals and were given to complaining that they were being harassed when their animals destroyed peoples' foodstuffs and were detained. In addition, Dangme fishermen did not take well to the "chieftaincy system" represented by the Headman and his Stool elders because they said such a system did not exist in their places of origin. In turn, some in the Dangme community complained about Tongu Ewe desire for excessive deference which they considered tiresome. In relation to roaming livestock, they felt that there were people who were arresting livestock on the least pretext in order to fleece livestock owners.

The roaming livestock problem, however, transcended community differences in all three settlements.[44] Another example was the problem of nets and fish thefts on the Lake. A respondent at Kpando Torkor, whose nets had been stolen several times, said it was a common occurrence although it was possible to catch the culprit because of differences in net repairing techniques (JA, Kpando Torkor). At Surveyor Line, one informant said there was suspicion that those involved in harvesting the nets of subsistence fishermen at night were

---

[43] Dangme fishermen were usually away on the Lake or if present, busy repairing their nets and, therefore, less willing to spend time on communal labour. They were also not in a position to police their livestock to ensure that they did not destroy people's farms or eat their foodstuffs. The more sedentary Ewe communities had a stronger presence in the settlement.

[44] At Kudikope it was manifested as an inter-community problem while at both Surveyor Line and Kpando Torkor it transcended such differences. At Surveyor Line, animal rearing was outlawed for many years but had now been restarted by certain individuals, including some of those in the leadership of the settlement. The Surveyor Line Unit Committee Secretariat has sent out summons on three complaints (17/10/98; 7/11/98; 26/11/98). Another entry in its books concerned three incidents in which a total of 5 goats had been caught. Panel members had gone to assess the costs of destroyed goods and the owners of the goats had paid (SL, 24/11/98).

professional fishermen looking for bait for their hooks. These kinds of suspicions affected relations between communities and resulted in retaliatory seizures of fishing equipment, especially when nets were destroyed in the course of theft.

In addition to differences in livelihood strategies, there were inter-community rivalries as a result of the growing confidence of the Dangme communities and their resistance of Tongu Ewe control of political and judicial institutions within particular settlements. This was fuelled by the perception that the land owners were taking their side. In recognition of the coming of age of the Dangme community, the landowners had allowed them to choose a leader. The Tongu community was not very happy about this development as it threatened their position of pre-eminence. One informant charged that the Dangmes did not respect them because they had more resources and the backing of the landowners.[45]

In addition to the community level conflicts, there were inter-personal conflicts between members of different communities and among members of the same community. Some of these arose from credit arrangements, thefts and assaults.[46]

In the early years of migration, some of the conflicts arising from fishing resulted in claims that many of the deaths on the Lake in the early years were either murders or of supernatural causes. Such suspicious occurrences were fewer now because settlements had established judicial processes. At Kpando Torkor, the Kpando Dzigbe chiefs had come to agree rules of conduct for the Lake with migrants and this had eased tensions (JA, Kpando Torkor).[47] More commonly these days, conflicts arising from differences in livelihood strategies were manifested in accusations and counter-accusations of insensitivity, self-seeking behaviour, jealousy, wickedness, immorality, lawlessness, arrogance and witchcraft. Community conflict resolution fora

[45] This lack of respect was also cited as the reason why Ewe women married Dangme men while Dangme women did not marry Ewe men along the Lake. However, there were relatively much fewer Dangme women around the Lake.

[46] Kpando Torkor case book entries, 1/9/99; 9/9/99; Surveyor Line case book entry, 3/10/98.

[47] There was one case of an alleged murder of a boy who had been taken as a fishing assistant by a fisherman in the books of the Kpando District Assembly. His father was petitioning the Assembly for an investigation into the death of his son on the Lake (Kwesi Gameli Medenu, Petitions File, Kpando District Assembly, 7/3/94).

such as the Headman and Unit Committee courts at Surveyor Line and Kudikope, and the joint Headmen/Unit Committee court at Kpando Torkor recorded several cases where people had been summoned to answer charges related to accusations of loose morals,[48] prostitution and witchcraft.[49]

Notwithstanding stated differences among migrant communities, they considered themselves ranged together against their hosts to whom they had to make payments for land. Migrant settlements, particularly those dominated by one community, were involved in various forms of co-operation with each other. Among Tongu migrants, funerals were an occasion for inter-settlement co-operation and solidarity involving several contiguous settlements and this was expressed through the funeral associations. In times of disaster, for example, accidents on the Lake, all neighbouring settlements would come together to organise rescue operations and recover and bury the dead. The Slater case, which is discussed later in the section on land disputes involving migrant communities, is an example of the inter-settlement co-operation on an issue which concerned all migrants, but which had particular resonance for the Tongu communities. With the institution of Unit Committees of the District Assembly, inter-settlement co-operation had acquired a new dimension as several settlements were gathered under one Unit Committee (UC). At the same time, there was more inter-settlement competition over issues such as where the ballot box was placed during elections, which settlement was the UCC's home, which UCC was closer to the ruling Party and which one had been able to secure more development projects.

Relations between migrant communities and officialdom contributed to inter-settlement tensions. An example was the decision by the VRA to employ young men from Surveyor Line as forestry officers to plant trees around the lake and police the ban on draw-down farming. For the first time since the ban on draw-down agriculture in the early 1990s, Forestry Officers destroyed farms at Surveyor Line and Kudikope in 1998. At Kudikope, which did not have any Forestry Officers, respondents complained that Surveyor Line people had come to destroy their crops. The Kudikope UCC raised concerns

---

[48] Surveyor Line case book entry, 5/2/99; Kpando Torkor case book entries, 17/8/99; 27/8/99.

[49] Kpando Torkor case book entry, 1/10/99.

about unevenness in the treatment of those who had farmed on Lakeside land, claiming that some people had been allowed to cultivate rice in spite of the ban while others had had their crops destroyed. Although he supported the ban on grounds that farming by the Lake was destroying the Dam, he had gone to report to the Forestry Department branch office that there was some corruption involved in enforcing the ban. In this, he was reflecting the tendency of the settlement and community leaders around the Lake to support officialdom. But perhaps, even more important, as a late migrant who had very little land around the Lake, the change in his life as a result of the ban was going to be minimal. In contrast, the UCC of Surveyor Line was unhappy about the destruction of the crops and the silence of the Headman of Surveyor Line whose children were among the Forestry Officers.[50] As he explained, however, no one had tried to stop the Forestry Officers because they had had ample notice and were only farming because others were doing it too (UCC, Surveyor Line).

Another example of how relations with officialdom created inter-community tensions was the government ban on fishing with the *adranyi*, a dragnet pulled from shore in the early 1990s. This was out of concern for its "sweeping" qualities; i.e. very young fish were harvested along with the large ones, thus endangering fish stocks in the Lake.[51] While some settlement heads were trying to enforce the ban, some of the more active fishermen were resisting. At Kudikope, the Tongu Headman argued in support of the ban, "we have never favoured *adranyi* because we do not want the fish to finish" (Headman, Kudikope). The fishermen on the other hand said they only caught insignificant quantities of small fish for use as bait for their hooks (*efe* or *efu*) and, therefore, were not endangering fish stocks. While the Tongu Ewe communities were emphatic that they were obeying the *adranyi* ban, the Dangme communities charged that they were involved in other illegal practices such as *atidza* and bamboo fishing. There were also regular accusations of DDT use across the different fishing communities.

---

[50] He felt that the Headman was not condemning the destruction of farms because his own children were working for the Forestry Department.

[51] This net was apparently popular because small nets were regularly caught in the tree stumps in the Lake. Also, some nets did not set uniformly because of the tree stumps thus allowing fish to escape after being caught in the net and the drag-net addressed these problems.

5. *Migrant Settlements and the Different Players in their Environment*

Migrant settlements had relations with various players in their environment—the State and the Volta River Authority, other migrant settlements, the local stools and communities[52] on whose land they had settled, and more recently the District Assembly. Different elements of these relations within the migrant environment were factors in the organisation of livelihoods, some positive, some negative and some not so clear-cut. Secondly, they were in some cases implicated in the changing relations between the migrants and their hometowns.

Relations with host settlements

> *Amedzrovi me hea anyigba nya o*
>
> (A stranger does not litigate over land (A.A, Headman, Kudikope).

Many settlements around the Lake such as Surveyor Line and Kudikope were established on land the government had acquired from local communities under the VRP for which local communities had not been compensated. The founders of migrant settlements sought permission from the chiefs of these communities to settle on their land. This enabled migrants to settle in peace and also to acquire farmlands outside the boundaries of state-acquired land. The local communities were also able to determine in important ways the character of migrant settlements. In the case of Kpando Torkor, although part of the land on which it was established was state-acquired land, its founders were asked by the Dzigbe chiefs to only build with palm fronds and thatch. It was only after several years when the contours of the permanent settlement were in place and the lack of security and incidents of deaths from snakebites were a problem that the building of more permanent structures started.[53]

---

[52] Communities were defined by any one or more criteria such as language, village of origin or main occupation. Thus respondents sometimes referred to intra-Tongu Ewe differences e.g. the differences between Mepe and Battor people as well as differences between Tongu Ewe and Dangme and other fishing communities in discussions about the players within their environment.

[53] It was only in the 70s that a carpenter constructed the first laterite-block house. While it was under construction, the midwife expressed her desire to rent it for her maternity home. According to the carpenter, the midwife's interest strengthened his hand in building what was the first permanent dwelling. This encouraged others to follow suit (Interviews with FD, Kpando Torkor). Even then, the early houses had very low walls because settlers believed that the wind would destroy high walls, a

These early attempts to control migrant settlements affected migrant livelihoods directly and indirectly. For example, at Kpando Torkor, improved security which came with the building of more permanent housing coincided with the rearing of animals (FD, Kpando Torkor). More indirectly, strictures such as the permanent housing ban, which increased migrant insecurities, contributed to keeping migrant settlements makeshift for long periods and perhaps encouraged the practice of building in hometowns among migrants. In settlements such as Kudikope and Surveyor Line, there were still no cement block dwelling houses at the end of the 1990s, while the practice was very recent at Kpando Torkor, a much more urbanised settlement.

By the end of the 60s, land became the single most important issue in migrant-local host relations. This was because the introduction and expansion of farming meant that additional farmlands had to be acquired from local communities to supplement draw-down agriculture, which had been on land owned by the VRA. In becoming farmers, Tongu Ewe migrants became vulnerable to local conflicts in land relations. Two categories of land—that immediately around the Lake which was used for settlements and draw-down agriculture (*tɔnu nyigba*) and that which was more or less distant from the Lake which was largely acquired as farmland by migrants (*kpodzi nyigba*)— were implicated in these relations. In relation to the land abutting the Lake, in the first three decades of migration, the migrants struggled to use the land without interference from local communities. Farms along the lake were typically small, on average between $\frac{1}{2}$ and $\frac{1}{4}$ an acre.[54] While it was prone to flooding every year and small in size, it was central to the food security of farming households and was the preferred farming land for those who could get it. Farming on a larger scale though, required the acquisition of land on higher ground.

As early as in 1968, there was a disagreement between Surveyor Line residents and the Anyaase chief when the latter demanded rent

---

belief encouraged by the landowners. A reason advanced by some informants for the ban on more permanent housing up to the early 70s was that the landlords of Kpando Torkor believed that the government was about to build "quarters" i.e. resettlement housing. Apart from the pressure exerted by settlers, the realisation that no "quarters" would be forthcoming helped to break their resistance to more permanent structures (Interviews with TN and FD, Kpando Torkor).

[54] Some farms though were as large as 2 acres and one respondent said his land was 4 acres, a claim that was plausible given that he was one of the early settlers and was a member of the power block at Surveyor Line.

for Lakeside farmlands and the migrants refused to pay.[55] The chief then threatened to prevent them from farming on land on higher ground if they would not pay rent on Lakeside farms. In one incident, farms at Surveyor Line were destroyed at the behest of the chief who was arguing that the stool had not been compensated for any government acquisition and, therefore, remained the true owner of the land. The police were called and the case went to Koforidua, the Eastern Regional Capital, and then to Accra. The paramount chiefs of Mepe and Ajena (as representatives of Surveyor Line and Anyaase people respectively) became involved. This particular incident was eventually settled out of court. However, the conflict over Lakeside farmlands took almost four years to resolve, and tensions have continued to simmer, flaring up now and again.

A demarcation exercise by the VRA around the Lake clarified the boundaries of the VRA's holdings. In all three settlements, there were references to the demarcation[56] as clarifying the ownership of land migrants were farming at any point in time. This strengthened the hand of settlers when confronted with demands by locals for rent. Interestingly, some of those resisting the payment of rent on land abutting the Lake were renting what they could not farm to fellow migrants on either cash or sharecrop basis.[57]

The relations between migrant communities and their hosts were some of the issues covered by the survey. In the survey, the majority of responses regarding relations with host communities were about peace and harmony. Another 7.3% of responses were about solidarity and the exchange of gifts. While fewer responses mentioned problems, the kind of problems that were mentioned confirmed what informants and respondents said during in-depth interviews. 13.5% of responses were about harassment, restrictions and imbalances in the relations between hosts and migrants. Another 11% of responses were about the impacts of chieftaincy disputes and conflicts among the hosts on migrant communities (Table 7.1.). Given that

---

[55] In addition, the chiefs attempted to collect rent for the use of the Lake, which they abandoned quite early when the fishermen refused outright.

[56] At Kpando Torkor, it was said that the "one mile square" from the Lake was VRA land. At Kudikope and Surveyor Line, they spoke of an area of 280 ft from the Lake.

[57] A respondent who had four acres of Lakeside land had rented a part of it for 50,000 cedis for the year.

Table 7.1: Relations with host communities by gender

Response	Absolutes			Percentages		
	Male	Female	Total	Male	Female	Total
At peace with each other	78	75	153	58.2	67.6	62.4
Harassment, restrictions, unequal relations	19	14	33	14.2	12.6	13.5
Join hands to mourn and exchange gifts	15	3	18	11.1	2.7	7.3
High rent of farmland and land for building	8	3	11	6	2.7	4.5
Their conflicts and chieftaincy disputes affect us	13	14	27	9.7	12.6	11
Give us land when we need it	1	2	3	0.8	1.8	1.3
Total	134	111	245	100	100	100

Note: Some respondents gave more than one answer.

several people had run away from conflicts among their hosts in the northern parts of the Lake and two of the three settlements had been affected by chieftaincy disputes among their hosts, this was not surprising. 4.5% of responses were about the high cost of farmlands and land for building. Interestingly, this was one of the few responses where the difference in subscription between men and women was significant (6% of male and 2.7% of female). Together, the responses which represented problems were 29% of the total number of responses.

Land controlled by host communities and intra-settlement relations

Migrants had no difficulty accepting the ownership and control of local chiefs with respect to the land on higher ground. For this category of land, dealings with landlord settlements, particularly the stools, were either conducted by individuals directly with the representatives of the stools and land-owning lineages as at Kpando Torkor or mediated by the Headmen of migrant settlements as at Surveyor Line and Kudikope. While these arrangements at Kudikope were partly because their land-lord chief lived a long distance away,[58] they also signalled that some level of trust had been built between the leadership of the settlers and

---

[58] The Apaaso Chief lived at Senchi, a three-hour journey from Kudikope because of the poor state of the roads. He and his people had been resettled as a result of the Volta River Project. His visits were occasional and the Headman visited Senchi to transfer payments and discuss land issues.

their landlords. At Surveyor Line, for example, the Headman showed people who wanted farmland which parts of the land were vacant. If they preferred another piece of land, they could go ahead and demarcate and use it as long as it was not another person's plot or did not encroach on any part of another's land. After the farm had been demarcated and planted, the Headman would verify the acreage and the rent would be paid accordingly. Some new migrants were given portions of land previously acquired by older migrants until they could secure their own more directly from the landowners.

Children could inherit their parents' farms and it was easier if they were farming with the parents in question or living in the settlement. However, the main conditions were that they continue to farm the land and pay the rent, failing which another person could be allocated the land.[59] In times of disputes over land, the Headman used his discretion and awarded the land to which of the parties was more likely to use it properly.[60] As the Surveyor Line Headman explained, "Some people cannot farm, but claim land so another person cannot use it" (TK, Headman, Surveyor Line).

With the ban on Lakeside farming instituted by the VRA in the mid 90s, much of the farmlands being used at Kudikope and Surveyor Line were those controlled by the Anyaase and Apaaso chiefs (the landlords of Surveyor Line and Kudikope respectively). For some years now, both chiefs had been demanding a change in tenancy arrangements from fixed cash payments to sharecropping, specifically, *abusa*.[61] The Apaaso chief had also indicated that he would review the 8,000 cedis a year being paid by fishermen. As recently as in 1999, a landlord chief was threatening to give the land to other people if the migrant farmers would not agree to sharecropping (UCC, Kudikope).[62]

---

[59] The Headman of Surveyor Line argued that while both male and female children ordinarily should be allowed to inherit their parents' farms, if they were not planning to farm seriously, the farm should go to any other interested party.

[60] Other considerations were whether either of the parties already had some farmlands and whether the farm had been abandoned, i.e. if it had not been cultivated for two years. The final principle was that no one had an absolute right to a particular plot of land (TK, Headman, Surveyor Line).

[61] The particular arrangement envisaged was that the landlords would sell the crop back to the farmer for a sum of money.

[62] Apart from acquiring his farming land through the Headman of this particular settlement, the UCC of Kudikope was on the delegation because of his political position.

The settlers had in turn signalled their unwillingness to change their land access arrangements, as the land was no longer as fertile as it had been. To a person, farmers preferred fixed cash payments, because a fixed portion of the harvest could be substantial (SD, Surveyor Line). Thus far, the Headmen were supporting farmers to resist the imposition of sharecropping arrangements. At Surveyor Line, farmers had been asked by the Headman to continue paying 30,000 cedis for one acre while at Kudikope, farmers with two acres were paying 20,000 cedis an acre. While no one had complied with the demand for *abusa* as yet, there were fears that sometime in the future, they would have to agree as other villages around the Lake were said to be doing so already (TAA, Headman, Kudikope; SD, Surveyor Line).

In relation to such lands, however, migrants were caught up in chieftaincy disputes within the host communities themselves, because the different claimants were demanding rent from the migrants. Both Surveyor Line and Kpando Torkor were experiencing this kind of situation at the time of the study. In one case, about 7 years after the Akosombo Dam, a large piece of land close to the Lake was given to an army colonel called Slater, who was a member of the then military government, by the Apaaso chiefs. Parts of this transaction involved the farmlands of some Kudikope and Surveyor Line residents. Slater decided to clear the land for farming and without notice to the farmers, a bulldozer came and cleared the farms. The affected farmers complained to the Apaaso chief who ignored them. A section of the affected farmers decided to pursue the case all the way to the seat of government in Accra. A group of aggrieved farmers and their supporters from neighbouring settlements (described by one informant as Mepe people) marched unto the Slater farm complex and slashed the tyres of tractors with cutlasses. Several informants said that they had gone to destroy Slater's property in retaliation for their losses. The Police were called in and many of those involved in the action ran away. The conflict raged on until the overthrow of the government caused Col. Slater to flee into exile.

In a second case, the Anyaase people, the landlords of Surveyor Line residents had a long-standing chieftaincy dispute. This involved two contenders to the stool and their supporters. Both chiefs had been gazetted at different times; i.e. they had received government recognition. The inhabitants of Surveyor Line were conflicted as to which chief to pay rent to. As the case went through appeals and

counter appeals, the Surveyor Line residents received an official direc-
tive to pay rent to one of the contenders. The majority complied.
The other contender, aggrieved by this development sued some
Surveyor Line residents, 7 men and 1 woman in the High court at
Koforidua to recover rent arrears of 2 years and an order that the
defendants pay him rent (Suit L46/98 dated 30th July 1998). This
group included the Headman, the deputy Headman, now also UCC,
and 3 members of one of the prominent Surveyor Line families—a
husband and wife and their adult son.

In the third case, a chieftaincy dispute among the Kpando Dzigbe,
the landlords of Kpando Torkor, had resulted in the courts placing
an injunction on land sales. However, land was being sold unofficially.
The uncertainty about land and land sales was affecting the growth
of Kpando Torkor. Those who already had farming and residential
plots were using them without paying any more rent and engaging
in new land transactions without reference to the landlords, and
those whose tenancies had expired continued to live on the land
without being asked to pay anything. Much of the crisis was in
respect of residential property that was at places where the chiefly
lineage owned the land. It was also more difficult to acquire new
land for building and farming outside the already existing boundaries of the Kpando Torkor settlement.

There was unhappiness about the uncertainties. As one leading
resident said, "The dispute creates confusion about who to pay for
the land and this has created many quarrels" (TG, Kpando Torkor).
The maxim about the Kpando Dzigbe chieftaincy disputes was that
migrants could not take sides. In addition to the Chieftaincy dispute,
there were complaints at Kpando Torkor that the Kpando Dzigbe
people were reselling land they had given to early settlers who had
given drinks as payment, but who were now too poor to build houses.
People from across the Lake who had money because they were still
able to fish were the beneficiaries of the resale of land.

The three cases highlight different sources of insecurity in migrant
settlements and are interesting in what they reveal about the various relationships within the migrant environment. The Slater case
at Kudikope was a good example of the interaction between national
political processes, local-migrant relations and migrant livelihoods.
Divisions and alliances in the Slater case were not simple dichotomies
between migrant and locals, State and locals against migrants or
migrants and the State against locals. Alliances were also continuously

shifting. At different points in time, the State gave support to a different side of the dispute. For example, both Slater and the migrants enjoyed police protection, and at one time were being supported by different police divisions. The VRA's somewhat passive support for the migrants reflected its own desire to assert its control over the Lake and the draw-down area without offending local chiefs who had not been compensated for the land.

Within the Kudikope community too, there were divisions. The Headman felt that while the loss of farms was regrettable, as migrants, farmers had no entitlements. Their only remedies were to look for alternative land or settle elsewhere along the Lake. The aggrieved farmers did not share this view as their actions showed. These disagreements deepened into mutual suspicion. One of the aggrieved farmers suspected that the Headman and his supporters were reporting his activities to Slater's people and would have given him up to the police if he had not ran away. The aggrieved migrants found support within the Surveyor Line and Pamproase communities where there were fellow Mepe people. They also said that some local people, including elders of the land-owning stool were supportive of them because they understood what it meant to lose one's farmlands.

The chieftaincy dispute affecting Surveyor Line had also generated intra-settlement tensions because a minority within the settlement continued to pay rent to the contender who had sued the headman and others. Harsh words had been spoken by each side although differences were being kept under control in the spirit of oneness stressed by the Headman. The Surveyor Line and Kpando Torkor cases showed how migrant livelihoods could be caught up in matters concerning their hosts. Thus while the land in and around migrant settlements was better than land in the Lower Volta in quantity and quality, the various troubles and institutional failures cumulatively were a threat to the livelihoods of farmers. Chimhowu's (2002) study of frontier settlements in Zimbabwe draws attention to similar issues. These disputes also had settlement level repercussions. As already indicated, Kpando Torkor's growth had been stymied by land conflicts.

Observances in relation to the land

As tenant farmers, migrants were expected to observe the land-use rituals and practices of the landlords. At Kudikope, farmers observed the Wednesday ban on digging the land with an implement. There had also been a Wednesday fishing ban in the past, but fishermen were no longer observing this. There was, however, still a ban on fishing on the last Saturday of every month. Also, menstruating women were not allowed to go to the river or cook for their fishing husbands. At Surveyor Line, there was a ban on farming every Friday as well as every 6th Friday to Sunday when the *Adae* (an Akan funeral observance) was celebrated by their hosts. Anyone who was caught contravening these regulations had to pay a fine of a sheep. One of the contestants to the Anyaase stool also ordered the killing of all the dogs at Surveyor Line because there was a shrine at Gyakiti, a nearby local settlement whose deity could not live with the barking of dogs.[63] At Kpando Torkor, when the Kpando Dzigbe stool had more control over the land in the early days, residents had to observe rituals related to the local yam festival. With the weakening of the Kpando Dzigbe hold over Kpando Torkor because of the chieftaincy problem as well as the christianisation of settlements, these rituals were replaced by annual church-based harvests to raise money for development projects.

When migrants were buried on the land of host communities, some mortuary rites specified by host communities had to be observed. At Kudikope, a ram had to be killed to purify the land before a burial, after which those involved had to wash their hands and feet from a bucket of water they carried with them before returning to the settlement. At Surveyor Line, for every burial on Anyaase land, a sheep had to be paid to the chief. Surveyor Line had now acquired a piece of Apaaso land for use as a cemetery. Also, a new road constructed by Surveyor Line residents to circumvent the Anyaase settlement allowed them to transport those dead persons who were to be buried in their hometowns without having to go through the Anyaase settlement and having to pay ritual fees. During funerals of important people in the host settlements, migrants in the vicinity, particularly their tenants, presented gifts of food and money and entertained mourners with drumming and dancing. There was not the same level of reciprocity on the part of the hosts in relation to

---

[63] It would appear that this ban was to curtail hunting because the bush fires were blamed on hunters setting fire to the bush to catch game. The reaction of the affected hunters had been muted because the action was in line with the government's ban on bush fires (Interview with UCC, Surveyor Line).

all the three settlements studied. Beyond land and the observance of rituals, there were other socio-economic relations between migrant and neighbouring host settlements involving the buying and selling of foodstuffs and fish.

Intermarriage between people from different communities in Ghana was the norm. However, the Lakeside was striking for the low level of intermarriages even between people of the same broad linguistic group. There were liaisons between migrants and locals and children were born, but there were no inter-marriages at Surveyor Line and Kudikope according to my informants. From the point of view of informants, intermarriages were not wise because of perceived differences in marriage culture, specifically the rights and responsibilities of the parties and the ease with which women of certain cultures sought divorce. Other reasons were that the local women were more interested in making money through these liaisons than in marriage. Interestingly, while at Kpando Torkor there were some marriages between Tongu migrants and their Kpando Dzigbe landlords who were also Ewe, some informants thought it was not wise, citing the more involved and onerous marriage rituals of the Kpando Dzigbe, particularly on the death of a wife or an in-law. While the rate of intermarriage was improving all the time at Kpando Torkor, adult migrants of all ages were still expressing a preference for marrying from one's own hometown (TA, Kpando Torkor).

The low levels of intermarriage were not restricted to relations between migrant and local communities. Among the different migrant communities at Kudikope, for example, there was also not much intermarriage. While a few Ewe women had married Dangme men, no Dangme woman had married an Ewe man. There were very few unattached women of marriageable age in the Dangme community because of their particular migration practices. Some respondents, however, insisted that the relative poverty of Tongu Ewe men and its attendant loss of respect were important in their inability to attract Dangme women.

Relations between migrant communities, the VRA and the District Assembly

At Surveyor Line and Kudikope, the District Assemblies were seen by settlement leaders as representing the government and the erstwhile ruling party, the National Democratic Congress and, therefore, allies in the struggle against the "host" chiefs. As one informant noted, "When they tried to collect rent from us for Lakeside farming and we refused, they wanted to prevent us from farming on higher ground. The District Chief Executive made it clear to them that the law was not on their side and so they stopped" (SD, Surveyor Line). Until the mid 90s, the VRA had also been seen as an ally in the struggle with host communities over Lakeside land. The pieces of paper on which the VRA had asserted its ownership of the land were highly valued by migrant community leaders and had been used as exhibits in court cases around demands for rent by local communities. While the VRA made it clear in these declarations that it would retrieve the land whenever the need arose, migrants did not expect this to ever happen. All that was to change sometime in 1996 when there was a major landslide in the gorge of the Akosombo Dam. It was blamed on erosion resulting from people farming on the slopes of the surrounding hills. It has been pointed out that the increased incidence of farming on marginal lands such as the steep hill slopes on the eastern side of the Lake was a result of the submergence of vast tracts of farmland under the Lake (Titriku, 1999).

The VRA, with government support, banned farming on the hill-sides and selected draw-down parts of the Lake to prevent further erosion, landslides and the siltation of the Lake. Having asserted the ownership and jurisdiction of the VRA against the claims of the local chiefs all these years, migrant settlements now had to contend with the impacts on their livelihoods of the VRA's exercise of ownership. There was a strong sense among the leaders of migrant settlements that they could not win this battle against officialdom, especially when the military and forestry officials had been called in to enforce the draw-down farming ban. Even more telling was the fact that their traditional allies such as the District Administration and the Member of Parliament for the area had signalled their endorsement of VRA policy (UCC, Surveyor Line; TAA, Headman, Kudikope).

While accepting that they could not win, many migrants disputed that draw-down farming was destroying the Dam in the absence of more than a statement to that effect and were suspicious about why the ban on draw-down farming was being imposed. Some said the problem was the lack of water in the Lake and not draw-down farming (IB, Kudikope). The claim that soil from farms was being blown by wind towards the Dam was also rejected by respondents (TK, Surveyor Line; UCC, Surveyor Line). Some informants argued that the solution to the Lake's problems lay with asking Burkina Faso to release water from its Dams upstream to ease the water shortages in the Volta Lake, and not in banning draw-down farming. Informants speculated that the ban on draw-down farming, which was mainly done by migrants, was to placate the mainly local hillside farmers who had to be stopped because of the landslides.

Much of the unhappiness about the draw-down farming ban was driven by fears about its impact on livelihoods. The special qualities of draw-down land, coupled with past and present troubles with the landowners created a sense of unease about the prospect of sole dependence on rain fed farmlands. Some respondents spoke about the prospects of hunger and starvation. Livestock keepers who were using the draw-down area for grazing their animals were also fearful about the implications of the planned tree-planting programme. The VRA had outlawed the cutting of leaves from trees, so cattle could not be kept in kraals and fed. The level of concern was such that some respondents said they would go to their hometowns if they lost the land while others mentioned the option of migrating to other parts of the Lake such as the Afram plains.

Issuing directives was not a satisfactory approach to policy change of such magnitude. Not surprisingly, the VRA's efforts to educate migrant settlements on how their activities were endangering the Lake and inculcating in them environmentally sound practices was not working well. Even more problematic were the alternatives being proposed to migrants. Settlements around the Volta gorge and elsewhere were advised to start farming mushrooms, snails and honey. This advice was being given without due regard for its implications for food self-sufficiency in migrant settlements. As well, it was not clear how these new products would secure livelihoods given the existing problems of markets.

Defying the ban was seen as a short-term but unsustainable strategy. Community and settlement leaders, especially those involved in the UCs, now derived their legitimacy from enforcing District Assembly and other official regulations within their settlements, often with the threat of police support. They were, therefore, unsure about how to approach this issue. Depending on their stance, influence and practice, some communities did not allow farming this year by the Lake while others did. Individual migrants for their part took a cat and mouse rather than a directly confrontational approach to this issue.

6. *Migrants and their Hometowns*

Migrants still considered themselves strangers after over four decades of founding and living in migrant settlements. This was in keeping with the way they were seen by their landlords. Especially in relation to land matters, migrants all over Ghana and elsewhere in Africa are often considered to be strangers no matter the length of their stay. This sense of not belonging was reflected in the makeshift character of living conditions around the Lake and the desire of certain migrants to maintain their roots in their hometowns. A clear majority of respondents considered their settlements around the Volta Lake to be their homes (78%), as distinct from their hometowns. Migrants continued to have links with their hometowns and the people living there. Among respondents, these links included attending the annual festival (7.8%), visiting family (49.5%) and sending remittances in cash and kind (4.6%). A significant 27.5% said that they had no links. The majority of respondents said they visited once a year (31.7% for male and 33.3% for female) and another 29.8% male and 31.5% female visited two and three times a year. A further 13.6% male and 10.5% female visited several times a year, or regularly. 9.6% male and 18.4% female never visited their hometowns (Table 7.2). The figure for those who had visited in the last year showed up interesting variations in this picture. Female respondents who visited three, four, five or regularly/several times a year, were about half the size of male visitors (48.3% male and 23.3% female). 9.6% male and 18.4% female had not paid any visits home.

Table 7.2: Number of visits to hometown a year

Number of Visits	Absolutes			Percentages		
	Male	Female	Total	Male	Female	Total
Weekly	3	2	5	1.9	3.5	2.3
Monthly	3	–	3	1.9	–	1.4
Regularly/several times	22	6	28	13.6	10.5	12.8
Five times	7	1	8	4.3	1.8	3.7
Four times	15	2	17	9.3	3.5	7.8
Three times	21	6	27	13	10.5	12.4
Two times	27	12	39	16.8	21	17.9
Occasionally	8	5	13	5	8.8	6
Once	51	19	70	31.7	33.3	32.1
None	4	4	8	2.5	7	3.6
Total	161	57	218	100	100	100

Table 7.3: Number of visits to hometown last year by gender of respondents

Length of stay	Absolutes			Percentages		
	Male	Female	Total	Male	Female	Total
Not Stated	–	1	1	–	1	.5
Weekly	2	1	3	1.4	1	1.4
Monthly	1	–	1	.9	–	.5
Regularly/several times	17	7	24	14.9	6.8	11.1
5 times	5	3	8	4.4	2.9	3.7
4 times	15	6	21	13.2	5.8	9.7
3 times	18	8	26	15.8	7.8	12
2 times	16	21	37	14	20.4	17.1
Once	29	36	65	25.4	35	30
Occasionally	–	1	1	–	1	.5
None	11	19	30	9.6	18.4	13.8
Total	114	103	217	100	100	100

This was in keeping with the observation by some respondents that women went to their hometowns fewer times because they were sometimes too busy with young children or without the resources to make these expensive trips. These visits were mostly for the festival (23.8% male and 29.7% female) and to attend funerals (26.7% male and 25.8% female). Another 32.5% male and 28.7% female travelled to visit family and friends. That only 4.1% male and 2.4% female respondents were engaged in economic activities in their hometowns confirms the observation that multi-spatial livelihoods that involved hometowns were more difficult to organise from around the Volta Lake. Those who paid visits home felt the weight of expectations, real or imagined, in relation to community, clan and lineage affairs.

Fundraising events were an important part of the annual festivals. One such event was the church harvest. As one informant at Kudikope said, "It is people from Dzigbe who pay the most during the harvest with cows, money and other things. This is how we show that we have done well" (IB, Kudikope). During and in between festivals, migrants also had to contribute to lineage compound projects. Some migrants considered these responsibilities onerous. As one migrant said, "Going to Asafotu is costly and prevents you from saving money. You become a stranger there and you have to buy everything. Funerals have to be paid for and there are old people to give small sums of money" (male respondent, Surveyor Line). On the other hand, the improvements in communication had given some migrants a sense they were in closer proximity to their hometowns and, therefore, could visit more often. As one said, "I have been to my hometown four times this year. It is not far anymore and not expensive so you can go". Annual visits have also been credited for injecting money into the downstream economy periodically, although the value of these flows has been disputed. Some consider them detrimental to the economic health of the Lower Volta.[64]

Migrants, hometowns and rites of passage

In addition to festivals which were a time for celebration and the performance of rituals related to work and prosperity and collective funerals for those who died during the year, deaths and burials were occasions on which the continuing links between migrants and their hometowns were displayed. Being buried at one's hometown was important to many migrants, but this desire was tempered with some realism about the financial implications of conveying dead people to their hometowns. Only those who could afford it or had children with the resources were able to do this. For those whose relations could not afford the journey, their lineages sent representatives from hometowns to assist with mortuary rituals. There were several persons who had no objection to burial in migrant settlements but were not sure their relations would agree (TKA, Kpando Torkor). Owning a house in one's hometown, a manifestation of attachment, was also related to the anxieties about death and burial. Busloads of friends from migrant settlements accompanied people to funerals in their hometowns on a regular basis and in addition to the migrant's own family house, general infrastructural developments at hometowns were among the positive factors that could impress them. In this connection, migrants' views about the current state of their hometowns tended to focus on infrastructure. The majority of respondents pronounced themselves pleased with developments in their hometowns such as the toilets, pipe-borne water, electricity, good roads and other services when asked to describe the state of their hometowns these days (66.8%). As one woman explained of the hometown house, "I built

---

[64] The introduction of large sums of money into an area of low productivity, it has been argued, has been highly inflationary, a situation worsened by the subsequent flight of such money from the area (Petition of the Tongu District Council, 1976).

it so that when I die, I can be laid in state in it. When I die, should people follow me home, they will see that I come from a place of note" (NV, Kpando Torkor). These were the words of someone who had no plans to retire to her hometown, did not express strong feelings about where she would be buried and was philosophical in her acceptance that she would not have a voice in the decision.[65]

Another rite of passage associated with the hometown was the formalisation of marriage even when the key parties such as the parents of the woman were migrants themselves. Some migrants maintained political and ritual linkages with their home communities. For example, the Headman of Surveyor Line, an elder of the Mepe stool, was regularly consulted on state matters. During the research period, he was away more than once at Mepe at the request of the paramount chief. Hometowns were also the places for solving longstanding, intractable and serious disputes. A case between a woman and her husband's brother, two migrants, which was heard at the Aklakpa Shrine in February 1999 was an example of such an intractable quarrel. In this case, the parties were in such bitter conflict that her brother-in-law accused the woman of witchcraft. As she could not get justice in their settlement on the Lake because her brother-in-law was the Headman there and tried to be both judge and jury in the case, she had brought the case to the shrine at Mepe. That the priest who was presiding over the proceedings was also a migrant did not change the sense that justice in the final analysis could be had only at the hometown shrine.

Changing relations between migrants and their hometowns

Relations between migrants and their home villages had changed over the years. At first, home villages were considered to be the best places for educating children. People still sent their children to their hometowns to attend school, but a number of factors had led to the dwindling of this practice. There were now more schools in migrant settlements and people were acknowledging the hardships children

---

[65] "Those who remain after I am gone will decide. We took two people home to bury in the last 4 months. They are likely to take me even if I say no. If they do not take me, my children will become laughing stock. People will say to them, 'recently when your mother died, you buried her in the bush'" (NV, Kpando Torkor).

had to endure in their parents' hometowns on their own or in the care of old grandparents or other close or distant kin. More and more, Lakeside migrants were sending their children to larger settlements around the Lakeside such as Kpando and Juapong, or further afield to Accra, Tema and Ashaiman to complete school and apprenticeships and to look for work. While respondents still had many relations, some quite close kin living in their hometowns, few of them were looking after these relations. The occasional gift of foodstuffs, fish and money might be sent or presented during visits, but most people did not see this in terms of looking after relations. Only 8.6% of male respondents and 3.8% of female respondents mentioned remittances as a link between themselves and their hometowns.

With the passage of time and the death of parents and close kin left behind, the links with hometowns have become tenuous. Even so, the emotional attachment and symbolism continued to be very strong and in times of crises of livelihoods, health or general well-being, returning to the hometown was an option.

Table 7.4: Number of households remitting people outside the community by gender of household head (migrant settlements)

	Absolutes			Percentages		
	Male	Female	Total	Male	Female	Total
NS	8	2	10	4.9	3.4	4.5
Remittance	58	16	74	35.8	27.6	33.6
No remittance	94	40	134	58	69	60.9
NA	2	–	2	1.2	–	.9
Total	162	58	220	100	100	100

Hometowns featured in many more retirement plans than would be actualised. This was because migrants were coping with conflicting imperative and changes in their situations. An important constituency driving these changes was the children who had been born and brought up in migrant settlements. For them, the hometown was not necessarily a village in the Lower Volta. At best, they had two hometowns. The first and the most accessible was where they grew up. This was even more so if they or their parents continued to live in the settlements of their birth and or childhood. The second hometown was the place in the Lower Volta they might visit once a year because of a funeral of kin, but a place for which they did not

always share their parents' affinity. Those children sent to hometowns who successfully completed their education tended not to come
back. Some parents were not unhappy about this. For one respondent whose daughters had learned trades they were practising in
various urban areas, she saw their not remaining at Surveyor Line
as a sign that she and her husband had been successful in bringing
up their children (AZ, Surveyor Line). Given the limited avenues for
practising artisanal professions, this view was understandable.

Several social organisations in migrant settlements such as the
funeral societies and development associations were hometown-based.
While hometown development associations were varied in terms of
their levels of activity and organisation, several respondents spoke of
paying levies for various projects back home. Some respondents were
becoming less enthusiastic about paying levies because of unhappiness
about accounting within the associations and the use of the money
by the recipients (TA, Kpando Torkor). However, some migrants
continued to make regular contributions towards the development of
their home villages. The improving self-organisation of migrants
through hometown associations of all kinds was making this source
of community support significant. Their projects included the improvement of schools and other infrastructure.

Table 7.5: Location of ex-household members living outside the community by
gender of respondent * (migrant communities)

	Absolutes			Percentages		
	Male	Female	Total	Male	Female	Total
Around the Lake	202	79	281	31.6	34.3	32.3
Juapong	2	0	2	0.3	0	.3
Ashiaman/Tema	39	14	53	6.1	6.1	6.1
Accra	82	40	122	12.8	17.4	14
Other Urban Areas In the Volta Region	71	29	100	11	12.6	1.5
Urban Areas Outside the Volta Region	44	11	55	6.9	4.8	6.3
Rural area in the Volta Region	55	13	68	8.6	5.7	7.8
Rural Area outside the Volta Region	49	14	63	7.7	6.1	7.2
The Lower Volta	88	24	112	13.8	10.4	2.9
Outside Ghana	8	6	14	1.2	2.6	1.6
Total	640	230	870	100	100	100

* Cumulative total of first three on the list of relations

There were also signs that people's networks were increasingly wider than the hometown base and the relationships networks were developing hand in hand with the rivalries and competition among the various communities within migrant settlements. Many migrants considered the Lower Volta to be more urbanised[66] than their Lakeside settlements. There was usually no irony in the joy expressed about the extension of electricity and potable water to their hometowns while migrants were living without these facilities. Apart from being pleased that kin and friends were experiencing improvements in their lives, it was important in these rivalries and politics of migrant settlements.

With the decline in livelihoods around the Volta Lake, some migrants were becoming interested in the establishment of multi-spatial livelihoods involving their hometowns. However, there were only a few such attempts at Mepe and Sokpoe. Wives and children were more useful in migrant settlements where migrants were farming than in the Lower Volta where farmlands were considered less productive. Migrants were more interested in land for building and were buying up plots at a pace that was creating many land conflicts.

7. Summary and Conclusions

In this chapter we discussed the wholesale migration of the Tongu Ewe from the Lower Volta to the Volta Lake in response to the Volta River Project. The chapter also argued that the situation of Tongu migrants today was shaped by the early processes of migration and establishment of migrant settlements. We argued that as a result of the establishment of unplanned settlements by migrants, infrastructure and services were very poor and this had a dampening impact on livelihoods. The chapter examined the political, judicial and socio-economic institutions and organisations within migrant settlements showing the ways in which migrants shaped these institutions. The place of these institutions in the organisation of migrant livelihoods was also discussed. In relation to governance institutions, we saw that the recent establishment of UCs in migrant settlement had

---

[66] Indeed, some of the central settlements and outlying villages in the Lower Volta had schools, electricity, health facilities and good quality water, facilities which continued to be absent in the majority of migrant communities.

resulted in the incorporation of a new power structure in the settlements. We also found that the UCs were exercising judicial powers
over a wide range of interpersonal disputes contrary to the laws
establishing them. This had resulted in complicated and sometimes
competitive relationships between the UCCs and the Headmen. The
concentration of powers represented by the overlapping membership
of the two institutions was observed, as were indications of possible
future struggles, conflicts and institutional problems arising from the
operations of the two institutions.

Among the Tongu communities, rites of passage concerning birth,
marriage and funerals continued to be conducted broadly according
to Tongu customs, according to informants. However, migrant life
had produced variations. The study observed that burial rites had
been modified to take account of the requirements and norms of the
landlord communities, the Christian churches and the funeral companies. The Churches also participated in funeral rites through burial
services and the drumming, dancing and the collection for the bereaved
family. While marriage rites were said to be similar to those at home,
very few marriage and divorce ceremonies were taking place in the
three settlements. It would appear that people preferred that marriage
rites take place in their hometowns. However, informal and yet to
be formalised unions were contracted day in, day out, and respondents
differentiated between a formal and non-formal union only when
asked, particularly when there were children between the parties. In
spite of the appearance of flexible attitudes towards marriage and
multiple relationships, the chapter argues that communities took such
a serious view of adultery that it was the kind of case which went
to the Headman's court.

A significant part of the chapter focused on relations established
by migrant communities and settlements among themselves and with
various players—the host communities and state agencies. We argued
that relations between and within migrant communities were characterised by co-operation, competition and conflict and were in some
cases affected by relations with local communities and officialdom.
Conflicts were manifested by accusations and counter-accusations of
insensitivity, self-seeking behaviour, jealousy, wickedness, immorality,
lawlessness, arrogance and witchcraft and this was evident in the
case load of the community conflict resolution fora in all three settlements. Migrants' relations with local settlements and officialdom were
important in migrant livelihoods, specifically in the acquisition and

use of land and the Lake and more generally in the sense of security of migrant settlements. The chapter concludes that migrant settlements had generally devised ways of living with their tenant status, striving, though not always successfully, to avoid being implicated in local conflicts. However, the economic and social ramifications of their relations with landlord settlements were an important subtext for migrant livelihoods. In relation to officialdom, the chapter discussed different aspects of relations between migrant settlements and the VRA and other government agencies. It was found that while the VRA was a useful ally in conflicts with local communities about the use of the land immediately adjoining the Lake, the VRA's own priorities of safeguarding the Dam and the Lake meant that its support could not be taken for granted. Its recent moves to ban draw-down farming and the cutting down of trees in certain parts of the Lake could be read in that light.

At the start of their large-scale out-migration from the Lower Volta, migrants maintained strong relations with the Lower Volta on account of the spouses, children and parents they had left behind. We found that with the passage of time and the deaths of remaining close kin in hometowns, migrants' relations with their hometowns became less specific in the sense that very few migrants were looking after people in the Lower Volta. The birth and upbringing of children in migrant villages had further complicated hometown allegiances and created distances that would probably become more significant in the next generation. As well, the deteriorating conditions around the Lake further reduced the ability of Lakeside migrants to contribute directly to livelihoods in the Lower Volta through remittances. At the same time, the insecurities of migrant life and persistent troubles with locals ensured that migrants continued to experience their status as strangers in a negative way. The result was continuing desire to maintain relations with the Lower Volta and its inhabitants. Thus, hometowns retained their value as places of ritual importance, a source of cheap labour, a refuge in times of crisis and a place to retire to or be buried at. This attachment was demonstrated by annual visits and financial contributions to hometown development associations and burial associations. These issues were important because migrants considered themselves and were considered to be strangers around the Lake, with all its implications. It was in this environment, a world apart from the sedate homogeneity of hometown communities, that migrants fashioned their post-dam livelihoods. Migrant livelihood activities and their organisation are the subject of the next chapter.

CHAPTER EIGHT

FROM MULTIPLE ACTIVITIES TO GROUP SPECIALISATION: LIVELIHOODS AT KPANDO TORKOR, SURVEYOR LINE AND KUDIKOPE

1. *Introduction*

This chapter examines the nature and organisation of livelihoods at Surveyor Line, Kudikope and Kpando Torkor. The chapter identifies both community wide and household level changes in livelihood portfolios since Tongu Ewe migrants settled along the Volta Lake in the 60s. The chapter tackles a number of related themes. The first concerns the deployment of pre-dam resources and technologies in the establishment of livelihoods in migrant communities. Capital items such as money, outboard motors, cattle and labour were all deployed in different ways by migrants. The findings from the three settlements suggest that these old resources were critical to the establishment and trajectories of post-dam livelihoods around the Lake and created differentiation among migrant communities. A second theme relates to the adaptation and modification of pre-dam labour relations to post-dam livelihoods. This was in evidence in the fishing industry but also pertained to other livelihood activities. Of particular interest was the establishment of household-based production systems in which women and men's productive and reproductive activities were more interconnected and interdependent than in the pre-dam days. This theme also focuses on the loss of production autonomy suffered by women and their strategies to survive within lakeside production systems. The deployment of old labour relations which involved yearly accounting and remuneration and the 3 for labour principle for post-dam livelihoods as well as the more intensive use of child labour in fishing communities is also tackled.

The chapter discusses the shift in Tongu Ewe migrant livelihoods from an almost total reliance on fishing to a specialisation in farming and the relegation of fishing to a supplementary activity. The nature and organisation of migrant livelihoods is tackled. Following this, social relations in the organisation of livelihoods, specifically those of class, gender and intergenerational relations, are discussed through the use of cases. The last section is the concluding one.

2. *Migrant Livelihoods Around the Volta Lake: Historical Perspectives*

In the last chapter, we indicated that the earliest Tongu migrants around Surveyor Line, Kudikope and Kpando Torkor did not farm. Instead, they concentrated on fishing, the processing of and trading in fish, for between three to five years of establishing migrant villages. They exchanged fish for foodstuffs with their hosts until their experiences of periodic food shortages and supply uncertainties led to the adoption of draw-down agriculture along the Lake. Soon, Tongu migrants became largely self-sufficient in food crops. Once settlements grew, farming was extended to land further away from the Lake, establishing rain-fed agriculture. A Surveyor Line resident recalls the establishment of farming as an important part of migrant livelihoods;

> Only three years after we came to fish, we began to farm. We had problems with food. We used to exchange fish for food from the local women. We were capable of farming and yet there were times when we ran out of food. So we began farming. We started by farming close to the banks of the Lake. It was clear that it was not going to be enough. Also, the Lake used to take the farms. When that happened, there was no food, so we decided to also farm on higher ground. We went and asked the chief. He agreed and gave us the land (CS, Surveyor Line).

Some of the barter practices established in those early years when fishermen did not farm have continued to the present because of a high level of specialisation in the livelihood activities. For many Tongu Ewe women, farming became an important livelihood activity although many still preferred the fish trade. As we indicated in the last chapter, farming resulted in changes in relations with the local communities, transforming many migrants from independent fishermen into tenant farmers.

The expansion of farming marked the beginning of a shift to a more sedentary and family oriented approach to livelihoods among Tongu communities. By the 80s, the inclusion of fishing and farming in many livelihood portfolios had been replaced by specialisation in farming across Tongu communities around the Lake. Those who remained in serious fishing had to move to more distant settlements across the Lake. These changes occurred as a result of a number of factors. Throughout the 1960s and 70s, Tongu fishermen had employed their pre-dam fishing practices on the Lake with reasonable success. As we have already indicated, while there was a lot of fish when the Lake was new, prices were not very good or stable. Therefore many fishermen did not maximise their catches. However, they were able to put up houses in their hometowns and buy a few cows. All that was changing and all around the Lake, there were complaints that fishing and farming were in decline. As one respondent noted, "we could get five to six basins of fish a day in those days. These days we cannot even catch enough to eat. Now we are going backwards" (Tongu Ewe fisherman, Surveyor Line).

With the decline of fish stocks in the Lake from the 80s, Tongu Ewe fishermen responded by intensifying their involvement in farming and in time, farming replaced fishing as an anchor livelihood activity for many of them. For the Tongu migrants, farming was now the most accessible option because it was still possible to do with relatively little capital into a migrant's old age, something which was less feasible with fishing which was more physically demanding and required a large capital outlay. This process was deepened by the adoption of seasonal fishing by some fishermen. In addition, some Tongu Ewe migrants took up animal rearing. Their animals, which included cattle, sheep and goats, proved a useful replacement for fish.[1]

The pre-dam organisational practices and technologies of the Dangme and others who had coastal fishing experience were better equipped for the maturing Lake. Their companies[2] began to use the outboard motors they had used at sea. This allowed them to travel longer distances to parts of the Lake not accessible by paddling and to remain all-year-round fishermen. The outboard motor was also very useful for cutting loose the nets which got caught in the numerous

---

[1] As one respondent explained, one cow could fetch them 2.2 million cedis (FD, Kpando Torkor).

[2] A Company was composed of a male head who owned the fishing equipment, a group of other male adults and children who participated in fishing and related activities such as net repairing and a few women who were involved in fish processing and marketing and also reproductive activities such as cooking and farming for the Company. At Kudikope for example, only 3–4 Tongu Ewe fishermen had outboard motors compared with over ten outboard motors in the Ningo community.

tree stumps in the Lake. As few Tongu Ewe fishermen adopted the outboard motor technology, Dangme and Fanti groups became the main fishermen on the Lake.[3] The failure of Tongu fishermen to adopt the outboard motor was initially because of its newness and subsequently because they could not afford it.

Later arrivals such as the Avenor Ewe and others from the neighbouring Republic of Togo specialised in working as farm labourers alongside their own farming. Migrants from the mid Volta who were mostly found at Kpando Torkor were traders and farmers with a few venturing into mainly hook fishing. Most of the shops at Kpando Torkor were owned by them. In their choice of livelihood activities, the later arrivals were reflecting their lack of fishing traditions. Several of those interviewed, including one prominent trader who had been at Kpando Torkor since the mid-60s had never before crossed the Lake (TKA, JK, and LKA, Kpando Torkor).

Some fishermen who had done well in the fishing boom days had branched into Lake transport and the sale of inputs and fishing equipment as well as consumer food items, drinks, clothing and drugs. One respondent, however, argued that the Lake transport was not profitable because of low fares and seasonal variations in traffic (MT, Kpando Torkor).[4] One result of the specialisation and the relatively good quality of farmlands was that many farming households were largely self-sufficient in the staple foodstuffs (maize and cassava) and also sold surpluses.[5] As one informant noted, "this land does not

---

[3] As one Dangme fisherman at Kudikope remarked acerbically, "the Tongu only have the name, but the true fishermen are the Ningos, Adas and Fantis". A project feasibility document for Kpando Torkor lists farming as the number one in order of importance with fishing and small scale industry and trade and business coming second and third respectively (GWSC/DANIDA, 1995). The decline in fishing among the Tongu Ewe was attributed to the costs of fishing equipment such as the nets and hooks. As one informant said, "only the rich can fish now" (TA, Kpando Torkor).

[4] This might account for low number of transport boat operators at Kpando Torkor. In 1999, only four boats were identified as coming from Torkor. There were some from across the Lake that plied the route between their settlements and Kpando Torkor.

[5] They only had to buy salt, sugar, oil and fish (if they did not fish at all) around the year and vegetables around December. Other regular non-food purchases were kerosene and soap as well as fishing and farming equipment. It was the shortages of these items which communities found very difficult to deal with. Particularly in periods of national shortages when the inaccessibility of migrant settlements worked against them, these goods were in very high demand.

need fertilizer. It is fertile already. We produce our own seedlings for planting and we do not use a tractor" (Headman, Kudikope). At Kpando Torkor, the possibility of irrigation agriculture was also a factor that encouraged specialisation in farming. While the total land under cultivation was quite small, for those farmers who applied for and were given irrigated land, planting two times a year, the demanding nature of farm maintenance and the lack of flexibility in the calendar of activities precluded serious involvement in non-farm activities.

Group specialisation did not imply an absence of multiple livelihood activities. Indeed, some of the most successful people in the three settlements had added various activities to their main undertakings to earn more money or to invest their savings. For example, activities such as the rearing of goats and sheep, keeping cattle with someone across the Lake or building rental accommodation were mentioned in addition to seasonal fishing, crop farming and trading. Some of the fishermen who had branched into Lake transport and trading continued to hire out their fishing equipment to their children and strangers. People living across the Lake who fished, farmed and reared animals were considered to be among the most successful migrants and informants confirmed the need for two or three livelihood activities especially because of the uncertainties of rain-fed farming.

However, the need to embark on multiple activities did not appear to be as urgently felt as in the Lower Volta. This was probably because each undertaking had more possibilities than the sum of possible engagements in the Lower Volta. Also, there were several persons, particularly those working for others who did not have the space or resources to diversify their activities until they had earned enough from their labouring activities.[6] For many of the fishermen's assistants, for example, their annual contracts and the practice of *gbedɔdɔ* (sleeping away from home) made independent engagements impossible. However, some of them, especially those who had grown up in the migrant settlements as opposed to being hired from the Lower Volta, established more flexible arrangements such as daily wages, which allowed them to pick and choose who to work with

---

[6] The hiring of labour was so widespread and established around the Volta Lake that at Kpando Torkor, prison labour had been used by some farmers until recently when the Prison Service established its own farms in the area.

and enabled them to engage in other activities. Also, several farm labourers had acquired their own plots while continuing to labour on others' farms as their way of diversifying their sources.

Currently, the Volta Lake fisheries were in a state of decline, a situation which had been unfolding for more than a decade due to a number of factors. One of these was the proliferation of aquatic vegetation in the Lake. As already mentioned, this was an early concern which occasioned extensive investigations and recommendations. Notwithstanding these efforts, aquatic weeds became a feature of the Volta Lake. A recent study found that their prevalence within the Volta Lake was between 1–10%, with a more extensive problem in the Kpong Head-pond because of its shallowness and numerous small islands.[7] De Graft-Johnson recently argued that although the spread of weeds was anticipated, preparations to arrest their proliferation were wholly inadequate (de Graft-Johnson, 1999). The high levels of migration to the Lake constituted a second set of factors. The attraction of the fishing boom coupled with the progressive decline of the Lower Volta resulted in levels of migration to the Lake which in time resulted in a higher than optimum density of fishermen, over-fishing and the high incidence of illegal fishing methods. The depletion of much of the tree cover in the Volta Basin (partly due to human activities) also had an added impact.[8]

By 1999 it was estimated that over 100,000 fishermen, fish processors and traders were involved in the Lake fisheries which were valued at an estimated US$120 million and over (Gordon, 1999; Kalitsi, 1999).[9] At the same time, researchers found that there were now too many fishermen on the Lake in relation to the fish stocks. According to Gordon, the optimum density of fishermen was 1–3 per square kilometre. Instead, the Volta Lake had over nine (9), a situation which could be worse given that the area of the Lake was actually less than 8,500 square kilometres because of recent years of drought in its catchment area. Thus the fisheries could be facing imminent

---

[7] See de Graft-Johnson, 1999, for a list of the different types of water weeds on the Volta Lake, the Kpong Head-pond and the Lower Volta.

[8] Interestingly, much of the fuel-wood was used for domestic purposes with only 1/3 going into commercial fish processing. This problem of deforestation, which began with the submergence of large tracts of forests, was expected to have long-term adverse effects on both the Dams and the fisheries.

[9] The number of fishermen was estimated at 80,000 in 1991, having grown from 18,358 in 1970, 20,615 in 1975.

collapse (Gordon, 1999, p. 80). This was a far cry from the 60s and 70s when as one employee of the Fisheries Department of the Ministry of Agriculture said, "There was a lot of fish and not many fishermen" (TN, Kpando Torkor).

The problem of over-fishing was complicated by the proliferation of illegal and very "efficient" fishing gear such as beach (*adranyi*) and purse seines, bamboo tubes and nets with very small meshes e.g. 3 mm as well as the *atidza* method of fishing (Titriku, 1999).[10] We discussed illegal fishing methods in relation to inter-community relations in the last chapter. It has been estimated that a startling 65–70% of fish landings were made with illegal gear (Gordon, 1999, quoting Braimah, 1992). Fishermen have attributed the popularity of illegal gear to the high costs and unavailability of approved fishing gear. But perhaps the most serious problem was the failure to plan for declining fish stocks until the early 90s when the problem was far advanced (Gordon, 1999; Braimah, 1999). This was the kind of institutional lapse which was common within the Volta River Project, due partly to the pre-occupation with hydroelectric power generation.

Fishing policy reflected these failures. Between the 60s and the early 90s, the Fisheries policies for the Lake were based on the idea that there was room to increase its exploitation. More recently, the recognition of the problems led to a policy review and new proposals for Lake fisheries management. One of the new policy measures being advocated was the involvement of fishermen in the management of fisheries, particularly with respect to the issues of illegal fishing gear.[11]

The poor infrastructure in migrant settlements, which was detailed in the last chapter, was also an important element in this regard.[12] With their history of being seen as beneficiaries of the Volta River

---

[10] *Atidza*, a method of fish farming had not been illegal in the Lower Volta. However, fears about debris choking dam turbines resulted in its ban on the Lake.

[11] Braimah, for example, has observed that surveillance takes up 80% of the cost of fisheries management. Therefore, to educate fishermen to understand the adverse long-term impacts of illegal gear on the fisheries and fishing community as a whole and, therefore, begin to police themselves and each other, was more economically advantageous (Braimah, 1999).

[12] For example, an Integrated Development of Artisanal Fisheries (IDAF) project at Yeji (1989–1996) found that all the 340 fishing villages in the Project were very poorly served with infrastructure and facilities. They had no schools, clean water, electricity, health facilities, markets, recreational facilities and alternative employment opportunities; communications were very poor, and many places were mostly only accessible by boat.

Project's fishing boom and their subsequent neglect by District Administrations and State institutions, migrant settlements have become poor relations of the older and more established neighbouring communities who themselves are only in slightly better shape.

Commentators such as Asafo also argued that the harsh living conditions of fisher-folk resulted in a "for survival" mentality towards the Lake. This implied that conservation and sustainability, which were not high on the agenda of the most active fishermen, could not be promoted without attention to their socio-economic conditions (Asafo, 1999).[13] These conditions provided the context for the organisation of migrant livelihoods, the focus of the next section of the chapter.

3. The Organisation of Livelihoods Activities Around the Lake

Fishing and farming around the lake

The main migrant livelihoods revolved around fishing, farming and the processing of and trading in fish and fresh and processed foodstuffs such as dried cassava, garri, groundnuts and beans. There was also some charcoal-making, but this was under threat in some of the settlements with the ban on tree cutting. While there was some animal-rearing in all three settlements, the bulk of cattle, sheep, goats and chickens were in villages across the Lake (Tɔgodo) and several respondents had one or two cows being kept for them in kraals there.[14]

Tables 8.1 and 8.2 below present the first two livelihood activities of household heads in the three migrant settlements studied. Caveats in the livelihoods literature apply here. The tables represent only the first two activities of heads of households. They say nothing about the activities of other members of the households. They also do not indicate the scale of activities and their labour relations. Because there are much fewer female household heads, women's livelihood activities are not properly represented. That kind of information will

---

[13] Under the IDAF project, income generation activities such as draw-down farming, woodlots, orchards, pottery, sheabutter processing and garri processing were being promoted to address some of these problems (Braimah, 1999).

[14] There were three cattle kraals at Kudikope with cattle belonging to their owners and a few others. Sheep, goats and chickens were also kept in small numbers. For ten years, animal-rearing was banned at Surveyor Line because it was considered a farming village. Although some people had now started, it was a source of tension in the community and they had been asked without success to pen their animals.

be presented in the discussion of the case material and informant interviews. However, the tables provide important information about livelihoods in these largely Tongu Ewe settlements. The first is that farming was the most important livelihood activity of the majority of both male and female household heads (44.1% male and 41.4% female). This finding supports the observed shift from fishing-anchored to farming-anchored livelihoods. Fishing was the first livelihood activity for 18.6% of household heads (24.7% male) and the second for 14.5% (19.7% male).

Table 8.1: 1st livelihood activity (earnings) of household heads at Surveyor Line, Kudikope and Kpando Torkor

Activity	Absolutes			Percentages		
	Male	Female	Total	Male	Female	Total
Working for someone	10	2	12	6.2	3.4	5.4
Artisanship	11	6	17	6.8	10.3	7.7
Trading (non foodstuffs)	10	9	19	6.2	15.5	8.6
Food trading	11	13	24	6.8	22.4	10.9
Farming	72	24	96	44.4	41.4	43.6
Fishing	40	1	41	24.7	1.7	18.6
Traditional Artisanship	–	1	1	–	1.7	.5
Other	7	1	8	4.3	1.7	3.6
Unemployed/Retired	1	1	2	.6	1.7	0.9
Total	162	58*	220	100	100	100

Note: The sample in migrant settlements was 116 male and 104 female.
These tables relate to household heads, which were 162 male and 58 female in the sample.

Table 8.2: 2nd livelihood activity (earnings) of household heads at Surveyor Line, Kudikope and Kpando Torkor

Activity	Absolutes			Percentages		
	Male	Female	Total	Male	Female	Total
Wage work	–	1	1	–	1.8	.5
Artisanship	4	2	6	2.4	3.4	2.7
Trading (business)	10	5	15	6.1	8.6	6.8
Food trading	2	9	11	1.2	15.5	5
Farming	48	7	55	29.6	12.1	25
Fishing	32	–	32	19.7	–	14.5
Retired	–	1	1	–	1.8	.5
Unemployed	1	–	1	.6	–	.5
Other	1	1	2	.6	1.8	.9
NA	64	32	96	39.5	55.2	43.6
Total	162	58	220	100	100	100

CHAPTER EIGHT

There was only one woman fishing in the sample. This also suggests that women were now largely absent from fishing.[15] From the survey figures, farming and trading were women's most important first activities—farming (41.4%), food trading including food processing (22.4%), trading (15.5%) and artisanal activities(10.3%) in that order. For their second activities, food trading (15.5%) and trading (8.6%) replaced farming (12.1%), the three activities representing the majority of women's second livelihood activities (Table 8.2). Male household heads on the other hand were mostly involved in farming and fishing, but an important minority were engaged in trading (6.2%), the food trade (6.8%) and artisanship (6.8%) (Table 8.1). Another 6% were involved in trading as a second activity although the figure in the food trade (1.2%) as a second activity was substantially lower. As we found during the informant and case interviews, men's involvement in the food trade was mainly the sale of their own foodstuffs either just harvested or also processed.

The two tables presented above (8.1. and 8.2) show that 39% of male household heads and 55.2% of female household heads were not involved in more than one livelihood activity. This, coupled with the fact that most second activities remained linked with farming and fishing, was in keeping with the suggestion that certain kinds of diversification were not feasible in frontier areas such as the Lake.

For farmers, farming was all-year round. Land in the immediate vicinity of the Lake was planted in January and harvested in August and September. The main crops grown on such land were cassava and okro and a small amount of rice. Sweet potato was popular in the early days because it was fast yielding (3 months) but was now a minority crop. It had been brought from the Lower Volta originally and farmed on land beside the Lake. Land on higher ground was planted in April and May and harvested in August and September in time for the second farming season which started in October, with the harvest in November and December. Crops that were farmed two times a year on higher ground were maize, groundnuts and beans. Cassava took a year to mature on higher ground.

---

[15] According to informants, a few women had been engaged in fishing in the sixties. It was now an almost exclusively male undertaking and the few women involved pre-financed canoes and nets, or hired people to fish for them for a share of the proceeds. More commonly, they were engaged in the processing and selling of fish.

Groundnuts and maize were in some cases inter-planted with cassava. The crops farmed at the edge of the Lake formed the basis for the household's food for several months because they matured quickly. A few people also grew non-staples such as sugarcane on their Lakeside farms. However, it was the crops grown on higher ground which were sold. Migrants planted annual crops because of land insecurity, soil quality and food culture.

Larger-scale farming was possible around the Lake because of the widespread use of hired labour, which was all the more important because tractors were not used much. There were also very modest experiments in irrigation agriculture in a few places such as Kpando Torkor and the Afram Plains. The Kpando Torkor Irrigation Project began several years ago as a government project complete with extension officers.[16]

There were about 150 (mostly men) at Kpando Torkor involved in irrigation agriculture.[17] They had to work from 6 am to 6 pm and this made other engagements difficult even though it was possible to hire labour for various activities on terms which included *abusa* i.e. 1/3 of the crop. A few farmers were supplementing government efforts by private irrigation. Each of them had a pumping machine, but they were sharing pipes. One of them had irrigated enough land to allocate small plots to between 20–30 people for 1/3 of their proceeds as rent (TA, Kpando Torkor).

Irrigation allowed farmers two crops a year. In the main season (the rainy season between March and June), crops included okro, maize, cowpeas and cassava grown on rain-fed land. In the dry season (October to December), it was mostly okro on irrigated plots and the crops were harvested in March. Farmers with irrigated plots used family and hired labour for preparing the land, planting, doing some of the weeding, spraying, moving the irrigation pipes around and harvesting. Several of those involved in farming tried to maximise their harvests by acquiring and cultivating different kinds of land on various terms. Draw-down and rain-fed land, privately irrigated and government irrigated land where it existed, each contributed something

---

[16] As at the time of the research, there was a farm manager, a technical officer, a pump attendant and a watchman, but no extension officer.

[17] The Project had started with over 100 acres with a total of 104 farmers, 25 of them women, each allocated an acre of irrigated land. At the time of the study, it had reduced to 25 acres.

to the livelihood portfolio—food security, the possibility of very high yields and good terms of trade, among other things. More commonly, farmers tried to augment their livelihoods by animal-rearing. However, apart from the interpersonal conflicts generated by animal-rearing in predominantly crop farming settlements, it took a few years for the investment in animals to start showing results and people did not always have the time. Once that happened though, the animals were a good way to build savings and could also be eaten when there were fish shortages. For women, rearing small ruminants and poultry was open to them in a way fishing was not. Charcoal-making remained another opportunity in the places where it had not been banned.

Fishing was still considered to be the best option for an anchor livelihood activity in situations where the fisherman had his own nets, canoes and outboard motors. "You have to have money when you are looking for money", one fisherman pointed out. Even then, there was an element of unpredictability because of the always present risk of fishermen losing their nets before they had finished paying for them. Nets were difficult to replace under such circumstances. Those fishermen without the necessary capital fished seasonally to supplement their farming or other more regular activities. Some Tongu fishermen were still practising itinerant fishing, chasing down reports of a good fishing season in different parts of the Lake. They would go for weeks, selling their catch at various markets around the Lake. The majority of Tongu Ewe fishermen, even the more sedentary, now sold most of their catch fresh. These responses to the paucity of the catch and the growth in marketing options loosened some of the interlocking relations organised around fishing.

The most capital-intensive activities associated with successful livelihood outcomes were service enterprises such as boat transport. Persons with 40 horsepower outboard motors and large boats could carry 100 passengers at a time. Some of those who had the capital had also ventured into road transport, but few had been successful and rotting hulks of broken-down vehicles were to be found in the various alleys of Kpando Torkor. Those persons trading in nets, fuel and consumer items in the market towns along the Lake also did reasonably well depending on their capital base and their clientele. These activities were male-dominated while women combined their farming with the processing and trading in foodstuffs and fish.

At Kpando Torkor, but not at Surveyor Line and Kudikope, there were artisanal services such as sewing, hairdressing and trading. People came from settlements across the Lake to enjoy these services. Some hairdressers also set up an itinerant practice, going from village to village. However, artisanal activities were not so well established as to be real alternatives to fishing and farming and they remained minority activities.

4. *Gender Relations and Marital Politics in the Organisation of Livelihoods in Migrant Settlements*

Background

Marital relations, labour relations among different categories of household members, relations between household members of the same sex and relations between children and elders within households together constitute the intra-household relations implicated in the organisation of livelihoods. In addition to establishing settlements, migrants established units for the conduct of their livelihood activities. What they established was related to whom they migrated with. In the early days, when fishing was organised by groups of migrant adult men with kinship relations, each of whom had one or two assistants, their households consisted of these larger corporations. Those who travelled with wives or female siblings incorporated women's productive and reproductive labour into the organisation of their fishing and their households. With the strong competition over resources generated by the presence of more and more people around the Lake, these cooperative systems soon gave way to more "individualised" approaches. This was not a neat or linear transition and as the cases discussed below show, younger men and women continued to work as assistants to older fishermen before gaining their independence. However, the scale of the production units became smaller among the Tongu Ewe. The residential patterns of migrant settlements reflected some of these changes. Older migrants tried to recreate the lineage compounds of their hometowns and as their sons grew, they encouraged them to build their homes close by. In some cases, sons worked with their fathers who then either retired or moved on to other things, while continuing to collect rent from their sons for their capital investments.

The earliest migrants either travelled in all male groups—fishermen and their assistants *(adegborviwo)* or in mixed groups with men, women and children. Male migration to the new Lake accompanied by their male assistants was in keeping with pre-dam practice. The pre-dam labour relations with these young males were adapted to the post-dam environment first in the fishing industry and later extended to trading and cattle rearing. Some of the reproductive functions of the male assistants were taken over by wives and other female kin who also brought female assistants to help them execute these functions. In the early years of migration, some migrants continued to go back to their home communities in the Lower Volta quite regularly for various reasons. For some it was to pursue the pre-dam livelihoods and for others it was to visit the children they had left behind in school. Several clam pickers also went back to pick clams for several years until the clams disappeared completely. This was because the clams guaranteed them the autonomy in production they were yet to construct in migrant settlements. Initially women were locked into household production relations that were more interdependent than the pre-dam arrangements in the Lower Volta. While under the Tongu Ewe marriage code men did support their wives with capital and equipment in return for labour, households were constructed on the basis of interdependent and autonomous relations of production and women had their own livelihood activities. As one informant noted, "Vume women had their pots, Agave women had their mats and we Mepes had our clams. We did not have to wait for the rains or follow men to Dzigbe to work" (MA, Surveyor Line).

Within the new environment, women's labour was critical to the execution of all Lakeside livelihood activities. As a result, they lost their autonomous livelihood activities with the result that their success became more dependent on the fortunes of their husbands or partners. As women became more established in the Lakeside environment, they struggled to establish their own livelihoods, but still within a framework of a production system in which the space for autonomous activities was more constricted for women. With the very good fish catches from the mid-sixties when the Lake begun to fill, many fishermen plunged into multiple marriages and liaisons and had many children. They rationalised this during the interviews in terms of their labour needs and the ease of life in those days. Several of the earliest migrants had four wives in their prime and more than twenty children.

Women's struggles for security in this new environment resulted in gender conflicts. It became common to accuse women of being on the perpetual lookout for the most successful fishermen to attach themselves to and thereby fuelling marital instability. Several of the younger respondents were brought up by grandparents and relations of either parent in the Lower Volta and other places around the Lake when their parents' marriages collapsed and each party went on to contract new relationships or to migrate to other parts of the Lake. Several respondents still had children living in different settlements around the Lake or in their hometowns being cared for by various relations.

Thus women's independent livelihoods of the pre-dam days were undermined by the central role of fishing in the livelihoods of migrants in the first two decades. While women's labour in fish processing and marketing and in care activities was critical for the success of fishing careers, fishing remained a male dominated domain and women were largely in support and subordinate positions. Large family sizes were seen as the key to success, failing which paid labour was used. This ideology continued to dominate the fishing industry. As one woman explained:

> The fish work is very difficult, so no one woman can do it. Some people have 2 to 3 canoes. Each of them has 4–5 boys so you need someone to cook for them, carry the fish from the boat to the village, clean it, smoke some and dry the rest. For this reason, fishermen have many wives and children. Even those women who leave their husbands end up with other women's husbands (MAA, Kpando Torkor, 23/10/99).

Thus, polygyny provided labour for fishing activities. While migrants continued to practise and justify polygamy, it was not on the scale of the past. Material conditions simply did not support that scale of existence. Polygyny was an ambiguous factor in the migrant livelihoods. It complicated the development of interdependent household production relations around the Volta Lake and contributed to heightened levels of marital tensions and instability compared with the pre-dam days. While there was no necessary connection between multiple marriages and marital instability, certain conditions of migrant life such as the absence of kin-based social organisations with their checks and balances, the presence of different communities and the more forceful economic ethos of migrant life affected gender and other social relations. One manifestation of this was a change in perceptions of men about women and vice versa. The same respondents who spoke fondly of the clam fishing women who as mothers, wives and lovers had held families together when men were away and had sponsored the education of many men, now spoke of greedy women always on the lookout for the fishermen with the largest catch. As one respondent put it, "women like to go where there is sweetness" (IB, Kudikope). Respondents spoke of instances where women had switched partners for economic reasons and there were cases in the UC records which suggested that accusations of sexual impropriety were an important manifestation and source of conflict (GA, Kudikope).

Women in turn spoke of the difficulties of polygyny, the destabilising impacts of marital instability, men refusing to sell their fish to their wives and preferring to sell to strangers with whom they tended to establish new liaisons while neglecting old relationships and children. Several of the fishermen who did not sell fish to their wives advanced a range of functional reasons, some historical, some contemporary, but generally relating to women's lack of trading and language skills, poor knowledge of the terrain, their tendency to take advantage of their relationship with the fishermen to cheat them or their lack of capital to be serious fish buyers. Whatever the reasons advanced, something profound happened in the migration from the Lower Volta to the Lake which transformed these selfless supportive women with years of clam-trading behind them into self-seeking, cheating, gullible and incompetent fish sellers. Apart from the potential marital tensions arising from women not having access to their husbands' fish, it also meant lower earnings from fish since the added value of processing could be lost to the household. Fishermen were beginning to acknowledge this, several of them complaining that middle women had made fortunes while their wives remained poor. However, the realisation had come too late for many of them.

The above conditions, coupled with several others, created the space for women to fashion more autonomous livelihoods. These included the changing sizes and cycles of households, the decline of fishing, the practice of itinerant fishing and the sale of much of the fish fresh. These together with the replacement of fishing by farming as the main livelihood activity reduced the need for women's labour in the processing and selling of fish and enabled them to gain more autonomy to farm and trade on their own account. However, the discourses around marriage and marital roles complicated women's attempts to make the kind of autonomous livelihoods that had been possible in the Lower Volta. Many of the older men still espoused the ideology that women had to support their husbands instead of working independently.

However, as the cases discussed below show, there were cases where women worked independently. Their ability to do so depended on factors such as their age, how long they had been in a particular marriage and whether they had independent roots in the migrant settlement they were staying in. Younger wives had to work to gain their independence and it was common to see the younger women working very closely with their husbands and in some cases their mothers-in-law or other more senior females in a fishing company. Especially where their husbands were themselves working for either or both parents or older siblings, wives had very little space for autonomy. Some younger women, however, did manage to organise their own livelihoods.

In spite of this growing autonomy, women's livelihood activities continued to be mainly derived from, and subordinated to what their husbands did. It was mainly the wives of fishermen who processed and sold fish. Depending on the arrangements between the couple, wives were either selling on their husbands' behalf or buying the fish and selling it at a profit for themselves. Many men preferred the former arrangement. In some cases, wives only processed the fish while the men did their own marketing. Women whose husbands were not fishing seriously mostly did not sell fish at all, particularly in the smaller villages such as Surveyor Line and Kudikope.[18] At Kpando Torkor, however, there were several women who sold fish who were single or whose husbands were not engaged in fishing. There were also some who bought fish from other people while their husbands sold to others. However, not all husbands were happy with their wives buying fish from others because of a widespread impression shared by both men and women that those who went there got

---

[18] Many women at Surveyor Line and Kudikope also processed cassava from both their own and their husbands' farms into garri and the proceeds were shared according to various formulae. The processing of foodstuffs had its particular labour relations that had elements in common with those of farming and fishing. Processing cassava was one activity in which many men were also actively engaged. In the cassava harvest period, the sight of two men, one the owner of the crop and the other his visitor, sitting together and peeling large mounds of cassava for processing was not uncommon.

involved with the fishermen. As one woman whose husband would
not let her buy fish from other fishermen put it:

> A woman who goes to Torgodo sleeps behind her husband's back.
> Some women do this to get fish to sell either on credit or at a lower
> price or free of charge. Some women even leave their husbands and
> move to Torgodo to stay with the men who supply them with fish.
> The fishermen say that every woman who goes there does this. They
> go there so they know what the married women are doing there (female
> respondent, Kpando Torkor).

In spite of the social disapproval, several women had built a career
in purchasing fish from fishermen and therefore making a living outside household-based production arrangements. Of course, it is arguable
that but for the social disapproval, more women would have done
this. It was hard and dangerous work travelling on the Lake from
village to village, week in week out. There was always uncertainty
about fish sources and prices because of fishermen's strategies to
maximise their profits in the face of the decline in fish stocks, seasonality in the availability of fish and the rising prices of inputs and
fishing equipment. When local fish traders took the fish to Accra to
be sold, they had to deal with the traders there who either sold the
fish on their behalf for a commission or from whom they rented
market stalls (MT, Kpando Torkor). Improvements in the availability of lake transport had made the turnaround time for fish-buying
trips across the Lake shorter and improved the availability and quality of fish. However, fish sellers sometimes had to both buy and sell
fish on credit and this meant very complex arrangements and the
constant danger of default and the breakdown of carefully nurtured
relationships which were critical to livelihoods.[19]

An important response to the uncertainties was the establishment
of relations in which traders pre-financed nets and equipment of
fishermen in return for preferential treatment. The arrangement, a
kind of loan transaction, meant that the fisherman sold his catch
either exclusively to the trader or she became the priority customer
until he had paid back the loan. Even when not indebted, some
fishermen sold to particular traders as a form of guarantee for future

---

[19] In addition to fish transactions, fish traders sometimes had to purchase various goods needed by fishermen living across the Lake such as mosquito nets, cloth
and salt to be repaid when accounts between them were sorted out.

access to capital. Just as fishermen complained about their wives cheating them, they also complained about the women with whom they had these arrangements. They charged that women sometimes discouraged them from paying their debts in order to prolong the exclusive sales relations. Fishermen were generally agreed that it was preferable to finance nets from selling livestock and other valuables than taking loans from potential and regular customers.

The fish traders in turn complained about the duplicity of fishermen. Around Kpando Torkor, respondents said fishermen simply disappeared across the Lake where they fished and sold to other buyers there to avoid their obligations on this side. Thus, it was considered a risky way of trying to make a living, especially since in several cases, the women had also acquired the nets on credit and, therefore, had debts to pay. In spite of these difficulties, the perception persisted that selling fish was the most lucrative female occupation around the Lake.

As a fish trader explained, things were more complicated than they appeared: "The Tɔgodo people are saying the asisiwo (literally, "regular customers", referring to the fish traders) are making more money than them. It used to be more profitable when the fishermen sold directly to us. Now our profit margins are low because their wives are also putting a marker on the price" (MT, Kpando Torkor).[20] In spite of the complications of the fish trade, some traders understood market trends and responded accordingly, taking a seasonal approach to the fish trading, for example. One of them observed, "I am not going to Tɔgodo at the moment because there is a lot of fish because of the floods. If you sell fish at this time, the price is low so you will lose. When the floods recede, I will then resume going to Tɔgodo. At that time, even a little fish will make you a lot of money. In the meantime, I am farming" (trader, Kpando Torkor). Fishermen and farmers on the other hand could not respond in the same way, especially if they were indebted to a trader. Fishermen could also lose their nets because of the trees in the Lake and when this happened, their situation became difficult. In the next section,

---

[20] From the point of view of fishermen's wives though, their more recent involvement in the marketing of fish was a positive development after years of struggle to improve their access to the proceeds of their labour. In any case, since the late 80s, very few Tongu fishermen were fishing in the quantities that required preservation. They sold most of their fish fresh. One estimate was that only 7 persons were fishing seriously at Surveyor Line (CS, Surveyor Line).

through the presentation of several cases, some of the factors shaping livelihoods in migrant settlements around the Volta Lake are discussed.

CASE 8.1: Raphael, young head of household, he and his wives work separately and cooperate (Surveyor Line)

Raphael, (33) was the head of a household made up of himself, two wives and five children between the ages of 13 and 3. He was born at Mepe and grew up there with his grandmother. In 1979, when he was in class five, he decided to come and live with his parents at Surveyor Line because of his grandmother's inability to maintain him and his siblings. He came and continued school, first at Anyaase, two kilometres from Surveyor Line and then at Ajena where he completed JSS 3. During his years of schooling, he lived with his parents and helped them to fish and farm when he was not in school. As an adult with his own family, he was still involved with helping them with their work and in return benefited from their resources (e.g. he was using his father's net to fish) and their status as a prominent Surveyor Line family. His two-room house was built across from his father's and next to his mother's rooms. His first wife Augustina lived in one of the rooms with her children and he lived in the other. The other lived in her parents' compound and only came to sleep when it was her turn to do so.

In 1995, he went to Ashaiman to stay with his elder brother to learn masonry. He graduated in 1997 and continued to stay with his brother whenever he was at Ashaiman. He had learned the trade from his father's brother's son and was now helping him to execute contracts at 10,000 cedis a day. At Surveyor Line he was also fishing and farming. In income terms, he earned more from fishing and farming than from building houses. He and his wives farmed separately. They helped him on his farm on Tuesdays and Wednesdays and did their own farming on the other days except Friday and Sunday. He also helped them if they called him to. Raphael was away from Surveyor Line between November and February working as a mason at Ashaiman near Accra. He would return in March and stay until October farming.

He had acquired the land he was farming, four acres, through the Headman at 30,000 cedis an acre and was farming all of it. The land consisted of five separate plots, all on higher ground, on which he was growing mainly maize, cassava and groundnuts. He estimated the consumption of his crop at 50% and sales at another 50%. He did not share his earnings from farming with his wives. His two sons helped him with his fishing by paddling the canoe when they were not in school. He sold his catch fresh at Akosombo. It was taken there by his spouses. A trip could earn about 20,000 cedis. He had a canoe, a net and a hook. His capital outlay was 1,250,000 cedis and he expected that his canoe would last ten years and his net two years and the hook one year before he had to replace them.

Augustina, Raphael's first wife

Raphael's first wife was 26 and was born at a nearby migrant settlement. Both her parents had died by the time she was 17 and she came to Surveyor Line to live with her mother's sister. Three years on, in 1993, she married Raphael. She was educated up to class six but had stopped school after her father died. She was now farming and trading in cooked food at Surveyor Line, Gbitikope and across the river. She also fried *garri* for sale at Gyakiti and Dzemeni.

When she first arrived, she helped her aunt to farm for a year. During this time, her aunt would buy her things as her reward. Her aunt then gave her 1/10 of an acre of the land to farm for herself. After that, she bought her own things and helped her aunt on her farm two days a week. She and her aunt grew cassava and groundnuts on their farms. When she married, she gave up the land. She and Raphael now had three children and the birth of each had been assisted by her father-in-law who was also a pastor.

When she first came to stay, she helped her husband on his farms. When her first child was 2, she acquired her own farm. She went to the bush and picked out what she felt was suitable land. It was about half an acre and she started with about a third of an acre and then added the rest to it over the two years. She was growing cassava and groundnuts. She paid the Headman 20,000 cedis as rent. In return for her help, her husband gave her 1/10 of an acre of his land. She and her husband also had a Lakeside farm which they had now given up because of the ban. She also purchased a part of her father-in-law's cassava crop to make *garri* this year. She would pay him only after she had sold the *garri*. She was not using hired labour for her farm.

She and her co-wife were working on their husband's farms on the same days and also fried his *garri* together. They cooked and slept with him in alternate weeks. They ate separately and whoever was cooking for the man slept in his room. Augustina was deeply unhappy about her husband's second marriage because she had had no idea about it until the other woman was pregnant and also, she feared it would affect her children's future adversely. She felt Raphael was too young and financially insecure to have two wives. She said he was already having difficulty buying basics such as soap and kerosene. She now had to buy those things for herself. Fortunately, they were self-sufficient in food because of their farming.

Sesi, wife number two

Sesi was Raphael's second wife. She was born at Mepe in 1969 and grew up with her mother's mother around Juapong in the Eastern Region. She began school there and in the fourth year of her primary education, she came to live with her parents at Surveyor Line to continue her education. When she was in form 1 at Ajena Secondary School, she gave up on school because she preferred trading and also could not cope with being beaten by teachers. She went to Dzemeni in 1984 to baby-sit for a fish trader for a year. She then went to Accra to work for an uncle (mother's brother) who sold drinks at an Accra suburb. She stayed for three years. In her last year, she began going to Sempoa on the Lake to purchase fish for her uncle's wife. After a year, they stopped when the fish trade was no longer good. In 1988, she began to trade in doormats on her own account because she was encouraged to start working for herself as she was old enough.

She bought the mats from Sokpoe and sold them in Accra. She came to Surveyor Line for a funeral in 1989 and bought some garri to go and sell. It worked well so she started buying and selling garri between Surveyor Line and Accra. This she did for two years. It was during this period that she met Raphael again and they began a relationship. In 1995, she gave birth to their first child at Surveyor Line. She had had to leave Accra because her uncle's wife was upset about the pregnancy. She came to stay with her parents. In 1999, she built her own kitchen, an elaborate shed with short walls behind her parents' home so she could begin to cook for Raphael. Before then, she would sleep in his room every other night. Now that she was cooking, it was every other week. She and Raphael were not formally married yet, although he had accepted responsibility for the baby and considered her his wife.

Even while she was pregnant, she was still buying garri and selling it in Accra. She was now farming. She had her own farm but did the two-day farm labour on Raphael's farm. Her farms were three separate pieces of about 3 acres on higher ground. She also had about half an acre of draw-down farmland. She hired labour to clear, weed and help her with her harvest. She grew cassava and groundnuts. She sold her own farm produce to buy tomatoes, kerosene and soap.

She and her co-wife helped each other. For example, Augustina had helped her to harvest her drawdown farm and she paid her 40,000 cedis for helping her make *garri* worth 150,000 cedis. However, they had tensions. Sesi said Augustina was not friendly and was unhappy anytime Sesi came to sleep with their husband. Sesi therefore had asked Raphael to build a separate house for her but he had refused because he wanted her to stay where he was. She found her mother-in-law to be supportive. She had her doubts whether she would be able to cope with the hostility of her co-wife and the hard work farming entailed. She had had to hire labour to the tune of 150,000 cedis that season alone. She also bought groundnuts worth 70,000 to plant, but the yield, a basket of groundnuts, was very poor. She preferred to trade and was hoping her uncle and his wife would allow her to go back to Accra to stay with them.

CASE 8.2: Bright, 35, marital instability and livelihoods (Surveyor Line)

Bright was 35, a farmer and fisherman and lived at Surveyor Line with his two wives and two children. He was born at Mepe after the Akosombo Dam and grew up at Surveyor Line. He did not have formal schooling and no recollection of living at Mepe. He lived with his father's older brother at Dzemeni Torgodo for about seven years, helping him with his fishing and farming. He returned some 15 years before the interview because he wanted to live nearer to his parents.

He was now fishing and farming on his own account. He farmed jointly with his two wives. He had three acres of land on higher ground and two acres by the Lake. At present, he was farming one and a half acres of Lakeside land and one acre of higher ground land. He rented the "higher ground" land through the Headman and was paying 30,000 for an acre a year. He was planting cassava and maize on his higher ground and cassava by the Lake. He was selling most of his produce and giving a third of the proceeds to his two wives. He had one assistant who was helping him to fish. He was paying the young man's parents 100,000 cedis a year for their son's services.

Bright, together with his wives, processed cassava from their farm into *garri*, which they made between four and five times a month. His wives then sold the *garri* at Akosombo and Dzemeni on Thursdays and Mondays. He gave them 1/3 of the earnings as payment for their contribution. Bright estimated the family's earnings from fishing at 60,000 cedis a month, farming at about 500,000 cedis a season and *garri* sales at about 200,000 a month. Bright had a four-room laterite-block house with a thatched roof. He had two kitchens built with the same material. He built the house years ago from his fishing and farming. He also had a house at Battor.

Bright's senior wife was Mercy. She was in her late 30s and was in the eighth month of her 5th pregnancy. She had had three children before coming to live with Bright. Mercy had been born at the Lake a year after the big floods (1964). Her parents were resettled a year later at Ampaem but they returned to the Lakeside where they were farming. Her mother was now dead but her father was still there. She lived with various people, kin and non-kin, as house-help for over five years at Lakeside settlements and so did not go to school. Her last position was at Buipe with a cousin whose husband was a fisherman with his own company with two boats. Here she helped to cook for the fishermen and smoke and salt fish as well. The company had twenty fishing assistants and they used "*adranyi*" (drag net) to fish. Accounts were made once a year. Her cousin bought her cloth from her earnings as the main cook of the Company. When she felt that she was now an adult and, therefore, capable of making a living on her own, she returned to her parents on the Afram plains and lived there for ten years. During this time, she married a man at Dzemeni Tɔgodo, a village that was one day's boat journey away from her parents' village and they had three children. She and others farmed on land belonging to the local communities. They did not pay rent, but contributed money to stool rituals and funerals.

She used to farm by herself, about half an acre of cassava, ground-nuts and beans. After her marriage, she began to farm with her hus-band and received a third of the proceeds as her share. She would sell the produce at various markets on the Lake. She used her money to buy personal items as well as salt, pepper and onions. They did not make *garri*. Her husband had a chain saw, which he used to cut wood for people. He would hire labour to clear the land and to harvest their crops. They paid the harvesters a third of what they harvested.

They were married for ten years. (Their first daughter, now 16 years old, was helping her to peel cassava during the interview). Her hus-band then decided to move to Kudikope to look for better prospects. She followed him there months after he left. He was marrying a new woman so he asked her to leave and kept their three children. She came to Surveyor Line, which was close to Kudikope and stayed with her uncle, her mother's maternal cousin. This was in 1993. Her daugh-ter followed her and came to stay. When she arrived, her uncle was living alone. He had children but they were staying with their mothers at three places. Soon after she moved in, they began a relationship.

Three years into their relationship when she had their first child, he started a new relationship. The new woman, Vicky, who was from Konkordeka, a neighbouring migrant settlement, came to stay at Surveyor Line. From then on, things began to go wrong with Mercy's marriage. She was sent home to Mepe by her husband to give birth to their child. After four months, her husband had not visited, so his brother gave her money for transport and she returned. He was not pleased to see her and spoke of his intention to divorce her. She called him before four different people, but he would not budge. It emerged during one of their now interminable quarrels that Vicky was responsible for his desire to terminate the marriage. She gave up on the relationship but continued living in the house. She could do this because they were related. He began to see her secretly again. He also started a new relationship with a third woman, Faustina. Vicky, who now had one child with him, left in anger and returned to Konkordeka. He mar-ried Faustina who had three grown children already and she came to stay. She was at present expecting their first child. Mercy was more comfortable with this new marriage because she was related to Faustina. She described her as her grandfather's child and her aunt. They were on good terms and although she had not resumed cooking for her husband, he would eat sometimes when she cooked. She and her new co-wife worked together. They made *garri* together and shared the profits after repaying their husband the money he had spent purchasing the cassava.

At present Mercy was farming on draw-down land. It was her husband's farm and about one third of an acre. Even at the height of the crisis in their relationship, he did not take the farm from her. She says it was because of their family relationship. Also, he had other land on higher ground that he was not using. The land had belonged to his father. As the only son of his father who had remained at Surveyor Line, he had control over those lands. His brother was working at a trans-national-owned banana plantation at Atimpoku near Akosombo. In spite of the draw-down farming ban, she still intended to farm the next year. If stopped, she would move to farm on higher ground.

Her husband was fishing mainly, but she was not buying his fish. Some Akan women from Gyakiti were his main customers. At first they used to farm the same piece of land for three years. For three years now, she was making her own farm on the land he had given to her. He was farming with his new wife on one plot. The marriage was not even a year old. She was not helping them on their farm and they did not help her either. She was cooking her own food from her own farm, but she could take food from his farm as the mother of his children. Mercy had no dealing with her two daughters who were with their father's mother at a Lakeside migrant settlement. She was afraid to contact them because she was afraid of her ex-husband.

CASE 8.3: *Lucy, livelihood disrupted (Surveyor Line)*

Lucy was in her 40s. She had been at Surveyor for only six months. She had come from another Lakeside settlement where she lived for many years. She was born at Mepe and brought to Surveyor Line by her parents when she was a child. They had settled at the Surveyor Line outgrowth, Gbitikope, where they were farming. Her father became the Headman of Surveyor Line. She did not go to school and instead helped her parents to farm. She met and married her first husband at Surveyor Line. They had two children. The marriage broke down and she went to live with her mother at a Lakeside settlement on the Afram Plains. She and her mother had one farm and worked together. Her mother died in 1990.

Lucy met and began a long relationship with a man residing in the settlement. They lived apart and she had her own one acre farm on which she grew maize and groundnuts. He was also farming and she used to weed for him two days a week and help with the harvest. His farm was 3–4 acres although they were growing the same crops. He also helped her with her farming sometimes.

Her father asked her to return to Surveyor Line. She was his eldest daughter and he felt that she was living too far away. She had responded to her father's demand to return because she was not properly married. While she did not cook for her husband, they had two children and he gave her money. Besides, she worked on his farm. They had been together for about ten years and his wife knew about her and so if he came to perform the marriage rites as he was promising, she would go with him.

The land she was farming had been given to her mother by her relations so she returned it to them when she left. She was hoping to start farming at Surveyor Line on land given to her by her father. He had given her 1/10 of an acre of cassava on higher ground but it was not yet mature. She was at the moment staying with her younger brother and his wife. Her brother had built her a house to live in and she was hoping to become independent soon.

She had been self-sufficient when she lived on the Afram plains but missed not having family there. Apart from her farming, she was burning charcoal. She grew groundnuts two times a year. She burned charcoal throughout the year, 15 bags a week, about 5,000 cedis a bag. Her profits were about 500 cedis on each bag. She also sometimes bought fish from the Bakpa fishermen when the fish harvest was good. She would smoke some and eat some fresh but it was mainly for food. She helped one fish trader to sell her fish sometimes for a fee, but she did not consider this to be her work. She had been told that charcoal burning was not possible here at Surveyor Line because of a government ban. She was a bit concerned about her prospects, but her father would not let her go back. She had brought 50,000 cedis from her earnings for her upkeep until she could earn something from her farming.

Only one of her four children was with her. She had had two more children with her second husband. The older two from her first marriage were at Mepe. The boy was in school and the girl was married and living with her husband. Her third child was at Dzemeni Torgodo helping Lucy's sister to trade. She was not in school and neither was the child with her. Her children were in different places not because she could not look after them but because one was staying with her sister and the other was with her husband's people.

These three cases together illuminate certain factors at play in the livelihoods that women of different ages were able to make for themselves within the framework of a polygynous marital system. Augustina and Sesi were younger women in a polygynous union who had some independence. This was partly related to the fact that their husband Raphael himself was not very established and had interests outside the settlement at Ashaiman near Accra. Augustina had first come to Surveyor Line as a minor dependent and then gained experience working independently before her marriage. She had married Raphael while he was still in school. Sesi had also been trading independently before the marriage to Raphael. There were interesting parallels and contrasts between Raphael's two wives. While one was from a rural background, the other had lived in Accra and wanted to go back there. Both had dropped out of school and, therefore, did not have formal training. Augustina had farming skills she was likely to use throughout her life while Sesi was more likely to trade in the future. Unlike Augustina, she had acquired a larger piece of land and hired labour to farm and was complaining about the tedium involved in farming. Both of them had strong family connections at Surveyor Line. After ten years, Augustina had the knowledge and connections to acquire land on her own as did Sesi whose parents were still living there. At the same time, they were engaged in working for their husband on his farm and frying his *garri*. Raphael's periods away and the set up they had established allowed them to engage in some independent livelihood activities. Augustina's remark that she had to buy her own soap and kerosene was likely to become a pattern in their relations especially since she had her own farming and food trading activities.

Raphael, Augustina and Sesi can be contrasted with Bright, Mercy and her new co-wife. All three were older than Raphael and his wives. However, Mercy and her co-wife were more dependent on their husband for land and other resources than Raphael's wives, mainly because they had come to Surveyor Line on Bright's account, thus the land Mercy was farming had been given to her by Bright. This was in spite of the fact that she had worked for many years in other parts of the Lake. Her livelihood and migration trajectories had been shaped by marital instability.

Even while quite young, women in polygamous marriages faced particular difficulties. Raphael's young household provides some insights into the issues. Augustina's fears for her children were based on the assumption that there would be many more children. Those fears might or might not be realised depending on how their lives turned out. For a more experienced woman like Mercy, polygamy and marital conflict had been very damaging. In spite of several years of making a living, Mercy had had to start all over again. Her various periods of insecurity were linked with marital breakdowns. In the recent case, her kinship ties with her husband had ameliorated what would have been a very difficult situation. In spite of being pregnant, she had to accept a subordinate position in relation to her husband's new wife. Again, it was fortunate that they were related. For others who were not so fortunate, it meant moving from settlement to settlement in search of stability. Mercy was slowly gaining some autonomy in her livelihood activities, but as a stranger in the settlement, she was relying on her husband for land. Because of their shaky rapprochement which was evidenced by the fact that she had not resumed farming and cooking duties, she was able to work fully for herself with the help of her daughter. She was in an unusual situation because most women who had their own work were still required to spend time on their husband's farm in addition to other paid and unpaid activities. This had to undermine their own farming unless they could hire labour. Two other days had to be spent observing the traditional one-day a week farming prohibition as well as the Christian convention of not working on Sundays. Not surprisingly, women had much smaller farms and it was common for them to be given small pieces of the land rented by their husbands. However, it allowed them access to their husbands' harvests and other resources and some women could earn additional money making garri for their husbands. Whitehead's (2002) argument for a more nuanced view of a woman's labour duty is relevant here. Indeed, one of my informants patiently explained to me the leverage that doing this labour, which could be done at a woman's own pace, gave women. However, a marriage had to subsist for a long time for women to realise the benefits of their contribution. Lucy's case shows how marital instability could disrupt women's livelihoods. For women who were single, divorced, separated or widowed making a livelihood could be very difficult because of the conditions around the Lake.

Lucy's livelihood had been disrupted by her move to Surveyor Line at the behest of her father. Her husband's failure to perform their marriage rites was interfering with her attempts at making a livelihood on her own terms. She had moved from one community where she insisted she was doing well, to be close to her father, brother and other family members. Some of her livelihood activities, especially the charcoal burning and the trade in fish, were not going to be possible at Surveyor Line. On the other hand, she was getting the help of kin to organise new activities. Lucy had been given land for farming by her father and a roof over her head by her brother. Even as she expressed the hope that her husband would come and perform the marriage rites so she could go back, she was realistic enough to begin to establish her own independent activities and make a life for herself and her son.

5. *Labour Relations Outside the Household in the Organisation of Livelihoods: Gender and Class in Practice*

The people who migrated as mature people did well. Those who came young or were born here have not done well. Their money is stuck here (Respondent, Kudikope).

Fishing was a group activity of necessity. Fishing groups varied in size from two-person outfits to those with tens of members, the larger ones known as Companies. The Company, which was mostly a feature among the Dangme communities, had a leader who was usually the procurer of the capital items—nets, boats and the outboard motors. These he purchased initially with his own resources or from money borrowed from his home village or from family members. Once the Company got off the ground, new equipment could be purchased from earnings although now and again an injection of fresh capital was needed. The Company Head kept records of daily earnings and expenditures even if he could not write. Accounts were usually made at the end of the fishing year to share the earnings. Accounting was more notional than real. In the past, there was a ritual which involved the whole Company, of sitting down during annual festivals to divide up the proceeds. These days, assistants were simply paid by the Head of the Company and then it was considered that accounts had been made.

Proceeds from fishing after everyday expenses such as food and fuel had been removed, were usually divided into two parts, one part for the boats and nets and one part for labour, or in three parts, two for the boats and nets and one for the labourers. The portion paid for labour, whether a half or third, was then divided among the fishing assistants—who were in the region of 4 and 6 for each boat. A portion of this was also given to the women who did the cooking, fish preservation and marketing for the Company. In practice, this distribution of proceeds to Company members was not in equal parts. It depended on age, experience, skills and the nature of the agreement reached with the head at the start of the contract. In the case of very young boys, accounts were made to their parents back at home annually or biennially depending on the agreement and if both parties were happy, the child could return to the same Company for a few more years. These days, assistants could also be employed on fixed terms irrespective of the Company's profit margins. Often however, they were not paid the agreed sums or at

the right time if things did not go well for the Company Head.
Several fishing assistants cited instances where they were paid less
because the Company Head had had to make unexpected personal
expenses during the year. In any case, the agreed sums were quite
small, particularly when they were a lump sum at the end of the
year. It would seem that with the exception of the children of the
Head of a Company, fishing assistants did not earn enough money
to enable them to save up to eventually buy their own nets and
boats. With the increasingly large capital outlays needed to set up
independent fishing as well as the decline in fish stocks, fishing assistants were in a very precarious position. Labour relations governing
other livelihood activities shared many of the features of those of the
fishing industry. Transport boat operators, trading assistants and those
helping women in the fish trade were also working under similarly
precarious conditions. For the women and girls who assisted the
wives of the Company Heads, their situation was complicated by the
semi-domestic and semi-formal nature of the productive and reproductive activities they were involved in.

The use of hired labour from other households and even other
places for land clearing, weeding, harvesting and processing crops
was also prevalent in all three settlements. There were men from
Togo and other parts of the Volta Region of Ghana who came periodically to the Lake to work as labourers during the clearing season. In the harvest periods however, the labour that was used tended
to be from other households within the settlements. In some cases,
the cassava was sold before being harvested. This allowed the buyer
to harvest and process the crop gradually in order to maximise his
or her returns. Agricultural labour for activities such as weeding had
clearer terms because they were one-off, bounded, easier to measure
and paid up front whether or not the investment could be recouped.
By the 1990s, with the uncertainties about rain-fed agriculture, farmers were complaining about the high cost of farm labour. To clear
an acre of land cost a farmer 40,000 cedis and another 20,000 cedis
for weeding. Harvesting payments were variable, but in one case,
one out of every eleven baskets of maize harvested was for the harvester. As farm labour could be combined with own account farming and other activities, it allowed farm-labourers much more flexibility
than fishing assistants who were in some cases also expected to assist
with farming in addition to the main activities for which they were
hired. The following cases describe the workings of some of the
labour arrangements around the Lake.

CASE 8.4: Samuel, migrated as an Assistant, Kudikope

Samuel, a Mepe man now in his 50s, came to Kudikope in 1993. He had been working at Asesewa selling nets when in 1979 and the early 80s, government directives under the coup d'etat regimes led by Flt. Lt. Jerry Rawlings banned traders such as him from trading in fishing nets. Although the ban was eased, it destroyed his capital base and after a few years of struggling, he decided to move to a farming area to secure some capital to get back into the fishing net trade. In all he had spent seventeen years at Asesewa. Before then, he had been at Ampaem on the Lake for seven years keeping shop for a Mepe man who sold nets. He had gone there after school and a year of teaching in the Lower Volta.

He was taken to Accra by his mother's younger brother who was to find him work. There, a Mepe man came and took him to Ampaem in 1969. He was paid yearly, fed and clothed and promised rooms in the house his master was building, as reward for his services. Indeed his master put up a three-storey house at Mepe but the rooms were never given to him. As he was quite young at the start of the relationship, he had been quite happy with the arrangement and worked hard. At the time, his master had very young children. Once they grew up, Samuel's services were no longer needed and so he was released by the master. As he recalls, "his attitude changed and he asked me to go and I did. I was afraid to demand that he fulfil his promises because he was a medicine man and believed to have the super-natural power to hurt others".

Samuel went back to his mother at Mepe to seek her help. She loaned him money left in her care by her paternal cousin who was a migrant in the Kpando area supplemented by contributions by herself and her sister who, like her, was farming at Mepe. He described the loan as a little money, but it allowed him to start something. He decided to try his hand at selling nets for himself at Asesewa because it was close to the Volta Lake and a reasonably large market town. This was in 1975. He began to trade in nets in several markets around the Asesewa area. He was able to acquire some credit from suppliers and was also able to extend credit to those of his customers who could not pay immediately. Before long, he had paid back the loan and gave some gifts in appreciation.

In 1977, he married a Kwahu woman from Mpraeso who had come to Asesewa to work. They had two children. He had already had a child with a Mepe woman who was staying with relations at Ampaem in 1974 while he was still with his master. He could not marry her while in the service of a master.

He had barely established himself in his trade when the Rawlings coup d'etat in 1979 disrupted his trade. When his work collapsed in 1982, he went to stay with his mother for a year to recover and then went back to Asesewa, this time to farm. He did this until 1992 when he decided to leave and try his fortune elsewhere along the Lake. When he left Ampaem, his wife also left and went to her people.

He had relations at Kudikope, some paternal cross cousins, and so he came here. He acquired one acre of rain-fed land and a much smaller plot (2/10 of an acre) of Lakeside land for farming. In time, he became active in community affairs, taught voluntarily at the settlement's school when there were no teachers and was now in the leadership of the settlement.

CASE 8.5: Korwu, fishing assistant, Kudikope

Korwu, a Mepe man of 37-years, was working as a fishing assistant to a Ningo fisherman. He was single, did not have children and did not attend any of the churches. He stopped school in class 3 because his mother died and he had no one to take responsibility for his education. Korwu was born at Mepe and he remembers that his mother used to sell things, but he was not sure what. He was the 7th born of his mother's eight children. Only three were alive today, two of them women staying at Mepe, one trading between Accra, the Lakeside and Mepe and the other a seamstress. He grew up at Mepe and was 18 years when his mother died. Once he dropped out of school, he decided to come to the Lakeside and went to a place near Nketepa. He did not know anyone there. On arrival, he went to the Headman and told him that he was looking for someone to work for. The Headman said he could stay with him until he found someone. He stayed for less than a month when a Mepe man took him on as a fishing assistant. They agreed that he would be paid a fixed sum after a year. When the year was up, he called his master before the chief who had been witness to the agreement and he was paid.

He and his master worked together in the boat, just the two of them. His work was to set the net and retrieve it from the depths of the Lake whenever it got stuck. Both of them repaired the net when it was torn. His master's wife smoked the fish and cooked for them. They worked from dawn to 12.00 noon each day.

He stayed for a few years. Then he became unhappy because he was not being treated well and he was not satisfied with the accounting. They were also no longer catching the amounts of fish they used to catch before and sometimes the catch was so poor that they did not get enough to eat. His master no longer paid him what was agreed and only gave him half the agreed sum for a four-year period. He, therefore, left the master's services after conveying his decision to the Headman too, pleading the deterioration of the catch.

He then went to Dzemeni in early 1997 to look for a new master. He approached a Ningo fisherman who had come to market from Kudikope and asked if he could become his fishing assistant. The man said he would think about it and came back after two weeks to offer him the position. They agreed that they would do the accounting at the end of the year, just before the Ningo Homowo festival. This was in the 8th month of the year. They divided the earnings into two, one part went to the boat and nets and the other half to the members of the Company (made up of seven persons including the boat-owner and his wife). In addition to Korwu, there were four children. The oldest, a fifteen-year old, was the son of the owner and the other three his relations. The boat owner as "father" of the four collected their earnings on their behalf. The year before, Korwu earned ¢200,000 and was yet to be paid for the year as his master had gone off for his hometown festival. All the assistants were paid the same amount even though they did not have the same skills. Some of the children were so young that they could not mend nets. Their main task was bailing water out of the boat. There were two boats and two nets. One of the boats was used mainly for hook fishing. All the six fishermen in the Company went to the Lake every day. The Company also had an outboard motor and they purchased fuel at Dzemeni. Their fishing grounds were all around the Lake.

The fish was smoked and sold at Dzemeni market by the wife of the owner of the boats. She bought the fish at a price determined by the Head of the Company paying for it only after returning from the market. Korwu's master had four wives and they worked for the Company in turns rotating every two years. When it was not their turn to work for the Company, they sold other goods or fish bought from other fishermen. Food expenditure was financed from the sale of stink fish, which was not part of the fish for which accounts were kept. In Korwu's view, the stink fish was very lucrative because it represented about a quarter (1/4) of the catch. Food expenditure could be extended to the replacement of clothing worn in the kitchen. Other everyday expenditure on health and clothes were bought out of the Company's earnings. For any other needs, a member of the Company could take an advance on their earnings. That year, Korwu had taken an advance to send to his father at Mepe. He also sent his yearly earnings to his father who was building him a house at Mepe. Korwu preferred earning a fixed sum every year to the accounting process, which resulted in variable earnings.

Korwu had never farmed seriously, although he sometimes helped on the farm when he was not on the Lake. The women did the farming when they were free while the men were on the Lake. They were not selling the foodstuffs from the farm because it was meant for food. Korwu lived in the Ningo quarter of Kudikope because he was working for a Ningo fisherman. This was the third year into his four-year contract and he was not sure if he had enough money to begin to fish on his own. According to him, you needed ¢2 million to acquire a boat and a net to begin. He went to Mepe only once in two or three years. Because he was an assistant, it was difficult for him to go there as often as he liked. Moreover, the monthly festival period was a very good time for fishing and the master liked to take advantage of this period. They went fishing seven days a week only resting when they were tired.

CASE 8.6: Agblemor, Head Assistant to a woman's boat, Kudikope

Agblemor was a 36-year-old Anlo Ewe man from Galosota. He grew up there and went to school for 10 years, but failed his middle school-leaving certificate examinations. That was the period of national food shortages and everyone was hungry, the teachers as well. They, therefore, did not teach them much that year. After school, he came to the Volta Lake in 1986 to a place called Akorkorma where he lived for three years with his mother's brother helping him with his farming and fishing. They used both basket traps and a net. His uncle did not pay him, but bought him clothes and food and his needs. He then went to Accra to live with another uncle to learn masonry. After one year of studying, he went to his hometown for the Easter and decided to return to Akorkorma because he was unhappy with the restrictions he had to live under in Accra. He was 20 then.

He did more fishing at Akorkorma for his uncle until 1991 when his uncle brought him to Kudikope. His uncle's sister needed Agblemor's services to assist her own fishing business. There were five of them—Agblemor, his aunt's son and three others, working with her canoe. Once they brought in the fish, they would clean it and she would smoke it and take it to the market. She accounted to them every two weeks. The earnings were divided into three, one for the boat and nets and two parts for the Company's workers after the cost of food and other inputs had been subtracted. Out of the 2/3, they paid the three boys varying sums according to their age and knowledge of work i.e. experience. In 1998 for example, one 20-year old was paid 120,000 for the year, an 11-year old earned 56,000, while a third 11-year old was given a goat that cost about 30,000. Every year, they would go and recruit boys from Juapong and other places in the Lower Volta. For the first time, there were no boys because there was a problem with the boat and they were yet to repair it. He also had a farm, one acre of cassava, pepper and maize. He rented the land from a woman at Gyakiti as an *abusa* tenant. His wife was making *garri* from his cassava and selling at Dzemeni market. She would give the money to him on her return from the market. After a year of staying in his aunt's room, Aglemor built a three-room house with the help of some people in the community whom he fed and bought drinks for in return for their labour. He lived close to other Anlo and Avenor people in the community.

In 1998, his wife had needed an operation, which cost about 1 million cedis. He had to borrow 300,000 of that amount and the rest came from his savings, which he had kept with someone in a nearby village, Ametsitsikope. He borrowed from a Ningo man because he could not raise the loan from his own community. He was still in debt as a result. That year would have been good but for his wife's illness.

While Agblemor was doing better here than at Akorkorma, it was still a precarious existence. He had originally planned to stay for a short while and go home, but the work had not been good. He felt that there was no longer the chance to make serious money at Kudikope. "The money has already been made. Those who came early have made the money and gone", he said. In the past, hook fishing had been good, but it was no longer the case especially since they had no outboard engines and, therefore, were forced to fish in shallow water. Paddling was tedious when the wind was high and they could not predict when that would happen on any day on the Lake. This was making their work difficult.

He was still thinking of gaining independence as a fisherman. He estimated that it could be done with 500,000 cedis which would make a canoe, one net and a hook (*efe*). It was important to have nets, hooks and basket traps because of the changes in fishing patterns every few months. When the Lake flooded in August, this was the basket trap season.

CASE 8.8: *Tseko, 45, Ningo Fishing Company Head, Kudikope*

Tseko at 45 started his fishing career first at Cotonou in Benin where he was an assistant to a master fisherman for one year and then to Yeji where he served another fisherman for two years. After this, he went to Kpando Torkor to work with two of his brothers, one older and one younger, in a partnership. With their savings from Yeji, they bought a boat and net and took eight children from families at Ningo. His third wife joined him at the Lake. There she smoked fish, sold it at the market and accounted to her husband's brother who kept the earnings. At first she was the only woman in the company, but Tseko's brothers soon married. The youngest of the three brothers was unhappy with the accounting and took his share of the business and left the company. The oldest and his wife then took over the marketing of the fish. Tseko demanded that his wife also be allowed to participate in the marketing of fish, but this brought acrimony. After an incident in which she was refused fish which she needed to procure treatment for her sick son, she left and returned to her grandmother. The problem had to be settled formally at home and Tseko's older brother was fined. The brothers settled their differences and decided to work separately. The business was again divided and Tseko began to work on his own. Sometime in 1975, he heard that Kudikope was good, so he went there with three wives, five children and the fishing assistants. There was already a group of Ningo fishermen living there. There again, someone sponsored his fishing for a few years and then he was finally free. These days his own children were working with him. He also had a 15-year-old boy he had hired. He did not render accounts to his own children, but their needs were provided for. He looked forward to a day when he would help them set up on their own, but that time had not come yet. He sold the fish to his wife who in turn sold it, keeping whatever she earned over and above his sale price.

Sometime in 1984, he began to use an outboard motor. These days he had six different nets for fishing and two outboard motors which were over ten years old. He believed they could be used for another five years with good maintenance and the availability of spare parts. A replacement 25-horsepower outboard motor would cost four million cedis. Tseko's fish was sold at Dzemeni and Marine markets once or twice every week by his third wife. They had regular customers at both places. The dead fish was salted to preserve it as stink fish. It paid for food, sundries and other everyday needs. However, whenever dead fish was a significant part of the catch, sometimes more than what could be smoked, Tseko's wife had to account for it. The household had a two-acre cassava farm for which they hired labour. On the days they did not go to fish, the men in the company would go to the farm.

Two of Tseko's children also had farms. Tseko's wife estimated the Company's earnings at 100,000 every two weeks. Tseko was not sure what he earned but his earnings enabled him to buy a car once, but it broke down. He also had a corn-mill and a bicycle and was building a cement blockhouse in his hometown. He hoped to buy some livestock (cows and goats) as part of his retirement plan although he expected his children to maintain him when he could not work anymore. Much of his equipment had been bought from his own earnings because he had a policy against borrowing money for work. However, his wife's father had given them a loan. Tseko, however, had regular customers who were good for the times when fish was not selling well.

These cases throw light on various aspects of labour relations around the Lake. One of these is the intersection of kinship and labour relations in livelihoods. Samuel's account (Case 8.4) is punctuated by the interventions of kin of different degrees of closeness at critical moments in his life. Kinship was the route through which he entered into a relationship which proved unrewarding. At the same time, family relations softened his fall and made recovery possible. It was a relation, entrusted to find him work who had arranged for him to work as an assistant to the Mepe man. The informal terms of the relationship had proved to be detrimental when after working for many years without much remuneration, the promises of future rewards did not materialise. Because of his youth and inexperience and the informality of the relationship, he had been content to work on promises. When they failed to materialise, he pursued no remedies for fear of supernatural sanctions. The fear of witchcraft was an important element in power situations, sometimes deployed to augment the power of the less powerful or to make invincible the already more powerful in any relationship. His mother's help was decisive anytime he faced a crisis whether as a source of credit or as a refuge, which allowed him to recover from a failed enterprise. It was family relations who had given him shelter when he first arrived and then helped him to settle at Kudikope and later establish himself as one of the settlement's leaders.

In the fishing community, labour relationships of a similar nature were even more common as the cases of Korwu (8.5) and Agblemor (8.6), who were around the same age, show. However, the two cases also demonstrate the variability in labour relations within the fishing industry. Between Korwu (Case 8.5) and Agblemor (Case 8.6), the latter was in the better position because he was the head fishing assistant to a woman boat owner. As we have already indicated, women boat owners did not have the same relationship with the Company as male owners. The benefits derived from the injection of capital into fishing were gendered. Thus Agblemor and other members of the crew could among them earn 2/3 of the proceeds.

Agblemor could be said to be reaping the rewards of serving his old master for many years by being promoted to become the head fisherman for this man's sister's boat. When he had worked for the man, he received no formal payment. Not all fishing assistants were rewarded in this way. In spite of his better situation, that his wife's illness left him in debt suggests that in spite of the fairer terms of his employment, the relatively small scale of their operation exerted constraints. However, independence was within his reach although he would have to operate on a small scale and face problems similar to what he had to deal with at present. On the other hand, he too would have assistants who would put in more labour than they would receive in wages. Korwu on the other hand, looked very far away from becoming a master fisherman. He was in his second stint as a fishing assistant. This time, he was working with a fisherman with an outboard motor and, therefore, with the potential to earn more money, but there were also more fishing assistants to be paid. Although he tried to send money home for his father's maintenance and for building a house, his situation was precarious and he had had to take an advance on his earnings during the year. His hours were also very long and he had no other livelihood activities unlike Agblemor who had a farm.

Korwu's account was also interesting in what it revealed about the ways in which Company Heads kept their declared earnings

down. In this connection, his employer was unusual in paying each
member of the crew the same amount irrespective of their ages and
contributions. Could this be because he was the one to whom the
share of the four minors was going as their "father"? In remarking
that the "stink fish", i.e. the sun-dried rotten fish, was outside the
official accounts in spite of being substantial sometimes, he was draw-
ing attention to another way in which fishermen rewarded their wives
without declaring this to the Company.[21] While the Head fisherman's
wives reaped the benefits of the under declaration of earnings in this
case, their having to do these rotating-two-yearly-stints with the
Company made their positions more precarious than it appeared.

Unlike Agblemor who was able to visit his hometown as often as
he desired and who had a wife and family, Korwu was the quin-
tessential fishing assistant who could not be seen to be acquiring
responsibilities while in the service of his master. He had even opted
to stay in his master's quarter of the community and had few dealings with fellow Tongu Ewe people. The accounts of other fishing
assistants (not presented here because of space constraints) suggest
that innovations developed by fishermen to improve their catch were
labour-intensive and made great demands on the assistants. Their
experiences of the accounting and pay practices demonstrate why
fishing assistants these days did not stand much of a chance to
become independent, particularly if they did not have the support
of fishermen fathers. From badly kept accounts to being paid in
instalments and master fishermen reneging on agreed terms, fishing
assistants were in a precarious situation.

The labour relations within the fishing companies were not simply between the company owners and their assistants. Intricately
involved in these relations were the women who cooked for the company and preserved the fish. Within the context of household production relations, women were engaged in fish preservation and sale
and in looking after the Company's food needs. Through this, they
became an added layer within what were complicated labour relations. Korwu's case, for example, raises this issue. In several other
accounts, the wives of Company Heads were considered by fishing
assistants as part of the exploitative edifice, conniving with their hus-

---

[21] This is buttressed by the fact that in other accounts, it was noted that when
the rotten fish came in large quantities, it became part of the official harvest and
had to be accounted for.

bands to cheat fishing assistants. As one young man who had completed two stints as fishing assistant said of them:

> If you don't have your own net, you will never do well. You have to accept the master's accounting. When there is a lot of work, they start misbehaving towards you. The women won't cook early and they will insult you at the least opportunity. Sometimes they will say you have misbehaved if you react to their provocations and they will fine you two bottles of drink. The various fines are then subtracted from your pay. You could also be tried and fined for quarrels or any kind of trouble you get into outside the work situation and all that is deducted from your earnings. If you sell a bit of fish for chop money, you can be accused of stealing and you could be sacked mid-season and even paid nothing (fishing assistant, 25 years old, Kpando Torkor).

As in these intersecting social relations, the reality was much more complicated. As already discussed, wives themselves were struggling to gain a foothold in the Companies and to receive a fair remuneration for their services in the context of marital instability. Thus, while their strategies to gain more resources through the control of dried rotten fish and their tensions with fishing assistants disadvantaged the latter financially, they were not simply part of a monolithic power structure within the fishing Company.

The lack of satisfactory remedies for bad fishing contracts was a serious institutional problem around the Lake. Samuel and Korwu's cases allow the examination of the options (or lack of them) of fishing assistants in what was an unequal relationship. While institutions such as the *Tɔkɔfia* mediated conflicts between fishermen and their assistants and the Headmen could mediate in the case of other livelihood activities, the power relations were such that most assistants left the employ of their masters in search of new labour relations rather than litigate to get redress. Given the numbers of people in need of such work around the Lake and the labour reserves represented by the Lower Volta and the coastal areas of Ghana, child and adult labour on such exploitative terms was not about to dry up.

All round the Lake, there were several Master fishermen who had been fishing assistants in their youth. Their success as fishermen depended on factors such as when they gained independence, their ability to save as assistants or to secure help on generous terms from relations and also, in some cases, from fathers. In addition, their ability to buy and use outboard motors as well as secure the labour of others on quite exploitative terms was critical. Tseko (Case 8.7), a Dangme fisherman at Kudikope, was an example of a fishing assistant who had made the transition to master. The main difference between Tseko who was in his mid 40s and Korwu and Agblemor who were in their late 30s and were still apprentices was their age and fishing traditions. By the time Tseko became an independent fisherman, the industry was still quite good. Tseko had been able to tap into the Dangme fishing company traditions and also buy an outboard motor at a critical time. Both Korwu and Agblemor did not see their trajectories in terms of owning outboard motors and having numerous assistants, partly because they came from a different fishing tradition. Tseko's insistence on not borrowing money to improve his livelihood activities reflects the sentiments of several of the fishermen interviewed. In addition or perhaps because of the consequences of indebtedness such as having to have a preferential trading arrangement with a creditor, there appeared to be a sense that there was something untoward about borrowing from strangers to upgrade livelihood activities. Even those who had had to take loans from kin to finance their activities would not contemplate such arrangements with traders.

Samuel's case also demonstrates the impact of national events and political upheavals such as the coups d'états of the 1970s and early 80s on rural livelihoods whose distance from the capitals might suggest otherwise. In some cases, they triggered migration to the Lake, while in others, they disrupted the livelihoods of especially traders. Time and context were also critical to livelihoods. As someone who gained independence long after the first wave of migration, Samuel's conditions for making a living were not as good as those of the first migrants and those who migrated when he did, not as assistants, but as independent operators. In the late 70s and 80s, a combination of the decline in fish stocks, government regulation banning traders such as himself disrupted many livelihoods.

Labour relations between women

Relations among women involved in the fishing industry was another dimension of the labour relations around the Volta Lake. Women who cooked and preserved fish for Companies were assisted by younger women and girls. Without several trusted assistants, the successes of some of the fish traders would not have been possible. The informalised and layered character of these relations made them potentially more exploitative than those between the master fishermen and their assistants. At the very least, fishing assistants were acknowledged as hired labour and terms with them agreed from the start, even if such terms were honoured more in the breach. Also in some cases, kinship between the parties meant that no formal terms and conditions were ever set. The assistants of the Company cooks were affected by the more ambiguous positions of their mistresses. Similarly, the assistants of fish traders had neither fixed terms nor conventions regarding terms. Lucky's case is an example of such a relationship.

CASE 8.8: Lucky, ex-fishing assistant, Kpando Torkor

> Lucky, 48 years old, a Sokpoe native resident at Kpando Torkor was born at Berekum in the Brong Ahafo Region where her mother and father were working as cocoa labourers. She grew up at Sokpoe where she finished middle school. She then went to commercial school in Accra and stayed with her mother's younger brother for three years. She completed her training in 1977 and taught at a primary school in Accra from 1977–1981. In 1982, owing to ill health, she went to live with her mother's sister to farm and sell fish at a market town in the Eastern Region. She married a man she met while she was in commercial school in 1979. After some years, the marriage broke down.
>
> She left the Eastern Region in 1983 and went back to Sokpoe. While at Sokpoe, she did no work. She left after a year and came to Kpando Torkor. The wife of her uncle (Auntie Mary), with whom she had lived in Accra, brought her to Torkor to assist her to trade in fish. Auntie Mary continued to live in Accra, coming to Torkor the day before a market day and leaving for Accra the day after the market day. She had pre-financed nets for people at Torgodo and Lucky and another assistant would go to different villages to collect fish in return. Lucky had three villages and she was collecting fish from eight Ada and Ningo fishermen. Auntie Mary was not working with Tongu fishermen because her past experiences with them had not been good.
>
> The fish Lucky collected was sold to Auntie Mary at an already agreed price. It was Lucky's responsibility to record the amount of fish she was given in a notebook. In August, when the fishermen were ready to go to their hometowns, they would come to Torkor and accounts would be rendered. Auntie Mary would pay them for their fish and they would pay her for the net. During the year, if they needed any money, they would come and collect it and Auntie Mary would record it against their earnings. When they returned from their festival, the cycle would start again. Lucky did this work for three years until 1987. She had now stopped working for Auntie Mary, but the work was still going on. At the time she stopped in 1987, their fish purchasing capital was one million cedis.

During the time she worked for Auntie Mary, Lucky was given money for food and maintenance the whole year. After accounts had been rendered with the fishermen, her aunt would give her some money. Lucky farmed to supplement her income, working on her farm during Kpando Torkor market days when her services were not required by her aunt. Auntie Mary, whose parents lived at Kpando Torkor, had a three-room laterite-block house which was plastered with cement, painted and roofed with thatch. Lucky was given a room in the house during her years of service. Since then, Lucky had hired her own rooms, three rooms for 6,000 cedis a month. She was growing maize and cassava on an acre of rain-fed land for which she was paying 10,000 cedis a year. When she began to work for herself, she also began to buy fish for sale at Kpando Torkor. She made a net for a fisherman but did not get much money so now she was no longer doing that. She did not have the capital to go to Accra to sell fish and fishermen, especially those across the Lake, did not give fish out on credit unless the buyer had bought a net for them.

Trading in fish was capital-intensive because buyers from Accra sometimes bought the fish on credit and the trader had to go and buy some more fish while waiting for them to pay. A basket of fish cost 500,000 cedis. While it was possible to take a loan from fellow migrants at Kpando Torkor, and there was also money left with people at Kpando Torkor by those living across the Lake to be loaned out, taking a loan could be risky. There was no guarantee of the availability of fish on each trip and the fish could go bad and land the trader in debt.

Lucky had also stopped going to Torgodo in order to make time for community leadership work having been elected to a position the year before. Since 1992, she had held some positions in community leadership. Not going to Torgodo meant that she could start farming more seriously. In addition, she was getting part of the 20% commission given to community leaders who were assisting with the collection of taxes. She also had three goats with her at Kpando Torkor and was hoping to buy more. She had recently acquired land to build a house but was yet to pay for it. With her own house, her animal rearing could be put on a more serious footing.

An important source of support for Lucky was the church. When she was ill recently, they gave her 1.5 million cedis towards treatment. She was also close to the catechist and a female church member from Agave. She felt so close to the church that she was thinking of making a net for a member of the church. For the past two years, since 1997, she had also been co-ordinating a small rotating credit scheme that used to have twenty members but now had sixteen. Every market day, they each contributed 5,000 cedis to be given to the member who needed it most. It was also possible to take a loan from the collection and a commission of 1,000 cedis was taken on each week's collection to be paid to the co-ordinator of the scheme. She was aware of the existence of similar credit arrangements within Kpando Torkor.

Lucky's household was made up of herself, her brother and the son of another brother. She had not married because she could not have children these days, having had one child twenty-six years ago. Her son had completed polytechnic and had a Higher National Diploma and was a teacher at a Kpong Dam Resettlement. He had attended secondary school at Koforidua and had never lived at Kpando Torkor because of his education.

Lucky's years as an assistant fish trader had not yielded much except experience which she was unable to put fully to use because of the lack of capital. While loans were available, she was wary of getting into debt and, therefore, had not availed herself of any of this money. Instead, she had put her relatively high level of education to good use by participating in settlement leadership structures. Through that she was receiving commission for tax collection. Her education also enabled her to coordinate a rotating credit scheme among a group of women. These sources were supplementing her farming and nascent livestock-keeping activities. Kinship relations had not been as helpful for Lucky as had church membership. While she had been at the receiving end of unfair labour relations underpinned by kinship, she had received financial support from the church in a time of illness. She was also expecting that the church would act as moral authority and arbiter of a net pre-financing arrangement she was considering with a fellow church member.

6. *Child Labour in Migrant Communities*

There were numerous minors working around the Lake who were in an even more vulnerable situation than the adults described above. In migrant communities, many young people helped their parents with livelihood activities in return for maintenance. Some children of school-going age worked to support their education in farming, fishing and the care of livestock. Some respondents, particularly the fishermen, had had their children working with them for years until they became adults themselves and were set up in their own fishing businesses. In certain cases, fathers handed over the business to their sons when they became too old or wanted to concentrate on other livelihood activities. These children had been taught skills and they inherited their father's equipment when he gave up fishing. They often organised their fishing in much the same way as their father,

using the same technologies and labour relations. With the spread
of formal education, the process of handing down skills and equipment to sons was becoming less common. Scores of young adult
males were found in classrooms along the Lake thus rupturing these
socialising and labour relations. However, high school dropout rates
meant that, depending on the stage at which they dropped out, some
children did take on their parents' livelihood activities, fishing, farming and trading. Some of these though, preferred to do it independently from their parents. The older fishermen have attributed this
to indiscipline. However, the high incidence of paid labour relations
within different livelihood activities along the Lakeside might be a
factor in children preferring to work for others for money instead
of future gains such as being set up in business or inheriting their
parents' activities and resources.

Several children brought up in migrant settlements left when they
finished school. This process of children growing up in migrant settlements and leaving as adults existed side by side with a movement
in the opposite direction which involved bringing children of poor
households from home-towns in the Lower Volta and elsewhere into
migrant settlements as "hired labour". As some of our cases demonstrate, this was one of the ways in which the fishing industry addressed
its labour needs. Thus, fishermen used the labour of other peoples'
children while their own children went on to other things. Farming
activities have also been affected by school. Many farmers now used
children's labour only periodically, and hired labour instead for several key activities. However, the education of farmers' children was
threatened by the relative poverty of their parents and in several
cases, boys and girls in school had been given small plots of land
on which to grow crops to help pay for their education.

The children recruited from the Lower Volta and elsewhere were
in some cases as young as eight years and working full-time for very
poor wages because they did not have particular skills. The gendered character of child labour had implications for the life-chances
of girls and boys in migrant villages and reproduced gender relations
in production. For example, a four-year stint as a cattle herder earned
a boy a calf. According to local wisdom, this was to safeguard education at a later stage. At the end of the period, the boy was expected
to return to his parents and be looked after in primary school. During
this period, he could engage in casual labour to help. In later years,

when the costs of schooling became high, the calf would hopefully have grown and multiplied enough to support him. It was not certain how many boys actually realised this vision as planned, since a cow could die or never have calves, but this view was entrenched within Tongu Ewe communities. It might have been popularised by parents and guardians in need or fearful of the future, but even those who on the face of it could afford to educate their children had embraced it. Thus a few of the herd boys were the children of kraal owners who were not on the breadline. One such child at Kudikope had been taken off fishing and put on the cattle herding schedule, the suggestion being that the rewards from cattle herding were superior to what was earned by fishing assistants, not to mention the dangers they faced each day they set off to the Lake.

For girls, there were no such opportunities for wage labour, even with all its problems from a growing child's point of view. A young girl in school who was having difficulty with school fees could expect to do some petty trading or generally help her parents in their work in the hope that her fees would be paid and she would be given daily pocket money. While around the Lake this translated into girls in school being younger than boys, they were also more vulnerable if parents or guardians decided that school was not affordable. Furthermore, it could be argued that the deliberation and planning which set boys to work to finance their future education was missing in the case of girls.

One result of migration and migrant life was that people tended to have both minor and adult children living in different places around the Lake and in the Lower Volta.[22] This phenomenon of children of the same parents leading different lives appeared to be more a function of marital instability and some of the implications of patrilinity than the inability to care for children, although increasingly, financial considerations were playing a part. There was no telling what would happen to the children when a relationship broke down. Often, the principle of patrilinity gave men legal control over their children even when they did not have the conditions to bring

---

[22] An example is Lucy (Case 8.3, Surveyor Line) who said, "Two of my children are at Mepe, the older boy is going to school while the younger is married and living at Mepe with her husband. One child is at Dzemeni Torgodo with my sister. She is trading for her and does not go to school."

them up themselves. It was common for children to live with their father's mother until they were old enough to decide where and with whom they wanted to reside. Depending on how acrimonious the breakup was, some women had no form of access to their children. If they contracted another marriage and more children were born, this could happen again.

For these and other reasons related to the larger political economy of the Lake, children's prospects in migrant settlements were not particularly good. Even where parents were willing and able to educate their children, the distances from schools and the generally low quality of schools in migrant settlements defeated them. The distractions for children were numerous and many of them succumbed. The teachers at Kpando Torkor observed that certain girls did not come to school on market days, and with mothers and guardians threatening to take them out altogether if teachers raised too many questions, it was considered prudent not to challenge them. The high age of children, especially the boys in primary school posed particular challenges for them and their fellow pupils. Parents were less inclined to look after adults in school and girls were more vulnerable to pregnancy, which in turn created new responsibilities, which further blighted their future prospects.

7. Older Migrants and the Decline in Livelihoods Around the Volta Lake

With the decline in fishing and the vicissitudes of rain-fed agriculture, migrant settlements lost their status as places where people could make a decent living and accumulate savings and property if they were hardworking. While livelihood activities were yielding more at the Lake than in the Lower Volta, there were visible signs that all was not well around the Lake. Literally, every household at Surveyor Line and the majority at Kudikope, were spending hours and days processing cassava and several had stacks of maize in their wooden silos. The low prices of foodstuffs such as maize and processed cassava (a tin of *garri* was 1,000 cedis), supported the observation that a good harvest was necessary but not sufficient for good livelihood outcomes. In all the migrant settlements, particularly Kpando Torkor, there were constant references to Tɔgodo residents who were able to fish, farm and rear animals and, therefore, were still able to enjoy much better livelihood outcomes in spite of their more difficult living conditions. A small minority of traders and service providers mostly found at Kpando Torkor who sold basic consumer goods such as sugar, rice, drinks, tinned foods and medicines, appeared to have the strongest basis for long-term security. Even then, those whose services were connected with the fishing industry, e.g. dealers in fishing equipment, experienced the fluctuations in the fishing industry.

Some of the inhabitants of migrant settlements, particularly the older ones, were visibly struggling. In spite of being past their active working life, they continued with low intensity activities such as animal rearing, collecting rent on housing and earnings on capital equipment and support from economically active children. Some of the older migrants were also vulnerable because many of their children were still living around the Lake and also having to cope with the decline in fishing and farming. The worst off were the old women who after all these years had nothing to show for the tons of fish they had preserved and sold on behalf of others. Few of them had property, cattle, nets, boats and outboard motors on hire from which they could continue to receive some money. At best they had land they farmed when they were strong enough to do so. Those who had adult children and siblings in the settlements lived with or close to them and were supported by them. The following cases examine the conditions of some of the older migrants.

CASE 8.9: Damali, early successes no guarantee of long-term security, Kpando Torkor

> Damali, who was born around the time of the first smallpox epidemic, was in her 80s from her own reckoning. She lived at Kpando Torkor where she and her husband and their four children migrated to soon after the Akosombo Dam. They were one of the earliest settlers there and experienced the constant movement to higher ground to escape the flooding of the Lake until the shoreline settled. She also recalled that the first "Stranger chief", Gbadagbali, then lived at a place called Aglama before it all merged into Kpando Torkor. She already had a track record of buying and selling fish and farming in a settlement on the Volta River where she had grown up as a child of migrant Bakpa (Lower Volta) parents. She had met her husband, a Bakpa man, there. The floods of the Dam drove them from there and they came to Kpando Torkor.
>
> On arrival, she continued with the fish trade. From early on, she bought her husband's fish as she did in the pre-dam days. In addition, she went around Tɔgodo buying fish from others with whom she had established buying relations. She then conveyed the fish, which

was mainly smoked fish but also salted and sun-dried tilapia, to an
Accra market where there were women who sold the fish and accounted
to them for it. These middle women were mostly Ga, but a few Tongu
women living in Accra were also involved. The arrangement of having fish sold for you was very widespread and quite well established
in the market. Going to Accra entailed making overnight trips sometimes and she was hosted for years by a fellow Tongu woman who
lived in Accra. Sometimes, she also sold the fish at Kpando Torkor
to other colleague fishmongers who then sold it in Accra. In addition
to fish, she sometimes sold preserved game purchased from hunters.
She used to save her money at the Commercial Bank at Kpando.

In some years she established net financing relations with fishermen.
The arrangement was that they would pay her back in instalments.
In the meantime, she still had to pay for the fish she purchased from
them. She had found the fish business rewarding, but it all depended
on the quality of relations with the fishermen and their families. As
she notes, "If the people are truthful, you can make money. I even
had enough money to buy land and build a house at Kpando Aziavi.
It was twelve rooms, laterite blocks, cement plastered with aluminium
sheets for roofing. I lived in one room and rented the rest. The people who gave me the land then gave it to a school. They paid us compensation. There were four of us involved, two from Kpando Torkor.
I was also able to buy two transport boats. I sold them when the work
stopped going well". Damali was also able to build a five-roomed house
of cement roofed with aluminium sheets at Bakpa.

Losing the house at Kpando was a big blow. She moved to Kpando
Torkor where she built a new house of laterite bricks plastered with
cement with a thatch roof. It had three rooms. She rented one and
left the other for "visitors" who included passengers on her boats who
had to sleep over. She built another four rooms for her children.
During her active working life, she had the children of relations living with her. She took three daughters of her brother who helped with
the household chores and fish preservation. All three of them never
went to school and became involved in fish buying on their own
account. In the days she used to travel to Torgodo, she would travel
with her assistants who carried the fish and cooked the meals. Another
young woman would remain at Kpando Torkor cooking for the four
to five men in the transport boat she owned. They were not paid
wages. Instead, they were clothed so in her words, they "would look
decent among their peers during festival celebrations".

She had her sons and other relations, "grandchildren" working for
her on her two transport boats. At the end of each month, they shared
the proceeds into three—one for the boat, one for the outboard motor
and the last part for the workers. She did not know in what proportions the workers share was distributed. Her son was in charge of sharing the proceeds. The proceeds were shared only after the money for
fuel and the daily maintenance of the crew had been subtracted. A

daily amount was given to those of the boys who were not fed by her. She had the boats for years and sold them three days before a serious boat accident at Amankwa Tornu.

She had been advised to sell the boats and buy a vehicle for the road. The vehicle she bought from the proceeds of the sale of the boats was so old that it did not work. It looked new, but was very old. She would have known if this was a boat. She gave a second vehicle to a "grandson" to run and share the proceeds with her. He went to Dzemeni and disappeared without rendering accounts in 1990. She reported this to the police but he was still at large. This happened about ten years before the interview.

She had bought cows out of her earnings years ago. She built a kraal and put the venture in the care of the son of a cousin. At one time, she was told there were nineteen cows. The numbers being reported kept on fluctuating and then she was told that some of the cows belonged to another person. The issue went to litigation and she ended up with four cows which she then left with another relation. Litigating over the cows cost her money and at her age, she was too old to find the resources to invest in any more ventures. These days, she had retired from fish selling and was farming a small piece of land by the Lake and receiving some support from her children.

CASE 8.10: Amenorvi, struggling after years of migrant life working with her estranged husband, Surveyor Line

Amenorvi was in her mid to late 60s, and was separated from her husband of many years although they both lived at Surveyor Line. She and her husband had arrived in the late 60s or early 70s. She had been born at Mepe and she was an adult, picking clams and farming when the Akosombo Dam had been constructed. When clam picking deteriorated, they came to Surveyor Line. He fished and farmed and sold his fish to the local Akan people. She farmed.

Her current household was made up of herself, her adult daughter, a young adult son and six children of her daughter who were between the ages of 15 and 2, the last two a set of twins. An 11-year old son of her daughter was not in school. They lived in a four-roomed laterite-block house with a thatch roof in a compound that used to belong to someone who had left the settlement. They had had to renovate the house with resources from her farming when they moved in about ten years ago. Amenorvi and her two children were farming separately, but helped each other with farm work, especially at the beginning of the farming season. The farms were on rain-fed land and hers was less than an acre. Her daughter who was 35 had an even smaller farm and her young 22-year-old son had $1\frac{1}{4}$ acres. They could not employ labour and so their farms were small. She grew cassava and groundnuts and sold about half the produce and used the rest for food. Her children also brought some of their food for the household's consumption.

Amenorvi also made *garri*, two or three times a month or when she needed money urgently, with cassava she purchased. She would make about 8–9,000 cedis worth of *garri* on each occasion. Her daughter sometimes helped her to peel the cassava and she sold it herself at Gyakiti if it was not much or across the lake at Dzemeni if there was at least a sack of it. She could not estimate her earnings from her farm, but thought it might be around 200,000 cedis a year. Because the garri was produced and sold in small quantities, she was not able to estimate her earnings. She was responsible for buying food, kerosene and soap while her children also contributed towards clothing.

James, Surveyor Line

Amenorvi's estranged husband, James, who was in his 70s was in a house by himself. He had completed middle school and he described himself as a farmer. He had been a fisherman once but was no longer fishing due to a hernia. His house was a two-room laterite block and thatch-roofed house. He stopped farming four years before due to ill health and was now rearing animals. He had about nine goats, five sheep, and eleven fowls. He bought some of the animals from Gyakiti and the goats he started with were a gift from his brother. He looked after himself from the proceeds of the sale of the animals at Dzemeni market. He sold two fowls or one goat or sheep at a time. He was responsible for his own food, soap, clothes, kerosene and drugs. He also did his own housework—sweeping, cooking cleaning, feeding his animals and taking them out to graze.

While James had a stronger resource base than Amenorvi, he could not afford treatment for his hernia. He also did not travel to his home-town for the festival this year for financial reasons. His closest friends were his elder brother's sons. His daughter who lived with her mother gave him cassava and corn dough and his grandchildren, his daughter's daughter and his son's daughter fetched him water. At Surveyor Line, he had four children and five siblings who were all farming and/or fishing.

James had first migrated to Kpong before the Dam. He and his wife used to work as farm labourers and his wife also collected fuel wood for sale. They then moved to another place called Aseso and began to farm on their own account. After the dam, they went to Kpong where he became a paid employee, a labourer of the Kpong Water Works. His wife persuaded him that there was money to be made fishing at Surveyor Line, so he left his job and they moved here. He was disappointed by what he found because according to him, the best fishing was already over. He bought himself a net and a canoe from his savings and fished with a colleague who earned a third of the proceeds while he earned—on account of owning the equipment. He sold his fish to Gyakiti people who came to Surveyor Line to buy it fresh. When his colleague left, he worked with his children who slowly mastered the fishing. His wife smoked the surplus after the sale here at Surveyor Line and took it to Akosombo. He also did some farming. Now that he could no longer farm, he had leased his farmland to some people to earn something from it. His connections in the fishing industry sometimes brought him fish to eat. However, things were hard for him now because of his ill health.

Damali's (Case 8.9) working life had begun auspiciously. She was not one of the women around the Lake who had been kept out of the fish trade on grounds that they had no experience selling fish to strangers. She plunged into fish trading from the beginning and bought fish from her husband and Torgodo fishermen. Even more interesting, she had access to savings facilities and did not have to rely on a relation to keep her savings as others had had to do. She was also successful in establishing the relationships in Accra for selling her fish. Damali had many children of her relations to provide critical, and in the case of the girls, unpaid labour for her fish trade and boat transportation business. However, in the end, she was left with very little after one or two bad business decisions and the dishonesty of a driver whom she described as a "grandson". Women had a particularly difficult time with investments in livelihood activities they did not and were not expected to know well because of the sexual division of labour. Both the transport and cattle business were not easy to manage at the best of times, and without some form of participation and close monitoring, it was extremely difficult. The loss of the house she was renting out at Kpando raises another dimension of the precariousness of livelihoods. While Damali was paid compensation, her future earnings as a landlady were curtailed and she was never able to reinvest in property on that scale.

Amenorvi (Case 8.10), the estranged wife of one of the early migrants at Surveyor Line, who was now living with her daughter and grandchildren, was having problems of survival. Her husband James was also old and ill, but with a stronger material basis for survival. However, she lived in the same space with her daughter and son and their children and, therefore, had a stronger call on their material and non-material support. James, on the other hand, lived alone and had to do most things for himself although his children supported him with foodstuffs and their children fetched him water from the river.

Amenorvi's situation was always less promising than Damali's. Her husband, who was disappointed with the conditions around the Lake when he arrived there after leaving wage work at Kpong, never established the scale of fishing from which she could also earn some money. Instead he sold his fish which he said was not much mainly to others and it was what they did not want which came to her. She had spent most of her working life around the Lake farming and processing cassava and now was farming land which was too small to guarantee enough food for the year. Living with her children was an advantage, but their situation was not promising. They themselves were engaged in rain-fed agriculture, one of them on an even smaller scale than Amenorvi. Together with her husband who did not farm but reared animals, they could have had a household with some synergies in their various livelihood activities. However, they had been separated for decades.

8. *Summary and Conclusions*

The chapter discussed the transformation of Tongu livelihoods from fishing, through the introduction of farming to the present specialisation in farming, food processing and trading. In spite of the decline in migrant livelihoods and the lower levels of diversification, people appeared to be doing better around the Lake than in the Lower Volta. This was because each activity—fishing, farming and trading, had a stronger base than similar activities in the Lower Volta. Of particular interest were the differences in the livelihood strategies of the various migrant communities, in particular the differences between the Tongu Ewe and Dangme communities. We argued that although the Dangme migrants arrived on the Lake later than the Tongu Ewe fishermen, their use of outboard motors and large "companies" with assistants made them more successful as fishermen. They were able to continue to fish in spite of the decline in fish stocks while the Tongu Ewe either completely dropped out of fishing or were doing it part-time, seasonally or on a scale too small to anchor their livelihoods.

In addition to the differences in community strategies, labour relations had created differentiation between different participants in the main economic activities of the Lake—fishing, farming, trading and services. Terms of remuneration, in particular the yearly accounting system, had been particularly disadvantageous for assistants although arguably, in the absence of savings facilities, it allowed them some opportunity for savings. However, that labour agreements were honoured more in the breach created an army of assistants who could not hope to graduate to become own-account operators. The widespread use of child labour especially in the fishing industry posed social and policy dilemmas, condemning many children to reproduce the very conditions which had driven them to wage labour at an early age.

For women, gender inequalities were an added factor in livelihoods. The particular forms that gender differences took were related to the male-centred character of migration and settlement. We argued that female and male migrants of the same age had very different trajectories within migrant settlements along the Lake. For various Tongu women, life in migrant settlements in spite of the opportunities for trading and farming represented a reversal of centuries of autonomous market oriented livelihoods. Migrant livelihoods were organised in more interdependent terms with women in supporting roles as cooks and fish preservers and traders with varied and indeterminate terms of remuneration. This created various obstacles to women's attempts to recreate the more autonomous livelihoods of the pre-dam days. The high incidence of multiple marriage and marital instability contributed to high levels of insecurity, which women suffered over and above what all migrants experienced. These factors as well as women's strategies to make their way in migrant settlements both within and outside the framework of marriage contributed to gender conflicts and the widespread ideological representations of women as unreliable self-seekers.

Kinship was an integral component of the intersecting social relations of migrant society. It was deployed by both men and women, sometimes in similar fashion, sometimes differently, in the organisation of livelihoods. Opening closed doors, making the unthinkable possible and generally oiling the wheels of social interaction in life and livelihoods, kinship was also the soil in which class and gender exploitation thrived. The decline in migrant livelihoods was most visible in the situation of older migrants. After many years of hard work, many had nothing much to show for their efforts. Their resources had been dissipated by poor institutional conditions, exploitative and unregulated labour relations and poor social security arrangements.

The study confirmed some of the findings in the literature. One of them concerns the difficulties of diversification and accumulation in frontier settlements in spite of the relative abundance of natural resources (Chimhowu, 2002). Secondly, although livelihoods were less diversified around the Volta Lake, they delivered better outcomes than in the Lower Volta where livelihoods were much more diversified.

CHAPTER NINE

CONCLUDING CHAPTER

Ne atikpo nɔ tɔme fe blave hā, metrɔ na zua elo o.

Even if a log remains in the river for twenty years,
it does not become a crocodile—Tongu Ewe proverb.

1. *Introduction*

This chapter brings together the main issues addressed in the book
and draws some conclusions, policy implications and areas for further investigation. The book, which is an account of the long-term
impacts of the Volta River Project, has focused on responses of downstream and lakeside communities, particularly in the area of their
livelihoods. The preceding eight chapters have tackled issues such as
the pre-dam conditions of the Lower Volta, specifically of the Tongu
Ewe communities, the conception and execution of the Volta River
Project and its predicted and actual impacts on communities of the
Volta Basin. Other issues considered include state policies and institutional attitudes to dam impacts and to the different categories of
dam-affected communities and their political responses to both dam
impacts and state policies. Four of the chapters of the book focus
on livelihoods in selected downstream and lakeside settlements.

In keeping with its conceptual framework, the study on which the
book is based combined a retrospective and prospective approach
using both quantitative and qualitative techniques. Instruments such
as a survey, case histories, in-depth interviews with key informants
and social groups, observation and the review of secondary literature allowed a comprehensive approach to the issues of dam-affected
communities with both scientific and policy relevance. The result is
a wide-ranging study linking the politics of the conception and implementation of the Volta River Project and state policies towards
affected communities with livelihood responses within two types of
affected communities. However, the approach has the limitation of
the loss of some depth on certain issues. For example, some of the

questions raised by the cases presented in the study were not pursued in detail. These include the issue of cultural repertoires and practices, religion and ritual in the organisation of livelihoods. Also, several disputes between community members heard at various shrines, chiefs' courts and unit committee arbitrations, though observed and recorded, could not be analysed in detail because of space constraints. Also missing has been the impact of bilharzia and other waterborne diseases on livelihoods. Some issues concerning expenditure and consumption within households were also not tackled in any detail. In spite of these gaps, the sheer volume of new data generated by the study has allowed downstream and lakeside communities to emerge from the mists of the unknown. Future researchers of these communities will have some background material and policy-makers can proceed with a fair amount of knowledge on the dynamics and workings of these communities, especially their livelihood activities and their organisation.

The chapter presents a summary and the main conclusions of the book. This is preceded by a situation of the Volta River Project in the wider perspective of the literature on large dams and the international politics of dams. This links what has largely been a study of national conditions with the debates and developments around large dams and their impacts.

2. *The Volta River Project in Wider Perspective*

Developments within the international context and the literature on large dams and affected communities provide a good background and framing for the conclusions of this book. This is because of certain significant developments in both the literature and the politics. The World Commission on Dams released its much-anticipated report in 2000. The Commission—a culmination of years of wrangling between academics, activists and the dam building industry on both sides of the Large Dams debates the world over—bears the hallmarks of these tensions in its composition, processes and report. However, the Report affirmed the rights of those already affected by Large Dams to redress. In addition, it set out processes through which they could proceed and enumerated some of the possible remedies they might pursue and how these could be funded. Most importantly, the Report's endorsement of various international human rights instruments reaffirms their importance for the protection of dam-affected people.[1] The Report draws heavily on the literature to which we now turn.

The Large Dam literature industry: Reflecting and catalysing the politics of large dams

A by-product of the Large Dam industry is the vast amount of literature it has generated. Goodland (cited in Morse et al., 1992) identifies ten issues of concern in the literature. These include the costs and benefits of dams and their measurements, the environmental and socio-economics questions, the situation of resettled communities and other affected communities and questions of politics—decision-making and participation.[2] Studies of large dams in Africa, Asia and Latin America date from the 1960s when their environmental and socio-economic impacts began to be felt.[3] The literature developed in two main streams—one which stressed the beneficial effects of dams and the other which focused on their negative impacts (Morse et al., 1992). From the 1970s, the literature on negative impacts grew exponentially (Farvar and Milton, 1972; Blackwelder, 1983; Goldsmith and Hildyard, 1984, 1986).

The debate entered a new stage when each stream in response to the other began to more seriously address the issue of costs and benefits of dams. Dam supporters argued that other sources of power such as coal, thermal plants, oil, natural gas and nuclear plants were potentially more problematic than hydro-electric power dams whose adverse impacts could be greatly minimised and their benefits maximised (Dixon et al., 1989). Other studies in this genre acknowledged

---

[1] They include the United Nations General Assembly Declaration on the Right to Development (1986), the Universal Declaration of Human Rights (1948) and the Rio Declaration on Environment and Development (1992) and are reproduced as Annex VIII of the World Commission on Dams Report (2000).

[2] The Goodland list contains transparency and participation, demand side management, efficiency and conservation; the balance between hydroelectric power and other renewable energy sources. It also includes the balance between rural versus urban supply; medium versus large projects; sectoral least-cost ranking and social and environmental criteria; storage versus run of river dams i.e. the land area lost to flooding; involuntary resettlement; project specific mitigation versus trade-offs and greenhouse gas emission damage costs.

[3] Some of this literature concerns the Akosombo Dam and the Volta Lake (Jopp, 1965; Scudder, 1965; Moxon, 1969; Chambers, 1970; Johnson, 1971; Kalitsi, 1973; Hart, 1980; Diaw and Schmidt Kallert, 1990).

some of the problems of water development projects such as dams and irrigation schemes but argued that they were vital for development (Jopp, 1965; Moxon, 1984; Obeng, 1969, 1975b, 1978). Even more controversially, dams were said to be a clean and renewable source of energy which could be used for various other purposes such as drinking water and irrigation and promote flood control and flow regulation (Goodland, 1994). Other potential benefits included the possibility of agriculture on land exposed by the fluctuations of the water levels of the lake, (Kalitsi, 1973), river transport, wildlife, tourism, water sports and health control (Paperna, 1969; Yeboah, 1977). An accepted across-the-board benefit of large dams in the literature is the significant increases in the fish in their reservoirs (Kumi, 1973; Linney and Harrison, 1981; Graham, 1986).

Critics of such claims pointed to the ever-present danger of siltation, dam failure and the incompatibility of various uses of dams. They also argue that the loss of animals and agricultural land from the submergence of land could cancel out the fish increases in reservoirs, which in any case tended to stabilise at lower than estimated levels after a few years (Cummings, 1990; Goldsmith and Hildyard, 1986).

These claims and counter-claims point to the difficulties of measuring the projected and actual costs and benefits of dams. Studies suggested that feasibility studies of dams often exaggerated their benefits while costs were played down to ensure positive returns (Paranjpye and Ganguli, 1980; Dogra, 1985). However, a number of practical problems with the cost-benefit approach have been identified. These include the non-materialisation of projected benefits (Morse et al., 1992; Kalitsi, 1973; Balon, 1978; Hart, 1980) and the criteria for deciding what benefits and costs to measure. Others were how to measure long-term and short-term effects and reversible and irreversible costs, and the over-reliance on market criteria to measure costs and benefits (McCaull, 1975; Repetto, 1986). Some of the problems of cost-benefit calculations are reproduced in Environmental Impact Assessments (EIAs) (Clark et al., 1984) and the monitoring regime of water resources projects (Blackwelder, 1983). Other studies have addressed the legal and financial difficulties of compensation, especially questions of legal processes, title to land, compensation of communal property, valuation of land and other resources and the computation of losses (Shrivastava et al., 1991). In spite of the difficulties with the costs and benefits of large dams, the literature is generally agreed on certain aspects of dam impacts.

The literature on negative effects classifies them into the physical, biological and human, while acknowledging the close interconnections of effects and their impacts (Biswas, 1978). Physical effects cited in the literature include the creation of artificial lakes or reservoirs leading to the submergence of agricultural land and forests with resources such as timber, fuel-woods, medicinal plants, food sources and animal life of a very wide variety (Cummings, 1990). There are also climatic changes (Kumi, 1973; Kassas, 1980; Cummings, 1990), siltation caused by the loss of vegetation and erosion (Linney and Harrison, 1981), flooding (Kalitsi, 1973), water-loss from evapo-transpiration (Kassas, 1980), water-logging and soil salinisation in the case of irrigation dams (Fahim, 1981). The biological effects identified in the literature include an upsurge in aquatic vegetation which has been linked with the observed increases in water-borne diseases such as schistosomiasis (bilharzia), onchocerciasis, gastro-enteritis and malaria (Johnson, 1971; Obeng, 1978; Biswas, 1978; Kassas, 1980; Blackwelder and Carlson, 1984; Cummings, 1990). Many of the diseases weaken infected persons, affect their economic and social situation and even cause death (Obeng, 1978).

While interest in the human or socio-economic impacts of large dams has been more recent, it has been very influential in the debates. Studies from Latin America and Asia abound with observations of the adverse effects of dams on indigenous people and riparian peasants as opposed to the benefits for aluminium companies and agribusiness (Cummings, 1990). Some studies have focused on protest movements to make the case about the differences between beneficiaries and adversely-affected communities (Cummings, 1990; Singh, 1991). Many of the studies have concluded that large dams are rarely in the interest of local populations in spite of "the vague logic of a national good" which has been the rationale of dam builders (Dogra, 1985). The issues have been analysed in terms of a fundamental conflict of interest between peasants and indigenous communities on one hand and state and industry on the other hand (Beckman, 1986; Graham, 1986; Morse et al., 1992).

The implications of resettlement for displaced communities have preoccupied much of the research on human effects (Scudder, 1965; Biswas, 1978). A few studies have noted the positive results of resettlement such as the provision of schools, post offices, clinics and markets (Kalitsi, 1973; Fahim, 1981). However, the conclusion of much of the writing on resettlements is that they have not been successful in addressing the challenges of displacement of whole communities from their ancestral lands as a result of their philosophical approach, poor planning and inadequate resources. Thus, resettlement has been known to often result in the loss of livelihood and self-sufficiency. (Kalitsi, 1973; Goldsmith and Hildyard, 1986; Cernea, 1990, 1996; The World Bank, 1993). This literature on affected populations inspired and was in turn nourished by political struggles over dams the world over and this can be seen in the more recent interest of the dam literature on anti-dam movements (Srinivasan, 1994; Parasuraman, 1993; Dwivedi, 1999, 2001).

International Politics and Large Dams: From Academic Debates and Peoples' Struggles to the World Commission on Dams

The protagonists in the political arena of the large dam debates and processes have been many and varied—governments, dam administration bureaucracies, academics, non-governmental organisations, dam-affected communities and their representatives, dam-building organisations, investment banks, the World Bank and the United Nations. These constituencies have, however, overlapped in membership and used each other's services in their particular interventions. The following account which attempts to link the protagonists and related struggles to the developing international politics may be somewhat generalised because the different players became active in different periods around the world. However, it allows us to identify key signposts in the debates on large dams and when different constituencies became significant players on the international arena.

In the 50s and 60s, in the most intense period of conceptualisation, design and planning of the Volta River Project, the most important players in large dam projects were governments, financiers and the dam-building industry. The industry was made up of various experts: engineers, construction companies, feasibility experts and various social and natural science experts who played a minor role. Communities to be affected by dams such as those to be physically displaced or *oustees*[4] were advised of their impending fate. They were

---

[4] Goodland (1997) adopted this term from the Indian literature. In the Ghanaian literature, they are commonly referred to as resettlers as though their actions were voluntary. We retain this latter usage, however for the sake of consistency, but use it interchangeably with the terms *oustees* and *displaced persons*.

then allowed to choose from already identified new locations, where and with whom they wanted to be resettled and were typically not adequately compensated for the trauma and inconvenience of resettlement. Goodland describes this limited involvement in resettlement site selection as primitive participation, which improved in the 1970s to consultation with oustees about the move and possible sites for resettlement. In the 1980s, he argues that the process moved from participation to consultation and oustees could even participate in hitherto out-of-bounds formerly purely "technical" decisions such as dam height and position on the river.

Another significant development in this period was the expansion of acknowledged dam-affected populations from the resettled to include their hosts, downstream and upstream communities and their organisations as well as the recognition of NGOs as stakeholders in processes generated by dam construction. The World Bank's 1996 Participation Sourcebook to guide the Large Dam Industry endorsed this expansion of affected populations (World Bank, 1996; Goodland, 1997).

A number of factors brought about these changes. One was a series of studies discussed in the last section that suggested that the industry had underestimated the impacts of dams by externalising many of the negative impacts and ignoring the long-term changes many ecosystems had experienced as a result of large dams. Foreshadowing these developments were reports of the violence and force that accompanied some early attempts at resettlement, the struggles between the resettled and their host communities and the growing self-organisation of dam-affected and dam-threatened communities. As more information on affected communities became available, controversies around specific dams and their local impacts grew into a global debate about the value of dams and a worldwide movement against large dams.

In the 1980s, this movement was boosted by the movement to centre stage of issues of environmental sustainability, which culminated in the United Nations Conference on Environment and Development (UNCED) in 1982. This event led to an exponential growth in public concern about the environmental and social effects of dams. A number of large dam Projects had to be shelved or postponed in both industrialised and developing countries.[5]

---

[5] For example, Sweden banned further hydroelectric projects on half of its rivers and Norway, which was very hydro—electricity dependent at the time, postponed

One constituency, which came under intense pressure for its role in the construction of large dams in this period, was the multilateral and bilateral financial agencies, in particular, the World Bank. Whilst the proportion of their investments was estimated at about 15%, they had become the focus of attention of the anti-dam lobby because of their strategic role in "spreading the technology, lending legitimacy to emerging dam projects, training future engineers and government agencies and leading financing arrangements" (World Commission on Dams Report, 2000). Also in the 1990s, the literature generated by resettlements was picked up by human rights lawyers who applied the principles of various UN instruments to argue that States had clear legal duties to dam-affected populations and were in breach of several of these (Paul, 1992; Shihata, 1993). The time of dam-affected communities and their supporters had come.

By the late 1990s, pressures against the dam industry were so intense that the demise of large dam building was being somewhat prematurely predicted (The Corner House, 1998). An international conference of dam-affected communities meeting in Curitiba, Brazil, in 1997 called for an "international independent commission to be established to conduct a comprehensive review of all large dams financed or otherwise supported by international aid and credit agencies and its policy conclusions implemented" (Greef, 2000, p. 49). In the meantime, in 1995, the World Bank under the leadership of a new President, James Wolfensohn, commissioned an internal evaluation by its Operations Evaluation Department (OED) of dams it had played a role in constructing and its operating procedures concerning dams. This was in response to the Bank having become a "major focus of criticism because of the number of problematic projects, including some of the biggest and most controversial, in which it had been involved." As well, it was in fulfilment of Wolfensohn's announced review of the Bank's development effectiveness on his appointment as president of the Bank (The World Conservation Union and World Bank, 1997). At a meeting in Gland, Switzerland, organised by the World Bank and the IUCN, the preliminary report, completed in 1996 and based on a desk study of 50 large dams in which the Bank had been involved, was heavily criticised as biased

---

all new HEP Dams. Intense controversies delayed the Sardar Sarovar on the Narmada River in India and planned dams in Nepal, China, Chile and Slovakia were the subjects of much controversy (Goodland, 1997, p. 71).

and flawed in methodology. The IUCN and the World Bank agreed to calls for an independent Commission and agreed to put up 10% of its estimated budget (Greef, 2000).

According to the World Bank, its rational for sponsoring the World Commission on Dams was "to depolarise the tense debates" (World Bank Annual Report 1999). While cynics argued that the Bank was trying to divert the struggles over large dams, the process it began took on an independent life. The Commission's starting point was how to build good large dams, but it allowed the possibility of a decision that a dam would not be built because its costs outweighed its benefits.[6] Through a process of forums, hearings, detailed case studies, country reviews, briefing papers, surveys and submissions, the Commission gathered a staggering amount of data on the financial, economic, environmental and social performance of dams and their alternatives. The Commission's Report was completed and launched in 2000.

The Report stated that dams had made important contributions to human development and their benefits had been considerable. However, it also stated that in too many cases, the price paid for these benefits, particularly in social and environmental terms, had been unacceptably high and unnecessary especially for displaced persons, communities downstream, taxpayers and the natural environment. Also, the lack of equity in the distribution of benefits had challenged the value of dams for addressing water and energy needs when compared with alternatives. Thus, dams had failed to satisfy the core values underpinning the goals of development such as equity, efficiency, participatory decision-making, sustainability and accountability (p. xxxiii). The most interesting aspects of the Report for our purposes was the extension of the notion of risk beyond governments and dam builders to include affected people and the environment. In the Report's proposed new policy framework, the problem of existing dams was explicitly addressed and it was recommended among other things that outstanding social issues, i.e. the problems of adversely affected populations, be addressed before any new dams

---

[6] The WCD's two objectives were "to review the development effectiveness of large dams and assess alternatives for water resources and energy development; and to develop internationally acceptable criteria, guidelines and standards, where appropriate for the planning, design, appraisal, construction, operation, monitoring and decommissioning of dams" (World Commission on Dams, 2000, p. 28).

be built. Another of the Report's recommendations was that affected populations become beneficiaries of the project and possible benefits discussed. In adopting a broader definition of affected populations, the Commission put the issues of downstream communities and migrant villages and their hosts firmly on the agenda. Also, the idea of affected communities becoming project beneficiaries, a novel and interesting approach to the issues of affected populations, was endorsed by the Report.

The Report, a consensus document signed by all 12 Commissioners who were from a broad spectrum of opinion about large dams,[7] was hailed as a victory for anti-dam campaigners as it gave voice to many of their criticisms of dams (Pottinger, 2000). The dam industry, however, was unhappy: the International Hydropower Association, for example, was quoted as saying in a press release that "the overall tone of the report is negative concerning the role of dams, generalising adverse impacts and understating well-known social and economic benefits" (Pottinger, 2000). The biggest threat to the Report though, came from the World Bank. Amid protests and accusations of bad faith from NGOs, it decided that "it would not adopt the WCD guidelines, but would only use them as a non-binding reference when considering new dams."[8] While the World Bank's stance has been damaging, future debates cannot sidestep the WCD Report which succeeded in moving the critique of large dams into the mainstream and strengthening the prospects of affected communities in this most contested terrain. Also, organised groups can use the Report to strengthen their position in debate and negotiations. The Report's endorsement of various UN instruments strengthened the hand of already affected communities and those to be affected in the future in their struggles to participate in decision-making about projects that affect them, secure the protection of their rights to basic needs and to redress and remedy if they suffer any adverse impacts.[9]

---

[7] Commissioner Medha Patkar of the Struggle to Save the Narmada River, India, also wrote a separate short comment, which was included in the Report.

[8] NGOs from 87 groups in 30 countries accused the Bank of bias in favour of governments heavily involved in the construction of large dams and demanded that it adopt the recommendations of the WCD (Bosshard, 2001).

[9] See also the Universal Declaration of Human Rights, 1948; the International Covenant on Economic, Social and Cultural Rights, 1966; the Convention on the Elimination of All Forms of Discrimination Against Women, 1979 and the Rio Declaration on Environment and Development, 1992. For a discussion of the importance of these human rights instruments for dam-affected people and others affected by development projects, see Paul, J, 1992 (a) and (b).

3. *Summary of Main Arguments and Findings*

The historical background

Three features of the pre-dam political economy of the Lower Volta played an important role in its post-dam trajectory. One of these was that it was based mainly on farming, fishing, clam picking and also small-scale trading in food crops and other consumer goods and artisanal and waged work. Secondly, the Volta River's variability, specifically its annual flooding around which the seasonal out-migration and key livelihood activities such as farming, fishing and clam picking were organised, played a critical role in the life of the Lower Volta. The third feature was the peripheral role of the Lower Volta in the export commodity-based colonial and post-colonial political economy of Ghana. These factors together fuelled the seasonal out-migration of its inhabitants to the cocoa growing, mining and fishing areas in the upper reaches of the Volta. By the 1960s, there were indications of growing differentiation within different economic activities and within the society as a whole as well as the growing importance of certain livelihood activities such as farming, creek fishing and clam picking. Decades of clam picking and long-distance trading by women were also producing changes in gender relations, but with strong continuities in various aspects of life. These continuities within the Lower Volta and the organisation of its livelihoods around a particular set of environmental and socio-economic conditions were to end quite abruptly with the Volta River Project.

The historical perspective adopted in the analysis of the conception and implementation of the Volta River Project was important in identifying the factors which shaped its relationship with affected communities. These included the imperatives of the post-colonial modernisation project, specifically the drive to industrialisation in a context of relative capital poverty of a newly independent country. It put Ghana in a weak bargaining position in the negotiation of the terms of the Volta River Project. The imbalance of power not only affected the Ghana government, but also those who had to rely on it to safeguard their interests, i.e. affected communities. This permeated project processes and agreements and resulted in issues of affected local communities being relegated to the background. In the sixties, this was made even easier by lack of information on the part of all the parties concerned about the long-term environmental and socio-economic impacts of such an undertaking.

In the conception of the VRP, three categories of communities to
be affected by the Dam—those to be physically displaced, those
whose lands were being acquired for resettlement and downstream
communities—were identified. The Preparatory Commission in 1956
made predictions about their losses and recommendations for redress.
The Commission's thinking was based on the assumption that most
dam impacts were amenable to correction. Many of its predictions
came to pass, but it also underestimated some dam impacts. After
the Akosombo Dam was constructed and the Volta Lake formed, its
fish-stocks surpassed the conservative estimates of experts for several
years. This fuelled mass out-migration from the Lower Volta and
the establishment of many villages along the Volta Lake. Aquatic
weeds became a serious problem not only on the Lake as predicted,
but also in the Lower Volta, where the Dam devastated the environment and natural resources causing a significant decline in livelihood
activities and in other aspects of life. The flawed predictions of the
Preparatory Commission, buttressed by the Reassessment Report
which had been commissioned a decade later to trim the costs of
the Project, took the issue of affected communities off the VRP's
agenda. This was with the understanding that dam impacts would
be tackled as part of the Ghana Government's development agenda.

In the absence of an institution designated and equipped for tackling the problems of dam-affected communities, it fell to the VRA
to address the problems. The organisation proved unequal to the
task and often was unable to reconcile the demands of producing
power with those of tackling the issues facing affected communities.
In relation to the specific question of livelihoods in the Lower Volta,
until recently the VRA ignored demands for compensation and resti-
tution in keeping with its general practice, but also because of a
long-held belief that the benefits of the Lake would make up for the
economic losses downstream. This supposition was based on a
superficial reading of the complicated relationship between migrants
and their hometowns and between the Lower Volta and its migrants.
In 1996, the VRA finally signalled a shift in policy by commissioning the Lower Volta Environmental Impact Studies. The studies
which sought to explore ways of addressing the environmental and
socio-economic decline of the Lower Volta are, however, not to be
seen as an admission of responsibility by the VRA. They are to
enable the organisation to concretise its preferred agency role in relation to affected communities. The Lakeside settlements did not fare

much better. Their problems became hostage to the VRA's concerns about the health of the Dams and the Volta Lake in the sense that only those which coincided with these concerns were addressed. Other serious problems such as poor infrastructure and the limited coverage of key services, depleting fish and other livelihood resources were largely ignored and have now become the responsibility of poorly resourced District Assemblies and the Department of Fisheries.

The resettlements, which received the most sustained levels of official attention, were found by the resettled to be inadequate for their purposes. The infrastructure provided them deteriorated quite quickly and the establishment of new livelihoods was hampered by the small size of land allocated them and the failure to successfully introduce mechanised farming to mitigate this problem. A few years on, the resettlements were handed over to mainstream government institutions as part of a process to normalise them. Their present state of dilapidation and hardships has been the subject of various studies, but as yet, there is no comprehensive programme for their rehabilitation.

Recent developments in the power sector such as the problems of keeping up with rising domestic consumption, concerns about rising tariff levels among consumers, the VRA's need for economic tariffs and the entry of private power producers into the sector, have created a more complicated climate within which to make demands regarding affected communities. In addition, the change in government and in the leadership of the VRA since 2001 has meant that communities might have to take their advocacy to a new set of players and begin all over again. Five years into the new dispensation and after the national conference to disseminate the findings and policy recommendations of the Lower Volta Environmental Impacts Studies, there is not much to show for policy changes in the Lower Volta.

Community differences: Complicating the policy climate

The study found evidence of decades of efforts of downstream communities to get the government to address dam impacts. This is contrary to the view in certain circles of dam-affected populations as passive and lacking clarity about their issues. However, community efforts were hampered by state neglect, the VRA's policy intransigence, the lack of clear channels for presenting grievances and institutional arrangements for addressing them. The most important problem though, was the lack of sufficient mobilisation within affected communities. The scale of out-migration and the "subject" political culture of rural communities in the early post colonial period were only two of several factors responsible for this.

Livelihood responses within the Lower Volta were another dimension of responses to the Dams, their poor outcomes being due to overwhelming problems such as the state of the Volta River and the land in the Lower Volta which were too serious to be addressed by household or community strategies. Out-migration of the Tongu Ewe from the Lower Volta to the Volta Lake especially, but also to other rural and urban areas in Ghana as response to the Volta River Project, was a third dimension of responses. The establishment of settlements along the Volta Lake without recourse to state planning processes resulted in very poor infrastructure and critical services with a dampening impact on livelihoods. The relations established by migrant communities and settlements among themselves, with their host communities and with state agencies, were characterised in different measure and at different times by co-operation, competition and conflict. These relations were critical to migrant livelihoods, specifically in the acquisition and use of land and of the Lake and more generally in the sense of security of migrant settlements.

The differences in the livelihood strategies of the different categories of dam-affected communities were an important dimension of the study. A complicating factor in the consideration of affected communities was the shifting identities and locations of some of their members. The livelihoods trajectories approach of the study showed that yesterday's re-settler could be today's lakeside dweller and tomorrow's downstream inhabitant. However, these changes were not lightly assumed and some options were no longer open. For example, people who were not resettled could not now become resettlers even though they could rent land allocated to resettlers and reside in resettlement villages. In addition, sections of the population retained only one of these identities for long periods of time. Moreover, the relationship between these three categories of affected communities was much more complicated, having undergone significant changes in the four decades since the Volta River Project. With the passage of time and the deaths of remaining close kin in hometowns, migrants' relationships with their hometowns became less specific and direct. Only a minority of migrants had dependants in the Lower Volta. The practice of migrants sending their children to the Lower Volta to school was dwindling for a variety of reasons. Increasingly, the children had to look after themselves because of the hardships being experienced by their hosts. With the economic decline of the Lake and its impacts on livelihoods, migrants also had a much reduced ability to support their relations and children in the Lower Volta. This was complicating hometown allegiances and loosening bonds, a process which was likely to become even more significant in the future. However, hometowns retained their value as places of ritual importance, a source of cheap labour, a refuge in times of crisis and a place to retire to or be buried at. In spite of the decline in migrant livelihoods and the fewer possibilities for multiple livelihood activities however, livelihood outcomes were better around the Lake than in the Lower Volta. This was because each of these activities— fishing, farming and trading—had a healthier resource base around the Lake than in the Lower Volta.

On part of the Lower Volta, the impacts of wholesale out-migration of the 60s were still being felt. This and the environmental and socio-economic decline had created differences between the Lower Volta and migrant communities. Although migrant villages were inaccessible, shabby and with woefully inadequate infrastructure and social services, they offered better economic prospects to their more vigorous populations than the Lower Volta, with its improved infrastructure, did for its ageing population. These differences in population structure, household composition, resource base and livelihood portfolios between Lakeside and Lower Volta settlements shaped the relationships between the two areas creating interdependencies and mutual, though not equal, levels of support. On the other hand, migration and migrant cultures had resulted in different categories of ex-migrants (retired, economically active and children) whose livelihoods were linked in specific ways to the Lake. This was because they had been organised to take advantage of the migration history of people and the migration culture of their communities. These included the use of old connections for long-distance trading, receiving remittances from children as well as rent and profits from resources left around the Lake. As well, a proportion of the foodstuffs and fish sold at markets in the Lower Volta was from the Lake.

Around the Volta Lake, there were differences between the Tongu and Dangme communities' approaches to livelihoods. Tongu migrant livelihoods, which began with only fishing and fish processing, were soon expanded to include farming which in time came to supersede fishing as the anchor livelihood activity. Although the Dangme arrived later on the Lake, their organisational strategies and their use of out-board motors made them more successful fishermen and allowed them to continue to fish in spite of declining fish stocks while the Tongu either completely dropped out of fishing or used it as sup-plementary livelihood activity.

Intensification and multiple livelihood activities do not necessarily mean adaptation to dam impacts

In the Lower Volta, two often inter-linked livelihood strategies— intensification of the use of pre-dam resources and involvement in multiple livelihood activities—were observed. The intensification of the use of pre-dam resources was a widespread response to the environ-mental changes. It took several forms which included changes in the method of exploitation of particular resources in order to improve yields or exploiting them as was done in the pre-dam environment but downgrading their significance in the livelihood portfolio. Other forms were the intensification of the exploitation of hitherto little-used resources, the wholesale adoption of activities leading to saturation and the deployment of old resources for new uses. Forms of intensifi-cation such as the increase in charcoal burning hastened tree cover depletion raising questions about the sustainability of some livelihood activities.

Intensification often went hand in hand with having multiple liveli-hood activities. While the practice of multiple activities pre-dated the Volta River Project, the restructuring of livelihoods in the post VRP era meant that the activities combined, their organisation and outcomes were quite different. Some activities such as clam picking and fishing were completely dropped from livelihood portfolios while some anchor activities became supplementary and vice versa. Farming, for example, suffered a general decline but its post-dam status depended on the nature of other livelihood activities being pursued by individuals and their households. Those engaged in artisanal services and wage work tended to replace farming with these as anchor livelihood activities while those engaged in extractive activities such as charcoal, firewood and mining rarely saw them as a replacement for farming. Trading activities which could easily be combined with and in some cases had a basis in farming, i.e. the sale of farm produce, did not affect the status of farming too much. On the other hand, the establishment of a shop or long-distance trading sometimes marked a shift of focus from farming to services.

Household level livelihood strategies and trajectories unfolded within a broader context of environmental and socio-economic processes. In the Lower Volta with its continuing environmental and socio-economic decline, livelihood outcomes were poor for most people irrespective of their strategies. This raised the question of the significance of multiple livelihood activities. As the livelihoods literature has demonstrated, the rationale and outcomes of multiple livelihood activities depend on the context, the activities in question, their scale and organisation. The discussion of livelihoods in the Lower Volta and around the Lake was rich with instances that demonstrated this ambiguity of multiple livelihood activities. In the Lower Volta, pre-dam multiple livelihood activities had been selected to fit with the seasonal cycle of the Volta River. This allowed households and their members reasonable outcomes in an environment that was rejuvenated naturally by the floods. Post-dam, with the dramatic restructuring of both the environment and livelihood portfolios, the principle of multiple activities was retained, but it involved a more random combination of activities which singly or in combination were unable to provide adequate livelihood outcomes and long-term security.

The study also confirmed that it was difficult to conduct multiple livelihood activities and accumulation in frontier settlements in spite of the relative abundance of natural resources mainly because of poor infrastructure and the absence of key legal, social and economic institutions. Thus around the Volta Lake, livelihoods were less diversified. However, they delivered better outcomes than in the Lower Volta. At the level of households, multiple activities had the possibility of good outcomes when they included activities with different resource bases, including different spaces, reasonably large households with several independent producers and with several strong activities.

In the light of the findings discussed above, the issue of whether adaptation to post-dam conditions had taken place in the Lower Volta and what conditions were responsible for adaptation or its absence were considered. The conclusion was that adaptation had not occurred in the Lower Volta. This was based on the finding that while the population decline of the area suffered after the Akosombo Dam had been arrested, it was still an area of net out-migration and a large proportion of its households showed the impacts of out-migration in their composition and structure. Studies including

this one found continuing environmental and socio-economic problems with adverse impacts on livelihoods. The reliance of the area
on imported food, the high costs of basic foodstuffs and the consumption of marine fish by a riverine population all pointed to the
fact that fishing and farming had not recovered from their disruption
of nearly four decades. Other findings which support this conclusion
were the widespread use of short-term credit for basic consumption
and the popularity of activities with questionable socio-economic or
environmental sustainability. Because the bases of livelihoods had
been undermined, many people were not doing more than surviving
in spite of their best efforts.

Part of the reason for the failure of adaptation was the limitations
of government policy. As other case studies have shown, interventions such as technologies, infrastructure and credit have improved
livelihood outcomes in downstream communities in the long-term.
The Lower Volta Environmental Impacts Studies (Volta Basin Research
Project, 1997, 1999) support the finding that adaptation of livelihoods had not taken place in the Lower Volta. The socio-economic
component of the studies found that the long-term neglect of dam
impacts and their interaction with human activities had worsened
the situation of dam-affected communities in that the major dam
impacts observed over the years had either remained the same or
become worse.

Social relations as a critical factor in livelihoods

The lack of adaptation notwithstanding, a small minority within the
Lower Volta was doing better than the rest in terms of their livelihood outcomes. The differences between them and the poorest households can be attributed to the resources they were able to command,
their ability to organise multi-spatial livelihoods, preferably from a
combination of urban and rural resources and their ability to secure
successful outcomes for each of their pursuits. Starting from a premise
that these differences had a basis in the social relations of livelihoods,
this issue was pursued in this book in some detail.

The examination of the social relations of livelihoods focused on
the specificities of class, gender, kinship and intergenerational relations in the context of long-term adverse environmental and socio-
economic change and responses. While social relations were key in
the organisation of livelihoods in both the Lower Volta and the

Lakeside, different aspects of social relations were examined in the two areas studied. In the Lower Volta, we observed the proliferation of and changing configurations of different kinds of households. This was an important issue because household characteristics such as size, composition and stage in developmental cycle were important for their ability to engage in multiple activities and also to secure good outcomes. While a household's size was complicated by its composition, those households with the best livelihood outcomes were reasonably large, with several adults with independent livelihood activities, with broad and in some cases multi-spatial bases and including artisanal activities and wage work. Many of the households headed by women did not fit this bill, as the larger ones were often organised around one main activity such as farming, baking or kenkey making, with high dependency ratios and supporting a host of people with varied and complicated relations with the head. One impact of large-scale migration was that households structured by a conjugal union were not the norm at Sokpoe and Mepe. Where there were conjugal relations however, marital co-operation around food crop production and the division of labour in production and expenditure were a critical element of livelihood strategies of households.

Households with a high proportion of children had fewer independent livelihood activities. However, children were critical for the organisation of reproductive and some productive activities. Within lineage compounds, the collective organisation of children for some reproductive activities allowed those with no children in their households to benefit from their services. There were also contradictory trends in the use of children for both productive and reproductive activities in the Lower Volta. On the one hand, the changing nature of the economy, the growing importance of formal education and the changing residential patterns in Sokpoe and Mepe were reducing the participation of children in unpaid labour within households. Other contributory factors were the changing composition of households and the commercialisation of some reproductive activities such as procuring water and fuel. On the other hand, more and more children, whether in school or apprenticed, had to work as casual labourers and petty traders to supplement their upkeep.

Labour relations within and outside the context of kinship allowed those with capital and equipment to secure the labour of others, including their children, other kin, hired labour and apprentices. These relations were less visible in the Lower Volta where the returns on exertions were smaller than around the Lake. However, their existence had even more import in the Lower Volta where even those who owned capital were having difficulties with survival, making the situation of those working for them even more precarious. Labour relations also created differentiation between different participants in the main livelihood activities of the Lake. Although arguably, the yearly accounting system of remuneration made some savings possible in the absence of savings facilities, labour relations did not favour the army of assistants involved in the different livelihood activities around the Lake. That agreements were honoured more in the breach did not allow the majority of assistants to become owners of their own equipment and tools for working on their own account. The widespread use of child labour especially in the fishing industry posed its own social policy dilemmas. The practice condemned many children to reproduce the lack of privilege which had created the situation where they were engaged in wage labour at an early age in the first place. It prevalence was part of the broader failure to regulate informal labour relations around the Volta Lake and in the rest of Ghana.

Relations between artisans and their apprentices were an important dimension of labour relations in the Lower Volta and in the larger settlements around the Lake. For artisans, apprentices' fees supplemented earnings while their free labour was useful for a variety of productive and reproductive activities. While apprenticeships allowed the possibility of multiple livelihood activities and also an escape from the limits of livelihoods based on natural resources, the terms and conditions of apprenticeships, the difficulties of survival during the training period and the low patronage of services resulted in high drop-out rates and discouraged potential apprentices.

Gender relations were a decisive element of the totality of social relations. The particular forms that gender differences took were related to the male-centred character of migration and settlement and the very different trajectories of female and male migrants of the same age and circumstances. For Tongu women, life in migrant settlements in spite of the opportunities for trading and farming represented a reversal of autonomous livelihoods centred on clam picking and long-distance trading. Migrant livelihoods were organised on more interdependent terms with women in supporting roles cooking, preserving and selling fish with varied and indeterminate terms of remuneration. This created various obstacles to their attempts to recreate the more autonomous livelihoods of the pre-dam days. The high incidence of multiple marriages and marital instability contributed to higher levels of insecurity for women. Their responses to these challenges contributed to gender conflicts and ideological representations of women as unreliable self-seekers always on the lookout for the most successful fishermen. Gender differences in the Lower Volta were framed largely by male absence and the higher dependency ratios of female-headed households. As well, the collapse of the clam industry had a devastating impact on the livelihoods of women.

In the Lower Volta, various elements of kinship were implicated in the organisation of livelihoods, from the basic advantages of rent-free accommodation through remittances from migrant relations to access to land, labour and capital. Just as it was in the pre-dam period, access to lineage resources was gendered and men had larger plots of land to farm and to rent out than women did. However, few male clan and lineage members benefited from the alienation of vast tracts of land by the leadership of these units. Instead, the competition and conflict over resources arising from these transactions was detrimental to the livelihoods of members of these collectives, both male and female. In the Lower Volta, close and loose kinship ties also smoothed credit transactions. However, those who could benefit from credit in the long-term were those who could honour their obligations. The widespread use of credit for very basic consumption and reproduction had an adverse impact on female traders whose capital base was usually very low. This also put pressure on the very kinship and friendship ties that made this possible in the first place.

Kinship was also an integral component of the intersecting social relations of migrant society. Both men and women, sometimes in similar fashion, at other times differently, deployed it in the organisation of their livelihoods. Opening closed doors, making the unthinkable possible and generally oiling the wheels of social interaction in life and livelihoods, kinship was also the soil in which class and gender inequalities thrived. The idiom of kinship informalised and fudged labour relations resulting in unclear terms and discouraging aggrieved assistants from seeking formal redress. The decline in migrant livelihoods was most visible in the situation of certain social groups. For example, older migrants, especially the women, often after many years of hard work, had nothing much to show for their efforts.

This was because their resources had been dissipated by poor institutional conditions, exploitative and unregulated labour relations,
multiple marriages and numerous children and poor social security
arrangements.

While both formal and informal organisations and networks were
useful in the organisation of livelihoods, the presence of formal organisations signalled a higher level of production and outcomes. They
enabled their members to access resources such as credit from a
wider universe than their own economies. Very few people at Mepe
and Sokpoe, but especially at Mepe, had the benefit of these associations. Instead, the majority of people were involved in funeral
associations which provided solidarity, money and entertainment in
times of bereavement. Informal networks provided access to various
resources, a key one being credit.

Young persons, whether in school or undergoing other training or
working casually or part-time, faced serious challenges of survival in
the Lower Volta. Among those with basic education, artisanal training was more patronised than higher education because it was more
affordable and had more definite outcomes. This was not a positive
development because of the very narrow range of training on offer
(especially for the girls) and the problems of saturation and poor
patronage. Most young people in training had to contribute to or
take charge of their upkeep. For those who were able to complete
their training, out-migration was an important strategy for realising
their investment. The situation of young people was a demonstration of the long-term reproduction of the livelihood crises of the
Lower Volta.

4. *Conceptual and Policy Implications*

This book contributes to the conceptual understanding of livelihoods
by providing empirical evidence and analysis on some debates in the
literature. One of these is whether the combination of different activities in an individual or household's portfolio is a sign of livelihood
adaptation. The conceptual framework also extends the notion of
responses beyond the traditional concepts of diversification and adaptation of the livelihoods literature. Thirdly, the interrogation of the
different social relations implicated in livelihoods, particularly within

its labour regimes, has generated some interesting insights into what intersecting social relations mean in practice in the organisation of livelihoods. These contributions are discussed below.

First of all, the study confirms the emerging position within the literature that the rationale, patterns and outcomes of diversification depend on factors such as environmental and socio-economic conditions, the state of institutions and infrastructure and the situation of particular households. Thus, while the presence of multiple livelihood activities is significant, what exactly it tells us has to be deciphered from examining livelihood portfolios in the light of these factors. Secondly, while the study of individual households might generate useful information about who is doing what and what their achievements are, livelihoods are better understood with reference to community, settlement and regional trends. Thus, for example, the practice of multiple activities can co-exist with a trend towards specialisation in a narrow range of activities.

The extended notion of responses adopted in the conceptual framework and the study's findings on responses confirmed our view that livelihood responses are more complicated than concepts such as multiple activities, intensification and adaptation allow for. Livelihoods involve activities and actions which address resource conflicts, resist or circumvent the strictures of other more powerful players within a livelihood environment, respond to material and normative conceptions of social security, state neglect and a regulatory vacuum. In certain cases, these considerations are important determinants of the kinds of activities selected, how they are combined and their outcomes. The study's contribution to the concept of adaptation has been to point out that the recovery of livelihoods have to be so generalised as to become the norm rather than the exception for adaptation to be said to have taken place. As well, the recovery of one activity out of several is not adaptation, unless it is so significant as to make up for the lack of improvement in others. The findings from the Lower Volta suggest that adaptation in situations of a drastic restructuring of the environment and livelihoods is almost impossible without some form of outside intervention directed at addressing environmental problems or circumventing their socio-economic impacts.

The findings from the application of the notion of intersecting social relations of class, gender, kinship and intergenerational relations to the study have generated a number of conclusions. One is that in situations of generalised crises in livelihoods, social relations play an even more significant part in differentiating livelihood outcomes. In particular, individuals and households which have the benefit of the labour of others are more likely to secure better livelihood outcomes than those who do not. Another implication is that while the findings confirm the position that certain social relations may be more significant than others under particular conditions and circumstances, they also suggest that because of the character of livelihood activities, gender differences in livelihood trajectories are particularly significant. Even the ability to derive gains from the ownership of certain forms of capital is gendered as is the structure and terms of labour relations. At the same time, within social organisations such as the fishing company, women's and men's positions are determined not just by their gender but by their relations with the head of the company, a source of both power and vulnerability.

Related to this issue is the question of autonomy and interdependence within household-based production. The study confirmed the position in some of the literature that household production combines elements of both autonomous and interdependent production, with the synergies from these arrangements contributing to livelihood outcomes for all parties, albeit to different degrees. Particularly in the migrant settlements, the study found that migration represented for women the transformation of largely autonomous livelihoods into much more interdependent relations structured around a hierarchically-structured male-dominated activity, fishing. That this disadvantaged women's livelihoods and increased their vulnerabilities is a further qualification of this thesis of mutual synergies. Furthermore, in a context of frontier cultures with features such as high rates of marital instability, male numerical, economic, political and social dominance only weakly mediated by kinship systems, women's disadvantages take on new dimensions. This suggests that it is not simply the balance between autonomy and interdependence, but the context within which livelihoods are being organised that determine their outcomes and trajectories. Some of these conceptual implications of the findings require further study before definitive positions can be reached.

A number of policy implications also arise from the analysis of livelihoods. One of these is that the problems of dam-affected communities have not and will not go away by themselves. Indeed, they can be worsened further by the continuing delay in addressing them as humans continue to interact with a deteriorating environment. Secondly, many of the fundamental problems are too large to be the responsibility of affected communities and their members. They require the intervention of the State and other agencies. For example, the poor state of the Volta River, particularly the problem of aquatic weeds, cannot be left to households or communities to resolve by communal labour. Beyond the issues of scale and seriousness lie matters of principle and legal justification which go beyond the VRA's notions of good corporate citizenship and moral responsibility. Simply put, while a State is able to deploy the resources of particular areas of its jurisdiction for the benefit of all under the principle of eminent domain, it has the duty to make good the losses suffered by those who were using the resources prior to their deployment. In the post World Commission on Dams (WCD) world, state responsibility for the problems of dam-affected communities has been strongly reaffirmed in terms of International Human Rights Instruments.

The specificities of affected communities imply that each kind of community requires particular measures and full attention. The fate of the Lower Volta, which fell off the agenda in spite of stated intentions to address its problems, point to the danger of a sequential approach prioritising some communities over others. After nearly forty years of equivocation, the main criteria for prioritisation should be the seriousness of impacts and past neglect. On those two counts, the Lower Volta is a priority, but not the only one. In the Lower Volta Environmental Impact Studies (Volta Basin Research Project, 1999), fears were expressed about Tongu Ewe migrants flooding back to the Lower Volta in order to benefit from interventions instituted there. Given our study's findings about the overlaps and changes in the status of resettled, migrant and downstream residents and the increase in the incidence of multi-spatial livelihood strategies, this is a difficult issue. It is much more complicated than the view that people who would otherwise not qualify for support might flood to an area to benefit from interventions there. Moreover, the Lakeside has issues of its own that require urgent attention and if tackled in tandem with the Lower Volta's problems, might reduce the danger of dual claims. That said, dual claims might be legitimate in cases where losses predated migration.

The inter-connections among dam-affected communities implies that proposed measures to address their problems need to pay attention to consistency so that one set of solutions do not exacerbate the conditions of others. The most fruitful approach is a comprehensive plan, which sees the problems of one kind of community as a dimension of a large problem of dam impacts. This is not to suggest that all problems must be tackled at once, but that they need to be kept in view even if they are being tackled sequentially. For example, the problem of child labour around the Lake cannot be solved without attention to livelihood issues in the Lower Volta and the unregulated labour relations that permeate the Lakeside and other parts of Ghana. In the same vein, the issue of aquatic weeds affects both health and livelihoods in the Lower Volta and therefore solutions have to keep this in mind. Another example of interconnectedness is the simmering conflicts around the use of the River, which cannot be addressed without attention to the decline in fish stocks, the weeds and the low water levels of the Volta. This is because of the role of these conditions in the creation of conflicts.

The demand for a "Marshall Plan" for the reconstruction of the Lower Volta is very relevant in this regard (Concerned Citizens, 2001). It requires an approach to the reconstruction of the Lower Volta which recognises the different levels of the problem—the environmental and other contextual issues, the institutional dimensions and the household level issues and their inter-linkages. However, it does not negate other more specific recommendations. For example, the Lower Volta Environmental Impacts Studies abound with useful recommendations for the Lower Volta which are relevant to any reconstruction plan for dam-affected communities. These include a programme of work creation, the dredging of the Lower Volta and its creeks, soil rejuvenation through treatment with clam shells to reduce its acidity, agro-forestry programmes and education and training programmes to prepare the youth for new work avenues. Other recommendations are the provision of roads, electricity, potable water, radio and telecommunications facilities to open up the Lower Volta. The studies also proposed the continuation of an experimental on-land aquaculture project at Ada to produce shrimps and crabs and serve as a learning centre for the area, a mangrove rehabilitation project and the introduction of animal traction (Volta Basin Research Project, 1999). In addition to endorsing some of these recommendations, the concerned citizens recommended a special desk at VRA to address the complaints of the Lower Volta, the assessment and payment of reparations to the people and the establishment of an Emergency Relief Fund (Concerned Citizens, 2001).

The differences between social groups in the Lower Volta and around the Lake imply that attention has to be paid to the implications of particular solutions for different social groups. For example, the VBRP's emphasis on shrimp culture has to take on board the consideration that most of its patrons would be men. On the other hand, clam culture, though more challenging, might be of greater interest to women because of its resonance with their pre-dam activities. Even in this case, their ability to benefit would depend on the technologies being developed for the activity. More broadly, solutions should benefit a broad range of social groups instead of exacerbating social differentiation and inequalities. In this connection, proposed measures should promote women's autonomous production as in the pre-dam period and tackle exploitative labour relations involving men and women especially around the Volta Lake, including the problem of child labour.

The idea of a special desk at VRA raises the issue of the institutional framework for addressing the problems of dam-affected communities. The Lower Volta Environmental Impact Studies have argued that the problems are too large and too costly for the Government of Ghana or the VRA to tackle singly. Therefore they recommend a stakeholder-pledging conference of the government, the VRA, donor agencies, NGOs and representatives of dam-affected communities to find the resources. Such a conference would be an important element of a programme to address the problems. However, the Government of Ghana has first of all to unequivocally accept responsibility for the condition of dam-affected communities. This implies taking the lead in addressing the institutional and resource challenges facing any reconstruction programme. However, much more than a special desk is needed. A new institution or a reformed institution whose central focus is the reconstruction of past, present and future affected communities of the Volta River Project is a necessary element in a comprehensive programme. The WCD guidelines for tackling the problems of dam-affected communities would be a useful starting point for determining its scope of work and orientation. New institutions raise the question of structure, legal and institutional character, relationship with the power generating and distribution institutions and the State and its resource base. It requires the recognition of dam impacts as an integral part of the costs of providing electricity and therefore ensuring that electricity tariffs provide the margins to pay for these costs on a regular and sustained basis. Donor resources while important and welcome cannot replace a sustainable source of core funding. The almost forty-year gap in responses also has to be computed and compensated from state development resources. This could form the resource base of a new or reformed institution and allow it to tackle the large and complicated task of the reconstruction of the Lower Volta and the problems of other dam-affected communities.

The idea of compensation and reparations for individual and community losses continues to exercise the minds of members of affected communities, as was found at Sokpoe and Mepe. The Lower Volta Environmental Impacts Studies made the same finding (Volta Basin Research Project, 1999). Given the time lapse and the narrow conception of compensation, it might be more fruitful to find some middle ground of paying some amounts to individuals, households and communities to show good faith, but reserving the bulk for the reconstruction of affected communities. However, decisions about the form and computation of compensation and other matters such as the elements and details of the reconstruction plan have to be made through democratic processes. This requires the participation of different social groups, especially those that have hitherto been absent from conferences and other deliberations on dam impacts, such as the women and youth.

These policy implications of the Akosombo and Kpong Dams are relevant to the proposed Bui Dam Project. While not binding, the WCD guidelines make clear that old problems have to be tackled before new projects are initiated. In our view, this not only promotes redress, but allows the relevant institutions to learn for the future. Indeed, Akosombo and Kpong have many lessons to offer the Bui Project. For example, the research approach pioneered by the Preparatory Commission might be modified and applied to the Bui project, not only to generate baseline information but to also ensure that the concerns of potentially affected populations have been heard and given serious consideration. Such communities also have to be supported with resources, expertise and the logistics to enable them to participate meaningfully in the design, implementation and management of the Project on the terms put forward by the World Commission on Dams Report. In particular, the recommendation that they become project beneficiaries is especially challenging and relevant.

There are a number of challenges in the policy context which make recommendations difficult to implement, or if implemented to have the desired outcomes. Fundamental shifts in policy directions such as what is being recommended are generally difficult to achieve. In the particular case, the problems are enormous and deep. As well, habits of close to four decades would be hard to break. This is especially because while the VRA has had the benefit of new thinking about affected communities, it has retained its deeply flawed approach to the issue. For example, the organisation participated in the processes leading up to the WCD and attended the Africa region's meeting of the Commission. However, there is no indication in its documents of whether or how the WCD Report is influencing its attitudes and policies towards affected communities. The bureaucratic culture of development institutions and the mobilisational approach to agenda setting in policy making in Ghana pose real dangers to whatever institution is established to tackle the affairs of communities who have suffered for so long. The problem of resources is serious and requires great political will on the part of the government to resolve. These challenges at the level of the State are compounded by the poor citizenship culture and low level of organisation among affected communities. The different power structures—the chiefs, the District Assemblies and Development Associations, have to work out more democratic and accountable ways of representing dam-affected communities.

Several developments in the power sector have thrown it into low level turmoil since the mid-1990s. These include the demand for power outstripping supplies leading to periodic power cuts. Related closely to this problem has been the VRA's inability to secure commercial rates for electricity from domestic consumers. These problems are being played out in a context of economic liberalisation and Structural Adjustment policies which have seen the entry of private power producers into what was a state-owned sector. Electricity for domestic consumers had been considered one of the clear benefits of the Volta River Project. However, it was only from the early 1990s that electricity was extended to large sections of Ghana under the National Electrification Scheme. The aims of the scheme included the creation of conditions for rural development through support for the development of essential services, increased employment and the reduction of rural urban migration (VRA, 1991; Yeboah, 1999). The significant expansion of local consumption of electricity under the Scheme had implications for supply, an issue the VRA outlined a strategy to deal

with in 1991. Its approach was to improve the generation capacity
of existing plants and prospect for additional sources of power. This
included the renovation of substations, transmission lines, communications and other major equipment. As well, there were plans to
explore more hydroelectric power (HEP) options, but also to reduce
Ghana's dependence on this source of energy by exploring alternatives such as natural gas and residual fuel (VRA, 1991). In 1997,
the VRA announced the commissioning and coming into operation
of the first 110 MW unit of the Takoradi Thermal Power Plant
(VRA, 1997).

Many of the larger dam-affected communities finally became connected to the national grid, thus addressing a longstanding griev-
ance. However, many households soon had problems paying power
tariffs and, therefore, maintaining their power supply.[10] And yet, the
power expansion programme depended on charging consumers economic tariffs. From the 1990s, the VRA's image as an efficient and
well-ran operation began to falter, partly because of its inability to
persuade past and present governments to endorse electricity tariff
increases. In a situation of falling real wages and soaring prices, there
were fears of a political fallout from high electricity prices. Thus,
the VRA for years did not receive economic returns on electricity
production and was owed huge sums by the Electricity Corporation.

In the early 90s, things began to change when the principle of
recovering the full cost of electricity supply from domestic consumers
was accepted by the then government (VRA, 1992). To avoid dramatic increases in tariffs however, the Authority was to adjust the
rates gradually. Also, the tariffs had to take account of "life line"
considerations to address the needs of the lowest category of income
earners (VRA, 1992, p. 10). With the view to regulating the energy
sector, a Public Utilities Regulatory Commission (PURC) was established in 1997.[11] Kalitsi argued that the PURC represented a lack

---

[10] The expansion also created new groups of affected populations and a new
round of demands for compensation for lost land, crops and buildings. The VRA's
preoccupation with these new groups did not leave it with much capacity for dealing with those who became affected more than three decades ago.
[11] PURC was established in a year described by the VRA Annual Report as one
"in which the Authority's efforts to obtain economic tariffs for electricity to meet
the cost of operating, maintaining and expanding our assets did not materialise".
This was due to the suspension of new approved tariffs announced by the Ministry

of consistency in government policy. At one level, VRA was expected to operate in a competitive environment, and yet it was hobbled in terms of its ability to fix power rates and, therefore, earn enough revenue to plan development projects (KK, Accra). There were also concerns that as the new Commission was dominated by consumers, it would be biased towards them to the detriment of the VRA's attempts to secure economic rates for electricity. What was not said was that as affected communities were also not properly represented, the PURC could not be expected to protect their interests.

That the question of electricity tariffs coincided with the expansion of electricity consumption beyond urban consumers has made the issue of affordability and equity important but unpopular among the producers and distributors of power. Affected communities which felt that they should not have to pay commercial rates for electricity now had to make their case in a context of market-oriented economic philosophies and VRA's anxieties about its very survival. At the same time, Kalitsi, for example, has argued that those benefiting the most had to pay enough to improve the conditions of those who were suffering negative effects. If this view would penetrate the State and the power bureaucracies, it would be a great step forward for dam-affected communities. The likelihood of this happening was however not so good.

As a response to the dwindling availability of concessionary loans worldwide and a World Bank- and IMF-directed Structural Adjustment Programme, the Government of Ghana invited private capital participation in the power sector. The VRA was, therefore, co-operating with private companies in power production. For example, the 110-megawatt expansion of the capacity of the Takoradi Thermal Plant was being financed jointly by the VRA and CMS Generation (CMSG), a power company from Michigan, USA. More such partnerships were envisaged in the future. The VRA also announced its agreement in principle with another American Company, Marathon Power Antares of Houston, Texas, to establish the framework for the joint development of a 300MW thermal plant in the Tema area. As well, the proposed Bui hydroelectric Power Project was expected to be built with private financing (VRA, 1998).

of Mines and Energy, because of public outcry. The PURC was subsequently set up to be responsible, among other duties, for approving rates chargeable for electricity (VRA, 1997, p. 11).

In 1998, the VRA established a number of limited liability companies.[12] In addition, it announced plans to reorganise itself to ensure the profitability of its various components (VRA, 1997). These moves were to reposition the organisation in the sector, make space for the independent power producers (IPPs) and perhaps to forestall the threat of divestiture.[13] The new companies, however, would continue to be subsidiaries of the VRA in the near future. As at 2005, the VRA had not yet shifted its business to those companies.

The presence of private capital in the energy sector was more than a shift in the nature of financing. The monopoly position of the VRA was reversed. Independent power producers to be licensed by the Energy Commission could now operate in Ghana.[14] The new regime has also freed the VRA of responsibility for ensuring that its power supply capability matches present and future demand for electricity. This was now the Energy Commission's statutory duty. Kalitsi has argued that the presence of private sector actors might also make it easier for the VRA to secure good prices for its power. For local communities, however, the introduction of independent power producers has complicated the picture for establishing responsibility and compensation for the impacts of the Dams. Those with old grievances now had to deal with new institutions and new situations.

There are many promising directions for future research on dam-affected communities. In the first place, the approach used in this study can be extended to the study of VRP resettlements, both old and new. As well, host communities would benefit from such attention. In relation to the gaps in our knowledge of the two kinds of communities tackled in this study, the issue of the implications of bilharzia and other water-borne diseases on livelihoods needs research. Child labour both around the Lakeside and the Lower Volta would benefit from more in-depth consideration as would the place and

---

[12] These companies, which were to take up the transmission and distribution of power were the National Grid Company Ltd. (GRIDCO), the Northern Electricity Distribution Company Ltd. (NEDCO), the Volta Telecommunications Company Ltd. (VOLTACOM) and the Takoradi Power Company Ltd. (TAPCO).

[13] The establishment of GRIDCO was to ensure open access to transmission-lines to all power-generating companies (KK, Accra).

[14] They could be private foreign, local or statutory organisations. Indeed, the Ghana National Petroleum Corporation (GNPC), a statutory corporation became involved in thermal power production. The GNPC has, since a change of government in Ghana in January 2001, ceased to be a player in the development of power.

meaning of certain cultural practices and repertoires in livelihoods. A comparative study of the different judicial fora and processes in Lakeside and Lower Volta settlements and their place in the organisation of livelihoods would deepen our understanding of livelihoods in the Volta Basin. The study's approach could also be used to provide some of the baseline information on communities to be affected by the proposed Bui Dam. For the Lower Volta and Lakeside communities though, time is running out and, therefore, future research has to be within the framework of tackling the identified issues. More delays would only exacerbate the precariousness of their living conditions. Notwithstanding the valiant attempts of the people who live in the shadow of the Volta River Project, not only will the log never become a crocodile, but it is in an advanced stage of rot and disintegration.

REFERENCES

Abhyankar, N.G. (1963), The regional planning of the Volta River Basin. *Volta Basin Research Project.*
—— (1964), The multi-purpose aspect of the Volta River Project. *Economic Bulletin of Ghana*, 8 (1).
Acquaisie, K.D. (2002), Who is representing local industrialists and the devastated communities in the Volta Project negotiations in Ghana, Ghanaweb, 31 May 2002.
Adams, W.M. (1985), The downstream impacts of dam construction: A case study from Nigeria, in Transactions of the Institute of British Geographers NS, Vol. 10: 292–302.
—— (1992), *Wasting the Rain: Rivers, people and planning in Africa.* Earthscan Publications Ltd., London.
—— (1993), Development's deaf ear: Downstream users and water releases from the Bakalori Dam, Nigeria, *World Development*, 21: (9) 1405–1416.
Addo-Ashong, F.W. (1969), The effects of flooding on the decomposition of wood. In: *Man-Made Lakes: The Accra symposium.* Obeng, L.E. (ed), Ghana Universities Press.
Aduamah E.Y. (1971), The Big Dam, *Legon Observer*, 6 (4).
Adu-Aryee, V.Q. (1985), The planning and execution of the Akosombo and Kpong hydroelectric project resettlement schemes. Institute of Social Studies, The Hague, the Netherlands.
Afriyie, E.K. (1986), Resettlement agriculture in Ghana—An experiment in innovation. In *Rural Development in Ghana*, Brown, C.K. (ed), Ghana Universities Press, Accra.
Agarwal, B. (1994), *A Field of One's Own: Gender and Land Rights in South Asia*, Cambridge, Cambridge University Press.
—— (1997), "Bargaining" and gender relations: within and beyond the household, *Feminist Economics Vol. 3 (1): 1–51.*
Agbodeka, F. (1992), *A handbook of Eweland, Vol. 1: The Ewes of Southeastern Ghana*, Agbodeka, F. (ed), Woeli Publishing Services, Accra.
Ahn, P.M. (1970), A brief progress report on work carried out by the University of Ghana Volta Basin Research Project on the Lake Drawdown Area, July 1968–February 1970. Technical Report No. 34, University of Ghana Volta Basin Research Project.
Amalric, F. (1998), The sustainable livelihoods approach: General report of the sustainable livelihoods project 1995–1997, Society for International Development (SID), Rome.
Amatekpor, J.K. (1970), Some investigations on soils, agricultural land-use, insect pests and plant diseases in the drawdown area of the Volta Lake. VBRP Technical Report, No. X 36, University of Ghana, Legon.
—— (1999), Soils and Land-Use in the Volta Basin: State of the Art, In: *The Sustainable Integrated Development of the Volta Basin in Ghana.* Gordon, C. & Amatekpor, J.K. (eds) Volta Basin Research Project, University of Ghana, Legon, Accra.
Amatekpor, J.K., Kufogbe, S.K., Anipa, B. and Duadze, S.E.K. (1999), Soils and land-use, *Volta Basin Research Project, 1999. Volta River Authority Lower Volta Environmental Impact Studies, Final Status Report for the Second Phase: May 1, 1998–January 31, 1999.* Prepared for the Volta River Authority, Volta Basin Research Project Secretariat, University of Ghana, Legon.

Ameka (2001), Ewe, In: Facts About the World's Languages: An Encyclopedia of the World's Major Languages, Past and Present. Garry, J. and Rubino, C. (eds), The H.W. Wilson Company, New York and Dublin.

Amenumey, D.E.K. (1997), A brief history. In: *A Handbook of Eweland, Vol. 1: The Ewes of Southeastern Ghana*, Agbodeka, F. (ed), Woeli Publishing Services, Accra.

Amoah, C. (1999), Water Quality *Volta Basin Research Project, 1999. Volta River Authority Lower Volta Environmental Impact Studies, Final Status Report for the Second Phase: May 1, 1998–January 31, 1999.* Prepared for the Volta River Authority, Volta Basin Research Project Secretariat, University of Ghana, Legon.

—— (1999), Overview of microbiological studies on the Volta Lake. In: *The Sustainable Integrated Development of the Volta Basin in Ghana.* Gordon, C. & Amatekpor, J.K. (eds), Volta basin research project, University of Ghana, Legon, Accra.

Anin, T.E. (2000), *Banking in Ghana*, Woeli Publishing Services, Accra.

Anipati III, Togbe. (undated), Memorandum submitted by Fiaga of Mepe Traditional Area to the Committee appointed by the National Redemption Council (Ghana Government between 1972–1975) to investigate chieftaincy matters in the Volta Region of Ghana.

Apt, N. (1992), "Trends and Prospects in Africa," *Community Development Journal*, Vol. 27 (2): 130–139.

Arce, A. and Hebinck, P. (2002), Life styles and the livelihood framework: problems and possibilities for development studies, paper presented at seminar on livelihoods, Cidin, University of Nijmegen, Nijmegen.

Aryeetey, E. and Harrigan, J. (2000), Macroeconomic and sectoral developments since 1970, in *Economic Reforms in Ghana: The Miracle and the Mirage.* Aryeetey, E., Harrigan, J. and Nissanke, M. (eds), James Currey, Woeli and African World Press, Oxford, Accra and Trenton.

Asafo, C.K. (1999), The role of the fisheries Department of the Ministry of Food and Agriculture in the Volta Basin. In: *The Sustainable Integrated Development of the Volta Basin in Ghana.* Gordon, C. & Amatekpor, J.K. (eds), Volta Basin Research Project, University of Ghana, Legon, Accra.

Atakpu, L. (2000), Dams, food security and livelihoods: Understanding the Nigerian experience, African network for environment and economic justice, Nigeria, WCD Regional Consultation Paper.

Ayibotele, Nii Boi (1999), Closing statements on the sustainable integrated development of the Volta Basin. In: *The Sustainable Integrated Development of the Volta Basin in Ghana.* Gordon, C. & Amatekpor, J.K. (eds), Volta Basin Research Project, University of Ghana, Legon, Accra.

Baerends, E. (1994), *Changing Kinship, Family And Gender Relations in Sub-Saharan Africa*, Women and Autonomy Centre, University of Leiden.

Bagachwa, M. (1997), The rural informal sector in Tanzania. In: *Farewell to farms: De-Agrarianisation and Employment in Africa.* Bryceson, D.F. & Jamal, V. (eds), African Studies Centre, Leiden, Research Series. 1997/10.

Balogh, T. (1956), Time and the Volta, Once More. *West Africa*, September 29 pp. 753–755.

Balon, E.K. (1978), "The Dubious Benefits of Large Dams", Ambio, Vol. 7, No. 2.

Bank, L. (1997), Of livestock and deadstock: entrepreneurship and tradition on the South African Highveld. In: *Farewell to Farms: De-Agrarianisation and Employment in Africa.* Bryceson, D.F. & Jamal, V. (eds), African Studies Centre, Leiden, Research Series. 1997/10.

Barnes, K. (1964), A Study of financial and economic consequences of Ghana Volta River project part one. Existent rural economy of the inundated Volta Basin.

—— (1966), *Economics of Volta River Project.* The State Publishing Corporation, Accra—Tema.

Beall, J. and Kanji, N. (1999), Households, livelihoods and urban poverty, *Theme Paper Three: ESCOR Commissioned Research on Urban Development: Urban Governance, Partnership and Poverty.*

Bebbington, A. (1999), Capitals and Capabilities: A Framework for Analyzing Peasant Viability, Rural Livelihoods and Poverty. *World Development,* 27 (12).

Beckman, B. (1986), Bakalori: Peasants Versus State and Industry in Nigeria. In: *The Socia and Environmental Effects of Large Dams, Vol. 2: Case Studies,* Goldsmith, E. & Hildyard, N. (eds), Wadebridge Ecological Centre.

Benda-Beckmann, F. Von, (1998), Social security and insecurity as a field of research and policy, CERES/CNWS/ASSR Summer School, Social Security and Insecurity, Amsterdam.

—— (1995), Rural populations, social security and legal pluralism in the Central Moluccas of Eastern Indonesia, in Dixon, J. and Scheurell, B. (eds), Social Security Programmes: A Cross-Cultural Perspective. Westport, Greenwood, (pp. 75–107).

Bequele, A. and Myers, W. (1995), First Things First: Eliminating Work Detrimental to Children. UNICEF/ILO, Geneva.

Bhalla, A.S (ed), (1992), *Environment, Employment and Development,* ILO, Geneva.

Birmingham, et al. (1966), The Volta River Project. In: *A Study of Contemporary Ghana. Vol. 1: The Economy of Ghana.* Allen & Unwin, London.

Biswas, A.K. (1978), Environmental Implications of Water Development for Developing Countries, in Widstrand, C. (ed), *The Social and Ecological Effects of Water Development in Developing Countries,* Pergamon Press, Oxford.

Blackwelder, B. (1983), Damming the world. *Not Man Apart,* October 1983.

Blackwelder, B. and Carlson, P. (1984), Fact Sheets on International Water Development Projects, Environmental Policy Institute, International Resources Project, Washington D.C.

Blaikie, P., Cannon, T., Davis, I. & Wisner, B. (1994), *At risk. Natural Hazards, People's Vulnerability and Disasters.* London: Routledge.

Bourdieu, (1977), *Outline of a Theory of Practice,* Cambridge University Press, Cambridge.

Braimah, L.I. (1999), Management of fisheries resources of Lake Volta. In: *The Sustainable Integrated Development of the Volta Basin in Ghana.* Gordon, C. & Amatekpor, J.K. (eds), Volta Basin Research Project, University of Ghana, Legon, Accra.

Bosshard, P. (2001), NGOs Protest World Bank Position on WCD Guidelines for Dams, World Rivers Review, International Rivers Network, Vol. 16. No. 2.

Brown, C.K. (1986), Urban bias and rural development in Ghana. In: *Rural development in Ghana.* Brown, C.K. (ed), Ghana Universities Press, Accra.

Bruce, J. (1989), Homes divided, *World Development,* 17 (7): 979–991.

Bryceson, D.F. and Jamal, V. (eds) (1997), *Farewell to farms: De-Agrarianisation and employment in Africa.* African Studies Centre, Leiden, Research Series. 1997/10.

Bryceson, D.F. (1997(a)), De-Agrarianisation: Blessing or blight? In: *farewell to farms: De-Agrarianisation and employment in Africa.* Bryceson, D.F. & Jamal, V. (eds) African Studies Centre, Leiden, Research Series. 1997/10.

—— (1997(b)), De-Agrarianisation in Sub-Saharan Africa: Acknowledging the inevitable. In: *Farewell to Farms: De-Agrarianisation and Employment in Africa.* Bryceson, D.F. & Jamal, V. (eds), African Studies Centre, Leiden, Research Series. 1997/10.

Bryceson, D.F., Kay, C., and Mooij, J. (2000), *Disappearing Peasantries? Rural labour in Africa, Asia, and Latin America.* Intermediate Technology Publications, London.

Cagatay, N. (1998), 'Gender and Poverty', *Working Paper 5,* Social Development and Poverty Elimination Division, New York: UNDP.

Carney, D. (ed), (1998) *Sustainable Rural Livelihoods: What Contribution can we make?* Department for International Development (DFID), London.

Carney, J. and Watts, M. (1990), Manufacturing dissent: Work, gender and the politics of meaning in a peasant society, *Africa Vol. 60 (2): 207–240.*

Cernea, M. (1990), Internal refugees and development-caused population displacement, Harvard Institute for International Development, Development Discussion Paper No. 345, note 5.

—— (1996), Bridging the research divide: Studying refugees and development oustees. In: Allen T. (ed) *In search of cool ground: war, flight and homecoming in Northeast Africa*, UNRISD, James Currey and Africa World Press, London, Trenton.

Chakrabarty, D. (1983), On Deifying and defying authority: Managers and workers in the jute mills of Bengal circa 1900–1940, *Past and Present*, 100, 124–46.

Chambers, R. (1970), *The Volta resettlement experience*, Chambers, R. (ed), Pall Mall Press Ltd., London.

—— (1997), *Whose reality counts? Putting the first last*, Intermediate Technology Publications, London.

Chambers, R. and Conway, G.R. (1992), Sustainable rural livelihoods: Practical concepts for the 21st century, Sussex, IDS.

Chanock, M. (1982), Making customary law: Men, women and courts in colonial northern Rhodesia. In: *African women and the law: Historical perspectives*. Hay, M. & Wright, M. (eds), Boston University Press, Boston.

Chimhowu, A.O. (2002), Extending the grain basket to the margins: Spontaneous land resettlement and changing livelihoods in the Hurungwe District, Zimbabwe, *Journal of Southern African Studies Vol. 28 (3): 551–573*.

Chisholm, N.G. (1982), Response of some rural communities in South-East Ghana to economic recession, Cambridge Monograph Series.

Clark, B.D. et al. (1984), *Perspectives on environmental impact assessment*, D. Rendel Publishing Co., Dordrecht.

Collier, M., Webb, R.H. Schmidt, J.C. (1996), Dams and Rivers: A Primer on the Downstream Effects of Dams, US Geological Survey Circular, 1126, Tuscon, US Geological Survey.

Concerned Citizens of the Tongu Area. (2001), Press statement on the Lower Volta environmental impact studies by the Volta River Authority through the Volta Basin research project of the University of Ghana.

Coppola, S.R. and Agadzi, K. (1977), Evolution of the fishing industry over time at Volta Lake, 1970–1976. In: *Volta Lake Research and Development Project. FAO Statistical Studies*. No. GHA/71/533.

Cummings, B.J. (1990), Dam the Rivers and Damn the People, Earthscan, London.

Darpaah, G.A., Addo, S. and Akomeah, J. (1999), Hydrobiology and fisheries aquatic resource development *Volta Basin Research Project, 1999. Volta River Authority Lower Volta Environmental Impact Studies, Final Status Report for the Second Phase: May 1, 1998–January 31, 1999*. Prepared for the Volta River Authority, Volta Basin Research Project Secretariat, University of Ghana, Legon.

de Bruijn, M., Van Dijk, H. (1999), Insecurity and pastoral development in the Sahel, Development and Change, Vol. 30, No. 1, January 1999, pp. 115–140.

de Graft Johnson, K.A.A. (1999), Overview of the weed problems in the Volta Basin. In: *The Sustainable Integrated Development of the Volta Basin in Ghana*. Gordon, C. & Amatekpor, J.K. (eds), Volta Basin Research Project, University of Ghana, Legon, Accra.

de Haan, L. (2000), *Livelihood, Locality and Globalisation*. Nijmegen University Press, Nijmegen.

de Haan, L. and Zoomers, A. (forthcoming), Development Geography at the Crossroads of Livelihood and Globalisation, in Journal for Economic and Social Geography.

de Zoysa, D.A. (1995), *The Great Sandy River: Class and Gender Transformation Among Pioneers Settlers in Sri Lanka's Frontier*, Ph.D. Thesis, Het Spinhuis Publishers, Amsterdam.

Denyoh, (1969), Changes in fish population and gear selectivity in the Volta Lake.

Department of State, (1964–1968), Foreign Relations of the United States, Volume XXIV, Africa, Ghana, Washington DC.

Derban, L.K.A. (1984), The health impacts of the Volta Dam, Ghana. In: *Perspectives on environmental impact assessment.* Clark, B.D. et al. (eds), D. Rendel Publishing Co. Dordrecht.

—— (1985), Ghana's Kpong Dam: A Case Study of Environmental Impact. Follow-up/Audit of Environmental Assessments Results Conference, The Banff Centre.

—— (1999), Public health aspects of the Volta Lake. In: *The sustainable integrated development of the Volta Basin in Ghana.* Gordon, C. & Amatekpor, J.K. (eds.), Volta Basin Research Project, University of Ghana, Legon, Accra.

Devambez, L.C. (1970), Some considerations on the improvement of fishing gear and fishing craft on lake fishing. *Volta Lake Research Project,* December 1970.

Devereux, S. (2001), Livelihood insecurity and social protection: a re-emerging issue in rural development. *Development Policy Review* 19, 4, pp. 507–519.

Diaw, K. and Schmidt-Kallert, E. (1990), *Effects of the Volta Lake resettlement in Ghana: A reappraisal after twenty-five years,* Arbeiten Aus Dem Institut fur Afrika Kunde, Hamburg, 1990.

Dickinson, H. (1982a), The Volta Dam: energy for industry? In: *industry and accumulation in Africa,* Fransman, M. (ed), Heinemann, London, Educational Books Ltd., Ibadan, Nairobi.

—— (1982b), Some population related problems in the Ghanaian economy, *The economic bulletin of Ghana,* Heinemann, London.

Dietz T. (1996), *Entitlements to natural resources: Contours of political environmental geography,* International Books, Utrecht.

Dixon, J. et al. (1989), "Dams and the Environment: Considerations in World Bank Projects", World Bank Technical Paper No. 110.

Dobson, F. (1963a), The Volta River Project: Its economic and financial progress, *Ghana Trade Journal, 1963.*

—— (1963b), Progress at Akosombo: Volta Dam takes concrete shape, *Ghana Trade Journal, July 1963.*

Dodoo, M. (1970), A Case Study of a Resettlement Town: New Mpamu. In: *The Ghana resettlement experience.* Chambers, R. (ed) Pall Mall Press Ltd., London.

Dogra, B. (1985), "Who Are Damned When Rivers Are Dammed?", *News From Fields & Slums,* NFS India, December.

Dorcey, T., Steiner, A., Acreman, M., and Orlando, B. (eds) (1997), *Large Dams: Learning for the past, looking at the future.* Workshop proceedings, IUCN/The World Bank, Gland Switzerland.

Drijver and Marchand (1985), The middle valley of the Senegal River (Senegal), *Case study in taming of the floods,* Drijver, C.A. & Marchand, M. (eds), Commission of the European Communities Centre for Environmental Studies, State University of Leiden.

Drijver, C.A. and Rodenburg, W.F. (1988), Water management at a crossroads: The case of the Sahelian Wetlands. Paper presented at the international symposium of hydrology of wetlands in semi-arid regions, Seville, May 1988.

Dwivedi, R. (1999), Displacement, risks and resistance: local perceptions and actions in the Sardar Sarovar, *Development and Change,* Vol. 30, No. 1, January 1999, pp. 43–78.

Dwivedi, R. (2001), Resource Conflict and Collective Action: The Sardar Sarovar Project in India, Ph.d. Dissertation, Institute of Social Studies, the Hague.

Ellis, F. and Freeman, H.A. (2002), Rural livelihoods and poverty reduction strategies in four African countries, *LADDER Working Paper No. 30.*

Ellis, F. (1998), Household strategies and rural livelihood diversification. *The Journal of development studies,* Vol. 35, No. 1, October 1998.

—— (1999), Rural livelihood diversity in developing countries: Evidence and policy implications, *Overseas Development Institute Natural Resource Perspectives No. 40.*

—— (2000a), The determinants of rural livelihood diversification in developing countries. *Journal of agricultural economics, 51 (2).*

—— (2000b), Capturing diverse livelihoods for policy purposes: a case-study from Tanzania, paper presented at the seminar perceiving livelihoods and mobility patterns amongst the poor in Africa and Latin America, African Studies Centre, Leiden, 12th October 2000.

—— (2000c), *Rural livelihoods and diversity in developing countries*. Oxford University Press, Oxford, New York.

—— (2001), Rural livelihoods, diversity and poverty reduction policies: Uganda, Tanzania, Malawi and Kenya, *LADDER Working Paper No. 1*.

Elson, D. (1992), "From survival strategies to transformation strategies: women's needs and structural adjustment." In *Unequal Burden: Economic Crises, Persistent Poverty, and Women's Work*, ed. L. Beerier & S. Feldman, Oxford: Westview Press.

Ennin, M.A. and Degraft Johnson, K.A.A. (1977), Studies on the ecology of Egeria radiata in the Lower Volta Estuary, Institute of Aquatic Biology, (CSIR) Publication No. IAB 76.

Ennew, J. (1994), Street and Working Children: A Guide to Planning, Save the Children, Development Manual, 4.

Esteva, G. (1997), Development, In The Development Dictionary: A Guide to Knowledge as Power, Sachs, W. (ed), Orient Longman., ertdEV g.

Faber, M. (1990), The Volta River Project: For whom the smelter tolled. In: *Towards economic recovery in sub-saharan Africa. Essays in honour of Robert Gardiner*. Pickett, J. & Singer, H. (eds).

Fahim, H.M. (1981), *Dams, People and Development: The Aswan High Dam Case*, Pergamon Press Inc., New York.

Fapohunda, E.R. (1987), The nuclear household model in Nigeria public and private sector policy: colonial legacy and socio-political implications, *Development and Change*, 18 (2) 281–294.

Farvar, M.T. and Milton J.P. (1972), *The Careless Technology: Ecology and International Development*, The Record of the Conference on the Ecological Aspects of International Development, convened by the Conservation Foundation and the Centre for the Biology of Natural Systems, Washington University, December 8–11, 1968, The Natural History Press, New York.

Fiawoo, D. (1961), Social survey of Tefle. Child Development Research Unit, Institute of Education, University College of Ghana, Legon.

Fine, B. (1999), The developmental state is dead-long live social capital, *Development and Change*, Vol. 30, No. 1, January 1999, pp. 1–20.

—— (1998), The Triumph of Economics: Or "Rationality" Can be dangerous to your reasoning. In *Virtualism: The New Political Economy*, Carrier, J. & Miller, D. (eds), Berg, London.

Foeken, D. (1997), Urban trajectories in rural livelihood strategies: household employment patterns in Kenya's coast province. In: *Farewell to farms: de-agrarianisation and employment in Africa*. Bryceson, D.F. & Jamal, V. (eds) African Studies Centre, Leiden, Research Series. 1997/10.

Folbre, N. (1986), Cleaning house, New perspectives on households and economic development. *Journal of Development Economics*, 22 5–40.

Francis, E. (1998), Gender and rural livelihoods in Kenya, the *Journal of Development Studies*, 35, No. 2, December 1998.

—— (2000), *Making a living: Changing livelihoods in rural Africa*. Routledge Press, London and New York.

—— (2002), Rural livelihoods, institutions and vulnerability in West Province, South Africa, *Journal of Southern African Studies Vol. 28 (3): 531–550*.

Franklin, B. (2001) Children's Rights: An Introduction, In The New Handbook of Children's Rights, Franklin, B. (ed) Routledge, London.

Fuchs, R.G. (1984), *Abandoned children: Foundlings and child welfare in nineteenth-century France*, State University Of New York Press, Albany.

Futa, A.B. (1961), The Volta River Project Part I. *The Economic Bulletin of Ghana*, 5 (1).
—— (1963), The Volta River Project Part II. *The Economic Bulletin of Ghana*, 3 (1).
—— (1983), Water resources development—Organisation of a resettlement programme. A case study of Kpong resettlement programme in Ghana. *Water International*, 8.
Gaidzanwa, R.B. (1997), Non-farm activities and gender in Zimbabwe. In: *Farewell to Farms: De-Agrarianisation and Employment in Africa*. Bryceson, D.F. & Jamal, V. (eds) African Studies Centre, Leiden, Research Series. 1997/10.
Geker, J. (1999), The effects of the Volta Dam on the people of the lower Volta. In: *The Sustainable Integrated Development of the Volta Basin in Ghana*. Gordon, C. & Amatekpor, J.K. (eds), Volta Basin Research Project, University of Ghana, Legon, Accra.
Geschiere, P. and Gugler, J. (1998), The Urban-rural connection: Changing issues of belonging and identification, *Africa*, 68, (3).
Ghai, D. (1992), Conservation, livelihood and democracy: social dynamics of environmental changes in Africa. UNRISD Discussion Paper, DP 33.
—— (1994), Environment, livelihood and empowerment, *Development and Change*, 25.
Ghana Statistical Service, (2002), Special Report on 20 Largest Localities, 2000. Population and Housing Census, Census Division, Accra.
Gladwin, C. (ed) (1991), *Structural Adjustment and African Women Farmers*. University of Florida Press, Florida.
Goldsmith and Hildyard, (1984), *The Social and Environmental Effects of Large Dams*. Goldsmith, E. & Hildyard, N. (eds), Vol. I, Wadebridge Ecological Centre, Camelford.
—— (eds) (1986), *The Social and Environmental Effects of Large Dams*. Goldsmith, E. & Hildyard, N. (eds), Vol. II, Case Studies, Wadebridge Ecological Centre, Camelford.
Goodland, R. (1977) "Environmental optimization in hydro development of Tropical Forest Regions", in *Man-made Lakes and Human Health*, Proceedings of the Symposium on Man-made Lakes and Human Health, Faculty of Medicine, University of Surinam, October 23–25, 1977, Paramaribo, Surinam.
—— (1989), The World Bank's new policy on the environmental aspects of dam and reservoir projects, *World Bank Report Series*, World Bank, Washington, D.C.
—— (1994), Ethical priorities in environmentally sustainable energy systems: A case of tropical hydropower. *World Bank Environment Working Paper 67*.
—— (1997), Environmental Sustainability in the Hydro Industry: Disaggregating the Debates, Overview Paper, In The World Conservation Union (IUCN) And The World Bank, Large Dams: Learning from the Past: Looking at the Future. Workshop Proceedings, Gland, Switzerland, April 11–12, 1997.
Gordon, C. and Amatekpor, J.K. (1999), *The sustainable integrated development of the Volta Basin in Ghana*. Gordon, C. & Amatekpor, J.K. (eds), Volta Basin Research Project, University of Ghana, Legon, Accra.
Gordon, C. (1999), An overview of the fish and fisheries of the Volta Basin. In: *The Sustainable Integrated Development of the Volta Basin in Ghana*. Gordon, C. & Amatekpor, J.K. (eds), Volta Basin Research Project, University of Ghana, Legon, Accra.
Gorman, M. (2002), Sustainable social structures in a society for all ages: exchanging experience between the developed and developing World, in Sustainable Social Structures in a Society for all Ages, Department of Economic and Social Affairs, United Nations, New York.
Government of Ghana (1963), *Statement on the Volta River Project*. Government Printer, Accra.
—— (1966), *Ghana Reborn*, Accra.
Government of the Gold Coast (1952), Development of the Volta River Basin: Statement by the Government of the Gold Coast on the Volta River Project and Related Matters. Printed by the Government Printing Department, Accra, Gold Coast.

Graham, R. (1982) The Aluminum Industry and the Third world: multinational corporations and under-development, London, Zed Press.
—— (1986), Ghana's Volta resettlement scheme. In: *The Social and Environmental Effects of Large Dams, Vol. 2: Case Studies*, Goldsmith, E. & Hildyard, N. (eds), Wadebridge Ecological Centre.
Graham, Y. (1989), From GTP to Assene: Aspects of industrial working class struggles, 1982–1986, in Hansen E. and Ninsin, K. (eds), *The State Development and Politics in Ghana*, London: CODESRIA.
Grant, F.C. (1965), Human aspects of bilharziasis in Ghana: Symposium on Bilharzia in Ghana. *Ghana Medical Journal* 4 (3).
Greeff, L. End of the road for the World Commission on Dams, Land and Rural Digest, September/October 2000, No. 14.
Grown C.A. and Sebstad, J. (1989), Introduction: Towards a wider perspective on women's employment. *World Development*, 17 (7): 937–952.
Guha, R. (1983) *Elementary aspects of peasant insurgency*, Delhi, Oxford University Press.
Guoldin H.M. (1972), Kinship networks in the migration process. *International Migration Review*, 6, (2) Centre for Migration Studies, New York.
Guyer, J.I. (1988), Dynamic approaches to domestic budgeting: Cases and models from Africa, In *A Home Divided: Women and Income in the Third World*, Daisy Dwyer & Judith Bruce (eds.), Stanford: Stanford University Press.
Guyer, J.I. and Peters, P.E. 1987 Introduction: Conceptualizing the Household: Issues of Theory and Policy in Africa. *Development and Change*, 18 (2).
Gyasi, E., and Enu-Kwesi, L. (1997), Agroecology. *Volta Basin Research Project, 1997. Lower Volta Environmental Impact Studies: Status Report for the First Phase: October 7, 1996–July 6, 1997*. Prepared for the Volta River Authority, Volta Basin Research Project Secretariat, University of Ghana, Legon.
—— (1997), Towards enhancement of agroecology disturbed by the damming of the River Volta in Ghana. Preliminary PLEC findings and mitigative suggestions in the Lower Basin, *PLEC News and Views*. No. 9 December 1997.
—— (1999), Agroecology. *Volta Basin Research Project, 1999. Lower Volta Environmental Impact Studies: Final Status Report for the Second Phase: May 1, 1998–January 31, 1999*. Prepared for the Volta River Authority, Volta Basin Research Project Secretariat, University of Ghana, Legon.
Gyimah-Boadi, E. (ed) (993), *Ghana under PNDC Rule*. Dakar: CODESRIA.
Halcrow, W. and Partners (1951), *Report on Development of the Volta River Basin*. Sir William Halcrow & Partners, London.
Hall, J.B. and Pople, W. (1968), Recent vegetational changes in the Lower Volta River. *Volta Basin Research Project Publication Number 39*.
Hall, J.B. (1970), Observations on the vegetation of the Lake Volta Drawdown Area. University of Ghana Volta Basin Research Project Technical Report, X 35.
Hance, W.A. (1958a), *The proposed Volta River Project: A Study in Industrial Development*. Harper, New York.
—— (1967), The Volta River Project: A Study in industrial development. In: *African Economic Development*. Hance, W.A. (ed), Harper, New York.
Hance, E. and Ninsin, K. (1989), *The State, Development, and Politics in Ghana*, Hansen, K. & Ninsin, K. (eds), London, CODESRIA.
Horowitz, M.M. and Salem-Murdock, (1991), Management of an African floodplains: A contribution to the Antropology of public policy. *Landscape and Urban Planning* 20.
Harris, O. (1981), 'Households as natural units', In: *Of Marriage and Market. Women's Subordination in International Perspective*, K. Young, C. Wolkowitz & C. McCullagh (eds), pp. 49–68, London: CSE Books.

Harriss, J.R., and de Renzio, P. (1997), Missing link or analytically missing?: The Concept of Social Capital, *Journal of International Development*, 9 (7): 919–971.

Harrigan, J. and Oduro, A. (2000), Exchange Rate Policy and Balance of Payments, 1972–96, in *Economic Reforms in Ghana: The Miracle and the Mirage*. Aryeetey, E., Harrigan, J. and Nissanke, M. (eds) James Currey, Woeli and African World Press, Oxford, Accra and Trenton.

Hart, D. (1980), *The Volta River Project: A Case Study in Politics and Technology*, Renwood Burn, London.

Hilling, D. (1965), The Volta River Project. *Geographical Magazine*, 37 (11).

Hilton, T.E. and Kowu-Tsri (1979), The impact of the Volta scheme on the Lower Volta Floodplains. *Journal of Tropical Geography*, 30.

Hinden, R. (1950), *Local Government and the Colonies*. London: George Allen and Unwin Ltd.

Hobsbawm, E. (1973), Peasants and Politics, *Journal of Peasant Studies*, 1 (1): 13.

Holden, (1969) Problems in forecasting sustainable yields from man-made lakes. In: *Man-Made Lakes: The Accra Symposium*. Obeng, L. (ed), Ghana Universities Press, Accra.

Hoover, R. (2001), *Pipe Dreams: The World Bank's Failed Efforts to Restore Lives and Livelihoods of Dam-Affected People in Lesotho*. International Rivers Network (IRN), Berkeley, California.

Hutchful, K. (2002), Ghana's Adjustment Experience: The Paradox of Reform, UNRISD: Geneva; James Currey, London.

Imam, A., Mama, A. and Sow, F. (1997), eds., Engendering African Social Sciences, CODESRIA Book Series, Anton Rowe Ltd., Chippenham, Wiltshire.

International Bank for Reconstruction and Development. 1960 Preliminary Appraisal of the Volta River Hydroelectric Project, Ghana. Restricted Report No. TO 249.

Jackson, C. (1996), "Rescuing gender from the poverty trap" *World Development* 24, No. 3: 489–504.

Johnson, S. (1971), A second look at the Volta Lake. *The Ecologist*, 1 (17).

Jopp, K. (1965), *Volta: The Story of Ghana's Volta River Project*, VRA, Accra.

Jubb, R.A. (1972), The J.G. Strydom Dam, Pongolo River, Northern Zululand: The importance of floodplain pans below it, in Piscator, Nol 86.

Kaag, M., Van Berkel, R., Brons, J. de Bruijn, M. Van Dijk, H., de Haan, L., Nooteboom, G. & Zoomers, A. (2003), Poverty is Bad: Ways forward in livelihood research, Paper presented at the Ceres pathways project seminar. Utrecht: Inter-university Research School for Resource Studies for Development.

Kabeer, N. (1994), *Reversed Realities: Gender Hierarchies in Development Thought*, London: Verso.

Kalitsi, E.A.K. (1973), Volta Lake in relation to human population and some issues in economic management. In: *Man-Made Lakes, Their Problems and Environmental Effects*, Ackermann, W.C. (ed), Washington D.C.

—— (1999), The role of Volta River Authority in the development of the Volta Basin. In: *The Sustainable Integrated Development of the Volta Basin in Ghana*. Gordon, C. & Amatekpor, J.K. (eds), Volta Basin Research Project, University of Ghana, Legon, Accra.

Kandiyoti, D. (1998), Gender, Power and Contestation: Rethinking Bargaining with Patriarchy. In: *Feminist Visions of Development: Gender Analysis and Policy*, Jackson, C. and Pearson, R. Routledge, London and New York.

Kassas, M. (1980), "Environmental Aspects of Water Resources Development", in Biswas, A.K. et al., *Water Management for Arid Lands in Developing Countries*, Pergamon Press, Oxford.

Katz, E. (1991), Breaking the Myth of harmony: Theoretical and methodological guidelines to the study of rural Third World Households, *Review of Radical Political Economics*, Vol. 23 (3&4): 37–56.

Killick, T. (1966), "External trade", In Birmingham, Walter et al. (eds), *A study of contemporary Ghana*, London: Allen and Unwin.

—— (1978), *Development Economics in Action: A Study of Economic Policies in Ghana*. St. Martin's Press, New York.

—— (2000), Fragile Still? The Structure of Ghana's Economy 1960–94, in *Economic Reforms in Ghana: The Miracle and the Mirage*, Aryeetey, E., Harrigan, J. and Nissanke, M. (eds), James Currey, Woeli and African World Press, Oxford, Accra and Trenton.

Kinsey, B. (2002), Survival or growth? Temporal dimensions of rural livelihood in risky environments, *Journal of Southern African Studies, Vol. 28 (3): 615–629*

Klumpp, K. and Chu, K.Y. (1977), Ecological Studies of *Bulinus Rolifsi*, the Intermediate Host of *Schistosoma Haematobium* in the Volta Lake, *W.H.O. Bulletin*. 55(6)

Konings, P. (1986), The space and rural class formation in Ghana: A comparative analysis. Monographs from the African Studies Centre, Leiden. KPI, London.

Koopman Henn, J. (1988), Intra-Household dynamics and state policies as constraints on food production: Results of a 1985 Agroeconomic Survey in Cameroun, In: *Gender Issues in Farming Systems Research and Extension*, Susan V. Poats, Marianne Schmink & Anita Spring (eds), Boulder: Westview Press.

Koopman, J. (1991), Neoclassical household models and modes of household production: Problems in the Analysis of African agricultural households, *Review of Radical Political Economics, Vol. 23 (3&4): 148–173*.

Kpikpi, J., Agudogo, D., Ansah, E., and Mensah, G. (1999), Health, in Lower Volta environmental impact studies, Final Status Report for the Second Phase (May 1, 1998–January 31, 1999), Report prepared for the Volta River Authority, Volta Basin Research Project, University of Ghana, Legon.

Kumekpor, T.K.B. (1997), Socio-Economics. *Volta Basin Research Project, 1997. Lower Volta Environmental Impact Studies: Status Report for the First Phase: October 7, 1996–July 6, 1997*. Prepared for the Volta River Authority, Volta Basin Research Project Secretariat, University of Ghana, Legon.

—— (1999), Socio-Economics. *Volta Basin Research Project, 1999. Volta River Authority Lower Volta Environmental Impact Studies for the Second Phase: May 1, 1998–January 31, 1999*. Prepared for the Volta River Authority, Volta Basin Research Project Secretariat, University of Ghana, Legon.

Kumi, E.N. (1973), Environmental effects of the Volta River project, 11th transactions of the international congress on large dams, Madrid, Vol. 1, 1973.

Kurien, P.A. (1994), Non-Economic Bases of Economic Behaviour: The Consumption, Investment and Exchange Patterns of Three Emigrant Communities in Kerala, India, *Development and Change*, 25, (4).

Kwei, E.A. (1965), The Spawning and the Growth of the Volta Oyster, *Egaria Radiata* (Lam), *Ghana Journal of Science*, 5 (2).

Lagler, K.F. (1969), *Man-Made Lakes: Planning and Development*. FAO, Rome.

Lawson, G.W. (1963), Volta Basin Research Project, *Nature*, Vol. 199, August 31, 1963.

—— (1967), *Sudd* Formation on the Volta Lake. *Bulletin de LIFAN*, Vol. 29.

—— (1968), Volta Basin research project. *Nature*, 199, August 31, 1963.

—— et al. (1968), A review of hydrobiological work by the volta basin research project 1963–1968. A paper presented at the regional meeting of Hydrobiologists in Tropical Africa, Makerere University College, Uganda 20–24 May 1968. Technical Report No. 26 Volta Basin Research Project, University of Ghana.

—— et al. (1969a), Observations on acquatic weeds in the Volta Basin.

—— et al. (1969b), Hydrobiological work of the Volta Basin Research Project, 1963–1968. *Bulletin de l'I.F.A.N. 31 (3)*.

Lawson, R.M. (1961), The Development of the Lower Volta. *The Economic Bulletin*, 7 (4).

—— (1963), The economic organisation of the *egaria* fishing industry in the River Volta. *Proceedings of the Malacological Society of London*, Vol. 35 Part 6.

—— (1967), Changes in Food Consumption in a Rural Community on the Lower Volta, 1954–1964, *Nigeria Journal of Economic and Social Studies*, 9 (1).

—— (1968a), Process of rural economic growth. A Case study of the change from a static to a transitional economy in the Lower Volta of Ghana 1954–1967. *Volta Basin Research Project Technical Report, No. 10 (27).*

—— (1968b), The Volta resettlement scheme. *African Affairs*, 67 (267).

—— (1968c), An interim economic appraisal of the Volta Resettlement Scheme. *Nigerian Journal of Economic and Social Studies*, 10 (1).

—— (1972), *The changing economy of the Lower Volta, 1954–67*, Oxford University Press, London.

Leach, M., Mearns, R. and Scoones, I. (1999), Environmental entitlement: Dynamics and institutions in community based natural resource management, *World Development*, 27, 2, pp. 225–247.

Leach, M., Scoones, I. and Mearns, R. (1997), The institutional dynamics of community-based natural resource management: An entitlements approach.

Ligon, F.K., Dietrich W.E., Trush, W.J. (1995), Downstream ecological effects of dams, in Bioscience, Volume 45: 183–192.

Linney, W. and Harrison S. (1981), Large dams and the developing world, social and environmental costs and benefits: A look at Africa, Environmental Liaison Centre, Nairobi

Lovett, (1989), Gender relations, class formation and the colonial state in Africa. In: *Women and the State in Africa*. Parpart, J. & Standt, K. (eds) Lynne Rienner Publishers, Boulder and London.

Lumsden, D.P. (1973), The Volta River Project: Village Resettlement and Attempted Rural Animation, The Canadian Journal of Africa Studies, Vol. VII, No. 1, 1973, 115–132.

Lyon, F. (2000), Trust, networks and norms: The creation of social capital in agricultural economies in Ghana, *World Development*, 28 (4).

MacDonald, G. (1954), Medical implications of the Volta River Project. Paper presented at the ordinary meeting of the Royal Society of Tropical Medicine and Hygiene held at Manson House, 26, Portland Place, London.

Manuh, T. (1993), Women, the State and Society under the PNDC. In Gyimah-Boadi, E. (ed), *Ghana under PNDC Rule*. CODESRIA. London.

Manuh, T. (1994), *Women's Rights and Traditional Law: A Conflict*: International Third World Legal Studies Association and the Valparaiso University School of Law.

—— (1995), *The women, law and development movement in Africa and the struggle for customary law reform*, International Third World legal studies association and the Valparaiso University School of Law.

Manuh, T., Songsore, J. and MacKenzie, F. (1997), 'Gender and land: The interface between legislative initiatives, customary tenure and land use management in Ghana' Research Report Submitted to IDRC, Canada.

Mbilinyi, M. (1989), This is unforgettable business. Colonial state intervention in urban Tanzania. In: *Women and the State in Africa*. Parpart, J. & Standt, K. (eds) Lynne Rienner Publishers, Boulder and London.

McCaull, J. (1975), "Dams of Pork", *Environment*, Vol. 17, No. 1, January/February.

McCaully, P. (1996), *Silenced Rivers: The Ecology and Politics of Large Dams*. Zed Books, London and New Jersey

—— (1997), A critique of "the World Bank's experience with large Dams: A preliminary review of impacts", Berkeley, International Rivers Network.

Meagher, K. and Mustapha, A.R. (1997), Not by farming alone: The role of income in rural Hausaland. In: *Farewell to Farms: De-Agrarianisation and Employment in Africa*.

Bryceson, D.F. and Jamal, V. (eds) African Studies Centre, Leiden, Research Series. 1997/10

Meagher, K. (2000), Veiled Conflicts: Peasant Differentiation, Gender and Structural Adjustment in Nigerian Hausaland. In: *Disappearing Peasantries? Rural Labour, in Africa, Asia, and Latin America.* Bryceson, D.F., Kay, C., & Mooij, J. (eds), Intermediate Technology Publications, London.

Meillassoux, C. (1978), Kinship relations and relations of production. In: Relations of production: Marxist Approaches to Economic Antropology, Seddon, D. (ed), Frank Cass, London.

Midgley, J. (1984), Social security, inequality and the Thirld World, Chichester: John Wiley & Sons.

Mikell, G. (1989), *Cocoa and Chaos in Ghana.* Paragon House, New York.

Ministry of Lands and Forestry, (1999), National land policy, Accra.

Moller, V. and Sotshongaye, A. (1999), "They don't listen": Contemporary respect relations between Zulu grandmothers and granddaughters/sons, *Southern African Journal of Gerontology, Vol. 8 (2): 18–27.*

Morse, B. et al. (1992), Sardar Sarovar: The report of the independent review, RFI, Ottawa.

Moxon, J. (1984), *Volta: Man's Greatest Lake,* Andre Deutsch, London.

Murray, C. (1998), Multiple livelihoods and social change. Working paper series: change livelihoods in Qwaqwa: Research questions and method of Study. Seminar held on September 10, 1998 at the Institute for Development Policy and Management, University of Manchester, Crawford House Precinct Centre, Oxford Road, Manchester.

—— (2000), Changing Livelihoods: The Free State, 1990s, *African Studies,* 59, (1), 115–142.

—— (2002), Livelihoods research: Transcending boundaries of time and Space, *Journal of Southern African Studies Vol. 28 (3): 489–509.*

Narotzky, S. (1997), *New Direction in economic anthropology.* Pluto Press, London.

Nicholas, M.S.O. (1970), Resettlement agriculture. In: *The Volta Resettlement Experience,* Chambers, R. (ed) Pall Mall Press Ltd., London.

Nkrumah, K. (1961), The Volta River Project. Statement delivered by Osagyefo the President to the National Assembly, Government Printer, Accra.

—— (1966), Speech by Ghana's Kwame Nkrumah at the Formal Inauguration of the Volta River Project, January 22, Akosombo, in Africa Report, Vol. 11, No. 4, April 1996, pp. 21–23.

Nugent, P. (1995), *Big Men, Small Boys and Politics in Ghana:* Power, Ideology and the Burden of History, 1982–1994, London, Pinter Publishing Ltd.

Nukunya, (1997), The land and the people. In: *A Handbook of Eweland.*

O'Laughlin, B. (2002), Agency and changing rural livelihoods: Forced labour and resistance in colonial Mozambique, *Journal of Southern African Studies Vol. 28 (3): 511–530.*

Obeng, L. (1969), *Man-Made Lakes: The Accra Symposium.* Obeng, L. (ed), Ghana Universities Press, Accra.

Obeng, L.E. (1973), Volta Lake: Physical and biological aspects. In: *Man-Made Lakes, Their Problems and Environmental Effects,* Ackermann, W.C. (ed), Washington D.C.

—— (1975a), Agriculture and water problems: The case of the Volta Lake. Institute for Development Studies, University of Nairobi, Occasional Paper Number 15.

—— (1975b), A major development project in Ghana: The Volta Dam, which brought economic gains, health problems and human stress. *Commonwealth.*

—— (1978), Starvation or Bilharzia? A rural development dilemma. In: *The Social and Ecological Effects of Water Development in Developing Countries.* Wodstrand, C. (ed), Pergamon Press.

Odegi-Awuondo, C. (1990), *Life in the Balance: Ecological Sociology of the Turkana Nomads.* African Centre for Technology Studies, Nairobi.

Odei, M.A. (1965a), Water use habits and Bilharziasis in Ghana: Symposium on Bilharzia in Ghana. *Ghana Medical Journal* 4 (3).

—— (1965b), Notes on the ecology of the snail hosts of Bilharziasis in Ghana: Symposium on Bilharzia in Ghana. *Ghana Medical Journal* 4 (3).

OED (1996a), World Bank lending for large dams: A preliminary review of impacts: Washington D.C. The World Bank.

—— (1996b), The World Bank's experience with large dams: A preliminary review of impacts: Profiles of large dams, background document, Washington DC, World Bank.

Ofori, I.M. (1973), Some problems of land tenure in new agricultural settlements. A case study of selected Volta River Authority settlements. Paper presented to Cocoa Economics Research Conference, 9–12 April 1973.

Okonjo, C. (1986), The concept of development. In: *Rural Development in Ghana.* Brown, C.K. (ed), Ghana Universities Press, Accra.

Onimode, B. (ed) (1989), *The IMF, the World Bank, and the African debt*, Zed Books, London.

Onori, E., McCullogh, F.S., and Rosei, L. (1962), Schistosomiasis in the Volta Region of Ghana. *Parasitology*, 57.

Painter, T.M. (1996), Space, time, and rural-urban linkages in Africa: Notes for a Geography of Livelihoods, *African Rural and Urban Studies*, 3 (1).

Panter-Brick, C. and Smith, M.T. (2000), *Abandoned children*, Cambridge University Press, Cambridge.

Paperna, I. (1969a), Snail Vectors of Human Schistosomiasis In The Newly Formed Volta Lake. In: *Man-Made Lakes, Accra Symposium*, Obeng, L. (ed), Ghana Universities Press, Accra.

—— (1969b), Aquatic weeds, snails and transmission of Bilharzia in the New Man-Made Volta Lake in Ghana.

—— (1969c), Studies on the Transmission of Schistosomiasis in Ghana: V. Transmission of *Schistosoma Haematobium* in the Forest and Savannah Zones of South East Ghana. *Ghana Medical Journal.*

—— (1969d), Studies on the Transmission of Schistosomiasis in Ghana. Ecology of Bulinus (Physopsis) Globosus, the Snail host of Schistosoma Haematobium in South-East Ghana. *Ghana Journal of Science*, 9 (1 & 2)

—— (1970), Study of the outbreak of Schistosomiasis in the newly formed Volta Lake. *Z. Tropenmed Parasitol*, 21, 411.

Paranjpye, V. and Ganguli, B.N. (1980), "Development of Water Resources In India. A Study of The Environmental and Social Problems Arising From a Medium Sized Irrigation Project in Maharashtra", *Commemorative Volume*, BARC. Bombay.

Parasuraman, S. (1993), 'The Anti-Narmada Project Movement in India: Can the resettlement and rehabilitation policies be translated into national policy?'. ISS Working Paper No. 161. The Hague: Institute of Social Studies.

Parks, R.W. (1960), The Volta River Project. A study of one of the major components of ghanaian economic development. A Thesis presented to the Department of Economics, Harvard College, Cambridge, Massachusetts.

Paul, J.C.N. (1992), Law and development into the 1990s: The need to use international law to impose accountability to people on international development actors, Third World Legal Studies, INTWORLSA and the Valparaiso University School of Law. Valparaiso.

—— (1992), The human right to development: Its meaning and importance. Third World Legal Studies, INTWORLSA and the Valparaiso University School of Law. Valparaiso.

Petr, I. (1966), Fish Population Changes in the Volta Lake over the Period January 1965–September 1966.

—— (1967), Fish population changes in the Volta Lake in Ghana during its first sixteen months. *Hydrobiologia* 30, September 2, 1967.

—— (1968a), Distribution, abundance and food of commercial fish in the Black Volta and the Volta Man-Made Lake in Ghana during its first period of filling (1964–1966). I. Mormyridae, *Hydrobiologia*, 32 December 1968.

—— (1968b), Fish Population Changes in the Volta Lake Over the Period September 1966–December 1967. Technical Report No. 23, University of Ghana Volta Basin Research Project.

—— (1971), Lake Volta: A progress report. *New Scientist and Science Journal*, 28 January 1971.

Phillips, A. (1989), *The Enigma of Colonialism*, James Currey, London.

Piesse, J. and Thirtle, C. (1999), 'Does non-farm income reduce rural poverty: a gini decomposition for the communal lands in Zimbabwe', draft paper presented to Conference of Poverty Strategies, Reading, April.

Pitcher M.A. (1998), Disruption without transformation: Agrarian relations and livelihoods in Nampula Province, Mozambique, 1975–1995, *Journal of Southern African Studies*, 24 (1) March 1998.

Pottinger, L. (2000), WCD Report Confirms social, economic and environmental harm from dams: World Rivers Review, International Rivers Network, Vol. 15, No. 6.

Poudyal, R. (1994), International Efforts to Ban Products that Use Child labour in South Asia, Save the Children, South Asia Regional Office, Briefing Paper No. 1, Kathmandu.

Preparatory Commission, (1956), The Volta River Project. Report of the Preparatory Commission, Governments of the United Kingdom and the Gold Coast, London.

Quartey, E.L. (1969), An address, In: Letitia Obeng (ed), Man-made lakes: The Accra symposium, A publication by the CSIR

Rado, E.R. (1960), The Volta River Project—Retrospect and prospect. *Economic Bulletin of Ghana*, 4 (2)

Ramsar Convention Bureau (1993), Towards the wise use of wetlands, edited by Davis, T.J., Ramsar Convention Bureau, Gland.

Ranger, T. (1989a), The invention of tradition in colonial Africa. In: *The Invention of Tradition*, Hobsbawn, E. & Ranger, T. (eds), Cambridge University Press.

Razavi, S. (ed) (1999), Shifting burdens: Gender and agrarian change under Neoliberalism, Kumarian Press Inc., Connecticut, USA.

Redclift, M. and Benton, T. (1994), Introduction. In: *Social Theory and the Global Environment*, Redclift M. and Benton T (eds), Routledge, London and New York.

Redclift, M. (1992), Sustainable Development: Exploring the Contradictions, Routledge, London.

Repetto, R. (1986), Skimming The Water: Rent-Seeking And The Performance Of Public Irrigation Systems, *Research Report No. 4*, World Resources Institute, December.

Risseeuw, C. and Palriwala, R. (1996), Introduction: Shifting circles of support. In: *Shifting Circles of Support: Contextualising Gender and Kinship in South Asia and Sub-Saharan Africa* Palriwala, R. and Risseeuw (eds), Sage, New Delhi.

Risseeuw, C. (1991), *Gender Transformation: Power and Resistance Among Women in Sri Lanka*, Manohar Publications, New Delhi.

—— (2000), Aging: A gendered policy concern in the South and the North, *Asian Journal of Women's Studies, Vol. 6 No. 2:11–44.*

—— (2002), Ageing: A Gendered Policy Concern in the North and South, in Sustainable Social Structures in a Society for all Ages, Department of Economic and Social Affairs, United Nations, New York.

Roberts, T. (1964), A Preliminary report of the fishes of the Volta with comments on the development of Ghana's Inland Fisheries. Technical Communications No. 9, University of Ghana Volta Basin Research Project.

—— (1967), A provisional check-list of the fresh-water fishes of the Volta Basin, with notes on species of possible economic importance. *West African Social Science Association Journal*, 12 (1) February 1967.

Roggeri, H. (1985), African dams: Impacts in the environment: The social and environmental impact of dams at the local level: A case study of the five man-made lakes in Eastern Africa, Environmental Liaison Centre.

Sawyerr, A. (1990), Some Legal Issues Arising from the Negotiation of the Valco Agreement in Tsikata, F. (ed), Essays from the Ghana-Valco Renegotiations, 1982–1985, Ghana Publishing Corporation, 1990.

—— (undated a), Renegotiation of the Valco Agreement: The background (discussion draft).

—— (undated b), Renegotiation of the Valco Agreement: Contribution to a theoretical interpretation (discussion draft).

Schram, J. (1967), Let the government do it: A study of social Anomie and Retreatism at a resettlement site. M.A. seminar paper, Institute of African Studies, University of Ghana, Legon.

Scoones I. (1998), Sustainable rural livelihoods: A framework for analysis, IDS Working Paper, 72, Brighton, Institute of Development Studies.

—— et al. (1996), *Hazards and Opportunities: Farming Livelihoods in Dryland Africa: Lessons from Zimbabwe*. Zed Books Ltd., London and New Jersey, in Association with the International Institute for Environment and Development, London.

Scott, J.C. (1978), *The Moral Economy of the Peasant: Rebellion and Subsistence in Southeast Asia*. Yale University Press, New Haven and London.

—— (1985), *Weapons of the Weak: Everyday Forms of Peasant Resistance*, Yale University Press, New Haven and London.

—— (1990), *Domination and the Arts of Resistance: Hidden Transcripts*, Yale University Press, New Haven and London.

—— (1976), *The Moral Economy of the Peasant: Rebellion and Subsistence in Southeast Asia*. Yale University Press, New Haven and London.

Scudder, T. (1965), "Man-made Lakes and Population Resettlement in Africa" in *Man-made Lakes*, Proceedings of a Symposium held at the Royal Geographical Society, London, 30th September–1 October 1965.

—— (1997a), Social impacts, in Biswas, A.K. (ed) Water resources: environmental planning, management and development, New York, McGraw Hill.

—— (1997c), Social impacts of large dams, in The World Conservation Union (IUCN) and The World Bank, Large Dams: Learning from the Past: Looking at the Future. Workshop Proceedings, Gland, Switzerland, April 11–12, 1997.

Sefa-Dei, G.J. (1992), Hardships and survival in rural West Africa: A case study of a Ghanaian community. *CODESRIA Monograph Series*, 3/92, Dakar.

Seiz, J.A. (1991), The bargaining approach and feminist methodology, *Review of Radical Political Economics, Vol. 23 (1&2): 22–29.*

Sen, A. (1984), *Resources, Values and Development*. Basil Blackwell, Oxford.

—— (1990), Gender and Cooperative Conflicts In*: Persistent Inequalities*. Tinker, I. (ed), New York, Oxford University Press.

—— (2000), Social Exclusion: Concept, Application and Scrutiny, Social Development Papers, No. 1, Office of Environment and Social Development, Asian Development Bank.

Shihata, I.F. (1993), Legal Aspects of Involuntary Population Resettlement in Cernea. M. and Guggenheim, S.E. (eds), Anthropological Approaches to Resettlement: Policy, Practice and Theory, Westview Press, Boulder.

Sims, R. and Casely-Hayford, L. (1986), Renegotiating the price and availability of energy. In: *Essays from the Ghana-VALCO renegotiations, 1982–85*, Ghana Publishing House, Accra, 1986.

Singh, R. (1991), The assault on the Sardar Sarovar Dam, 5th December 1990 to 28 January 1991, Other India Press, Mapusa-Goa

Sklar, L., McCully, P. (1994), Damming the rivers: The World Banks's lending for large dams, Working Paper 5, Berkeley, International Rivers Network.

Slater, R. (2002), Differentiation and diversification: changing livelihoods in Qwaqwa, South Africa, 1970–2000, *Journal of Southern African Studies Vol. 28 (3): 610–629.*

Songsore, J. and Denkabe, A. (1995), *Challenging Rural Poverty in Northern Ghana: The Case of the Upper West Region,* Centre for Environmental Development, Unit SMU, The University of Trandheim, Report No. 6/95.

Srinivasan, B. (1994), 'Dissent and democratic practice: Attack on NBA office', *Economic and Political Weekly 29 (18): 1058–9.*

Srivastava, U.K., Seethuraman, S.P., Mehta, S.S. (1991), Compensation to Canal-Affected People of the Sardar Sarovar Narmada Project, Report of the Indian Institute of Management, Ahmedabad.

Staudt, K. (1986) 'Women, Development and the State: On the Theoretical Impasse', *Development and Change, 7: 325–33.*

Tamakloe, M. (1968), New Mpamu: case study of a Volta River Authority Resettlement Town. *Ghana Journal of Agricultural Science, 1 (1).*

Tamakloe, M.A. (1994), Long term impacts of resettlement: The Akosombo dam experience in Cook, C.C. (ed), Involuntary Resettlement in Africa, Africa Technical Series, Washington DC, World Bank.

Taylor, B.W. (1973), People in a rapidly changing environment: The first six years of Volta Lake. In: *Man-Made Lakes, Their Problems and Environmental Effects,* Ackermann, W.C. (ed), Washington D.C.

The Corner House (1998), Dams on the rocks: The Flawed economics of large hydroelectric power dams, Briefing No. 8.

—— (1998), Missing the Point of Development Talk: Reflections for Activists, Briefing No. 9.

The International Labour Organisation, (1996), Child Labour: Targeting the Intolerable: Report VI (1), Sixth Item on the Agenda, International Labour Conference, 86th Session, 1998, ILO, Geneva.

The World Bank, (1993), Early Experience with Involuntary Resettlement: Impact Evaluation on Ghana Kpong Hydroelectric Project (Loan 1380–GH), Report No. 12141, Operation Evaluation Department, Washington.

—— (1986), Participation Source Book, Washington.

—— (1999), Annual Report.

—— (1997), Annual Report.

The World Conservation Union (IUCN) and The World Bank, (1997), Large Dams: Learning from the Past: Looking at the Future. Workshop Proceedings, Gland, Switzerland, April 11–12, 1997.

Thomas, D.H.L. and Adams, W.M. (1999), Adapting to dams: Agrarian change downstream of the Tiga Dam, Northern Nigeria, *World Development,* 27 (6)

Titiati, E.K. and Gilbert, M. (1969a), A report on the fishing methods conducted on Volta Lake. (Unpublished Report) Volta Lake Research and Development Programme.

—— (1969b), Some considerations on the open water fishery on Volta Lake. (Unpublished Report) Volta Basin Research Project Archives.

Titone J. (2001), Bui Dam threatens hippos and humans, World Rivers Review, International Rivers Network, Vol. 16, No. 4.

Titriku, P.K. (1999), Agriculture in the Volta Basin: Problems and prospects. In: *The sustainable integrated development of the Volta Basin in Ghana.* Gordon, C. & Amatekpor, J.K. (eds) Volta Basin Research Project, University of Ghana, Legon, Accra.

Togbi Anipati III (undated), Memorandum submitted by the Fiaga of Mepe traditional area to the committee appointed by the National Redemption Council to investigate chieftaincy matters in the Volta Region of Ghana.

Togonu-Bickersteth, F. (2002), What can we borrow from one another, in Sustainable Social Structures in a Society for all Ages, Department of Economic and Social Affairs, United Nations, New York.

Tongu District Council (1976), Report on the General Effects of Akosombo Dam on the Life and Property of the People of the Tongu Area, Petition to the Government of Ghana and the Volta River Authority, 26th May 1976, Sogakope.

Trager, L. (1998), Home-Town linkages and local development in South-West Nigeria. Whose Agenda? What Impact? *Africa*, 68 (3).

Trussell, D. (1992), *The Social and environmental effects of large dams*, Volume 3: A review of the literature, Wadebridge Ecological Centre, U.K.

Tsikata, D. (1994), Gender, livelihood and ecological change in The riverine communities of the Lower Volta Basin: An exploratory study of Tefle and Mepe. M.Phil Thesis, Department of Sociology, University of Ghana.

—— (1997), Gender Equality and the State in Ghana: Some Issues of Policy and Practice, in Imam, A.M, Mama, A. and Sow, F. (eds) *Engendering African Social Sciences*, CODESRIA Books, Dakar.

Tsikata, F.S. (1986), Dealing with a Transnational Corporation: The Ghana-Valco Renegotiations, in *Essays from the Ghana-Valco Renegotiations, 1982–85*, Tsikata, F.S. (ed), Ghana Publishing House, Accra.

UN (United Nations) (1947), Universal declaration on human rights, New York, United Nations.

—— (1986), Declaration on the right to development, New York, United Nations.

United Nations Development Programme, (1968) Preliminary Findings, Report of Study into Flooding in the Lower Volta and Keta Areas, 19/12/1968.

Van Der Geest, S. (1997), Between respect and reciprocity: managing old age in rural Ghana, *Southern African Journal of Gerontology, Vol. 6 (2): 20–25.*

Van Landewijk, P.W. (1988), The best-laid schemes. A story of resettlement: The Kpong Hydroelectric Project, Ghana. Doctoral study on the sociological impact of resettlement in the Kpong hydro electric projcct, Ghana, Sub-faculty of Non-Western Sociology, Leiden University.

Volta Basin Research Project (1997), Lower Volta environmental impact studies, status report for the first phase (October 7, 1996–July 6, 1997), Report prepared for the Volta River Authority, University of Ghana, Legon.

—— (1999), Lower Volta environmental impact studies, final status report for the second phase (May 1, 1998–January 31, 1999), Report prepared for the Volta River Authority, University of Ghana, Legon.

—— (undated), Clearance of vegetation in the Volta by burning. Volta Basin Research Project, Legon.

Volta River Authority (1987): Annual Report, Accra.

—— (1988), Annual Report, Accra.

—— (1989), Annual Report, Accra.

—— (1990), Annual Report, Accra.

—— (1991), Annual Report, Accra.

—— (1992), Annual Report, Accra.

—— (1997), Annual Report, Accra.

—— (1998), Annual Report, Accra.

—— (undated), Environmental Management of the Volta Lake Basin in Ghana, unpublished document of the VRA.

Volta River Project (1956), *II Apendices to the Report of the Preparatory Commission.* Published for the Governments of the United Kingdom and of the Gold Coast by her Majesty's Stationery Office.

Wheelock J. and Oughton, E. (1996), The household as a focus for Research, *Journal of Economic Issues*, 30 (1).

White, B. (1996), Globalization and the Child Labour Problem, Institute of Social Studies, Working Paper Series, No. 221.

Whitehead, A. and Kabeer, N. (2001), Living with uncertainty: Gender, livelihoods and pro-poor growth in rural Sub-Saharan Africa, *IDS Working Paper 134.*

Whitehead, A. (1981), "I'm Hungry Mum," The politics of domestic budgeting. In: *Of Marriage and the Marke: Women's Subordination in International Perspective.* Wolkowitz, C. and McCullogh R. (eds), CSE Books, London.
—— (1985), Effects of Technological Changes on Rural Cultures: A Review of Analysis and Concepts. In: *Technology and Rural Women.* Ahmed I (ed), Allen and Unwin, London.
—— (1998), 'Gender, poverty and intrahousehold relations in Sub-Saharan Africa small holder households: Some lessons from two case examples', background paper for 1998 SPA report.
—— (2000), Continuities and discontinuities in sustaining rural livelihoods in North-Eastern Ghana. Working Paper No. 18, Multiple Livelihoods and Social Change, Institute for Development Policy and Management, University of Manchester.
—— (2002), Tracking livelihood change: Theoretical, methodological and empirical perspectives from North-East Ghana, *Journal of Southern African Studies Vol. 28 (3): 575–598.*
Widner, J. and Mundt, A. (1998), Researching Social Capital in Africa, *Africa* 68, (1), 1–24.
Williams, P. (1991), The Debate Over Large Dams. The case against it. *Civil Engineer,* August 1991.
Woodman, G. (1985), 'Customary Law, State Courts and the Notion of Institutionalisation of Norms in Ghana and Nigeria', in A.W. Allot (ed) *People's Law and the State:* Foris Publications.
World Commission on Dams (2000), Dams and development: A new framework for decision-making. The report of the World Commission on Dams. Earthscan Publications Ltd., London and Sterling, VA.
Yanagisako, S.J. (1979), Family and household: The analysis of domestic groups, *Annual Review of Anthropology,* 1979, 8: 161–205
Yeboah, F.K. (1977), Some considerations for the comprehensive development of River Basins—The Volta Basin Experience in Ghana. Paper presented at the Conference on Kainji Lake and River Basin Development, 11–17 December 1977, Ibadan, Nigeria.
—— (1999), Mitigative actions taken by V.R.A. on Dam affected communities. In: *The Sustainable Integrated Development of the Volta Basin in Ghana.* Gordon, C. & Amatekpor, J.K. (eds), Volta Basin Research Project, University of Ghana, Legon, Accra.
Young K., Wolkowitz, C. and McCullagh, R. (1981), *Of marriage and the market,* London: CSE Books.
Zoomers, A. and de Haan, L. (2002), Development geography at the crossroads of livelihood and globalisation (forthcoming).
Zoomers, E.B. (1999), Livelihood strategies and development interventions in the Southern Andes of Bolivia: Contrasting Views on Development. In: *Linking Livelihood Strategies to Development,* KIT—Press (Royal Tropical Institute, Amsterdam, The Netherlands.

Laws Cited

Constitution of the Fourth Republic of Ghana, (Promulgation) Law, 1992, PNDCL 282.
Volta River Development Act, 1961, Act 46.
Local Government Act, 1993, Act 462.
Courts (Amendment) Act, 2002, Act 620.
Local Government (Urban, Zonal and Town Councils and Unit Committees) (Establishment) Instrument, 1994, L.I. 1589.

INDEX